The original publication was made possible through a grant from
Government of Canada Human Resources Development,
Meeting Professionals International and the MPI Foundation.

Revisions and reprinting were made possible by the MPI Foundation

MEETING PROFESSIONALS INTERNATIONAL
3030 LBJ Freeway Suite 1700
Dallas, TX 75234-2759 USA
Tel: 1.972.702.3000
Fax: 1.972.702.3070
www.mpiweb.org

First Edition, 1st Printing, MARCH 1997
Second Edition, 1st Printing, DECEMBER 2003
Second Edition, 2nd Printing, March 2006

ISBN 0-982009-0-7

Meetings and Conventions:
A Planning Guide
With 2006 Updated Forms

Original Authors: Dr. Don McLaurin and Ted Wykes

Guide Review Task Force
Sandy Biback, CMP, CMM, Toronto
Angela Harvey, CMP, Ottawa
Rita Plaskett, CMP, CMM, Toronto
Jean Silzer, CMP, Calgary
Helen Van Dongen, CMP, CMM, Toronto

MPI Foundation Liaison:
David DuBois, CMP, CAE, Executive Vice President, Dallas

Acknowledgements

The MPI Foundation would like to thank the following people and organizations
for their support and contribution to the revision of this book.

Abrahamson, Ruth, CMP

Adams, Candy, CTSM, CME, CEM, CMP, CMM

Accepted Practices Exchange, Convention Industry Council (APEX)

Cambridge Suites Hotel

Canning, Cris, CMP

Corbitt, Ann

Davey, Clark

Delta Chelsea Hotel

Eisenstodt, Joan

Endean, Tahira, CMP

Exposoft Solutions Inc.

Fairmont Royal York Hotel

Feldman, Roni, CMP

Ford, Carol

Foster, John S. Esq.

Garland, Ian

Gravelle, Michelle, CMP

Halfacre, Roger, MTS, CTC

Howe, Jonathan

InfoLink: The Conference Publishers

International Association of Exhibition Management (IAEM)

Joiner, Amanda, CMP CMM

JR Daggett & Associates

MacCusworth, Frances

Meetings & Incentive Travel Group

NearSpace Inc.

Pini, Alan, CMM

Scaillet, Didier

Shock, Patti J.

Silzer, Niesa

Sklarz, Helen

Speakers' Spotlight

TelAv Audio Visuals

The STRONCO Group of Companies

World Youth Day 2002

The Task Force gratefully acknowledges Diane Stefaniak, CAE, without whose
vision and pioneering spirit the original text would never have happened.

Preface

No matter where you are in the world, somewhere near you, a meeting is taking place. Society's thirst for knowledge through lifelong learning and the desire for social interaction will continually create the need for conferences, meetings and special events.

For the thousands of meetings being staged around the world every day, someone is responsible for the arduous task of planning and staging it. A meeting, by definition, is a gathering or coming together of people. Meetings may be simple (executives of a company in a board room) or they may be complex (days of various activities taking place in several different locations). The purpose of any kind of meeting will not be achieved if there has not been a competent person in charge of the planning, scheduling and implementing the event - namely, the meeting professional.

Meetings and Conventions: A Planning Guide has been planned and written with the meeting professional in mind. It is intended to be a resource for experienced professionals and a learning tool for beginning professionals. The original book was an outcome of a project between Meeting Professionals International and the Government of Canada Human Resources Department. This two stage project resulted in a set of occupational standards for the meeting manager and the meeting coordinator which were published in 1994. The occupational standards were revised in 2000. The textbook **Meetings and Conventions: A Planning Guide** was the second stage of the standards project to provide a textbook based on the occupational standards. The original textbook was published in 1997.

For the purposes of this publication, and for ease of use, there are several consistent sections for each chapter. Each chapter has the following elements - key terms, learning outcomes, chapter content, chapter review, test your knowledge, checklists, conference journal as well as roles and responsibilities for the meeting manager and the meeting coordinator.

Regarding roles and responsibilities, it is assumed that in some circumstances, only one person plans and executes a meeting. In other situations, the meeting manager may have an assistant, a coordinator, who implements many of the elements of the meeting plan. Each chapter contains a breakdown of the tasks between the two roles. In most cases, individual tasks are discussed within the related chapter. However, in order to control the volume of the textbook, information on all identified tasks is not included.

Throughout the book, the terms, event, conference and meeting will be used interchangeably to indicate the function that the meeting professional is planning. The terms delegate, attendee and/or participant are also used interchangeably to denote for whom the function is planned or those expected to attend. Meeting Professional is used to describe any individual involved in the meeting industry, encompassing meeting planners, meeting managers or coordinators and planning staff. Also, the terms, host organization and sponsoring organization are interchangeable. For the purposes of this book, we have chosen host organization to avoid any confusion with "conference sponsors".

The conference journal provides a look at the sequence of events of planning one conference. It is intended to assist the learner in seeing theories put into action. Industry insights have been provided for a similar purpose. The checklists and templates have been provided in two locations - within the text and also on a CDROM attached to the back cover. While the textbook is copyrighted by Meeting Professionals International, the checklists are not. All checklists and templates may be copied and reformatted to meet your own professional needs.

We are confident that all meeting professionals will find value in some or all of the book as they plan the myriad of details and tasks necessary to implement and execute a successful conference or meeting.

MPI Guide Review Task Force
June, 2003

Table of Contents

Chapter 3 Program Development

Chapter 4 Site Selection

Chapter 5 Negotiations and Contracts

Chapter 6 Risk Management

Chapter 7 Speakers

Chapter 8 Marketing and Media

Chapter 9 Trade Shows

Chapter 10 Sponsorship

Chapter 11 Registration

Chapter 12 Meeting Logistics

Chapter 13 Technology

Chapter 14 VIPs

Chapter 15 International Meetings

Chapter 16 Post Event Activities

Chapter 17 Human Resources And Professionalism

Meeting Objectives

INTRODUCTION

Establishing meaningful and measurable goals and objectives is the first step to planning and managing a successful meeting. The aim of this chapter is to familiarize the meeting professional with developing objectives and using them effectively. Fundamental to the understanding of successful objective design is a discussion of return on investment (ROI).

LEARNING OBJECTIVES

After completing this chapter, the learner will:

- differentiate between goals and objectives

- understand the value of identifying and writing goals and objectives

- understand the role objectives play in successful meetings

- write objectives

Ensure you understand and can apply the following terms:

- Attendee
- Conference
- Delegate
- Event
- Goal
- Measurable
- Meeting Objective
- Participant
- Return on Investment

Refer to the glossary for further clarification of the key terms for this chapter.

ROLES AND RESPONSIBILITIES

MEETING MANAGER

○ Research and analyze background information

- Review a history of prior meetings
  - ○ acquire information about the function and culture of the organization holding the meeting
  - ○ determine previous budgets and changes affecting them (e.g., corporate changes, changes in economic climate, personnel changes)
  - ○ gather, read and interpret history, evaluations, printouts, timelines, and statistics of previous meetings
  - ○ identify ways to improve the impact and results of past activities
  - ○ determine the role of unions and management as defined in collective agreements
  - ○ identify labour laws and government agencies which enforce them
  - ○ review previous attendee and VIP profile(s)
  - ○ review return on investment of previous meetings

- Analyze trends and prices
  - ○ identify current marketplace costs and the latest technology/software
  - ○ recognize and use networking opportunities to identify the best practices, programs and procedures used by other organizations
  - ○ monitor trends, new concepts, innovative practices, and anticipated challenges for the organization(s)' committees

- Determine expectations and needs
  - ○ meet with sponsoring /organizing individuals, staff, volunteers or committees
  - ○ conduct a needs analysis
  - ○ identify the expectations of attendees, the organization and sponsors in writing
  - ○ recognize the differing needs, backgrounds, concerns, goals, abilities, responsibilities, demographics, lifestyles, degree of commitment, learning styles, motivations, concentration, and interests of meeting attendees, even within a group which appears to be homogeneous
  - ○ conceptualize requirements in a clear, prioritized manner

- Review the policies of the organization(s)
  - review the goals/mission of the organization
  - review the organizational policies and procedures

○ Define Meeting Objectives

- Determine the objectives of the meeting
  - identify the various purposes for holding a meeting (e.g., educational, training/development, motivational, and/or financial)
  - demonstrate sensitivity to organizational image, sensitivity to market (e.g., not-for-profit)
  - ensure consistency of organizational goals and meeting objectives
  - clarify the objective(s) of the meeting

- Record Objectives
  - establish criteria by which a good meeting objective may be measured
  - recognize both hard (measurable) and soft (not measurable) objectives
  - write objectives which are measurable, understandable and easy to read
  - communicate objectives to appropriate personnel

- Align all decisions with the meeting objectives
  - recognize the need to reinforce meeting objectives at every opportunity
  - ensure that all decisions are consistent with meeting objectives (e.g., theme, décor, entertainment, program)

- Determine the meeting format
  - identify the various types of meetings (e.g., conference, convention, congress, council, clinic, symposium, seminar, forum, retreat, workshop, lecture etc.)

- Profile the targeted attendee
  - define demographics (age, sex, profession, average income, point of origin, interests, accompanying persons, who pays, and other pertinent details)
  - define the type of attendee (mandatory, voluntary, recreation)

- Establish the need for reports
  - determine the reporting requirements
  - develop processes related to data collection and distribution
  - determine the involvement of professional recognition
  - develop policies and procedures related to professional recognition of attendees

○ plan for administration related to continuing professional education (e.g., CEU's [continuing education units] and CME's [continuing medical education])

MEETING COORDINATOR

○ Research background information

- Review a history of prior meetings
  - ○ review information about the function and culture of the organization
  - ○ gather, read and interpret history, evaluations, printouts and statistics of previous meetings
  - ○ review previous attendee profile(s)

- Identify trends and prices
  - ○ identify current marketplace costs and the best technology/software
  - ○ recognize trends, new concepts, innovative practices, and anticipated challenges for the organization(s)' committees

- Review expectations and needs
  - ○ review the results of a needs analysis
  - ○ review the expectations of attendees, the organization, and sponsors
  - ○ recognize the differing needs, backgrounds, concerns, goals, abilities, responsibilities, demographics, lifestyles, degree of commitment, rates of learning, motivations, concentration, and interests of meeting attendees, even within a group which appears to be homogeneous
  - ○ review language and cultural requirements
  - ○ research the need for reports

- Review the policies and procedures of the organization
  - ○ review the goals/mission of the organization
  - ○ review organizational policies and procedures

○ Review meeting objective(s)

- Research the attendee profile
  - ○ obtain pertinent details as required

- Demonstrate an understanding of the objectives of the meeting
  - review the purpose(s) for holding the meeting
  - review both hard (measurable) and soft (not measurable) meeting objectives
  - recognize the need for all decisions to be consistent with the meeting objectives

- Align all activities with the meeting objectives
  - ensure that all meeting objectives are met
  - follow the language and cultural policies
  - follow the organizational policies and procedures related to the environment

WHAT ARE GOALS AND OBJECTIVES?

Goals are long-range targets that may be projected years into the future. A corporate goal might be

To be the most profitable global hotel company.

Objectives are short-range targets that are specific to one event. Each event should move the organization toward its stated goal. An individual meeting will have one or more objectives that are measurable. For example,

To increase corporate group business by 10% in the current fiscal year, by holding a training meeting for all North American sales staff.

Once objectives have been established, before an event can be planned, the meeting professional must have some preliminary information about the organization and prospective attendees, as well as expectations for the event.

EFFECTIVE OBJECTIVES MAKE PLANNING EASIER

Actual phrasing of all objectives is an important task that must be undertaken before the planning process can begin. When objectives are written, they:

- assist in the orderly planning and management of a meeting

- supply a basis for measurement and evaluation

- help define the major areas of responsibility and tasks (job descriptions)

- ensure everyone involved has a clear understanding of desired outcomes

SAME MEETING: DIFFERENT OBJECTIVES

The host organization will probably have different objectives than the meeting professional, while the attendees will have distinct objectives of their own. Here are three examples:

Host Organization

- to generate $100,000 net profit on the conference in the current fiscal year

Meeting Professional

- to process and confirm each delegate registration within 24 hours of receipt

Attendee

- to learn three new tools to enhance office productivity

It is important for the meeting professional to distinguish between the organization's objectives and the planning objectives, though most meetings will have some of each.

WRITING EFFECTIVE MEETING OBJECTIVES

- A good objective must be **SMART**:
  - **S**pecific   to increase sales
  - **M**easurable to increase sales by 10%
  - **A**chievable   to increase sales by 10% (rather than 50%)
  - **R**elevant   a sales meeting should have a sales-related objective
  - **T**imely   to increase sales by 10% by fiscal year end

- Objectives begin with the word "to", followed by a verb.

- Objectives must be easily understood by all stakeholders.

- Objectives should clearly state who is responsible for their completion, avoiding dual responsibility and ensuring accountability.

- Objectives should be recorded in writing, with copies distributed to those who will needto refer to them.

ASSESSING MEETING OBJECTIVES

The following presents a methodology for testing meeting objectives. After applying the criteria the meeting professional should be able to test all future objectives.

- Is the objective SMART?

- Can those who must accomplish it easily understand it?

- Is the objective challenging enough, while still achievable and realistic?

- Is the objective consistent with basic company and organization policies and practices?

- Can accountability for final results be clearly established from the objective?

RETURN ON INVESTMENT

Contributed by Jim Daggett, JR Daggett & Associates

It is increasingly important to evaluate and measure the effectiveness of meetings. Return on Investment (ROI) is key to determining and demonstrating the value of your meetings. It is based on the objectives of the meeting and impacts all other aspects of the meeting. There are five steps to the process of determining ROI.

The first step in the process is to determine the stakeholders of the meeting. Each different stakeholder group may have different objectives. For example, stakeholders should include the organization sponsoring or producing the meeting.

The objectives of the host organization may be:

- financial (they deserve to know whether dollars invested were well spent)

- marketing related (to determine who their message reached)

- performance based (increases in attendees, exhibitors, sponsorship, etc.)

- how well the meeting's and other stakeholders' goals and objectives were met.

Other stakeholders include:

- attendees (what did they get from the expenditure of time, money, etc.?)

- exhibitors (how well were their marketing dollars spent on the exhibit and/or sponsorship in direct relation to what they achieved from their participation?)

- facility and other vendors (was their ROI positive?), etc.

Each of these stakeholder groups participate in the meeting for different reasons and must be able to demonstrate the results of their expended resources at the completion of the meeting.

Financial and performance objectives are fairly simple to measure. However, the objectives must be specific enough to determine the extent of success. For example, increasing attendance is not a SMART objective, but increasing attendance of professional member registrants by 20% over the previous year is, and the results can be evaluated easily.

The second step is to set and specify the meeting's objectives. This step will set the stage for the ease and success of measuring your meeting's value. Having a measurement aspect of an objective is the only way to easily determine if the objective was met. Objectives should be determined for every aspect of the meeting and for each different stakeholder group.

The third step in the ROI process is to come up with tools that will measure the success of achieving the specific objectives. If objectives are detailed and contain an element of measurement, they should be fairly easy to measure and determine if, in fact, the objectives were achieved and to what degree. Tools that can be used include pre- and post-tests; questionnaires/surveys; focus groups to determine specific information retained or behaviours changed; results that changed after the meeting, such as performance, sales; or any combination of these.

Other measurements include financial (budgets) and performance (registration, exhibits, sponsorship, etc.) data that is, at face value, easily measured.

The fourth step in determining the ROI of meetings is to develop the content of the meeting to support the objectives and to be measurable at the conclusion. SMART objectives should have been developed in step one. And measurement tools were developed for each objective in step three. Now it is time to make sure that the meeting contains the framework to achieve success.

Determining the program content and delivery are keys to that achievement.

The program content, substance, purpose, and messages are what make the biggest difference to organizations' host meetings because they are what the participants take back and use to effect the desired change. Measuring the extent to which the meeting positively affected the participants is what actually proves effectiveness. A meeting professional who contributes to the development, communication and measurement process is adding value and maximizing meeting effectiveness to assure return on investment for all stakeholders - attendees, exhibitors, suppliers, and the meeting host.

Similarly, if networking is a goal of the meeting, food and beverage events (breaks, receptions, lunches, etc.) should be designed to foster networking and to measure the results.

The fifth and final step in the ROI process is to demonstrate the results. Compiling measurements and applying them directly back to the specified objectives will show whether or not the meeting was a success, based precisely on what each stakeholder group desired to achieve from their participation in the meeting. This reporting step should not be overlooked or underestimated. After all, if the stakeholders are not shown the results of their participation, they may not participate in the future.

Depending on their specific objectives and interests, you may need to present results to each stakeholder group somewhat differently. For example, the management of the host organization may want to see a formal presentation, including charts and graphs, indicating levels of success; while attendees and exhibitors may only require a summary of the results. Regardless of the delivery format, results and measurements (both positive and negative) should be communicated to each stakeholder. If certain objectives were not met, recommendations for changes to future meetings to insure achievement or improvement should be included.

Determining those who have a stake in the outcome of the meeting; writing SMART objectives for each stakeholder group and every aspect of the meeting; establishing measurement tools to evaluate, assess and quantify results; providing the meeting's content to specifically achieve objectives; and demonstrating and communicating the results are all important steps in showing the success and effectiveness of meetings.

~ A Conference Journal ~

Author: Helen Sklarz, Sklarz Management Services

In celebration of the millennium, two not-for-profit associations decided to combine their respective conferences and trade shows in an effort to present a unique and unprecedented event.

Two years in advance of the proposed meeting, a committee comprised of senior management and volunteers from both organizations began monthly meetings to establish the objectives and management roles in this new arena. Basic issues that were generally taken for granted had to be reviewed and redefined. For example, they now had to ask themselves how management and financial decisions would be made and who would manage the logistics of the conference. As well, how would revenues be generated and shared? It became very apparent within the first planning year that the two organizations, although sharing the same objectives for the outcome of the conference, had very different ideas about implementing the event. It also became clear that, although both organizations managed their respective events successfully, the desire to explain "our way" to the other group had to change to discussions of "the new way of doing things".

A new conference planning team, comprised of equal support from both organizations, was established. An equitable organizational structure was developed. Next, goals and objectives needed to be defined.

It was decided that this joint meeting would need to redefine the standard industry conference and trade show and blend the conference objectives of a national association with 3,000 attendees with those of an association with 7,000 attendees. If successful, the goal was to conduct a joint venture of this nature some time in the future.

The conference committee objectives were as follows:

- to plan and conduct a unique and unprecedented industry event for 12,000-15,000 attendees from around the world

- to conduct a fully integrated industry conference and trade show over an entire week, not two conferences held back to back

- to ensure that 120 - 140 speaker presentations would span the needs of attendees from both associations throughout the week

- to identify and implement different presentation formats of interest to delegates, in particular, through the use of technology

- to ensure that both trade shows had equal opportunity and direct access to delegates, in a prime location near conference sessions, as each association's trade show would continue to be managed as an independent event

- to offer informal education opportunities through networking

- to combine all social events and space them throughout the week to ensure attendance by members of both associations. This was a very sensitive issue as each group had a long history of conducting their awards or gala evenings on a specific day of the week, with a certain order of events.

- to minimize the expense for delegates who normally went to both conferences by setting a registration fee that was fair and equitable

- to share sponsorship and registration revenues equitably and to earn, at a minimum, the same net profit as derived from their own conference had they run it independently

The planner's objectives were:

- to ensure that the new vision proposed by the planning committee would be carried out efficiently and economically

- to develop a new conference team with additional meeting coordinators and suppliers

- to maintain expenditures within budget

- to revise existing methodology and implement complementary systems throughout the conference

To help organizers measure the Return on Investment (ROI), they also decided to conduct a formal evaluation of attendees onsite, through the use of a professional marketing company. This would ensure sufficient representation from exhibitors, delegates and sponsors to help determine the value of the conference from each perspective.

MEETING OBJECTIVES CHECKLIST

PRELIMINARY QUESTIONS

☐ Determine demographics of audience

- what are the categories of job or professional responsibilities?
- how familiar with the subject(s) are the members of the group?
- what are the attendees' expectations?
- is it a homogenous group? Are there guests?
- how sophisticated are they about communication techniques? travel?

☐ How many stakeholder groups are involved with the meeting? What different objectives does each group have? Are any objectives common to all?

☐ Identify the anticipated or desired behaviour of the audience after the meeting, (e.g., how should they do things differently?)

☐ Identify necessary tools to be provided to the audience

- information
- training
- motivation
- change in job concept
- technical information

☐ What can the audience gain from the event? How can this be measured?

CHAPTER REVIEW

- **GOALS** are long-range targets that may be projected years into the future.

- **OBJECTIVES** are measurable short-range targets that apply specifically to the event that will assist in the planning and management of a meeting by indicating the expectations of everyone involved and supplying a basis for measurement and evaluation.

- **OBJECTIVES** should always be SMART: specific, measurable, achievable, relevant, and timely.

- **OBJECTIVES** should be clearly worded to avoid confusion and should specify who is responsible.

- **RETURN ON INVESTMENT** is the process of:

  1. determining meeting stakeholders

  2. specifying the meeting objectives

  3. determining tools to measure the level of success in meeting these objectives

  4. developing measurable content that meets the objectives

  5. demonstrating results

- A **CHECKLIST** for developing meeting objectives is a useful tool when meeting with stakeholders. The provided checklist should be modified in accordance with personal experience and individual situations.

TEST YOUR KNOWLEDGE

The following self-test will indicate the level of understanding and knowledge gained from this chapter. Solutions to all self-tests can be found in **Appendix A.**

1. Meeting objectives need not be written.

    ☐ True   ☐ False

2. Goals are long-range targets set by the organization, while objectives are short-range and apply to the immediate event.

    ☐ True   ☐ False

3. Objectives should include information on measurement and timing, and should be realistic and relevant to the needs of stakeholders.

    ☐ True   ☐ False

4. Meeting objectives can be used as a basis for post-event evaluation.

    ☐ True   ☐ False

5. Objectives may be written in any format, as long as both meeting professional and organization agree.

    ☐ True   ☐ False

6. Meeting objectives must specify who is responsible for completion of the task.

    ☐ True   ☐ False

7. Organization goals are:
    (a) measurable, short-range targets specific to the event
    (b) geared toward the increase in knowledge the attendees will acquire at an event
    (c) long-range targets that may be projected years into the future
    (d) dependent on the wishes of those attending the event

8. Meeting objectives are:
    (a) verbal requests from the organization regarding an upcoming event
    (b) long-range targets that may be projected years into the future
    (c) achieved when the attendees are "charged up" and ready to go when they leave an event
    (d) measurable, short-range targets specific to the event

9. Goals and objectives should be developed and written to...

   (a) indicate the expectations of event attendees

   (b) provide a means of measuring attendee reaction and evaluating the event.

   (c) outline the expectations of key stakeholders involved, supplying a basis for measurement and evaluation

   (d) all of the above

   (e) none of the above

10. An effective objective should:

    (a) guide the actions of planning and management

    (b) consider all organizational variables

    (c) be clearly written

    (d) provide the basis for meaningful post-event evaluations

    (e) all of the above

11. The "best" written objective below is:

    (a) To increase membership by holding a training session, at a cost of no more than $20,000.

    (b) To spend a maximum of $20,000 training sales staff to use new techniques whichwill increase membership by 10%.

    (c) To produce a 10% increase in membership by the end of the fiscal year by trainingthe sales force to use new telemarketing techniques at a maximum cost of $20,000.

    (d) To increase membership by 10% before the end of the fiscal year through a trainingsession.

12. Describe how the use of objectives can make an event more effective.

    _____

    _____

    _____

13. Describe the 5 steps involved in determining a meetings return on investment.

    _____

    _____

    _____

    _____

NOTES

_____
_____
_____
_____
_____
_____
_____
_____
_____
_____
_____
_____
_____
_____
_____
_____
_____
_____
_____
_____
_____
_____
_____
_____
_____
_____
_____
_____
_____

Chapter 2

Budget

INTRODUCTION

The purpose of a budget is to achieve the maximum benefit from the resources available to an organization over a period of time. A budget is a numerical expression of the established policies, plans, and objectives pertaining to all aspects of operation. Designing an event budget requires the meeting professional to translate the event goals and objectives into financial terms.

The event budget is a business tool - a working document that communicates and controls income and expenses throughout the entire planning process. During the initial planning stage, budget estimates are a framework, based on general calculations of some of the revenue and expense items. As specific details, such as meeting sites, program elements and other factors become finalized, so do their respective costs. The budget should be a conservative but realistic representation of anticipated revenues and expenses. Generally, a certain degree of flexibility in the budget amounts should be expected and constant review of this changing document is always necessary.

Ensure you understand and can apply the following terms:

- Accrual accounting
- Break-even
- Budget philosophy
- Budget reconciliation
- Chart of accounts
- Contingency
- Fixed cost
- Gratuity
- Guest room pick up
- Indirect cost
- Room block
- Variable cost

Refer to the glossary for further clarification of the key terms for this chapter.

LEARNING OBJECTIVES

After completing this chapter, the learner will:

- develop a budgetary philosophy

- define revenue and expense categories

- identify fixed, variable and indirect costs

- understand the difference between cash and accrual accounting

- use break-even formulas

- manage cash

- develop cost control strategy

- develop a registration fee structure

ROLES AND RESPONSIBILITIES

MEETING MANAGER

○ Determine financial objectives

- Determine the financial goal of the meeting
  ○ develop a financial philosophy (e.g., break-even/profit/deficit)
  ○ conduct a cost-benefit analysis
  ○ set financial guidelines for budget flexibility

- Determine any restrictions and special conditions
  ○ determine any restrictions (e.g., registration fees, space available, separate registration for social program)
  ○ determine cash flow with currency fluctuations, rate of exchange and deposit requirements in mind
  ○ determine any special discounts (e.g., for "early bird" registrations or for multiple registrations)
  ○ determine the tax structure in the meeting's locale including any applicable tax rebates
  ○ determine credit card commissions and bank charges in the meeting's locale

- ○ determine "taxable benefit" implications
- ○ determine special financial considerations (e.g., complimentary policy, royalties, package prices)

○ Prepare and manage a budget

- Relate budget items to the objectives of the meeting
  - ○ ensure that the objectives of the meeting are reflected in the budget

  - Define budget components
    - ○ define budget line items
    - ○ determine current marketplace costs
    - ○ apply the formula for determining registration fees, given the desired profit
    - ○ identify revenue components
    - ○ identify expenditure components, including fixed and variable
    - ○ incorporate inflation into current budget figures
    - ○ incorporate taxes and gratuities in expenditures
    - ○ determine hidden costs (e.g., overtime and power drops)
    - ○ incorporate interest on revenues
    - ○ develop internal audit procedures and schedule regular reviews of the budget to analyze budget variances

  - Draft a budget
    - ○ use a chart of accounts
    - ○ calculate no show percentages
    - ○ build flexibility into the budget
    - ○ identify cash requirements
    - ○ use budget planning checklists and worksheets which allow for tracking projected and actual revenues and expenses
    - ○ provide a detailed breakdown of revenues and expenditures
    - ○ build a contingency fund
    - ○ submit the budget for approval as required

  - Monitor and adjust the budget
    - ○ maintain financial accountability
    - ○ monitor revenues and expenditures
    - ○ adjust the budget as needed
    - ○ oversee the daily financial flow

- Develop financial procedures as required

- Establish financial policies and procedures
  - write policies and procedures for petty cash
  - write policies and procedures for banking onsite cash
  - develop credit, cancellation and refund policies
  - determine controls for procurement and inventory
  - arrange for payment by credit cards
  - identify deposit policies and procedures for cash, credit card payments and cheques
  - create a budget handbook with clear, easy-to-read financial policies and procedures, guide of all calculations, a line by line rationale, and backup quotations

- Plan cash flow management
  - prepare a cash flow chart
  - determine cash flow systems including interim financing
  - set up accounts and floats

- Plan and oversee cost control strategies
  - determine spending and signing authority
  - determine committee spending limits
  - provide guidelines to prevent theft and abuse

- Identify and plan for tax considerations
  - determine savings due to tax exemptions or refunds
  - determine procedures for issuing tax receipts and rebates
  - maintain records using standard accounting procedures
  - determine tax implications (e.g., withholding, exemptions)

- Determine banking procedures
  - maximize opportunities for investing revenues
  - determine the need for interest-bearing accounts
  - set up accounts and controls as per the policy of the organization
  - establish foreign banking procedures as required

- Determine a foreign exchange policy
  - use sources of current information on the rate of exchange

- ○ obtain the best currency rate
- ○ investigate the need for and option of buying futures
- ○ calculate the effect on profits of foreign exchange discounts and service charges
- ○ anticipate the effect on cash flow and the budget of foreign currency transactions
- ○ write a "fair exchange" policy for accepting fees in foreign currency
- ○ identify the time implications involved when banks process foreign cheques
- • Distribute information on exchange rates
  - ○ produce guidelines for attendees, organizers and exhibitors
  - ○ communicate the location of currency exchange outlets

○ Comply with tax requirements

- • Administer applied tax(es)
  - ○ apply knowledge of the tax-exempt status of non-profit organizations
  - ○ recognize exemptions from sales tax
  - ○ contact sources of current information about tax obligations
  - ○ complete the appropriate forms and reports
  - ○ comply with filing and safeguarding requirements
  - ○ remit tax on prescribed dates

- • Communicate applicable rebate, exemption and deduction opportunities
  - ○ identify tax rebate opportunities
  - ○ inform meeting attendees about tax deduction opportunities
  - ○ provide the necessary forms

○ Prepare financial reports

- • Compile all payables and receivables
  - ○ approve and sign all invoices for payment
  - ○ reconcile revenues and expenditures in a timely manner

- • Prepare and present reports
  - ○ develop a format for financial reports
  - ○ evaluate financial performance
  - ○ complete a Profit and Loss statement
  - ○ prepare a Variance Report

- Analyze financial reports and propose changes
  - analyze financial reports and propose future changes to budgetary and management practices

- Determine sources of funding
  - identify the types of sponsorships/subsidies/funding available
  - identify if any potential sponsorships conflict with meeting sponsor(s)
  - identify in kind services (e.g., people, skills, equipment, space, services)
  - determine the level of participant funding and other sources of funding
  - write a prospectus and solicit sources of funding

MEETING COORDINATOR

- Assist in the preparation of the budget
- Review any restrictions and special conditions
  - review any planned restrictions (e.g., restrictions to registration fees, restricted space available, separate registration for social program)
  - review any planned discounts (e.g., for "early bird" registrations, or for multiple registrations)
  - review relevant tax provisions and "taxable benefit" implications

- Review financial considerations for the meeting
  - review the sponsorship and subsidy arrangements made
  - review the financial goal(s) of the meeting
  - review revenue and expenditure budget components
  - review budget guidelines

- Gather and review financial data to produce a budget
  - gather and communicate data related to revenues and expenditures

- Adhere to the budget

- Manage revenues and expenditures
  - order and authorize expenditures as per the budget and/or cash flow
  - adhere to the chart of accounts, levels of authority and signing authorities
  - ensure that guarantee commitments correspond with the budget
  - document revenues and expenditures in detail

○ Administer revenues and expenditures

- Adhere to financial policies and procedures
  - ○ process credit card payments
  - ○ follow cash flow systems (e.g. purchase orders, invoicing, financing, and banking)
  - ○ manage and ensure the security of accounts and floats
  - ○ use defined bank deposit procedures
  - ○ control areas of risk and access to revenues
  - ○ provide financial tally sheet(s) as required
  - ○ follow facility policies and guidelines for amounts re: tipping and distribution of gratuities
  - ○ maintain records of gratuities and honorariums distributed
  - ○ adhere to defined tax procedures

○ Reconcile accounts

- Complete accounting and reconciliation
  - ○ adhere to the defined schedule
  - ○ track and communicate budget component variances
  - ○ identify and communicate all outstanding accounts
  - ○ maintain and update documentation required for the budget handbook

○ Assist in the preparation of financial reports

- Gather and review financial data

○ gather data
  - ○ confirm the accuracy of financial transactions

- Prepare and communicate preliminary reports
  - ○ draft variance reports
  - ○ communicate reports to management

- Follow-up on outstanding accounts
  - ○ identify and follow-up all outstanding accounts (payables and receivables)

ESTABLISHING A BUDGETARY PHILOSOPHY

The budgetary philosophy of the event must be determined before fees can be set or any dollars spent. A clear understanding of the budgetary philosophy for your event will guide the host organization and/or meeting sponsor in making financial decisions throughout the planning process. There are three main budgetary philosophies:

Profit
- event revenue budgeted is to be greater than event expenses
- profit is determined either by attendee or the entire event

Break-even
- total revenue is budgeted to equal total expenses
- event revenue sources such as registration, exhibit fees and sponsorship are designed to cover all expenses

Deficit
- event expenses are budgeted to be greater than event revenue
- employer sponsored event where no registration fees are paid\

PREPARING A BUDGET

In developing an event budget, the meeting professional must estimate the number of attendees and the related revenues and expenses. An event history will provide the most useful information, but may not be available. Knowledge of attendee demographics and the proposed program can guide the planner in the absence of a detailed event history. This must be combined with knowledge of the economy and current trends.

Before planning the budget for an event, obtain:

- past financial reports on the same or similar event

- financial objectives

- date(s) (flexibility here may enable cost savings)

- location(s) and venue(s)

- anticipated number of attendees

- more than one estimate for significant expense items (e.g., meeting space, audio visual equipment, food and beverage)

- marketing requirements

- type of food and beverage, and special events

- number of speakers and projected expenses

- costs to be paid by attendees

- anticipated registration and exhibit fees, if appropriate

- anticipated sponsorship

- relevant economic trends

BUDGETING PROCESS

Once the budgetary philosophy has been established, the budget development process typically follows this order:

- identify expenses

- identify potential revenue sources and amounts

- establish registration and exhibit fees, if required

- compare net revenue projection to financial objectives (adjust budget if necessary)

IDENTIFY EXPENSES

Cost estimates should be as accurate as possible. The meeting professional can get quotations from several sources and should rely on information from previous (or similar) events. Use a budget handbook for each event where calculations and backup quotations can be kept in an organized manner for reference during the planning and staging of the event, and for future events.

Selection of categories is event specific and will vary with individual event characteristics and personal style. Expense categories commonly used by meeting professionals include:

- administrative overhead

- food and beverage

- registration materials

- marketing

- speaker travel, expenses, and honoraria
- audio visual equipment
- signs, posters, and banners
- staff travel and expenses (planning and onsite)
- media
- tips and gifts
- taxes
- printing and photocopying
- office furniture and equipment
- communication charges
- meeting space rental
- insurance
- décor and flowers
- supplies
- car rental
- labour charges
- staffing services
- shipping and/or freight charges, customs brokers fees
- postage, mailing house
- photography
- session recording
- complimentary and staff registrations
- ground transportation
- gratuities and services charges
- guest rooms

- air or rail transportation

- credit card processing fees

- entertainment

- translation and interpretation

- education credit fees

- services for persons with special needs

- trade show related expenses

- foreign currency exchange

- contingency

IDENTIFY REVENUES

Whether event revenue is anticipated depends on the budgetary philosophy.

Potential sources of revenue include:

- internal allocations from the organization's budget

- grants

- registration fees

- exhibit fees

- sponsorships (cash or in-kind)

- event related merchandise sales

- investment interest

- cancellation or other administrative fees

- advertising

When determining event revenues, record calculations and assumptions, especially when estimating the number of attendees and exhibitors. It is wise to be conservative when estimating revenue.

ESTABLISH REGISTRATION AND EXHIBIT FEES

FIXED, VARIABLE AND INDIRECT COSTS

Meeting expenses will fall into one of three categories:

1) fixed

2) variable

3) indirect

Fixed costs do not change with the number of attendees. Fixed costs are calculated as a total amount, not on a per person basis, and include:

- audio visual

- marketing

- signage

- cancellation insurance

- speakers

- translation and interpretation

- meeting space rental

Variable costs change directly with the number of attendees, are calculated on a per person basis, and may include:

- food and beverage

- onsite materials

- guest room accommodation

- transportation

- gratuities

Indirect costs are costs that are not tied to individual attendees, can be fixed or variable, and may include:

- staff time

- overhead costs

- general cancellation insurance

For the purposes of break-even analysis, indirect costs are grouped with fixed costs.

BREAK-EVEN OR ZERO-BASED BUDGET

When an event is expected to generate at least enough revenue to cover all expenses, a break-even analysis or zero-based budget will help the meeting professional determine the minimum registration fee or the minimum paid attendance that will accomplish this equal balance.

To determine the break-even registration fee, when the number of attendees is known:
- determine fixed costs
- determine total variable costs (variable costs per person x number of attendees)
- find total costs (add fixed costs and total variable costs)
- determine break-even fee (total costs / number of attendees)
  $ = (fixed costs + [variable x number of attendees]) / number of attendees

To determine the break-even number of attendees, when the fee is known:
- determine fixed costs
- determine variable costs per person
- find contribution margin (registration fee - variable costs)
- determine break-even number of attendees (total costs / contribution margin)
  # = fixed costs / (registration fee - [variable cost/number of attendees])

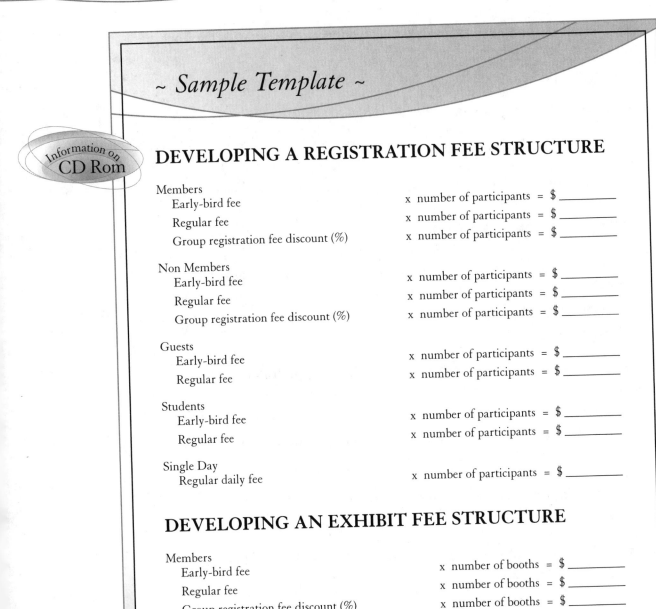

~ Sample Template ~

Information on CD Rom

DEVELOPING A REGISTRATION FEE STRUCTURE

Members
   Early-bird fee   x number of participants = $ _____
   Regular fee   x number of participants = $ _____
   Group registration fee discount (%)   x number of participants = $ _____

Non Members
   Early-bird fee   x number of participants = $ _____
   Regular fee   x number of participants = $ _____
   Group registration fee discount (%)   x number of participants = $ _____

Guests
   Early-bird fee   x number of participants = $ _____
   Regular fee   x number of participants = $ _____

Students
   Early-bird fee   x number of participants = $ _____
   Regular fee   x number of participants = $ _____

Single Day
   Regular daily fee   x number of participants = $ _____

DEVELOPING AN EXHIBIT FEE STRUCTURE

Members
   Early-bird fee   x number of booths = $ _____
   Regular fee   x number of booths = $ _____
   Group registration fee discount (%)   x number of booths = $ _____

Non Members
   Early-bird fee   x number of booths = $ _____
   Regular fee   x number of booths = $ _____
   Group registration discount (%)   x number of booths = $ _____

When you have drafted your expenses and the revenue numbers as described above, compare these numbers to your financial objectives to ensure that they accurately reflect your philosophy. If expected profit is too low, cut back on your expenses, re-evaluate the fees, or implement a higher fee for late or onsite registration. If expected profit seems high, before lowering fees, check that expenses are reasonable and accurate.

~ *Sample Template* ~

STATEMENT OF REVENUE AND EXPENSES

Information on
CD Rom

The statement of revenue and expenses compares transactions over a period of time, and reflects the year to date. Comparison of actual to budgeted revenues and expenses indicates which areas of an event are over or under budget.

SAMPLE REVENUE AND EXPENSE STATEMENT

For: **The Big Event**   **Date: dd/mm/yy**

	Actual year-to-date	Budget year-to-date
REVENUE		
Allocations/Grants/Contracts	$ 13,000	$ 13,000
Function fees	1,000	1,200
Registration fees	9,000	8,000
Exhibit fees	4,600	4,500
Merchandising	150	—
Advertising	3,875	4,000
Sponsorships	4,800	3,000
Investment interest	25	—
Total Revenue...................	**$36,450**	**$ 33,700**
EXPENSES		
Program devel. & production	$23,200	$ 22,000
Administrative	15,600	16,000
Personnel	5,200	4,000
Food and Beverage	—	—
Registration	1,100	—
Promotion	2,800	3,500
Participants and Speakers	300	1,000
Transportation	1,500	—
Audio visual	—	—
Translation and Interpretation	—	—
Exhibitions	—	—
Total Expense....................	**$ 49,700**	**$ 56,500**
Income Over Expense...........	**($ 13,250)**	**($ 22,800)**

BASIC ACCOUNTING PRINCIPLES

CASH ACCOUNTING

Cash accounting recognizes revenue when it is deposited, and expenses when they are actually paid out. This accounting method is primarily used for personal accounting, and may not give an accurate overall financial picture of your event, as it does not account for revenues or expenses that have been committed to (by signing a contract, for example) but not yet taken place. Cash accounting would not record additional revenue that you have confirmed and are expecting (such as a sponsor payment) or expenses that are currently due but for which no cheque has yet been issued.

ACCRUAL ACCOUNTING

Accrual accounting recognizes revenue when it has been committed to, earned or is due, even if it has not yet been received. It recognizes expenses when an order is placed or a commitment such as a contract signing takes place, even if payment has not yet been made. This system provides a more accurate and up to the minute overall financial picture of your event on an ongoing basis.

COST CONTROL STRATEGIES

When developing cost control strategies, experience, expense tracking and accountability are important assets to possess.

Use a file to record calculations and backup quotations for future reference. The meeting professional should also collect and store all orders, contracts, invoices, cheque stubs/copies, and payment receipts, categorized by functional group. All invoices must be checked against the budget to ensure accuracy or identify discrepancies. Check that all charges are in agreement with contractual arrangement, and whereever possible, work out the necessary corrections on site, immediately.

Always get financial agreements in writing. The meeting professional should have documented (not verbal) agreements with the following suppliers/partners as well as any other vendors:

- air transportation providers

- ground transportation providers

- sponsors

- catering services

- unions

- audio visual equipment suppliers

- entertainers

- exhibitors

- presenters/speakers

- facilities/sites

- printers

- tour operators

- exhibition services contractor

- registration personnel

The meeting professional will need some degree of flexibility to deal with unexpected occurrences. This can be accomplished by building in a contingency of 5% to 10% of the total budget, to deal with unexpected events, inflation, currency exchange, misplaced or miss shipped items, and other emergencies.

Signing authority is the authority to issue cheques or commit to additional expenses on behalf of your event suppliers and should be limited, preferably to authorized personnel within the organization. Tight control of signing authority ensures that the meeting professional has sole responsibility for cash disbursements. The meeting professional should conduct a daily review of the organization's master account with venues and other major suppliers while onsite at an event to ensure that no unauthorized expenses have been included.

Finally, to ensure that you also control tax related expenses, contact appropriate taxation departments to determine where and if the event has tax-exempt status. If host or participating organizations are tax-exempt, they may require that specialized forms and reports be completed and issued to the appropriate agencies. Some organizations will be tax exempt for items purchased onsite.

Information on CD Rom

CASH FLOW

Once the final budget has been approved, you will need to examine and plan for the timing of your inflows and outflows of funds. To create a cash flow, divide the total budget into monthly increments that reflect when revenue for specific items is estimated to be received and when expenses are expected to be paid. Evaluate the monthly results to determine if there are any months in which you will have a negative cash flow (less money available than is required to pay your expenses). If this does occur, you will need to manage payment dates and accounts receivable to ensure that cash is always available when required to meet your financial obligations.

~ Sample Template ~

SAMPLE CASH FLOW FOR AN OCTOBER EVENT

	April	May	June	July	August	Sept.	Oct.
REVENUE							
Allocations/Grants/Contracts	$1,000	$2,000	$5,000	$5,000	$5,000	$10,000	$50,000
Function fees	–	$200	$400	$600	–	$2,000	$4,000
Registration fees	–	$1,000	$2,000	$5,000	$23,500	$48,000	$62,000
Exhibit fees	–	$500	$1,000	$3,000	–	$500	$20,000
Mechandising	–	–	–	–	–	–	$7,500
Advertising	–	–	$1,000	$3,000	$5,000	$5,000	$2,100
Sponsorships	–	–	$2,000	$1,000	$1,000	$5,000	$10,000
Investment Interest	–	–	–	–	–	–	$200
TOTAL REVENUE	**$1,000**	**$1,500**	**$11,400**	**$17,600**	**$34,500**	**$70,500**	**$155,800**
EXPENSE							
Program Devel. & Production	$2,000	$4,000	$6,000	$10,000	–	–	$40,000
Administrative	$4,000	$4,000	$4,000	$4,000	$4,000	$4,000	$4,000
Personnel	$1,000	$1,000	$1,000	$1,000	$1,000	$1,000	$1,000
Food and Beverage	–	–	–	–	–	–	–
Registration	–	–	–	–	–	–	–
Promotion	$1,000	$1,000	$1,000	$500	$1,500	–	–
Participants and Speakers	–	–	$1,000	–	–	–	–
Audio Visual	–	–	–	–	–	–	$7,000
Transportation	–	–	–	–	–	–	–
Hospitality	–	–	–	–	–	–	–
Translation and Interpretation	–	–	–	–	–	–	–
Exhibitions	–	–	–	–	$5,000	–	–
TOTAL EXPENSE	**$8,000**	**$10,000**	**$13,000**	**$15,500**	**$11,500**	**$5,000**	**$52,000**
Income Over Expense	($7,000)	($8,500)	($1,600)	$2,100	$23,000	$65,500	$103,800
Cumulative Cash Flow	($7,000)	($15,500)	($17,100)	($15,000)	$8,000	$73,500	$177,300

Break-even point

CASH MANAGEMENT

The meeting professional may wish to open an event specific bank account if the meeting is large with significant revenue expected from onsite registration. Receipts can be transferred at the end of the event to the host organization's account.

This may not be necessary when onsite revenues are not expected to be significant or where cash can be deposited with the event facility as an advance toward the master account charges. This avoids security issues involved with the transport of cash and may even earn a discount from the facility for early cash payment.

Consider bonding all personnel involved with the handling of cash, cheques and credit cards.

Registration personnel should receive detailed procedural instructions and a daily tally sheet for each person who handles funds that includes:

- amount of each transaction

- method of payment (if by cheque or traveller's cheque, include cheque number)

- type of registration (e.g., full meeting, reception, guest program, special function)

- number of tickets issued

- applicable discounts, if any

- complimentary items (e.g., badges, tickets)

International funds exchange can be avoided by insisting that fees be paid in local currency or by credit card. When the event involves a large number of international delegates, the meeting professional may decide to accept international funds for the attendee's convenience. If this is the case, be sure to obtain the daily exchange rate when accepting onsite funds. If international funds are accepted for pre registration, be aware that the exchange rate may change significantly between receipt of fees and settlement of accounts.

When cheques are received in international funds, they are not actually added to the event account until the domestic banking institution has received funds from the international banking institution. As exchange rates do fluctuate, this time lag involves risk. Most banks will apply service charges for handling international currency transactions. Find out what these charges are and when they are applied.

It may be necessary to pass these extra fees on to the registrant, and in some cases, professional assistance from banks or currency exchange firms may be needed. Notify international delegates well in advance of international currency exchange rates and restrictions.

POST EVENT ANALYSIS

Post event financial analysis is performed to evaluate the event and to draw conclusions for future events. This is called budget reconciliation. It is important to determine in which categories costs were over or under budget. The overall numbers may look reasonable, but problem areas may be present that should be corrected for future events. To reconcile your budget, you should undertake the following tasks:

- compare actual revenues and expenses with planned results to determine both positive and negative variations

- analyze these differences to determine the cause of the variance, and potential solutions, if appropriate

- recommend changes in financial policies or procedures for future events as appropriate

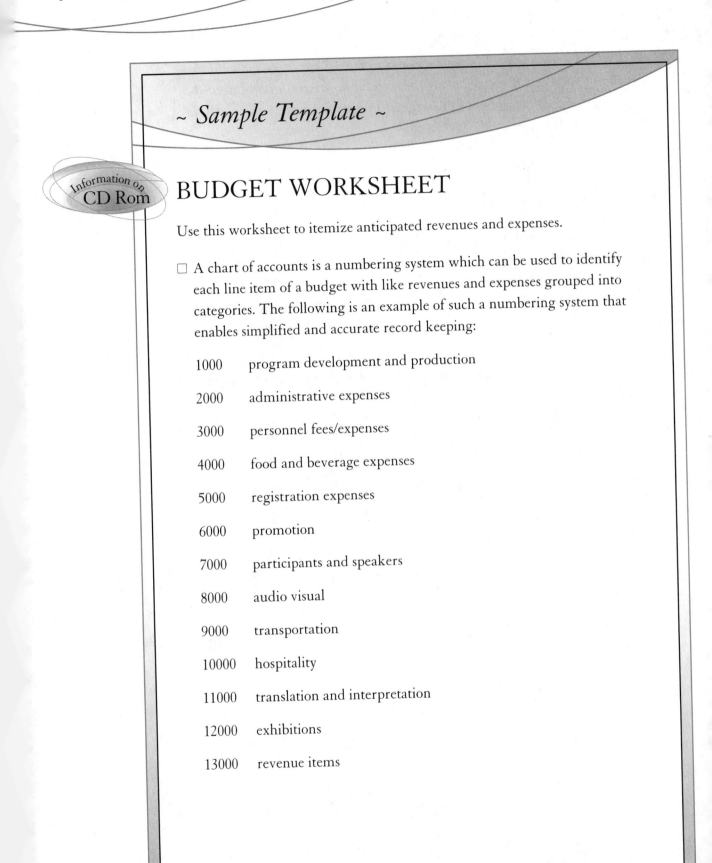

~ Sample Template ~

Information on
CD Rom

BUDGET WORKSHEET

Use this worksheet to itemize anticipated revenues and expenses.

☐ A chart of accounts is a numbering system which can be used to identify each line item of a budget with like revenues and expenses grouped into categories. The following is an example of such a numbering system that enables simplified and accurate record keeping:

1000	program development and production
2000	administrative expenses
3000	personnel fees/expenses
4000	food and beverage expenses
5000	registration expenses
6000	promotion
7000	participants and speakers
8000	audio visual
9000	transportation
10000	hospitality
11000	translation and interpretation
12000	exhibitions
13000	revenue items

~ Sample Template ~

☐ Program development and production
- abstract printing, distribution, selection _____
- program production _____
- board and committee travel _____
- board and committee lodging _____
- security _____
- gifts _____
- awards _____
- ribbons _____
- social functions
  - tickets _____
  - opening receptions _____
  - banquet _____
  - awards _____

SUBTOTAL: _____

☐ Administrative expenses
- gratuities _____
- telephones and long distance charges _____
- miscellaneous postage _____
- miscellaneous copies _____
- secretarial services _____
- office furniture rental _____
- computer/printer rental _____
- copy machine rental _____
- shipping to/from event _____
- meeting room rental _____
- insurance _____

~ *Sample Template* ~

- legal fees   —————
- photography   —————
- decorations   —————
- signs   —————
- flowers   —————
- taxes   —————

SUBTOTAL: —————

☐ Staff/volunteers
- professional fees   —————
- travel (air/ground)   —————
- accommodations   —————
- food and miscellaneous expenses   —————
- complimentary registrations   —————

SUBTOTAL: —————

☐ Food and beverage (plus tax and gratuity)
- opening reception   —————
- breakfast day one   —————
- morning break day one   —————
- lunch day one   —————
- afternoon break day one   —————
- dinner day one   —————
- breakfast day two   —————
- morning break day two   —————
- [repeat for each day]   —————

SUBTOTAL: —————

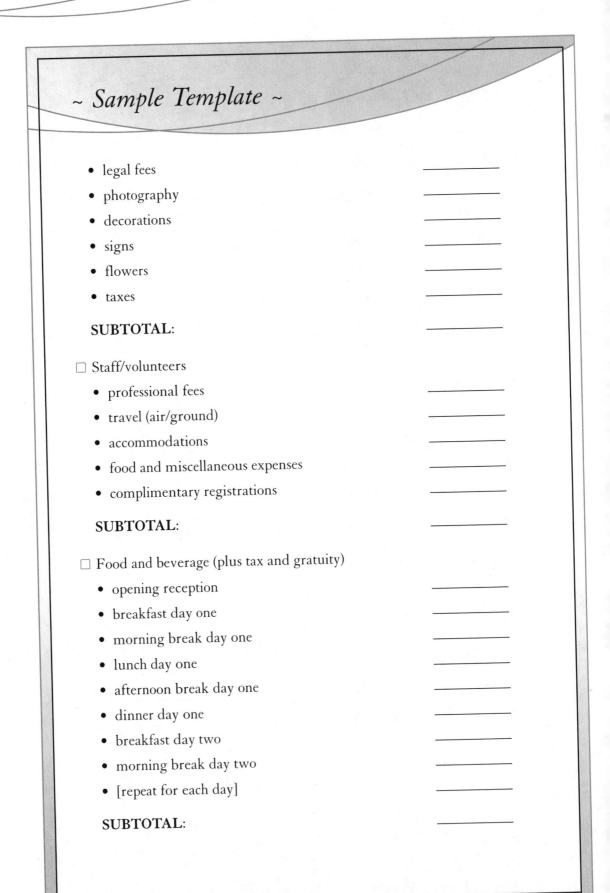

~ *Sample Template* ~

☐ Registration expenses

- advance registration forms   _____
- onsite registration forms   _____
- receipts   _____
- envelopes for advance registration forms   _____
- postage for advance registration forms   _____

SUBTOTAL: _____

☐ Promotion

- program announcement (art, printing, paper)   _____
- mailing lists/labels preparation   _____
- program announcement envelopes   _____
- postage for program announcement   _____
- event letterhead   _____
- event chair's letter preparations   _____
- event chair's letter envelopes   _____
- event chair's letter postage   _____
- ad preparation   _____
- advertisement placement   _____
- media release preparation   _____
- media release postage   _____
- posters   _____
- complimentary registrations   _____

SUBTOTAL: _____

☐ Program participants

- speaker one   _____
- hotel accommodations   _____

~ *Sample Template* ~

- travel expenses (air)   ————
- travel expenses (ground)   ————
- food and miscellaneous expenses ————
- honorarium   ————
- [repeat for as many speakers as are participating] ————

SUBTOTAL: ————

☐ Audio visual

- microphones   ————
- sound system   ————
- recording equipment (audio) ————
- recording equipment (video) ————
- technicians   ————
- spotlights   ————
- screens   ————
- monitors   ————
- slide projectors   ————
- overhead projectors   ————
- data projectors   ————
- LCD tablets   ————
- VCRs   ————
- chalkboards/whiteboards   ————
- flip charts   ————
- carts, stands, easels   ————
- mixers   ————
- accessories (remotes, dissolves, extension cords) ————
- supplies (markers, chalk, transparencies, tape) ————
- setup and teardown labour and service charges ————

SUBTOTAL: ————

~ *Sample Template* ~

☐ Transportation/shuttle service

- VIP pickups   _____
- car rentals   _____
- tours   _____
- general group transfers   _____

SUBTOTAL: _____

☐ Hospitality/attendees

- meet and greet (airport)   _____
- welcome hospitality suite   _____

SUBTOTAL: _____

☐ Translation and interpretation

- simultaneous interpretation   _____
- communication equipment   _____
- translation fees   _____
- printing fees   _____

SUBTOTAL: _____

☐ Exhibitions

- promotion, prospectus   _____
- decorator, drayage   _____
- security   _____
- space rental   _____

SUBTOTAL: _____

TOTAL: _____

~ *A Conference Journal* ~

Conference details had never been discussed when the associations decided to host a joint meeting but several issues were brought to the forefront with the need to develop a conference budget.

For example, they noted that there was disparity in conference fees charged to members between the associations. One charged $450 while the other had a set member fee of $175 for attendance at sessions only. Other differences also became very apparent. One group was successful in obtaining individual sponsorships of $100,000 while the other rarely saw donations exceed $35,000. More than 20 tours were offered in one guest program while the other had experienced success with five; shuttle service had been the norm for the national group but not with the international association.

The budget process forced the planning committee to translate the conference goals and objectives into financial terms. They began by identifying all events and functions that had the potential to earn revenue, since there was an established history related to fees as well as sponsors ready and willing to continue their relationship with the associations. They included all of the various registration categories, revenues from tours, the spouses program and revenues for pre conference seminars. Through in depth analysis and discussion they came to a mutual agreement on registration fees and the number of breakouts, tours and events they would hold. Then, to finalize the formula, they established the quantity or anticipated attendance. Since they could not pinpoint attendance, they decided that a single budget would not provide them with the information they needed so they developed three scenarios on a single spreadsheet that they defined as low (10,000 delegates), realistic (12,000 delegates) and high (15,000+ delegates).

Each budget scenario had to reflect a substantial profit for the joint event, which was to be shared equally by the associations. As is the case with many not-for-profit associations, the profits generated from educational conferences was used for the administration of association needs throughout the year and enabled them to conduct other member services that did not generate their own revenues. They also decided that they would only share in the profits from the joint conference, leaving the trade show component as two stand alone events with separate budgets, marketing plans, booth sales and management.

To develop expenses for the joint conference, they combined their existing budgets, using their most recent conference figures and included an amount for inflation. This proved to be unsatisfactory in certain circumstances because the conference was different from their past experience. At this point, they decided to obtain quotations from their suppliers, and in some cases, seek new suppliers. It was also necessary to identify an approval process for the budget and confirm the responsibility of the meeting manager. They decided that the meeting manager would be responsible for sourcing suppliers, preparing the request for proposal, evaluating the proposed costs, and conducting final negotiations with suppliers. The subcommittee responsible for a particular event reviewed the costs obtained by the meeting manager in advance of a presentation to the full conference planning committee. This committee then decided whether or not they wanted to commit to the expense. Signing authority was delegated to a handful of executive members of the committee, the meeting manager and the executive directors of both associations.

They wanted to prepare a budget that reflected conservative revenues and realistic expenses. Reflecting on the first draft of the budget, they realized that their desire to conduct an unprecedented event would fall short of their financial objectives to ensure a profit. Since they could not accurately predict attendance or sponsorship revenues, they decided they would need to pare down some of the costs related to individual events. They went back over proposals from suppliers to see what was not vital to the success of the event and began to minimize expenses without eliminating any events or detracting from the function.

There were certain fixed costs such as room rentals, insurance and staff salaries that could not change. Other costs such as food and beverage, décor and technology had greater flexibility because suppliers had been asked to create the event of a lifetime, and incorporated very creative ideas through the use of a range of materials, all of which equated to greater cost. For example, one of the decorators for the gala recommended chair covers as part of the overall theme. This would have created a beautiful effect in the room; however, it was decided that this was not crucial to the theme and the décor would still be effective if they eliminated this component.

Finally, after months of adding, deleting and fine-tuning, they had a workable budget that was sent to the board of directors of each association for final approval. As supplies and services were acquired and contracts signed, they kept a watchful eye on expenditures to ensure that they were in-line with the approved budget. Managing the budget also meant that at every conference planning committee meeting, there was a budget review and analysis conducted to compare the budgeted figures to actual expenditures. Revenues were also watched closely to determine if there was something else that could be done in terms of more pro-active promotion or a different sales approach, if they fell short of their goal. There were occasions throughout the year that an expense would arise that had not been taken into account at the start and, if significant, it was reviewed by the conference planning committee and subsequently submitted for approval to the board of directors.

This was an exhaustive process at the outset but well worth the time and energy because the firm establishment of the budget early on provided guidelines for purchases throughout the many months to come. Had this not occurred, the two associations might have shared a very large deficit instead of the intended profit at the end of the conference.

CHAPTER REVIEW

☐ Prior to developing an event budget, it is necessary to gather general information regarding attendees, host city, and event objectives. This can be obtained from the host organization, previous experience, or in consultation with other meeting professionals.

☐ Budget philosophy of the event must be determined:

- break-even
- profit
- deficit/loss

☐ Sources of event funding vary with the type of event:

- corporations - allocation from company budget
- associations - event generates revenue
- donation or sponsorship - funds, goods, and services

☐ Budget development strategy:

- determine expense categories and amounts
- identify sources of revenue
- establish registration and other fees
- compare revenues to expenses and adjust as required

☐ Fixed and Variable Costs budgetary method allows for break-even analysis.

☐ Fixed costs do not change with number of attendees, and include:

- promotion
- signs
- speakers
- meeting room rental
- insurance

☐ Variable costs vary directly with the number of attendees, and include:

- food and beverage
- taxes and gratuities
- onsite materials
- guest bedroom accommodations

☐ Indirect and hidden costs are present, and must be incorporated into the budget.

☐ Cash basis accounting is a very simple accounting method that recognizes revenue when it is deposited, and expenses when they are actually paid.

☐ Accrual accounting gives a more accurate financial picture of the event since revenue is recognized when is it earned, and expenses recorded when they are committed to.

☐ Cash flow analysis assists in evaluating the inflow and outflows of funds and ensures that sufficient money is readily available to meet financial commitments.

☐ The meeting professional must take steps to manage cash and provide registration personnel with detailed procedural instructions and daily tally sheets.

☐ Special consideration must be given to foreign funds; if they will be accepted, how they will be processed, and what service charges will be incurred.

☐ Cost control strategies must be in place, and depend on a well kept budget handbook, tracking, accountability, and experience.

☐ Post event financial analysis (budget reconciliation) is performed to evaluate the financial success of the event and to draw conclusions for future events.

TEST YOUR KNOWLEDGE

The following self test will indicate the level of understanding and knowledge gained from this chapter. Solutions to all self tests can be found in **Appendix A.**

1. The break-even budget is the only budget philosophy.
    ☐ True   ☐ False

2. Accrual accounting gives a more accurate financial picture than cash basis accounting.
    ☐ True   ☐ False

3. Accepting foreign currency payments is a simple process that is greatly appreciated by event attendees.
    ☐ True   ☐ False

4. Signing authority should be given to staff members to reduce the meeting professional's work load.
    ☐ True   ☐ False

5. Break-even analysis is used with the fixed and variable costs budgetary method.
    ☐ True   ☐ False

6. The event master account with the facility should be reviewed by the meeting professional:

    (a) every day at the event   (b) before and after the event   (c) on last day of event
    (d) after the event   (e) this task can be delegated to staff member

7. Sources of revenue for an event include:

    (a) registration fees   (b) exhibition fees   (c) sponsorships
    (d) company budget   (e) all of the above

8. The following are fixed costs except for:

    (a) promotion   (b) signs   (c) onsite materials
    (d) speakers   (e) all of the above are fixed costs

9. Hidden or indirect costs include:

    (a) staff time   (b) telephone equipment and calls   (c) labour and setup charges
    (d) insurance   (e) all of the above are hidden or indirect costs

10. How are revenue and expense items determined for an event budget?

_____

_____

_____

11. Why is the event budget so important to the meeting professional?

_____

_____

_____

12. List five cost control strategies available to the meeting professional.

_____

_____

_____

_____

13. In your own words, state the importance of performing a post event financial analysis.

_____

_____

_____

_____

_____

_____

14. What is the benefit to the meeting planner of undertaking a cash flow analysis?

_____

_____

_____

_____

_____

Program Development

INTRODUCTION

Meeting professionals are becoming more responsible for the quality of the education content of their meetings.

Once meeting objectives have been determined, the meeting professional can begin the process of designing an appropriate program. Much of the success of subsequent steps in the meeting planning process will hinge on careful attention to the design and development of the meeting program. It is at this stage that the meeting professional begins to allot times and formats to the various program elements. As well, the meeting professional begins the process of incorporating any themes into various planned activities, ensuring the theme is carried through all elements. From this point, the meeting professional begins to solicit speakers and determine meeting space requirements. Other elements of program design include planning for off site events, social activities, guest programs and food and beverage functions.

Ensure you understand and can apply the following terms:

- Breakout session
- Concurrent session
- General session
- Guest program
- Meeting agenda
- Meeting history
- Meeting theme
- Plenary session
- Speakers bureau
- Themes

Refer to the glossary for further clarification of the key terms for this chapter.

LEARNING OBJECTIVES

After completing this chapter, the learner will:

- understand adult learning principles

- understand the complexity of meeting design

- distinguish between different types of sessions

- understand the importance of delegate demographics

- understand the resources available to help select guest speakers

- incorporate themes into various program elements

- understand how the program format determines meeting space requirements

- gain an appreciation for the complexity of working with volunteers and committees

ROLES AND RESPONSIBILITIES

MEETING MANAGER

○ Develop the program

- Clarify the needs of participants
  - ○ recognize and understand adult learning styles
  - ○ survey prospective attendees
  - ○ recognize participants' needs for learning, knowledge, concentration, relaxation, comfort, excitement, pride, and networking, and reconcile needs with the goals and objectives of the meeting
  - ○ determine the need for and format of proceedings
  - ○ determine the requirement for educational credit and appropriate sources of credit

- Define program themes
  - ○ develop a dynamic program, choosing major themes or tracks which meet the objective
  - ○ recognize the need for a meeting design which creates favorable conditions for participants (both formally and informally)

- Develop the program to meet defined objectives
  - consult with those responsible for the content development of the program
  - adhere to budget guidelines and incorporate sponsorships
  - determine the presentation modes
  - determine staging requirements
  - design the pace, tempo and style of the program
  - ensure that the program matches meeting objectives and space available
  - recognize the sequence in which program decisions are made
  - determine length of sessions and schedule the program for variety
  - prepare a "preliminary" program incorporating all ancillary programs
  - incorporate legislative issues into plans (e.g., annual general meeting)
  - determine the format of materials to support/reinforce other presentation techniques and when to distribute them

- Develop a guest/youth program

  - Determine the need for a guest/youth program
    - use a questionnaire to determine a profile of guests who will attend
    - review histories of previous meetings

  - Determine the objectives of a guest/youth program
    - evaluate the questionnaire and the organization's objectives

  - Develop the program
    - research the unique character of the meeting location
    - source, negotiate and contract destination suppliers and services
    - recognize legal requirements involved
    - schedule planned activities

  - Plan information packages
    - develop itineraries, brochures and tickets
    - prepare and distribute an introduction script to program participants
    - follow up and evaluate

○ Develop social events

- Determine the need for a social program
  - ○ research the need for social events
  - ○ review histories of prior meetings and attendee profile
  - ○ determine the goals of social events as they relate to meeting objectives

- Develop the events
  - ○ determine the availability of various options of location, timing and program
  - ○ determine the need for and use of suppliers and services
  - ○ contract and schedule social events
  - ○ preview entertainment groups
  - ○ co-ordinate social events with other program components

- Manage the requirements of entertainers
  - ○ recognize types of entertainment
  - ○ determine the need and criteria for entertainment based on meeting objectives
  - ○ evaluate and recommend entertainment
  - ○ ensure appropriate setup to meet entertainers' needs
  - ○ discuss tax, immigration and legal considerations
  - ○ arrange a briefing session, emphasizing the sensitivities of the audience
  - ○ meet needs of entertainers for information, equipment, services and accommodation
  - ○ prepare a written agreement/contract and riders
  - ○ follow up and evaluate

- Develop pre and post programs
  - ○ determine the need for pre and post social programs, given the meeting objectives and attendee profile
  - ○ determine the need for and use of suppliers and services
  - ○ develop tours, vacation packages, extended stay opportunities and recreational opportunities
  - ○ co-ordinate pre and post activities with the program
  - ○ write pre and post program itineraries and brochures
  - ○ provide suppliers information about attendees
  - ○ design information packages

MEETING COORDINATOR

○ Implement the program

- Review the program and its objectives
  - ○ recognize how adults learn and factors which affect learning
  - ○ review the program, its major themes and the meeting objective(s)
  - ○ review the critical path for the program

- Fulfill responsibility for all elements of the program logistics
  - ○ deliver the program as outlined in the brochure
  - ○ use checklists and the conference résumé

- Co-ordinate proceedings
  - ○ co-ordinate and distribute proceedings

- Respond to last minute requests and changes
  - ○ demonstrate an understanding of the capabilities of facilities/suppliers
  - ○ adjust the program as necessary
  - ○ communicate changes

- Identify and solve problems related to the program
  - ○ brief staff and facility employees on changes
  - ○ hold daily briefing meetings as required
  - ○ monitor group dynamics

○ Implement the guest/youth program

- Review the objectives of a guest/youth program
  - ○ review the profile of family members and guests who will attend
  - ○ review planned events

- Deliver the program
  - ○ work with tour companies
  - ○ carry out the guest/youth program activities
  - ○ distribute information packages

- Prepare information packages
  - ○ develop itineraries, brochures, and tickets
  - ○ prepare and distribute an introduction script to program participants
  - ○ follow up and evaluate

○ Implement the social program

- Review the social program
  - ○ review the objectives of the social program
  - ○ review planned events

- Deliver the program
  - ○ co-ordinate entertainment
  - ○ distribute information packages

- Meet the needs of entertainers
  - ○ follow defined policies, procedures and contracts
  - ○ provide appropriate setup, equipment, services, information, accommodation, and aids required

- Co-ordinate pre and post activities with the program
  - ○ write pre and post program itineraries and brochures
  - ○ implement all logistics of pre and post programs

PROGRAM PLANNING

Program planning can include planning and coordinating literally every component of a meeting or educational offering. Today's meeting professional is expected to plan a program that will deliver a significant return on the organization's investment. While social events and networking are still important components of a successful meeting, employers are unwilling to send attendees to a meeting that does not have a reputation for quality educational programming. Additionally, as technological advances such as video conferencing, CD-ROM, and the Internet make communication and learning more accessible and efficient, organizations must offer meeting attendees training they can't easily get in their own home or office.

As a result, meeting professionals are becoming more responsible for the quality of the education content at their meetings. A meeting professional's duties must include designing program formats, assisting in speaker selection and maintaining quality controls over presentation materials.

KEY COMPONENTS FOR ASSEMBLING A PROGRAM PLAN

Once the meeting objectives have been established, additional research is necessary to identify the needs of the group. Collecting demographic information about meeting attendees is a prerequisite to:

- selecting a location for the meeting

- determining the appropriate length of the meeting

- potential audience size

ATTENDEE CONSIDERATION

Demographic and other kinds of information can also help with the selection of program content to meet the established meeting objectives. A good place to begin the research is to examine available information from past meetings:

- were a large percentage of the attendees from the local or regional area around the convention site, or from a geographically dispersed audience?

- where are the majority of the attendees located?

- what are the common characteristics that attendees possess?

- do family members or guests attend?

- are recreational activities important to the group?

Answering these questions and gathering as much information as possible is a key step in designing a successful meeting program.

CONSIDER THE PROFILE OF THE ATTENDEES

The special needs of attendees are important to identify before establishing meeting objectives. Consider if they:

- are from another country

- have a physical limitations

- have dietary restrictions

- have holiday and religious observances

Past meeting evaluations are extremely beneficial for determining preferences of the audience:

- What type of accommodations will please attendees?

- How important are local attractions?

- Are recreational activities important to the overall satisfaction?

- How important are shopping and eating establishments?

It is important to determine the likes and dislikes of the potential audience to help program scheduling. Any information that is available about the preferences of meeting attendees will provide a clearer understanding of their expectations. Consider the following questions as examples:

- Do attendees learn best in interactive workshops where they can express their views, or do they prefer to hear from experts in a lecture format?

- Are scheduled meal functions expected by the attendees, or will they want to explore area restaurants?

- Do attendees expect a program during a meal, or do they prefer free time to network with their colleagues at these times?

PROGRAM DEVELOPMENT

If it is customary to do so, a meeting title and theme is selected before content is developed.

The meeting professional should establish a template for the entire conference that details all major time blocks. These may include:

- plenary sessions

- workshops

- concurrent sessions

- refreshment breaks

- meals

- social events

- trade show

- registration hours

- tours

Once the timing has been established, the number of each type of session will be known. The program development committee can then begin to confirm topics and speakers for each session slot.

Consider the attendees' preferences and experience levels, and program something for everyone. Varying the format of the educational program will keep attendees interested.

It is important to consider the time it takes to get attendees from one location to another. Distances between events and the number of participants dictate the amount of time that must be allowed. The number of restrooms and telephones that are available should also be a consideration in determining break length.

WHY HAVE A THEME?

The theme chosen for an event is a common thread, linking the program, food, décor, and entertainment to one central motif. The theme may be requested by the host organization, or may be left to the meeting professional. Not all events require a theme. Those that do should set a clear tone for the events. The event theme should reflect established objectives.

ADULT LEARNING

Adult learning is the theory and study of how adults learn.

Arranging the educational content is becoming a standard job function of today's meeting professional. Although knowledge of adult learning skills should be developed, meeting professionals don't need to become experts in adult learning and instructional design. The meeting professional should understand:

- how to design effective learning objectives for adults

- how to design program formats that deliver to the established objectives

- when and how to access resources in adult learning, such as internal trainers, communication experts or design and production specialists

CHARACTERISTICS OF THE ADULT LEARNER

- Adults have extensive life experiences that tend to structure and limit new learning. Learning should focus largely on transforming or extending the values, meanings, skills and strategies acquired from previous experiences.

- Major pressures for change come from factors related to social and work roles, expectations and a personal need for continuing productivity and self-definition.

- Adult learning peaks when the content requires the learner to solve a problem. It is best accomplished when the learner is actively involved in finding a practical solution.

- Adults possess an organized and consistent self-concept and self-esteem that enables them to participate as an entity separate from other entities with the capability of acting independently.

- Because of their responsible status in society, adults are expected to be productive.

- Adults need to be actively involved in the learning process. They will respond when their maturity is acknowledged and factored into the learning exercise.

APPLICATION OF ADULT LEARNING PRINCIPLES

Factors that can affect the learning environment of adult learners are:

Physical – the physical arrangement of the furnishings, the space between attendees, and the interface of learner/facilitator and learner/learner greatly impact the learning and interaction that occur.

Social – adult learners need time to process information. Providing breaks and networking opportunities in the program will allow learners time to reflect on and share with others what they have heard.

Emotional – adult learners are motivated to participate in educational activities that will benefit them by the conscious need to take ownership of their learning.

Physiological – presentations that draw on real life experiences that the adult learner can relate to or imagine are critical to capturing their interest.

Psychological – to assist adult learners in becoming strategic thinkers, better listeners and generally open to new ideas in the learning environment, the pressures and distractions of daily life must be removed.

The role of the meeting professional is to understand the impact these factors have on adult learners and use that knowledge to create an optimum learning environment for meeting attendees. For example, in creating a program that is conducive to learning, the meeting professional should be aware of such things as the arrangement of the meeting room (physical); the time available for attendees to process the information they receive (social); their motivation or objectives for attending this meeting (emotional); and the real-world examples they will take away from the meeting (physiological). Removing distractions and eliminating interruptions during the meeting will ensure the attendee has a positive psychological experience.

Adult learners learn best when they actively participate in learning activities that take these principles into consideration.

> **HOT TIP** You create a high impact session using the case-study approach. Have an industry member describe, in five minutes maximum, a problem they faced and how they solved it. Leave five minutes for questions and dialogue then move on to the next speaker. If you choose good speakers, you can include up to eight and still hold the audience.

(All Hot Tips contributed by Meetings & Incentive Travel Group, Rogers Publishing)

SESSION FORMATS

FORMAT	DESCRIPTION
Breakout	small group sessions within a meeting, organized to discuss specific subjects
Concurrent sessions	multiple simultaneous topics covering a wide range of interest
Exhibit/trade show	event at which products and services are displayed
General/Plenary Session	general assembly for all persons actively involved in a meeting
Labs	replicate working environment with equipment to practice or learn new skills
Tours/Site Visits	trips to related sites or industries
Workshops	seminars emphasizing free discussion, exchange of ideas, demonstration of methods and practical application of skills and principles; also, meeting of several persons for intensive discussion

INSTRUCTIONAL STYLES

FORMAT	DESCRIPTION
Case study	simulated situation; attendees work with others in groups to practice or apply skills
Lecture/paper	discourse given before an audience, especially for instructional purposes
Panel	several speakers (e.g., four is a manageable number) with different perspectives on the same topic; may include a moderator
Poster sessions	display boards placed around room with visual informational presentations; often scientific and accompanied by the author
Product demonstrations	one or more persons showing how a particular product functions
Round table discussions	approximately 8-10 attendees with a group leader; informal discussion of issues or exchange of ideas
Talk show	moderator interview with 2 to 3 experts often with different perspectives

SESSION TIMING

Consider the following as a guideline in determining how much time should be allowed for various styles or formats:

Lecture	45-60 minutes including 15 minutes for question and answer
Panel	45 - 60 minutes (10-15 minutes each panelist), including 15 minutes question and answer
Lunch with speaker	90 minutes - 2 hours
Breaks	20 minutes for 50 people or fewer
	30 minutes for 50+ people
Dinner	30 minutes per course
Reception	(prior to dinner) 30 minutes to 1 hour
Reception style dinner	1 - 2 hours

Time allowances for people movement between sessions, assuming all sessions are located in one building:

up to 100 people	5 minutes
100-500 people	10 minutes
500-1,000 people	15 minutes

~ Sample Template ~

Information on
CD Rom

SAMPLE – PROGRAM AT A GLANCE

MONDAY

12:00 noon – 8:00 p.m.	Registration Desk & Information Booth
12:00 noon – 8:00 p.m.	Hands-On Labs
2:00 p.m. – 8:00 p.m.	Exhibit Showcase
2:00 p.m. – 6:00 p.m.	New Products Lab, Usability Lab, and Education Lab
6:00 p.m. – 8:00 p.m.	Reception in Exhibit Showcase

TUESDAY

7:00 a.m. – 5:30 p.m.	Registration Desk & Information Booth
7:00 a.m. – 8:20 a.m.	Continental Breakfast
8:30 a.m. – 10:30 a.m.	General Session
10:30 a.m. – 10:50 a.m.	Break
10:30 a.m. – 2:00 p.m.	Exhibit Showcase
10:30 a.m. – 4:30 p.m.	Hands-on Labs
12:00 noon – 1:00 p.m.	Birds-of-a-Feather Lunch
1:05 p.m. – 2:05 p.m.	Breakout Session
2:15 p.m. – 3:15 p.m.	Breakout Session
3:00 p.m. – 4:30 p.m.	Exhibit Showcase
3:15 p.m. – 3:40 p.m.	Break
3:40 p.m. – 4:40 p.m.	Breakout Session
4:30 p.m. – 9:00 p.m.	Welcome Reception and Partner Fair

WEDNESDAY

7:00 a.m. – 5:30 p.m.	Registration Desk & Information Booth
7:15 a.m. – 8:20 a.m.	Continental Breakfast
8:30 a.m. – 9:45 a.m.	Keynote Address
9:45 a.m. – 5:30 p.m.	Hands-On Lab and Documentation Lab
9:45 a.m. – 2:00 p.m.	Exhibit Showcase
9:45 a.m. – 10:10 a.m.	Break
10:10 a.m. – 11:10 a.m.	Breakout Session
11:20 a.m. – 12:20 p.m.	Breakout Session
12:25 p.m. – 1:25 p.m.	Lunch with Guest Speaker
1:30 p.m. – 2:30 p.m.	Breakout Session
2:40 p.m. – 3:40 p.m.	Breakout Session
3:00 p.m. – 5:30 p.m.	Exhibit Showcase
3:40 p.m. – 4:05 p.m.	Break
4:05 p.m. – 5:05 p.m.	Breakout Session
7:00 p.m. – 11:00 p.m.	Off-Site Event – Beach Blast

SOCIAL EVENTS

As with so many other aspects of the meeting, social events can add significantly to the overall success in achieving the objectives of the meeting. Social events can include meals, receptions, recreational activities or pre and post conference tours. Social events too, should be planned keeping in mind the overall theme of the meeting and the objectives for the event.

The quality of pre and post meeting tours offered can often be the added incentive that encourages participants to attend and to bring guests. Whether it be a one day excursion to tour the area surrounding the chosen destination or a three day package added to the end of the conference, closely working with a destination management company can alleviate much of the added work of planning these types of activities.

HOT TIP

Be Hip to Local Events

When writing your program guide, consider including a listing and schedule of seasonal events happening in the host city. Highlight extracurricular ideas such as sports or cultural events, concerts, festivals or local heritage gatherings. The appeal of local events and attractions can be an important lure to potential attendees. Schedule smartly though, you don't want delegates skipping out of the conference early.

GUEST/YOUTH PROGRAMS

Many conferences include separate programs for guests or children attending with the delegate. The meeting professional designs programs for these individuals based on direction from the host organization. These programs often run parallel with the educational content. Often there is a nominal fee for these events.

They can include city tours, sporting events, shopping, expeditions, museum visits, and other events that highlight the destination.

Youth programs should be managed by qualified supervisory personnel. All programs should be designed around the anticipated interest of those expected to attend.

CONTINUING EDUCATION CREDITS

Many professional groups and organizations offer their members the opportunity to earn continuing education units (CEUs) when they participate in formal education programs. CEUs are non-academic, meaning they are administered by the organization or professional group hosting the educational meeting or event. CEUs are earned through successful completion of a predetermined number of hours in an accredited program.

Each organization establishes a minimum number of CEUs which must be earned by one individual in a year. This requirement ensures that members remain current with new developments in their respective fields of specialization and/or maintain their professional certification.

WORKING WITH PROGRAM COMMITTEES

Committee members should be selected on the basis of their dependability, accessibility and knowledge of the subject matter. A chairperson should then be selected from this group who has the ability to maintain organizational control and be confident enough in the program planning process to delegate responsibilities.

Prepare a comprehensive resources workbook and send it to committee members before the first planning meeting. This workbook will include:

- meeting objectives

- brief history of the program structure including guest programs, tours, food and beverage functions, and social events

- evaluation summary of previous program

- pertinent facts for upcoming event (dates, location, anticipated attendance)

- relevant planning deadlines

~ A Conference Journal ~

Since they were working with two very successful annual events that, over the years, had been designed to meet the learning objectives unique to each association, creating a program for the millennium conference was not as difficult as it might seem.

They began with the education component. They noted what worked and what didn't for each group and then began to plan a new event taking into account the best of both worlds. Of course, a number of adjustments and refinements had to be made. For example, the national group usually conducted eleven concurrent sessions while the international association managed four. They settled on five concurrent sessions, primarily due to venue restrictions of limited meeting rooms small enough to accommodate breakout sessions.

These two conferences were generally based on a technical conference format. Typically, technical conference formats have short, topic specific informational sessions, usually 20 minutes in duration with a brief Q&A period following. The attendees do not relocate but rather the next speaker enters to present in the same fashion.

These concurrent sessions were designed to be 20 minutes in length, generally with a single speaker from within their industry, who provided updated information on a new technique, system or discovery. This is quite different from the usual structure of a session that may be 60 to 90 minutes in length and cover a single topic in depth. They also created an area outside each of the meeting rooms where the speaker could go to answer questions from participants without disrupting the flow of the sessions. It was imperative that no speaker took longer than his/her allotted time.

What they could not agree upon was the structure of the general session so they created a completely new concept for a single, 90 minute session that was held each morning and included a panel of experts of a particular topic combined with the use of an audience response system. This technology had never been used before by either group but they were very enthusiastic about its potential. The sessions were interactive and the information obtained from the instant audience response technology was monitored and a report developed that had the potential to be used in the planning of future programs for their industry. It was thought that this would help them meet their objectives to create a unique and unprecedented event and increase the use of technology.

Once the overall design of the sessions was in place, they began to look at the social side of the conference and created joint events designed to flow throughout the five days of the conference. They wanted participants to stay for the whole week so selecting the time of a particular event was all part of the strategy. Networking was an important objective that was met through the development of various casual receptions held throughout the week. Delegates were also invited to attend an awards banquet, which provided seating in reserved tables for corporations or individuals. This formal evening provided networking for delegates, spouses and business partners as well as an opportunity to support their peers who received an award at the event. The gala was usually held on the final evening of the conference as a closing banquet; however, during the millennium conference it was planned for the middle of the week to maintain the enthusiasm of the delegates. The guest program was also designed to run daily for the five days of the conference. As well, they conducted formal sit down luncheons on four of the days, each with a twenty to thirty minute presentation from a key individual from within their industry. At another luncheon, they followed a long standing tradition of one of the organizations that held a reception style networking luncheon. Although delegates had to line up at buffet stations, they never seemed to mind as this gave them opportunity to meet friends and colleagues.

One of the difficulties in the development of this program was the determination of projected attendance for sessions, meals, events and room blocks at hotels. They were able to review prior attendance; however, this was to be a very different event, so projections were more complicated. They needed enough space for 10,000 people which was likely to be the minimum number attained by just conducting their meeting jointly; however, they hoped to reach their objective of 12,000 to 15,000. As a starting point, they used the limits of the venue and set each room to its maximum seating capacity. Later on, as ticket sales progressed, they made appropriate adjustments.

The planning committee was large, comprised of a minimum of one individual from each association to sit on subcommittees that included both staff and volunteers. The meeting manager and meeting coordinators were assigned to each of the subcommittees to assist with program planning and logistics. The planning committee made all of the overall decisions, by consensus, after thoughtful consideration of the input provided from the subcommittee. There was a subcommittee for each element of the conference with a chair and sometime a co-chair to share the burden of a large task such as the development of the sessions.

As the program committee came up with creative ideas, it was the responsibility of the staff to source suppliers for entertainment, décor and flowers, audio visual support, and any other special services that were required. Meetings were set up with suppliers to identify the most suitable product or service, cost and availability. The meeting manager also determined how to best utilize available space at the venue, to ensure that there was sufficient room for two trade shows, social events and sessions.

It took time to create an overall program design that was thought to be the most effective program for the majority of individuals, keeping in mind the conference objectives and the limits of the venue. Ultimately it was accomplished through the efforts of many individuals.

PROGRAM DEVELOPMENT CHECKLIST

☐ Profile of attendees identified

- history of past conferences reviewed
- organizational / industry affiliations identified
- primary educational programs preferred
- expected level of social programs

☐ Secure record of previous conferences including

- projected vs. actual attendance
- number, types of functions
- size, setups of rooms
- speakers and topics covered
- types of sessions e.g., interactive, case studies, panel discussions, etc.

☐ Meeting theme and title determined

☐ Program committee members identified

- roles and responsibilities for committee members identified
- background material prepared and distributed to committee

☐ Program format developed

- will it include:
- plenary sessions
- workshops
- concurrent sessions
- refreshment breaks
- meals
- social events
- trade show
- registration hours
- tours

☐ Timing of the conference program schedule reviewed

☐ In developing a schedule for each function, ask:

- Is the function primarily business or social?
- Are musicians, entertainers, emcees required?
- Will the timing conflict or overlap with other events in the facility?
- What is the expected attendance at each function?

☐ Program at a glance developed

☐ Adult learning principles considered and applied

☐ When programming social events consider:

- Does the event or activity fit in with the overall program design and the purpose of the meeting?
- Will the event carry out the meeting theme?
- Will it promote attendance?
- Will it motivate participants?
- Will it provide relaxation and diversion for the participants?
- Will it promote networking, social interaction and informal conversation between participants?

☐ Pre and/or post tours

☐ Guest and/or youth programs

☐ Continuing education credits:

- affiliated and accrediting organizations identified
- applications for accreditations completed
- processes for providing attendees completed credits identified

CHAPTER REVIEW

Program planning begins by examining the demographics of your attendees and creating a profile of them. It is important to consider the likes and dislikes of attendees when planning your program. Gathering this information will allow you to better meet attendee expectations.

Program planning involves establishing a template of how all major time blocks will be used. This time may be filled with any of all of the following types of activities:

- plenary sessions
- workshops
- concurrent sessions
- refreshment breaks
- meals
- social events
- trade show
- registration hours
- tours

Program planning may also include the development of a theme, which creates a common thread, linking food, décor and entertainment to one common motif.

Adult learning is the theory and study of how adults learn. Understanding and utilizing the physical, social, emotional, psychological and physiological factors that impact adult learners and implementing these into the design of your program can result in a significantly improved learning environment. Adult learners learn best when they actively participate in activities.

Educational sessions should be designed with a variety of different formats, to help maintain attendee interest and attention. Some common formats include:

- general/plenary sessions
- breakouts
- concurrent sessions
- labs
- workshops
- tours/site visits
- exhibit/trade show

In these sessions, a variety of instructional styles, with appropriate time allocated for each, will also assist in maintaining attendee interest. Some instructional styles include:

- case study
- lecture/paper
- panel
- poster session
- product demonstration
- round table discussion
- talk show

Social events and guest or youth programs can add significantly to the overall success of your program and provide additional reasons for delegates to attend. In addition, many professional organizations offer the opportunity to earn continuing education units (CEU's) when they participate in the educational portion of the program. These CEU's demonstrate that members are remaining current and maintaining their professional designations. These non-academic credits are administered by the organization hosting the meeting.

A program committee can assist in the program planning process. Members of the committee should be chosen based on their dependability, accessibility and knowledge of the subject matter and should be provided with a comprehensive resources workbook containing appropriate background information to assist them in completing their tasks.

TEST YOUR KNOWLEDGE

The following self test will indicate the level of understanding and knowledge gained from this chapter. Solutions to all self tests can be found in Appendix A.

1. Guest programs usually revolve around social or recreational activities.

    ☐ True   ☐ False

2. Meeting objectives should shape the format of general and concurrent sessions and workshops.

    ☐ True   ☐ False

3. Most programs should include a mix of plenary and breakout sessions.

    ☐ True   ☐ False

4. Attendee profiles are a useful tool to help design the meeting format.

    ☐ True   ☐ False

5. A plenary session is the same as a:

    (a) breakout session

    (b) panel discussion

    (c) general session

    (d) product demonstration

6. Collecting demographic information about meeting attendees is a prerequisite to:

    (a) selecting a location for the meeting

    (b) determining the appropriate length of the meeting

    (c) determining potential size of the audience

    (d) all of the above

7. Which of the following is NOT considered to be a variable that affects the individual in the learning environment?

    (a) physiological factors

    (b) previous education

    (c) psychological factors

    (d) social factors

8. Roundtable discussions are considered to be appropriate for adult learners because:

   (a) they present an opportunity for everyone's input

   (b) all participants become more involved in the topic

   (c) they help build relationships amongst participants

   (d) all of the above

9. Explain what is meant by the term self-directed learner.

   _____

   _____

   _____

   _____

   _____

   _____

10. How might physical arrangements of an educational event have an impact on the learning that occurs?

   _____

   _____

   _____

   _____

   _____

   _____

11. If 75 attendees are being asked to participate in a one hour session, how long a break should be given at the end of the session?

   _____

   _____

   _____

   _____

   _____

   _____

NOTES

Site Selection

INTRODUCTION

Selecting an appropriate site is of primary importance to the success of the meeting. The location, features and amenities of the venue will all influence the meeting professional's ability to deliver a successful event and the attendees' ability to achieve their objectives.

LEARNING OBJECTIVES

After completing this chapter, the learner will:

- determine factors that will influence meeting destination decisions

- evaluate the appropriateness of meeting facilities being considered

Ensure you understand and can apply the following terms:

- Ancillary
- Facility
- Familiarization tour
- Meeting history
- Meeting host
- Participant expectation
- Participant profile
- Physical requirements
- Property
- Request for proposal
- Site inspection
- Site selection
- Supplier
- Total meeting value
- Venue

Refer to the glossary for further clarification of the key terms for this chapter.

ROLES AND RESPONSIBILITIES

MEETING MANAGER

○ Review meeting objectives

○ Determine criteria for selecting a site and/or for evaluating function space based on meeting objectives

- Clarify the role of other individuals/groups in site selection

○ Develop the meeting format

- Set the meeting length, desired dates, day(s) of the week, pace, and tempo
  ○ estimate attendance, ratio of men/women, age groups, multicultural status and local attendees who will not require guest rooms
  ○ match the number of attendees with the meeting's objective(s)
  ○ match the meeting format with meeting objectives
  ○ consider pre and post program requirements
  ○ determine food and beverage theme possibilities
  ○ indicate the number of general sessions, concurrent sessions
  ○ allot time for setup and tear down of registration, general session, expositions and meeting offices
  ○ determine the selection of date availability
  ○ determine specific dates and times for move-in and move-out
  ○ define arrival and departure dates and expected patterns, times

○ Determine the physical requirements

- Specify requirements
  ○ match requirements with meeting objectives and the program planned
  ○ define site requirements: size, location, utilities, facilities, amenities, services, number, type and cost of meeting rooms required and when, room layouts, audio visual needed, expositions, access requirements, service areas required (e.g., for registration), equipment, recreation, services for those with special needs, crowd control, number/type/cost of guest rooms, food and beverage, VIP and hospitality suites, technology
  ○ determine meeting rooms needed (how many and when)
  ○ identify meeting room setup requirements

- identify services required and compare/match with services provided
- allocate space
- communicate requirements

○ Define attendee expectations

- Develop a participant profile
  - consider the number of attendees and guests, their point of origin, their expectations, their spending patterns, the need to change/rotate the meeting locale, pre and post meeting and social opportunities
  - determine dietary, cultural, and religious restrictions/observances
  - evaluate the age range of attendees and average age, the accompanying guests or family members, need for a family/guest program, importance of local attractions/cultural/recreational opportunities, availability of shopping and restaurants

- Evaluate the site to ensure that special needs may be met
  - determine special needs
  - assess if facilities, services and equipment meet special needs
  - prepare a checklist to determine if the site is barrier free
  - evaluate move-in/move-out, seating, parking, washrooms, companion rooms, telecommunication services, identification, access, elevators, entrances, ramps, emergencies, food and beverage, audio visual and accommodations to determine if special needs can be met

○ Select meeting destination and type of facility

- Research destinations and sites
  - determine the advantages and disadvantages of various destinations
  - consider the availability of suppliers and the adequacy of the infrastructure of the destination
  - determine the limitations involved in site selection and confirmation
  - create a checklist for site inspection

- Define possible sites
  - match the meeting's location and environment with the meeting's objective(s) and point of origin of the attendees
  - consult meeting facilities guides and other publications as applicable to determine the sites available

- research possible sites
- use online services and web sites
- determine time limitations involved in site selection and confirmation
- identify policies (e.g., accommodation, meeting space, preferred vs exclusive suppliers, food and beverage (caterers), unions, hidden costs)

- Determine site requirements
  - match meeting objectives and site requirements
  - select from among the options available
  - determine the basis for booking (hourly, daily or 24 hours)
  - make tentative bookings and agree on an option date
  - advise on the decision making process and realistic timeframes
  - determine what criteria will dictate destination and type of facility (objectives, physical requirements, political/economic factors, sponsoring organization)
  - consider travel time and expense
  - decide first on the destination and then the type of facility
  - compare facilities' advantages and disadvantages to objectives, physical requirements

- Evaluate the options

  - Consult with local bureaus and other resources
    - determine the services local bureau(s) can provide and fees involved
    - obtain references for similar-sized events

  - Send out RFPs (Request for Proposal)
    - prepare and distribute RFPs to selected site options

  - Evaluate various sites
    - determine union and labour/management relationships and contract deadlines
    - assess anticipated impact of other site occupants, pre, during and post (e.g., on sound, distractions, crowd control, cleanliness, signage, groups mingling, security, privacy, competitive companies)
    - assess if there will be any construction/renovation underway in and outside the facility during your meeting, and identify events which could conflict or enhance
    - compare services required and those provided
    - determine the quality of service offered, professionalism, and credibility

- ○ contact facility sales offices/centers and arrange site visits with qualified sites
- ○ obtain/create all necessary cost analyses and compare costs
- ○ determine the need for outside services
- ○ determine availability of media requirements
- ○ conduct room inspections using tools to compare published data with personal findings (e.g., space availability)
- ○ conduct and record site inspection findings for an objective comparison
- ○ identify possible room setups, their advantages and disadvantages
- ○ complete an environmental audit using a checklist and compare the site's environmental policy and practices to those of your organization
- ○ request references and consult with other meeting professionals who have used the site
- ○ ensure that the needs of those with special needs are met
- ○ source resources available to assist
- ○ consider alternatives
- ○ inspect the sites as determined by a short list

○ Address special requirements

- • Meet special need requirements
  - ○ determine the official language(s) of the meeting
  - ○ establish cultural needs related to attendees, the facility, the program and the organization
  - ○ recognize attendee requirements related to foreign country, physical limitations, dietary restrictions, holiday, political and religious observances
  - ○ recognize the political, religious, language and cultural implications of the meeting destination

○ Plan to address special needs
  - ○ determine and plan to meet the requirements of those with special needs
  - ○ determine special needs from registration forms
  - ○ communicate special needs to the facilities
  - ○ ensure that equipment meets the requirements of those with special needs
  - ○ plan for special needs (e.g., parking, move in and move-out, seating, washrooms, companion rooms, telecommunications services, identification, access, elevators, entrances, ramps, emergencies, food and beverage, auido visual, accommodations)

MEETING COORDINATOR

○ Research sites and suppliers

- Prepare relevant history and documentation
    - ○ compile statistics on past meetings for comparison purposes (including past attendance, guestroom pickup, food and beverage revenue)
    - ○ develop a meeting profile including past venue floor plans and photos to assist in communicating needs
    - ○ prepare an RFP (Request for Proposal) outlining accommodation requirements, meeting rooms with square footage (meters) requirements, food and beverage requirements
    - ○ establish contacts with the CVB (Convention and Visitors Bureau)
    - ○ collect and communicate information on the destination, facilities and suppliers

○ Assist in site selection

- Allocate meeting room space and setup requirements
    - ○ use a checklist to confirm room requirements
    - ○ verify when rooms are needed
    - ○ verify that rooms meet requirements related to space, audio visual, interpretation, food and beverage, entertainment, exhibits, translation, and amenities
    - ○ confirm that meeting objectives are served by room setups
    - ○ inspect guestrooms
    - ○ use a checklist to confirm accommodation requirements
    - ○ verify how many, type and when guest rooms are needed
    - ○ verify that guestrooms are available and meet requirements related to special needs

- Participate in site evaluation
    - ○ consult with various resources
    - ○ prepare bid evaluations
    - ○ participate in decision making related to sites and suppliers
    - ○ make recommendations

○ Implement meeting space and setup requirements

- Design floor plans
    - use charts to scale and planning aids to match room size and attendees, and to indicate room arrangements (e.g., position of furniture, seating arrangements)
    - demonstrate awareness of the number of attendees who can be seated, given room size and other considerations such as number of aisles, seating style, head table, lectern, fire regulations, exits, etc.
    - recognize various room setups, seating arrangements, their advantages and disadvantages, to make the best use of space available

SITE SELECTION CONSIDERATIONS

The site selection process is much more than simply choosing a destination and facility for a meeting. The wrong site can compromise even the most well planned, attended and designed event. To effectively select the optimal site, the meeting professional can follow six basic steps:

1. identify meeting objectives

2. develop the meeting format

3. determine physical requirements

4. define attendee expectations

5. select meeting destination and appropriate type of facility

6. issue request for proposal to venues of desired type

1. IDENTIFY MEETING OBJECTIVES

The meeting objectives will guide the meeting professional in identifying the potential sites.

2. DEVELOP THE MEETING FORMAT

The overall schedule or flow of events is described in the meeting format. This planned program should indicate the number of general sessions and simultaneous or concurrent sessions that are required. When developing the meeting format, do not forget to allow time for setup of registration area, exhibits and meeting staff offices.

3. **DETERMINE PHYSICAL REQUIREMENTS**

Meeting history will assist the meeting professional in determining the physical requirements.

- Preferred dates
  - specific dates or time period
  - religious, and/or statutory holidays
  - scheduling conflicts with associated organizations
  - seasonal facility rates
  - local labour laws
  - planned construction/remodeling/renovations in and around the site
- Attendance
  - anticipated attendance
  - meeting history
  - growth projection for future
- Guest rooms
  - total number of sleeping rooms each night
  - number of rooms required for staff members, speakers, exhibitors, and others
  - arrival and departure pattern and flight schedules
  - smoking vs non smoking
  - percent of single vs double room occupancy
  - number of suites
  - hospitality suites for entertaining (number, size)
  - average cancellation percentage
  - average no show percentage
  - average room rate for the event
  - attendee expectations for room rates
- Meeting space
  - number of meeting rooms required
  - number needed simultaneously
  - room set up styles
  - audio visual needs
  - space in or near meeting rooms for refreshment breaks

- Food and beverage events
  - service seating styles
  - number
  - timing
  - estimated attendance at each event
  - previous attendance at similar functions
- Exhibits
  - area required (square meters/feet)
  - time necessary for setup/tear down of displays
- Registration
  - area required
  - space necessary for additional services (restaurant reservations, tours, local information, video/audio tape sales)
- Ancillary space
  - storage space
  - rooms needed for conference office
  - media
  - technical setup room
  - speaker preparation room
  - special lounge areas
  - hospitality room
  - spouse/guest/children program rooms
  - committee or other meeting rooms
- Other logistical considerations
  - special needs
  - interpretation booths
  - loading dock

4. DEFINE ATTENDEE EXPECTATIONS

Understanding the profile of the attendees is an important factor in site selection. Gathering demographic information on the attendees ensures the meeting professional will consider the preferences, age, interests and other factors in researching potential meeting sites.

5. **SELECT MEETING DESTINATION AND APPROPRIATE TYPE OF FACILITY**

The destination for a meeting may be dictated by meeting objectives and physical requirements, by political and economic factors, or the sponsoring organization may dictate the general location. When choosing the destination, consider travel time and expense for maximum number of potential attendees.

Once the destination has been selected, the meeting professional must decide on the type of facility. Each of the following types of facilities have advantages and disadvantages, so select the one that is most compatible with the established meeting objectives, physical requirements and attendee profile. See page 85 for a chart summarizing site selection considerations.

6. **ISSUE A REQUEST FOR PROPOSAL (RFP)**

The RFP allows the meeting professional to communicate the meeting needs to a small selected group of potential properties.

CONTENTS OF AN RFP

Introduction
The introduction provides general information about the host organization and the event:
- scope of organization (international, national, regional)
- demographics of anticipated attendees
- background on the event (who, what, when, where, why)
- previous dates of the event (if any)
- previous attendance numbers
- previous hotels, venues used
- contact person and information of person who will manage RFP process

Required from Hotel, Venue
- number of copies of RFP to be forwarded
- client references
- ease of access (rail, air, car)
- deadline date for receipt of RFP
- notification to those submitting RFP's

Event Dates
- preferred dates of event

- beginning date (including set up days)
- closing date (including tear down day)
- dates to avoid (statutory holidays, etc.)

Guestroom Block Requirements

- number of bedrooms required
- check in dates
- check out dates
- peak night(s)
- types of rooms (single/double/suites)
- staff rooms required
- complimentary bedroom policy required

Meeting Space

- tentative schedule
- 24 hour hold if required
- staff office if required
- meeting space required for:
- plenary sessions
- breakout sessions
- office space
- speaker ready room
- exhibit space
- food and beverage functions

Food and Beverage Functions

- overview of food and beverage events
- confirmation of pricing

Miscellaneous

- support services needed
- tentative set ups required for each meeting room
- pre conference/post conference events/tours
- guest/youth programs
- special needs

EXHIBIT SITE SELECTION

Site selection for an exhibition must consider the expectations of delegates, the host organization, and of course, the exhibitors. The meeting professional must take into account additional factors if a trade show is to be included with a conference.

First the accessibility of the location needs to be determined. The ideal exhibit site has positive traffic flow through the exhibit area, and is located adjacent to meeting rooms, registration and food and beverage areas. If attendees have to travel some distance to view exhibits, attendance on the trade show floor will suffer.

Physical accessibility for the setup and tear down of exhibit materials also needs to be considered. While most convention centers and hotels can accommodate trucks at their receiving area, some older facilities have elevators that may not be of sufficient capacity to handle heavier exhibits.

If the meeting professional determines that the space being considered is accessible, the next step is to evaluate the adequacy of the actual exhibit space. The meeting professional should have some estimate of how many exhibits can be expected. If previous similar trade shows have taken place, past records are a valuable tool for providing this kind of information. In North America, booths are measured in 10 foot by 10 foot units (100 square feet per booth). In order to estimate how much gross square footage is needed for the trade show, multiply the amount of square feet needed for booths by two in order to account for aisles, unusable space, columns, etc.

Example: Note: For the purposes of this chapter, Imperial measurements are being used.

> 50 booths @ 100 sq. ft. per booth
>> = 5,000 net square feet x 2 (unusable space)
>> = gross square footage needed (10,000 sq.ft.)

Choosing the correct size of exhibit space can have an influence on the success of the trade show. Too small a space, gives the illusion of heavy traffic, but also restricts movement and communication, while too much space gives the appearance of light traffic, which can lead to dissatisfied exhibitors.

If a facility appears to have enough space, the next area of concern to inspect is the actual specifications in terms of utilities, ceiling heights, columns, stairwells, and floor loads. A floor plan will have to be developed to indicate where booths will be placed based on the position of columns and other obstructions. Newer facilities are generally free from obstructions, but exhibit halls and ballrooms in older facilities may present some physical challenges. Low ceilings, low entrances and chandeliers may all restrict the height of displays allowed and will also contribute towards poor acoustics.

EVALUATE THE OPTIONS

Following an analysis of proposals received, the meeting professional can reduce the potential destinations and types of facilities to a short list. Requests for Proposals (RFP) or the Meeting Prospectus are usually prepared and sent to the local conventions and visitors bureau or facilities in the desired destination(s). Providing as much of the following information as possible in the RFP will result in receiving proposals from facilities who can accommodate the event. See page 94 for a chart summarizing site selection considerations.

The meeting site evaluation process takes time and should be thoroughly conducted. A variety of resources exist to aid the meeting professional in this task:

- local convention and visitors bureau

- local chamber of commerce

- site information resources (trade publications, direct mail/marketing companies, regional offices of hotel chains, online searches)

- industry colleagues, website, facility references

The facility will respond with a proposal and detailed information about the property and its availability for your meeting.

When evaluating facilities keep in mind the objectives of the meeting, such as square footage required for special activities, public space, meeting room setups and capacities, and audio visual needs.

> ## HOT TIP
> If you're scoping out a certain city or facility, ask for a list of people who have recently held a meeting or conference there. The most candid and willing comments are from people who have been in your shoes previously.

THE ROLE OF THE CONVENTION AND VISITORS BUREAU (CVB) IN THE SITE SELECTION PROCESS

CVBs offer invaluable services to the meeting professional and can save the meeting professional time, especially during the site selection process. CVB staff are dedicated professionals who cover a specific clientele or market sector. When the meeting professional establishes contact with the CVBs, the appropriate manager is assigned.

The local CVB representative can assist the meeting professional in assessing the suitability of conference and convention centers and nearby hotels by:

- circulating meeting specifications contained in the Request for Proposal to member facilities that can accommodate the meeting requirements

- requesting all properties send information back to the meeting planner or CVB

- providing contact information and setting up meetings with suppliers and facilities who provide the types of services the meeting requires

- accompanying the meeting professional on the site inspection tour

- following up with meeting professional and facilities to ensure all information has been received and understood

- providing up to date information on planned developments in the respective city/area

- providing pre event promotional materials on the destination in the form of CD ROM, video, maps, brochures, etc.

- providing guidance in terms of a dollar 'range' for room rates in the given city during the time the meeting is scheduled

- providing the names of contacts for referrals.

- providing tour guides for your companion programs

- sending an "ambassador" to a prior event to promote the city

- providing welcome materials to attendees, including discount passes to local restaurants, attractions and shops

THE SITE INSPECTION

Inspecting the site in person is the best way to assess the condition of a facility and to ensure the needs of the meeting will be met. Because site inspection is a time consuming and potentially expensive undertaking, visit only those destinations and properties under serious consideration. Most convention and visitors bureaus can schedule appointments with various facilities and will often provide a representative escort for the actual site inspection tour. If requested, the CVB will provide references of other groups of a similar size that have used their city.

POTENTIAL FACILITY COMPARISON

Meeting professionals should consider using alternative meeting venues. Local university campuses, cruise ships and off-season resorts are just three examples of alternative venues that are available. While each have their own unique limitations they also offer many advantages that can't be found in some of the more traditional venues.

When the meeting professional is fortunate enough to find more than one destination/facility that can accommodate a meeting, a simple means of comparison is necessary.

There may be one overwhelming criterion that dictates the choice (such as cost), or a systematic decision method can be used such as assigning a number or letter rating to checklist responses. As an example, on a scale of 1 (excellent) to 5 (poor), Facility A rates a 2 in the area of customer service while Facility B rates a 4. It should be noted that it is up to the individual meeting professional to determine the relative importance of each of the above factors. Similar checklists and systems can be developed when considering various suppliers or offsite venues at the meeting location.

ROOM SETUPS

The arrangement of chairs (and tables) in the room will depend on the objective of the function and, naturally, determine the size of room required. For example, a training program will require a different room setup ("classroom" or "schoolroom" style) than an awards dinner ("banquet" or "rounds") or board meeting ("boardroom" or "U-shape" or "hollow square"). Consideration must also be given to other requirements in the room such as food and beverage, audio visual and staging. The following diagrams illustrate a variety of options.

SITE SELECTION CONSIDERATIONS

Type of Facility	Advantages	Disadvantages
City Center/ Luxury Downtown Hotel	• Business hotels geared to groups and leisure market • Central to downtown • Increased amenities and services	• Parking expensive • More potential for crime • Distance from airport (time & cost) • Expensive room rate, especially peak season • Meeting must have sufficient guest room to meeting space ratio • May compete with larger meetings and conventions • May not feel as 'intimate' for delegates
Resort	• Relaxed environment in which attendees feel removed from day-to-day pressures • Location – provides less distraction for attendees • Greater potential for exclusive buyout • Well suited for retreats, incentives and programs where delegates have time to enjoy facilities • Extensive recreation facilities • Attractive 'off season' rates (Mar/Apr/Nov) • Range from upscale (offering a lot of amenities) to more rustic feel • Off season rates and delegate/group meal plan can save money	• High rates in peak season (limited ability to negotiate) • Extra charges: porterage fees, gratuities mandatory • No 6:00 p.m. hold; deposits paid in full prior to event (Resorts don't accommodate 'walk-ins') • Cancellation penalties may be 7 days-2 weeks out; • Location – distance from major airport (additional time/transportation required = additional money) • Suppliers of equipment and services critical to the success of the meeting must be available within the facility or nearby. • Location – may not be easily accessible
Conference Center	• Conference "specialists" (60%+ of business from conferences) • Provides total meeting environment including function rooms, equipment, sleeping rooms, dining rooms and recreation areas on a 24-hr basis	• Accommodations and amenities may be minimal

Type of Facility	Advantages	Disadvantages
Conference Center (continued)	• Staffed with professionals who are prepared to serve meeting professionals and participants (registration, furniture, equipment) • Self-contained, can handle small conferences (max 400 people) • If conference large enough, can contract entire facility, thereby reducing conflicts that may arise at a convention center • State-of-the-art audio visual equipment and full-time technical staff in house	
Convention Center	• Designed for large multi-group, multi-purpose use • No sleeping rooms or recreation areas • Usually limited food & beverage outlets • Extensive meeting space of varying capacities (congress halls, exhibit halls, breakouts, offices) to hold events that won't fit into a hotel or conference center • High ceilings • Usually has own in-house catering • Technologically 'wired' • May have one or multiple hotels physically connected to them	• No guest rooms (minimal negotiating power) • Charge for meeting space rental • Depending on distance from meeting hotel, cost and availability of shuttle bus service may be a primary consideration • May be heavily unionized • May have exclusive contracts with suppliers (limits flexibility to negotiate/bring in preferred suppliers) • Complicated contracts • Liability issues. Require proof of insurance. • In-house staff not available to move materials/install banners etc. • May restrict the location/available space for hanging banners due to other conventions inhouse • Require full payment upfront • Minimum food and beverage outlets • Minimum guest services available (restaurants, lounge, gift shop)

Type of Facility	Advantages	Disadvantages
Airport Hotel	• Close to airport – saves time • Excellent space for brief, business only meetings, or one day sessions requiring easy in/out airport access • Complimentary shuttle bus service is often available to/from airport hotels	• Location – away from downtown & city attractions/restaurants • Location/surroundings/views • Noise can be a factor • For longer stays – attendees may feel confined in this environment
Suburban Hotel	• Free parking • Closer to airports • Outside of main downtown core – less traffic • Sports and recreational facilities nearby • Small, intimate • Caters to business, rather than leisure traveler	• Large suburban hotels may have limited space for exhibits and other events • Limited attractions and restaurants in the area • May have too much of a similar feel to other suburbs – don't offer the unique flavor of the central city
Boutique Hotel	• Ability to 'customize' amenities & product offering for the group • Recommended for small, high profile, VIP or incentive groups or individual business travelers	• Limited meeting room space overall • Usually no large meeting room
All Suite Hotel	• Well suited for families (rooms larger, often with kitchenette, separate living room, bedrooms/multiple bathrooms) • Many have additional facilities (washer/dryer, microwave) • Great value for money • Cost effective for extended stays	• Distance from convention centers (could be several blocks, or driving distance only) • Usually no restaurant (or restaurant is not full service) • No large meeting space (possibly 1-2 small rooms for 20 people)
Cruise Ship	• Ocean going vessels that cater to conferences, rather than tourists • Full ship charter can be perceived as one of the most prestigious reward vehicles • Well suited for incentive trips • Reinforces company unity • Extensive array of activities and facilities available	• May not be suitable for attendees with mobility issues • Attendees may feel 'captive'. • Need a large group to justify a full ship charter • Success could be impacted by poor weather/sea conditions

Type of Facility	Advantages	Disadvantages
University or College Campus	• Inexpensive	• Some may restrict use to faculty and student conferences only • Non-academic groups can expect to be charged a higher fee • Seasonal – really only available when students are not on campus • Minimal onsite personnel to assist meeting professional
Theme Park	• Often offer all the elements needed for a good conference in addition to the amenities of a resort or park	• Sponsors may perceive venue as better suited to recreation than business meeting
Public Buildings/ Sports Facilities	• Range from prestigious to undistinguished halls and sports facilities • May have theaters with tiered seating • May be able to accommodate elaborate stage productions/launches/entertain-ment	• Usually restricted to certain types of activities • May be heavily unionized • May have ability to cancel event if facility required by dignitaries
In-company Sites	• Convenient for participants and speakers • Contributes to the prestige of the conference • Allows senior level people to attend who otherwise may not travel	• Could provide a lot of 'distractions' for participants (checking voicemail, email during breaks/lunch)

BOARDROOM SEATING

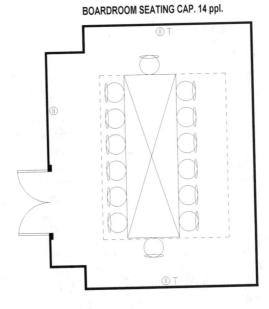

Appropriate for small groups discussing specific topics.

CLASSROOM SEATING

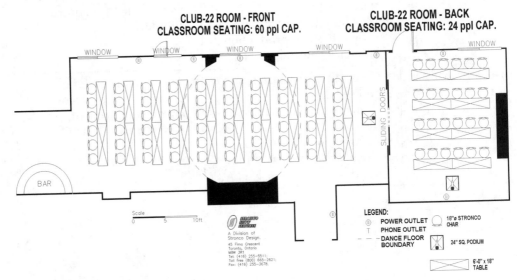

Appropriate for medium to large sized groups, with speaker(s) at the front.
Tables to allow participants to take notes.

DINNER ROUNDS SEATING

CLUB-22 ROOM - FRONT
ROUNDS SEATING: 74 ppl CAP.

CLUB-22 ROOM - BACK
ROUNDS SEATING: 28 ppl CAP.

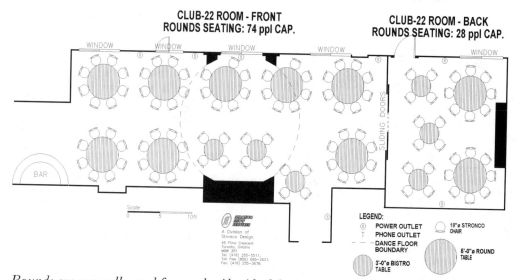

LEGEND:

⑪	POWER OUTLET	18"⌀ STRONCO CHAIR
T	PHONE OUTLET	
— —	DANCE FLOOR BOUNDARY	6'-0"⌀ ROUND TABLE
	3'-0"⌀ BISTRO TABLE	

Rounds are generally used for meals. Also ideal for workshops and small group discussions.

HOLLOW SQUARE SEATING

HOLLOW SQUARE SEATING CAP. 18 ppl.

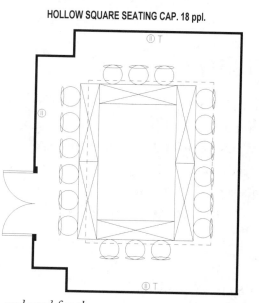

Similar to boardroom and used for the same reason: accommodates more people.

THEATRE SEATING

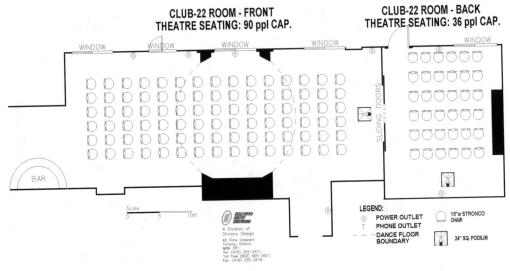

Generally used for large groups, with speaker(s) at front of room; plenary sessions.

All diagrams contributed by The STRONCO GROUP of Companies.

TRAFFIC FLOW

The meeting professional must anticipate traffic flow through all aspects of the event, and develop techniques for crowd control during peak movement times. Meeting rooms may be on several levels with limited escalator, elevator, or stairway connections. Several large capacity meeting rooms may open onto a hallway. The magnitude and type of event will determine traffic flow and control measures. The following generally create the biggest impacts on traffic flow:

- event registration

- entering and exiting function rooms

- travel time between sessions

- navigating trade shows

- receptions and refreshment breaks

- special functions

- travel between event and accommodation locations

TRAFFIC FLOW DURING REGISTRATION

The event registration area is often the delegate's first onsite experience of the meeting. Long lines, cramped space and disorganization here can make a first impression that may be difficult to overcome. Consider the following when evaluating the event registration area:

- How many stations are needed during event registration?

- Will pre-registered attendees be processed separately?

- How long will event registration be conducted?

- What is the peak amount of registrants expected at any one time?

- How will lines be formed? Will stanchions be used?

- How will the number of people permitted into the registration area be controlled?

ENVIRONMENTALLY CONSCIOUS MEETINGS

Meetings use up many resources from paper to printer cartridges to paper/plastic dishes, fuel and much more.

Here is a brief checklist to help you make your meetings environmentally conscious (adapted from an MPI initiative www.mpiweb.org/resources/greenmeetings):

- Ask the meeting facilities if they recycle:
  - aluminium containers and cans
  - coat hangers
  - corrugated boxes
  - fluorescent lamps
  - glass bottles
  - kitchen grease
  - newspaper
  - organic waste
  - paper

- plastics
- printer cartridges
- sterno (liquid fuel)
- tin cans

- Does the facility have water conservation programs in place?

- Does the hotel have a plan in place for towel and linen changing?

- Are recycle bins in each bedroom?

- Submit rooming lists, settle master accounts and send other documents by email

- Plan food and beverage events minimizing the use of disposable items

- Plan menus focused around abundant locally produced ingredients

- Recycle toner cartridges and other items from your onsite office.

- Register online and confirm registrations online

- Limit printing of handouts. Use other forms such as CD's or DVD's

- Instruct facility to place recycling bins in meeting rooms and hallways

- Print all materials on recycled paper

- Donate surpluses to local shelters, etc. where permitted by local regulations

- Consider having meeting locations near each other to limit transportation requirements

- Plan vehicle use and routing to maximize efficiency and to minimize driving

- Use cloth instead of paper napkins

- Serve food with edible garnishes, to minimize waste

- Contact local schools, shelters, retirement homes to determine their needs for leftover products from tradeshows, etc.

- For shipping, use recyclable biodegradable shipping and packing materials- paper and corrugated boxes vs polystyrene and plastic wrap

- Recycle badges and plastic inserts

- Use double-sided copies

SPECIAL NEEDS

The meeting professional should plan to meet any special needs of participants, including:

- person with a visual impairment (low vision and blind individuals)

- person with a hearing impairment (hard of hearing, deaf)

- person with a physical disability

- wheelchair users

- dietary restrictions, food allergies

The event registration form should include a special needs section where attendees can list any special needs, and the meeting professional should strive to include all communicated special needs. The meeting professional will also consult with the host organization for anticipated special requirements of the attendees.

BARRIER-FREE DESIGN

Although many facilities are quick to state they are wheelchair accessible, it is necessary for the meeting professional to look first hand for a barrier-free design. A meeting professional without a checklist may miss important details. For example, a restroom that has a wide entrance, flat floor surface, and grip bars may appear to be barrier-free, but if the doors to the stalls open inward, it may not be possible for a wheelchair to enter the stall and have the door close. This may be overlooked by someone not familiar with barriers to wheelchair users. If this same facility had large stalls, or if the doors opened outward, the restroom would be considered barrier free.

PUBLIC WASHROOMS

The meeting professional should consider having a wheelchair user who is knowledgeable about barrier-free design accompany them on the site inspection tour, or try to do the inspection from a chair themselves. Contact a disability group or independent living center for recommendations of facilities that are known to be barrier-free and a list of those to avoid.

Make sure washrooms are available on every level the event occupies. As previously mentioned, look for wide entrances, flat surfaces, washroom doors that open out, check that locks and door latches work, and that grip bars are secured, not loose. Faucets should be easy to turn on and off, either motion sensitive or push-on, and pipes under sinks must be enclosed.

PARKING

Make sure the site has more than one space reserved for people with disabilities, that this area is close to the entrance, and that it is shovelled during winter. Look for built in ramps where steps or uneven surfaces are found.

RAMPS

Ramps should be present as an alternative to steps or changes in floor levels. A rise to run ratio of 1 to 12 is the minimum acceptable; 1 to 20 is preferable, but unfortunately, 1 to 5 seems to be common. Where the ramp slope is steep, have one or two people ready to assist the wheelchair user up or down the ramp. Ramps should be covered with a black rubber mat for optimal traction. Make sure ramps are shovelled during winter events.

Portable ramps generally consist of two strips that are usually wide enough, but slip if they are not secured at top. Portable ramps are not as easy to use as built in ramps and are considered by wheelchair users to be adequate for one or two steps, but horrendous for five or six steps. If portables must be used, make attendees aware that ramps are portable well in advance of event. They may choose to have two people assist them up instead.

ELEVATORS

When inspecting a facility, look for elevators that provide access to all levels. Many wheelchair users have found themselves forced to take freight or service elevators, along with garbage or laundry. This is an extremely negative experience for an attendee or presenter to have to go through. Freight elevators may have to be used, in which case, have an escort ready, make the ride as quick and easy as possible, have attendees or speakers transported without garbage or laundry. When elevators are necessary, make sure they are designed for wheelchair access and operation and that floor numbers and call buttons are marked in Braille.

MEETING ROOMS

The site inspection should determine if the facility has barrier-free meeting rooms. Look for ramped access to all meeting levels, doors that meet minimum barrier-free access requirements, automatically opening doors, and barrier-free elevators.

Once the meeting room passes inspection, the setup must be barrier-free as well. When setting up chairs in a meeting room, look for ramped access. A common occurrence is for facility staff to set up the entire room with chairs, allowing no room to move a wheelchair and no place to seat wheelchairs. Specify seating for more than one wheelchair, in a good position for viewing the presentation. The meeting professional can enable wheelchair users to participate in question and answer sessions by having a person walk a cordless microphone around the room, rather than having the audience ask questions from a tall standing microphone and/or podium.

The meeting professional must not overlook the possibility that an event presenter will be a person with a disability. Stage access can be difficult, if a ramp is not present, or is very steep, or if there are too many chairs and not enough room to manoeuvre a wheelchair. Audio visual aids should be placed within reach of the speaker, or have an aid available to place overheads, etc. It is difficult and uncomfortable for a wheelchair user to give a speech at a tall podium with the microphone pointed down. Instead of a tall podium, have a table available with a microphone and space for paper and water.

Some meeting professionals feel that the onus is on the person with a disability to make others aware of their needs, but it is the meeting professional who is responsible even if special needs are not known ahead of time and only last minute accommodations onsite can be made. To avoid this situation, the meeting professional should consider special needs when selecting a site (for example, make barrier-free access a necessity independent of communicated special needs), and the meeting professional should give all persons involved with an event the opportunity to communicate any special needs.

GUEST ROOMS

Look for facilities that have more than one barrier-free room and more than one bed in the room. The bathroom should be large, with doors opening outward, square shaped for easiest access, have grip bars, and easy to use faucets. Look for venues equipped with emergency devices (red lights, etc.) and TTY phones in guest bedrooms.

PUBLIC TELEPHONES

Barrier-free events should include public telephones equipped with amplifiers for the hearing impaired, that are at wheelchair level. Investigate the possibility of TTY (computer interface) phone hook up.

GUIDE DOGS

If event participants are visually impaired, guide dogs may be accompanying participants on the property, into meeting rooms, dining and function rooms and accommodation rooms. Guide dogs often need to find a patch of grass, so have a suitable location, or an escort/volunteer person available to take the dog. Have someone greet the participant with a visual impairment and acquaint them with the site.

DIETARY NEEDS

Make provisions for special dietary needs during all food and beverage functions, including:

- healthy heart (low fat, low salt)

- vegetarian (be specific)

- diabetic

- food allergies

- kosher, halal, etc.

Posting ingredient signs on buffet items will accommodate those with food allergies such as nuts, meats, seafood and dairy products. Serving staff should be able to answer questions about ingredients and preparation of served foods.

Help wait staff identify special needs delegates at meals. Attendees can be given a ticket or card detailing their particular requirement (e.g., shellfish allergy, kosher). The planner can affix a sticker to the attendee's name badge. For gala events, special needs delegates can be given a flower or boutonniere. However it is handled, be sure special needs attendees understand that they are responsible for ensuring they identify themselves to their server.

COMMUNICATION NEEDS

Readers and Sign Language Interpreters

Readers and sign language interpreters are not the same and do not provide interchangeable services. A sign interpreter provides oral meaning in different languages, including sign. A reader's function is to read information to visually impaired participants.

A sign language interpreter visually interprets words to a hearing-impaired person.

Practice indicates that two to four persons per day, per position, will be required to staff each special service, to allow these individuals to work 20 minutes on and 20 minutes off.

INTERNATIONAL ICONS

 denotes accommodation for persons who use a wheelchair for mobility.

 denotes accommodation for persons who are deaf or hearing impaired.

denotes accommodation for persons who are blind or visually impaired.

~ *A Conference Journal* ~

Once they had the basic outline of the conference program, it was time to consider the venue, or in this case, venues. There were four primary factors in their search, with the first being the selection of the city. Through a collaborative effort, they selected a city that appealed to both associations. The national association identified a location where they had experienced the greatest attendance in the past, while the international group wanted to ensure that the chosen city had the greatest concentration of suppliers, prospective sponsors, exhibitors, and attendees.

With anticipated attendance of 12,000 in five concurrent sessions, daily general sessions for at least 1,000 participants in theater style seating and social functions with numbers in excess of 1,000 plus staging, they decided that their program needs would be best met by a convention center. Since there was also an ancillary education component, the potential requirement for additional space at a hotel, in close proximity, was also recognized.

The third deciding factor was the need to accommodate two large trade shows that had to be situated adjacent to sessions with easy access to participants, to ensure the success of the show. Each show needed approximately 150,000 - 200,000 square feet for booths, special show features and storage, two full days in advance to move in and a minimum of two and a half days of viewing time for delegates. As well, the second show needed unrestricted ceiling height, high floor load capacity and accessibility to a number of loading docks for large transport trucks carrying heavy equipment. Since the conference structure determined only five full days, this meant that each show would need to be in a completely separate area to provide sufficient time for the second show to setup in readiness for the grand opening midweek.

Another important issue for the joint meeting committee was that the majority of guest rooms had to be located within a 5 - 15 minute walk from the main conference site. Fortunately, they were able to identify five or six suitable hotels that surrounded the convention center.

Many other considerations were taken into account in their final determination such as the general layout of the facility for ease of use, ample parking, accessibility to nearby restaurants, safety, attractiveness of the facility, sufficient elevators to ensure traffic flow to exhibits and meeting rooms, barrier-free access, adequate service levels for a group of this size, and quality of the food and beverage.

They began their decision making process with a site visit of all of their options. With the convention center proposed as their main site, they obtained a layout of the floor plans and room by room, plotted the conference components they had previously identified in the available space. This particular convention center was comprised of two separate buildings, located one behind the other and linked by an internal walkway and series of escalators. They began with the north building, which had nearby restaurants and local attractions and was considered to have better access to public transit. There was ample room for the education sessions, luncheons, registration area, conference offices and one of the trade shows. Since so much space was allocated to the large general session, there was no room for the evening social events or the second trade show. They also discovered that this older building could not meet the rigid physical requirements of the second show.

They considered looking at space at one of the hotels in the area but the meeting rooms were not large enough nor could they accommodate the trade show. The external environment was another consideration as they had selected March in North America as optimal for attendance for their industry, but it would not be the best time of year for delegates to be walking back and forth from the hotel to the convention center.

Eventually, they came back to look at the second building of the convention center. They agreed that if they utilized both buildings, this facility met all four of their main criteria and many, if not all, of their other secondary considerations. Although slightly unusual, and perhaps not ideal, as it was quite a walk between buildings, they felt confident that this was a workable solution.

The planning committee knew from the start that the choice of venue was somewhat limited for the size of the group and complexity of the program. They realized early in the process, that a single facility would not meet all of their requirements and that they needed to be flexible and creative to make it work. For example, once they began to develop conference details and work out the logistics, they decided to move the entire conference (registration, sessions and luncheons) to the south building midweek to be adjacent to the second trade show.

SITE SELECTION CHECKLIST

The following checklist serves as a basic guideline of what should be observed and noted when conducting the site inspection of facilities. Over time meeting professionals may develop their own comprehensive list particular to their groups needs, however these basics should be of concern to every meeting professional.

DESTINATION

☐ Accessibility

- ease and cost
- proximity to airport
- barrier free access
- taxi/limousine service
- parking space
- shuttle service
- airport assistance
- adequate number of flights to destination
- seasonality of destination (peak vs. off-season)

☐ Environment

- local attractions
- shopping
- recreation
- restaurants
- climate
- appearance
- safety
- economic conditions
- reputation of area/facility for hosting meetings

☐ Facility

- efficient, friendly staff
- attractive, clean lobby
- registration desk easy to locate
- sufficient space and personnel in relation to guest rooms

- ability to handle peak check in/check out times
- sufficient elevators for peak demand
- message and information center
- guest services
  - drugstores
  - banks
  - emergency services
  - giftshop
  - concierge
  - safety deposit boxes
- comfortable, clean bedrooms
  - condition of furniture
  - bathroom amenities
  - adequate lighting
  - closet space and hangers
  - smoke detectors
  - fire exit information clearly posted
  - mini bar
  - data port
  - dual line telephone
- well lit and clean hallways
- beverage and ice machines on each floor
- service elevator accessibility
- size of standard versus deluxe room
- availability of executive floor offering special guest services
- barrier free designed rooms
- number and type of suites and availability of suite floor plans
- reservations procedures and policies
- room category classifications
  - nonsmoking
  - view
  - other
  - hospitality
- bedrooms available for early arrivals and late departures
- current convention rate and rack rate for individual guests
- check in and check out hours
- cheque cashing policies

- types of credit cards accepted
- refund policy
- dates of any planned renovations or labour contract negotiations
- changes in facility ownership being discussed
- availability of health club, hours and cost
- telephone access charges
  - long distance
  - local
  - calling card
  - 1-800
  - internet connection
- key system for guest rooms
- adequate parking space
- facility emergency plan
- emergency exits clearly marked

☐ Meeting space

- number of meeting rooms required
- formal program
- committee meetings
- business meetings
- estimated attendance for each session
- seating style
- audio visual needs accommodated
- space for refreshment breaks, receptions, dinners, etc.
- pre and post meeting space required
- barrier free access
- meeting room amenities (notepads, etc.)

☐ Food and beverage

- outlets
- appearance and cleanliness
- cleanliness of food preparation areas
- adequate staffing at peak times
- service levels

- prompt and efficient service
- variety of menus
- cost range
- reservations policy
- feasibility of setting up additional outlets

☐ Group functions
- quality and service
- diversity of menus
- guarantees
  - guarantee policies
  - when guarantee is required
- number prepared beyond guarantee
- costs
  - taxes
  - gratuities and/or service charges
  - projected price increase by time of event
  - extra labour charges
- alcohol laws
- cash bar policies
  - bartender cost and minimum hours
  - cashier charges
  - drink prices
- special services
  - tailored menus
  - theme parties
  - unique refreshment breaks
  - food substitutions available
  - table decorations
  - dance floor
- size of banquet rounds (8 or 10 people)
- room service
  - hours of operation
  - diversity of menu
  - prompt and efficient telephone manner
  - prompt delivery
  - quality

☐ Conference offices
- support services available from CVB
- experienced suppliers
  - audio visual
  - exhibit service contractors
  - staffing services
  - security
- sufficient space for furniture and equipment
- lighting
- proximity to meeting space
- electrical outlets
- telephones and internet connections
- secure after hours
- barrier free access

☐ Equipment
- table sizes
- chair styles and quantity available
- risers
- podiums
- lecterns
- easels
- table linens
- flags

☐ Exhibit space
- other meeting space
- food service areas
- restrooms
- telephones
- other portions of meeting
- sufficient time for move-in and move-out
- condition of facility
- ceiling height & rigging points
- pillars & electrical supply

- décor
- supplemental lighting
- first aid station
- office space
- crate storage area and policies
- communications access

☐ Other concerns
- does the site fit the other requirements of the meeting?
  - adequate parking
  - shopping nearby
  - local entertainment and attractions
  - children's activities
  - other
- outside vendors
  - equipment
  - decorations
  - services
  - supplies
- associated events or functions held in conjunction with meeting
- exhibitors
  - block rooms separately
  - hospitality functions
  - increase total meeting value

☐ Additional sources of information
- chamber of commerce
- CVB
- organization records
- business publications and trade journals
- individual facilities
- hotel chains' national sales office
- professional/peer information
- personal contacts
- online networks/websites
- referrals

SPECIAL NEEDS

☐ Space for special needs on registration/pre-registration forms, including:

- visual impairment
- hearing impairment
- mobility impairment
- dietary requirements
- language interpretation requirement
- other

☐ Interpreters

- working language of destination
- sign
- other languages according to need

☐ Translators

- working language of destination
- other languages according to need

☐ Readers

☐ Barrier-free design

- entrances
- lobby, corridors, and public areas
- elevators
- public restrooms/toilets
- guest/sleeping rooms
- exterior of facility
- reserved parking
- hard surface driveway or path connecting parking lot to entrance
- obstruction free: no curbs, steps, or level changes in excess of 1.2 cm (1/2")

☐ Outside ramp to elevated entrances

☐ Entrances

- swinging or automatic sliding doors minimum 90 cm (36") wide
- revolving door or entrance equipped with specified alternative

☐ Lobby, corridors, and public areas

- carpet depth does not hamper use of wheelchairs, walkers, or similar devices

☐ Elevators

- raised or Braille indicators located a maximum of 54" above floor
- call buttons
- large enough for wheelchairs to enter, turn, and exit
- access to all floors
- conveniently and centrally located
- number of elevators and their locations
- equipped with light-up and sound signals to announce arrival
- waiting areas, corridors, and halls similarly equipped

☐ Public restrooms/toilets

- entrances a minimum of 90 cm (36") wide
- doors easily opened
- easy access to toilet stalls (no narrow vestibule or powder room)
- one or more toilet stalls for wheelchair user
- toilet stall equipped with grab bars and a minimum width of 90 cm (36")
- door swings out of stall
- door a minimum of 83 cm (33") wide
- washbasins with lever or push button handles
- ample knee space beneath wash basin (75 cm or 30" minimum), pipes covered
- soap dispensers easily reachable from wheelchair (maximum 120 cm or 48" above floor)
- towel dispensers easy to reach (maximum 120 cm or 48" above floor)
- mirrors hung no more than 100 cm (40") above floor

☐ Guest/sleeping rooms

- doors a minimum of 90 cm (36") wide, swinging out
- light, heating, and air controls located a maximum of 54" above the floor
- flashing lights for telephone and alarm system
- bathroom large enough to provide easy access to all fixtures
- bathtub equipped with grab bars or shower that will accommodate entering and exiting

☐ Meeting rooms

- ramped access to all levels
- doors meet access requirements
- automatically opening doors
- barrier free setup
- room to manoeuvre wheelchair
- wheelchair seating
- wide aisles
- wireless microphone

☐ If presenter is person with a disability

- ramp access to stage
- room to manoeuvre wheelchair on stage
- audio visual aids accessible to speaker
- table with microphone, space for papers and water

☐ Public telephones

- equipped with amplifiers
- at wheelchair level
- TTY phone hook up

☐ Guide dogs

- tour of site
- location of nearest patch of grass

☐ Dietary needs

- healthy heart
- vegetarian (what kind?)
- diabetic
- religious observance
- allergies

CHAPTER REVIEW

- Six key steps to site selection include:
    1. identify meeting objectives
    2. develop the meeting format
    3. determine physical requirements
    4. define attendee expectations
    5. select meeting destination and type of facility
    6. evaluate the options

- Request for Proposal (RFP) allows the meeting professional to communicate the meeting needs to a pre-screened group of potential properties

- The RFP should include:
    - name and type of sponsor organization
    - meeting participant profiles
    - approximate dates of the meeting
    - length of meeting
    - number of sleeping rooms of each type needed
    - destination and facility requirements
    - support services needed
    - meeting history
    - meeting format
    - required number and size of meeting rooms
    - food and beverage requirements
    - range of rates sought
    - request for references
    - reply deadline
    - date of notification of decision

- A site inspection visit is the best way to assess the condition of potential facilities and ensure that the needs of the meeting will be met

- The local convention and visitors bureau can be of assistance during the site selection process by:
  - setting up appointments with facilities
  - providing a representative escort for actual site inspection tour
- providing contacts for reference checks
- providing assistance with conference and convention centres and determining suitability of nearby hotels

TEST YOUR KNOWLEDGE

The following self test will indicate the level of understanding and knowledge gained from this chapter. Solutions to all self tests can be found in Appendix A.

1. Convention and Visitors Bureau will help co-ordinate site inspections.

   ☐ True   ☐ False

2. The destination chosen for the meeting will be influenced by the availability and quality of local suppliers.

   ☐ True   ☐ False

3. When considering appropriate destinations, the meeting professional must be primarily concerned with satisfying the needs of the sponsoring organization.

   ☐ True   ☐ False

4. The primary purpose of a site inspection is to assess the condition of a facility and ensure it meets the needs of the meeting.

   ☐ True   ☐ False

5. The meetings objectives are not a significant consideration when choosing an appropriate meeting destination.

   ☐ True   ☐ False

6. University campuses and museums can provide viable alternatives to traditional meeting sites.

   ☐ True   ☐ False

7. Which of the following factors are critical to the site selection process?

   (a) organizational budget

   (b) expectations of the meeting participant

   (c) meeting objectives

   (d) all of the above

8. An RFP is typically generated to:

   a) record pertinent meeting data

   b) track meeting expenditures

   c) solicit bids from potential suppliers

   d) market the meeting to participants

9. Explain the difference between a conference center and a convention center:

    _____

    _____

    _____

    _____

    _____

10. Develop a 5 point checklist for appraising the suitability of potential meeting destinations.

    _____

    _____

    _____

    _____

    _____

    _____

11. List 5 items a meeting professional would look for when evaluating the barrier free accessibility of a potential meeting facility?

    _____

    _____

    _____

    _____

    _____

12. What physical and dietary restrictions should you be prepared to accommodate at your selected meetings facility?

    _____

    _____

    _____

    _____

    _____

NOTES

Negotiations and Contracts

INTRODUCTION

In the process of planning and delivering a successful event, the meeting professional will enter into numerous contracts with many suppliers. During the negotiation process, the meeting professional will negotiate with the representative who has the authority to make decisions on behalf of the venue or supplier. A contract results when all requirements and provisions required by both parties, have been mutually satisfied. Compromise on the part of both parties will undoubtedly be necessary.

Understanding the business value of the meeting, as well as the value of the goods and/or services required, is important information that will aid the meeting professional in negotiation.

Ensure you understand and can apply the following terms:

- Attrition clause
- Cancellation clause
- Force majeure
- Hold harmless
- Indemnification
- Liquidated damage
- Service levels
- Slippage
- Walk policy

Refer to the glossary for further clarification of the key terms for this chapter.

LEARNING OBJECTIVES

After completing this chapter, the learner will:

- understand the three components of a legal contract

- understand the effects of the contract on the financial situation of the conference/event

- prepare for negotiations

- negotiate successfully with various suppliers

ROLES AND RESPONSIBILITIES

MEETING MANAGER

○ Negotiate and finalize contracts

○ Negotiate rates and services

- compile a relevant history in preparation for negotiation

- negotiate contracts for goods and services (e.g., audio visual, suppliers, speakers, facilities, and entertainers)

- prepare for negotiation by researching pricing structures, previous users, policies and competition

- follow the correct negotiation steps and sequence to achieve a mutually satisfactory situation

- determine and respect company/internal policies regarding negotiations and contracts (e.g., restrictions on the use of outside contractors vs in house services)

- establish negotiating priorities

- set policies and procedures which will be applied consistently during negotiation (e.g., cancellation/ attrition clauses)

- recognize, document and communicate the history of your business and its value to the supplier

- establish and carry out a tendering process

- anticipate hidden costs

○ Complete contractual agreements

- ensure a written contract for all goods and services

- negotiate various types of contracts: lease, service and sales

- take action on contractual deficiencies

- include penalties by either party in applicable clauses (e.g., cancellation and attrition)

- question and interpret contractual terms and their implications, especially financial

- include protection from construction, renovation, or changes in ownership

- determine the contractual terms needed for liability reasons

- ensure that all details are clearly defined and agreed upon, leaving no room for misinterpretation

- ensure that all points negotiated are included in the final contract

- have contracts reviewed by a legal authority as required

- arrange signing of contracts and letters of agreement

- recognize the need to adjust contracts (e.g., based on registration numbers and other contingencies)

- confirm, finalize and communicate all contractual agreements to accountable parties

- distribute contractual agreements as applicable

○ Monitor contracts

- ensure contract adherence

- monitor and communicate changes which impact on the contract

MEETING COORDINATOR

○ Assist in preparation for negotiations

- Prepare relevant history
  - ○ compile statistics on past meetings
  - ○ compare past meetings including attendance, guestroom pickup, food and beverage revenue
  - ○ Respect contractual agreements
  - ○ Adhere to contracts on site
  - ○ review all documented contractual agreements
  - ○ demonstrate an understanding of contract details and expectations
  - ○ ensure contract compliance
  - ○ Communicate with and monitor facilities and suppliers
  - ○ provide information and updates
  - ○ monitor services

PREPARING TO NEGOTIATE

Most meeting and event negotiations are based on the total business value the meeting represents to the supplier. The greater the perceived potential revenue, the more leverage the meeting professional has for lower rates or concessions.

The meeting history is the most accurate tool to determine and communicate the value of a meeting. However, when there is no prior event history to refer to, negotiations become more difficult for the meeting professional - the facilities and suppliers are generally more cautious in their approach. In any event, focus on the information that is available, for example:

- meeting objectives

- space requirements

- guest rooms

- function space

- off-site function space

- meeting profile

- attendees

- food and beverage functions

- meeting format

- projected budget

- anticipated logistical requirements

- program content

- expected interest to potential attendees

- history from any similar meetings

HOT TIP

Leave Long Lead Times

It's a good rule of thumb to remember that 90 percent of negotiation happens in the last 10 percent of the time allotted to plan a conference or meeting. It's only when deadlines approach that actual agreements are reached and concessions made. Days always seem shorter when there's a time crunch, so give yourself some peace of mind and plan accordingly.

NEGOTIABLE ITEMS

When it comes to negotiating for meeting and event services, everything but taxes is negotiable. The following list details the most commonly negotiated items. Before entering into a negotiation, understand what elements are necessary to the success of your meeting and what would be nice to have, if your supplier will agree. You should give up the nice to haves before the must haves.

FOOD AND BEVERAGE

- hospitality suites and receptions

- minimum increase in food and beverage prices

- upgraded selections

GUEST ROOMS

- guest room rates (discount off published prices)

- increase complimentary room ratio (ensure cumulative rather than per night)

- complimentary guestroom for site inspection

- complimentary guestroom for move-in

- complimentary presidential or executive suite during the meeting for the meeting host

- complimentary room for meeting professional during the scheduled event

- VIP room upgrades at the group rate

- speaker and staff rooms discounted during the meeting

- ability to reduce guestroom block without liability

- room block reservation cutoff closer to meeting date than typical 30 days and rooms sold after cutoff date sold at the group rate

- optional or reduced service charges for bell service and housekeeping

- VIP amenities

- satellite check in with extra bell staff available

- free or reduced parking fees or valet service

- complimentary turndown service

- complimentary daily newspaper

- pre and post conference guestroom rates at conference rate

- toll free access, free telephone local calls

MEETING SPACE

- waiver or reduction of meeting room rentals for a guaranteed food and beverage expenditure

- waiver or reduction of exhibit space rental fees with adequate guest room block

- house telephone at registration within secured meeting office

- pads, pencils, candies, Kleenex, easels, corkboards, chalkboards, whiteboards

- complimentary room setups and resets as required for program

- complimentary or discounts for onsite services

- 24-hour meeting space rates

- additional utility charges (electrical, cleaning)

OTHER SERVICES

- children's programs and child care services

- house limousine or shuttle service to nearby attractions

- guarantee of specific service levels for all food outlets and functions

- free self mail registration and preprinted promotional brochures

- reduced or complimentary corkage charges

Industry Insight

Contributed by John S. Foster, Esq. Atlanta Georgia. All Rights Reserved. Reprinted with permission.

Recent disputes between meeting sponsors and hotels reaffirm the principle that it's better (and cheaper) to stay out of trouble than to have to get out of trouble. The best way to avoid controversies and lawsuits is to write a contract that clearly specifies the intent of the parties and is legally sufficient. The following are 10 guidelines to assist both meeting professionals and suppliers.

1. Understand the five legal elements of a contract:

   - offer

   - acceptance

   - consideration

   - recorded in writing

   - legally competent parties

2. Understand the proper way to revise a contract or proposal:

   a) strike out terms in the original and write new terms in the margin; both parties must initial and date all changes.

   b) place new terms in an attached addendum

   c) rewrite the original with new terms

3. Understand how to sign contracts correctly. The principal has primary liability for the performance of the contract. An authorized agent of a company or association binds the company or association to the terms of the contract.

4. Avoid "to be negotiated" clauses and always define your terms.

5. Understand how to negotiate and manage an attrition clause; negotiate and manage the following variables:

- review dates
- percentage of slippage allowed
- how damages, if any, will be calculated

6. Understand the elements of a cancellation clause and the concept of damages (versus penalties). Damages are defined as lost profit (or additional expenses) but not lost revenue. To determine damages, parties to a contract may agree to specific sums or to a formula. Terms that attempt to penalize one or more parties are not enforceable.

7. Spell out terms for deposits, both group and individual.

8. Understand option deadlines and the mailbox rule. Contract proposals contain option deadlines, a date by which the other party must accept the proposal in order for a contract to be formed. The mailbox rule specifies that a valid acceptance to a contract occurs when it is signed and put into a mailbox, not when the contract is received by the other party.

9. Recognize and understand indemnification and hold harmless language when you see it. If the contract contains an indemnification clause, you need to understand what risks and responsibilities you are being asked to assume. Don't agree to indemnify and hold harmless other people or entities for their negligence.

10. Understand the merger clause. This clause states that the entire agreement of the parties has been merged into the final contract and cannot be changed without each party's written consent.

CONTRACTS

Contracts should be reviewed by legal counsel before being signed by the meeting professional or host organization. Ensure all negotiated goods and services are included in the final written contract.

ELEMENTS OF A HOTEL CONTRACT

- Parties entering agreement:
  - if an agent is signing the contract, make sure the principal party is identified

- Dates of event

- General considerations:
  - billing and master accounts
  - unavailability of primary facility for event (e.g., labour strikes, building inaccessible)

- Guest rooms
  - number of rooms (in each category, if applicable)
  - room rates
  - confirmation policy
  - guarantees
  - deposits
  - early departure fee
  - check in/check out policy
  - room block adjustment policy
  - complimentary rooms
  - reservations procedures
  - billing
  - credit arrangements
  - room upgrades
  - rooming block pickup report

- Food and beverage functions
  - date of functions
  - function space
  - setups
  - price guarantees
  - staffing ratio
  - service of alcoholic beverages and corkage
- Meeting space
  - meeting schedule with meeting rooms and hours specified
  - approval requirements prior to venue changing space
  - equipment
  - public space
  - noise
  - conflicting groups
  - setup time
  - room rental rates
  - room diagrams
  - outdoor functions
  - exhibit space and charges
  - keys
  - coat check
  - registration space
  - onsite office
- Renovation/construction
  - notice of planned construction and construction schedule
  - postpone/reschedule construction when it interferes with meeting or guest comfort
  - right to cancel contract without liability if group determines construction will unreasonably interfere with its event
- Compliance with local laws
- Accessibility

- Parking and shuttles

- Service levels

- Signatures of authorized parties

- Miscellaneous
  - choice of law/forum
  - dispute resolution

~ Sample Template ~

SAMPLE HOTEL CONTRACT

Today's Date: Monday, October 29, 2001   Status: Tentative
Organization: ABC Group   Meeting Name: ABC Conference
Contact: John Smith   Title: President
Address: _____
Telephone: _____   Fax:_____

**NAME OF HOTEL
CONTRACT**

ACCOMMODATIONS				
MAY 2002	10	11	12	RATES
	FRI	SAT	SUN	SGL/DBL
Standard Guest Rooms	100	80	50	$125.00 Cdn
Total Guest Rooms	100	80	50	
Add $10.00 for each additional person for triple and quadruple occupancy.				

Rates quoted are based upon the information provided at the time of booking. Subsequent changes may affect the rates quoted. These rates will be subject to applicable Provincial Sales Tax (PST) on accommodation, currently five percent (5%) and the Goods and Services Tax (GST) at seven percent (7%). Rates do not include housing processing fees, commissions or rebates.

Complimentary Rooms: We will extend one (1) complimentary standard guestroom for every fifty (50) paid guestrooms occupied per night. This scale is based on a non cumulative basis. Complimentary credits apply to the cost of the guestroom and taxes only.

~ *Sample Template* ~

Room Upgrades: We will extend to your board of directors, seven (7) upgrades from standard guestrooms to deluxe guestrooms on the Club Floors at the negotiated rate of $125.00/night.

One Bedroom Junior Suite: We will extend to the chairman of the board a one bedroom junior suite at the negotiated rate of $125/night. (Junior suite is not located on the Club Floor.)

METHOD OF RESERVATION	CUT-OFF DATE
Individual 1-800-HOTEL or 111-111-1111 Room Block under "ABC Group" Check-in time is 3:00 p.m. / Check-out time is 1:00 p.m.	The cut-off date for your guestroom block is April 10. Prior to April 10, and if the group block is not sold out, individual group members are entitled to the group rates based on guestroom type availability. Reservation requests received after April 10 will be accepted on a space available basis only, at the Hotel's published rate.
BILLING	
Individuals responsible to settle their own accounts upon checkout	

GUESTROOM ATTRITION CHARGE

If the Group reduces but does not cancel its Confirmed Room Nights "230", the Group agrees to pay the Hotel, as liquidated damages, and not as a penalty, an amount based on the following provision:

From date of signature until four (4) months before the arrival date, the Group may reduce its Confirmed Room Nights "230" by fifteen percent (15%) without charge.

From three (3) months until one (1) month before the arrival date, the Group may reduce its Confirmed Room Nights "230" by an additional five percent (5%) without charge.

~ *Sample Template* ~

For shrinkage over and above this allowance, the Group agrees to pay $125.00 for each unused guestroom night blocked. Charges will be added to and payable as part of your Master Account.

If the Hotel resells all of part of the unused guestrooms, revenue received by the Hotel from the guestroom resale will be deducted from the amount owed by the Group for the shrinkage. The Hotel has no ability or obligation to sell guestrooms within the Group's guestroom block prior to selling other than available guestrooms.

MEETING, EXHIBITS AND FUNCTION OUTLINE

Meeting Room Rental:

We would be pleased to discount the meeting room based on the number of paid guestrooms occupied and catering revenue generated during your meeting. Total meeting room rental based on your current program is $8,725.00 (retail) before discount.

For every fifty (50) guestrooms paid per night (non-cumulative basis), we will deduct $250.00 from your total meeting room rental.

Total meeting room rental before discount:		$8,725.00
Minus guestroom discount	($250.00 X 4)	$1,000.00
Total meeting room rental including guestroom discount		$7,725.00

In addition, for all food and beverage functions catered by the Hotel currently estimated at $27,000.00 (excluding applicable taxes and gratuities), we will offer you an additional discount based on the scale below:

Food and Beverage Revenues	Discount	Total Rental
Less than $14,000	No discount	$7,725.00
Between $14,000 to 16,999.00	50%	$3,862.50
Between $17,000 to 19,999.00	75%	$1,931.25
More than $20,000	100%	complimentary meeting space

~ Sample Template ~

The following table is based on your proposed program. A more detailed breakdown will be provided once we receive a confirmed program from you.

Date	Start Time	End Time	Function	Room	Setup	Pax	Room Rental ($)
May 10	8:00 AM	11:59 PM	Tradeshow Setup	Ballroom	Table Tops	75	4,000.00
May 10	1:00 PM	4:00 PM	Meeting	Room A	Theater Style	125	975.00
May 10	4:00 PM	6:00 PM	Registration	Foyer		2	
May 10	6:00 PM	7:00 PM	Reception F&B	Convention Level Foyer	Reception Style	225	
May 10	7:00 PM	11:00 PM	Buffet Dinner	Grand Salon	Rounds of 8	225	
May 11	8:00 AM	5:00 PM	Registration	Foyer		2	
May 11	10:00 AM	5:00 PM	Tradeshow	Ballroom	Table Tops	75	2,500.00
May 11	12:00 PM	1:00 PM	Buffet Lunch	Grand Salon	Rounds of 8 – Semi circle	225	
May 11	5:00 PM	10:00 PM	Teardown	Ballroom			
May 11	5:00 PM	10:00 PM	Themed Dinner	Grand Salon	Rounds of 8 – Semi circle	225	
May 12	8:00 AM	4:00 PM	Registration	Foyer		2	
May 12	10:00 AM	12:00 PM	General Meeting	Ballroom C	Classroom	125	1,250.00
May 12	12:00 PM	1:00 PM	Lunch	Ballroom B	Rounds of 8 – Semi circle	125	
May 12	1:00 PM	4:00 PM	Meeting	Ballroom C	Classroom	125	
May 12	6:00 PM	11:00 PM	Banquet	Ballroom D	Rounds of 8 – Semi circle	125	

Exhibitor Storage - The D and E Rooms are being held May 9 - 11. Rental is based on a 24-hour hold ($300/day for each room)

~ *Sample Template* ~

Exhibit Space Charges and Description

Function space has been set aside for the Group's exhibit area consisting of tabletop exhibits. It is understood that exhibit setup will commence at 8:00 a.m. on May 10 with the show opening at 10:00 a.m. on May 11. Dismantling will begin at 5:00 p.m. on May 11 and will be completed by 10:00 p.m. on May 11. Exhibit setup and tear down time to include piping, draping, electrical hook-up, and drayage, plus any other contracted time.

Scheduled setup and tear down times have been established to ensure timely access for all of our customers. Function space must be vacated within contracted times as outlined. Penalty charges for additional labour to facilitate timely removal and clean up are as follows: $500.00 first hour or portion thereof, $200.00 for each additional hour or portion thereof.

Our convention services department will review your exhibit/display requirements floor plan and decide which services will need to be contracted to an outside decorator/drayage company. The Hotel is not equipped with storage space to receive, store and handle exhibit materials.

You may also anticipate additional charges for maintenance, labour and power, depending upon exhibitor requirements. Specific charges will be determined at the point at which your requirements are finalized.

It is the responsibility of the meeting planner that the exhibit hall is completely clean on departure. If the exhibit area is not left in its original condition (e.g., completely clean and clear of any exhibit material or debris), a cleaning charge will be assessed. The cleaning charge (if applicable) will be determined by the number of people (housemen) and their wage multiplied by the number of hours necessary to clean the area. Under our current union agreement, if we require bringing a person to the Hotel, the minimum of wage will be four (4) hours. For extensive cleanup where a garbage container/crusher/compactor is required, an additional charge of $2,500.00 will be applied to your master account.

~ *Sample Template* ~

Exhibitor's Contract

It is necessary that a copy of your proposed exhibitor's contract be submitted to our Convention Services department prior to its printing and distribution. This will ensure that both your Group and the Hotel are protected and that your exhibitors have received complete information and instructions.

Please incorporate the following "Hold Harmless" clause into your exhibitor's contract:

"The exhibitor assumes the entire responsibility and liability for losses, damages and claims arising out of injury or damage to exhibitor's displays, equipment and other property brought onto the premises of the Hotel and shall indemnify and hold harmless the Hotel agents, servants and employees from any and all such losses, damages and claims."

The exhibitor acknowledges that the Hotel does not maintain insurance covering exhibitor's property and this is the sole responsibility of the exhibitor to obtain business interruption and property damage insurance covering such losses by the exhibitor. A copy of the insurance policy will be forwarded to the Hotel three (3) months prior to the Group's arrival. Failure to do so will be an infringement of the contract and the Hotel will not be liable to any loss due to this infringement.

The Hotel suggests that the Group hire its own security from the time of move-in to the time of completion of tear down on a 24-hour basis. The Hotel is not liable for any loss due to the infringement of this clause.

Food and Beverage

We will confirm the prices for catered events three (3) months prior to your arrival date. Food and beverage prices are subject to applicable Ontario tax, currently at eight percent (8%), Provincial Sales Tax (PST), seven percent (7%) Goods and Services Tax (GST), and taxable service (gratuity) charge of fifteen percent (15%). All alcoholic beverages are taxable at ten (10%) PST, seven percent (7%) Goods and Services Tax (GST), and fifteen percent (15%) for Gratuities.

~ *Sample Template* ~

All food and beverage service to the Group's organization within the Hotel must be provided by the Hotel and served by Hotel personnel, in accordance with the Hotel's prevailing prices for such services. For hospitality suites, food and beverage must be purchased through the convention services department, when finalizing your function.

We require a meeting and banquet guarantee attendance figure not later than three (3) days, seventy-two hours, prior to each event.

Alcoholic Beverages

If alcoholic beverages are to be served in the Hotel's function space or hospitality (or elsewhere under the Hotel's alcoholic beverage license), the Hotel will require that beverages be dispensed only by its employees and bartenders. The Hotel's alcoholic beverage license requires the Hotel to: a) request proper identification (photo ID) of any person of questionable age and refuse alcoholic beverage service if the person is either underage or proper identification cannot be produced; and b) refuse alcoholic beverage service to any person who, in the Hotel's sole judgment, appears intoxicated.

A setup charge and a clean up charge will apply to hospitality suites. This will be added to the function invoice. A minimum of two hours for setup and two hours for clean up will apply ($17.00 per hour for a minimum of four hours).

Food and Beverage Cancellation Policy

Should the Group find it necessary to cancel any of the food and beverage functions listed above, the Group will be responsible for the Hotel's loss of revenue as follows:

300 Days to 91 Days	25% of Anticipated Function Revenue
90 Days to 61 Days	50% of Anticipated Function Revenue
60 Days to 31 Days	75% of Anticipated Function Revenue
30 Days or less	100% of Anticipated Function Revenue

~ *Sample Template* ~

Food and Beverage Attrition

The group may reduce the attendance for any or all of its food and beverage functions only once as outlined in the following scale:

From 10 months to 4 months prior to the function date the Group may reduce its food and beverage estimates per function by up to 30% without charge.

OR

From 3 months to 61 days prior to the function date the Group may reduce its food and beverage estimates per function by up to 20% without charge.

OR

From 60 days to 30 days prior to the function date the Group may reduce its food and beverage estimates per function by up to 15% without charge.

OR

Less than 29 days prior to the function date the Group may reduce its food and beverage estimates per function by up to 10% without charge.

The Hotel reserves the right to reassign function space in the event that there is a reduction of more than 30%. Any reductions greater than the above numbers will result in the application of additional function room rental based on the reduction in revenue from the affected function(s).

In the event that the final guaranteed number for any or all confirmed function(s) falls more than 10% below the most recent estimate provided by the Group (see above), the Group agrees to pay the Hotel as liquidated damages and not as a penalty an amount based on the following scale:

Between 75% and 90%	5% of the anticipated revenue as of 29 days in advance
Between 65% and 75%	15% of the anticipated revenue as of 29 days in advance
Between 50% and 65%	20% of the anticipated revenue as of 29 days in advance
Below 50%	25% of the anticipated revenue as of 29 days in advance

~ *Sample Template* ~

ALL REDUCTIONS IN ESTIMATED NUMBERS MUST BE COMMUNICATED TO THE HOTEL IN WRITING.

Insurance Liability/Indemnification

The Hotel and the Group each agree to carry adequate liability and other insurance protecting itself from any claims arising from any activities conducted at the Hotel during the meeting/convention. Each of the parties hereto shall protect, defend, indemnify, and save harmless the other, together with their affiliates and employees against and from all claim, damages, losses, and expenses, including but not limited to attorney's fees and cost by reason of any suit, claim, demand, judgment or cause of action initiated by any person, arising or alleged to have arisen out of the performance of their respective obligations under this Agreement.

CANCELLATION

Should the event not be held at the Hotel, the Group will pay the Hotel, as liquidated damages, within thirty (30) days after written notification to the Hotel of the transfer or cancellation as follows:

300 days to 90 days	25% of total revenue of peak guest room night and 50% of total meeting room rentals
89 days to 30 days	Total revenue of peak guest room night and 100% of total meeting room rentals
Less than 30 days	total revenue of peak guest room night, catering revenue and all function space rentals

Impossibility of Performance

This contract will terminate without liability to either party if substantial performance of either party's obligation is prevented by an unforeseeable cause reasonably beyond that party's control. Such causes include, but are not limited to, acts of God; regulations, or order of government authorities; fire, flood or explosion; war, disaster, civil disorder, curtailment of transportation

~ *Sample Template* ~

facilities or services necessary in order to hold the meeting; any delay in necessary and essential construction or renovation of the Hotel; strike, lockout, or work stoppage or other restraint of labour, either partial or general, from whatever cause.

ADVANCE DEPOSIT/PAYMENT

We require a non-refundable deposit of $1,000.00 to secure this space on your behalf. As a first time client, we will require payment based on the following schedule:

Upon signing of the contract	$1,000.00 (non-refundable)
By January 25	$2,500.00
By March 28	$2,500.00
End of Event	Balance Due

The deposit can be made by certified cheque payable to the Hotel or by credit card.

Card Member's Name:
Credit Card Number:
Expiration Date:
Authorized Signature:

BILLING

Groups who wish to request direct billing should complete a credit application four weeks prior to the event to allow sufficient time to receive approval from our credit manager. All charges to be applied to the Master Account must be signed by an authorized person immediately following the event. The Group's authorized person and Hotel representative will meet at the conclusion of the event to approve these charges.

~ Sample Template ~

The outstanding Master Account balance is to be paid upon receipt of invoice, which will include the appropriate breakdown and detail of charges. A 1.25% per month finance charge will be added on balances that are delinquent or paid after thirty (30) days of date of invoice.

OPTION DATE

As the final hotel selection will be completed by September 21, we will continue to hold the abovementioned guest rooms and public space on a tentative basis until September 21. However, if between now and the option date, another group requests this space and is willing to confirm on a definite basis, we will request an earlier decision. We will request this decision in writing and the Group will have seventy-two (72) hours to reply to the Hotel. Should the Hotel not receive any notification from the Group with respect to this, the Group will forfeit its entire tentative guest room and public space reservation. If a decision is not made by September 21, the Hotel will notify the Group in writing that all arrangements are cancelled. To guarantee rates quoted, the availability of sleeping room requested, and all other items, this contract must be signed and returned to the hotel by Friday, September 21 or the rooms may be cancelled.

_____

Hotel Representative   Title   Date

_____

Organization's Authorized Signature   Title   Date

KEY CLAUSES OF A HOTEL CONTRACT

CANCELLATION
Provision which specifies the respective penalties that apply if cancellation occurs for failure to comply with the terms of the agreement.

ATTRITION
Also known as 'Slippage'. The provision that provides for payment of damages, by the meeting sponsor, when the contracted percentage of guest room nights, food and beverage and meeting space is not fulfilled.

The Convention Industry Council (CIC) was selected by the meetings, convention, and exhibition industry to manage *Project Attrition* – a project created to implement a course of action that addresses the concerns of all parties. Refer to www.conventionindustry.org/attrition/project_attrition.htm

INDEMNIFICATION
Also known as the 'hold harmless' clause. Stipulates that neither party will hold the other responsible for any damages, theft to materials, or equipment owned or rented by either party; also guarantees that one party will take responsibility for damages assessed as the result of another party's inaction.

FORCE MAJEURE
Also known as the 'Acts of God' clause. Releases both parties from liability in the event of an occurrence which is out of their control.

UNINTERRUPTED USE OF PREMISES
Protects the meeting sponsor from any changes with respect to ownership, condition of the hotel, renovation or construction to the property. Implies that all service outlets will be fully operational at the time of event.

DEPOSITS
Method, frequency and amount of monies owed prior to the event. May be refundable/non refundable up to a certain amount or a certain date. Can apply to both groups and individual attendees.

WALK POLICY

Stipulates the action to be taken should a guest, who is holding a confirmed sleeping room reservation at a hotel, be required to relocate to another hotel, due to overbooking.

CUT OFF DATE

The date on which the facility will no longer hold sleeping rooms at the contracted group rate. Rooms are released back into the facility's inventory for sale to the general public.

DAMAGES, INSURANCE AND LIABILITY

Stipulates the procedures, penalties and rights of the party causing damage to the facility. Liability insurance coverage is required by most event sites up to a specified amount. Facilities will request that the meeting host obtain, maintain and provide proof of insurance coverage in sufficient amounts for any liabilities.

~ A Conference Journal ~

Ultimately, a contract should reflect the mutual agreement between the host organization and the supplier of a specific product or service. The millennium event was no different from any other organization in its desire to negotiate the best possible rates for the conference.

Once an appropriate supplier was identified, negotiations by the meeting professional took place (with the exception of all marketing and communications as these were conducted by staff who were professionals in this field). The provision of every service or product requiring significant financial investment necessitated a formal contract. This was crucial for the combined organizations, as well as for suppliers, who had worked with one organization but likely not the other.

From the host organizations' perspective, their plan was to obtain the best product, while keeping costs in line with the approved budget. As much as suppliers were willing to compromise in an attempt to meet the needs of the host organization, negotiations sometimes required compromise by both parties. There was nothing to be gained by negotiating rates so low that they were in jeopardy of diminishing the quality of the product provided or reducing service. It was the meeting professional's desire to have a win/ win situation for everyone. As well, it was important to maintain the special client/supplier relationships with existing suppliers that had taken years to build.

The most difficult agreements to develop were the hotel contracts, with respect to the room blocks themselves and room block attrition policies. How could they block sufficient space for a potential attendance of 15,000 and, at the same time, protect the organization from overbooking and facing attrition penalties? Since there was history, they began by simply combining the initial contracts of both organizations that had been prepared years in advance and then estimated a realistic increase to arrive at a block at each hotel. Then they tested the attrition clause to determine what the outcome would be should they experience a shortfall. The result was that they were at risk for hundreds of thousands of dollars.

Not wishing to put themselves at risk and yet satisfy their need to locate and protect a sufficient number of bedrooms for their delegates, they decided to go directly to the hotels for advice. They invited representatives from all of the properties in which they intended to obtain room blocks, as well as representation from the local Convention and Visitors Bureau. They explained the situation and their desire to be fair and equitable to everyone concerned including suppliers, hosts and attendees. A second situation to contend with was that one association enjoyed preferred rates as a result of being annual clients at several of the selected hotels, while the other, who came to that city only once every five years, was given a different, higher rate. Now that they had combined their events, their aim was to combine the rates and offer the best possible rate to conference attendees.

Once they understood the situation, all of the hotel representatives rallied behind the host organizers and extended their full support. The lesser rate was extended across the board and fair contracts were ultimately negotiated. Clauses were revised enabling them to reduce the guestroom block without liability several months prior to the event. The room block reservation cutoff was established closer than 30 days to the meeting date and some of hotels continued to sell rooms at the group rate after the cutoff date.

As a result, delegates enjoyed preferred rates in a major centre; the host organization lowered their financial risk and the suppliers benefited from high occupancy over a five day period, that normally had a lower bedroom pickup.

NEGOTIATIONS CHECKLIST

Have the following information available to effectively communicate the total business value of the meeting:

☐ Previous meeting history

☐ Anticipated use of facility foodservice outlets

- room service
- lounges/bars
- snack bars
- dining rooms

☐ Profile of attendees

- number
- demographics
- spending habits
- utilize historical data

☐ Room occupancy pattern

- number single rooms/suites
- number double rooms/suites
- multiple room occupancy ratios
- no show factor
- pickup and total room nights history

☐ Length and time of stay

- arrival and departure pattern of participants
- pre- and post-meeting stays
- consider scheduling the meeting on slower or lower occupancy days of the week
- consider off season and shoulder season bookings payment responsibilities
- hotels anticipate more revenue when meeting sponsor pays the bill

☐ Space pattern

☐ Transportation needs

- shuttles to off-site activities
- auto rental
- parking
- limousine services

CHAPTER REVIEW

When preparing to negotiate with a venue or other supplier, it is important that the meeting professional be able to demonstrate the total business value of the meeting, in order to have leverage to obtain lower rates or other concessions. This value can be demonstrated by using the meeting history, or where one does not exist, by presenting a detailed list of meeting specifications.

All items in a contract, with the exception of taxes, are negotiable. Discounts, concessions, upgrades or complimentary goods or services can typically be negotiated for food and beverage, guest rooms, meeting space or other services.

Contracts should be reviewed by legal counsel before being signed by the meeting professional or host organization. It is important that the meeting professional be familiar with, and able to negotiate all key elements and clauses of a hotel contract including:

- fees

- cancellation

- attrition

- indemnification

- force majeure

- uninterrupted use of premises

- deposits

- walk policy

- cut off dates

- damages, insurance and liability

TEST YOUR KNOWLEDGE

The following self test will indicate the level of understanding and knowledge gained from this chapter. Solutions to all self tests can be found in Appendix A.

1. Contracts should always be reviewed by legal counsel before signing.

    ☐ True ☐ False

2. Rates in hotel contracts are negotiable, all other terms of the agreement are set by the hotel and cannot be amended.

    ☐ True ☐ False

3. The correct way to revise a contract is to:

    (a) strike out terms in the original and write changes in the margin. Both parties must initial and date all changes.

    (b) place new terms in an attached addendum

    (c) rewrite the original with new terms

    (d) all of the above

4. Which of the following is not considered a basic rule of good negotiating?

    (a) obtaining the best possible price should be the meeting professional's only goal.

    (b) everything is negotiable

    (c) get everything in writing

    (d) don't be embarrassed to ask

5. Which of the following clauses is typically not included in a contract?

    (a) cancellation policy

    (b) hold harmless clause

    (c) agreed upon rates

    (d) holding rooms in excess of block

6. Which of the following is the best way to demonstrate the total business value of your meeting to a supplier?

    (a) your meeting budget

    (b) the size of your hotel bedroom block

    (c) your meeting history

    (d) your skill in negotiating

7. List the 5 legal elements of a contract.

_____

_____

_____

_____

_____

8. List 10 items that could be negotiated in a hotel contract to obtain more value for your meeting.

_____

_____

_____

_____

_____

9. Give an example from personal experience where you were involved in negotiating for better pricing or service. Considering the information in this chapter, how would you approach this negotiation differently the next time?

_____

_____

_____

_____

_____

NOTES

Chapter

6

Risk Management

INTRODUCTION

The meeting professional should be prepared for a variety of emergency situations, including:

- fire

- medical

- weather

- labour issues

- unexpected occurrences such as medical, terrorism, etc.

Event facility staff should already have procedures established for situations such as fire, medical emergencies, demonstrations or protests, and should be able to provide assistance. Be sure to ask about the existence of these policies and procedures during the site inspection. Once the venue has been contracted, request a copy for inclusion in the meeting résumé. Other problems can arise during a meeting that may not be considered emergencies but can be very disruptive if not handled properly. The meeting professional should be prepared to manage any crisis, with the appropriate assistance.

Ensure you understand and can apply the following terms:

- Confrontation

- Demonstration

- Risk management

Refer to the glossary for further clarification of the key terms for this chapter.

LEARNING OBJECTIVES

After completing this chapter, the learner will:

- anticipate the potential risks to a meeting and its attendees

- know what information to request of the venue and supplier representatives

- evaluate the level of risk and plan appropriate responses and responsibilities

ROLES AND RESPONSIBILITIES

MEETING MANAGER

○ Develop a risk management plan

- Determine the need for risk management planning
  - ○ establish the need to minimize losses and manage registration growth
  - ○ do a risk analysis on a timely basis

- Develop and use a risk management plan
  - ○ establish risk management policies
  - ○ identify possible risks and plan to manage them
  - ○ ensure reporting of all incidents
  - ○ define a level of authority for each element of the risk management plan
  - ○ incorporate contingencies related to facilities, labour, attendees, currency, supplies, services and special needs
  - ○ communicate the risk management plan on a timely basis
  - ○ identify and obtain insurances required (e.g., types and amounts)
  - ○ ensure compliance with government regulations and bylaws
  - ○ plan for managing risks related to the service of alcohol
  - ○ incorporate security necessary for services, property and equipment

MEETING COORDINATOR

○ Implement the risk management plan

- Demonstrate an understanding of insurance coverage
  - ○ recognize personal responsibility related to insurance and liability
  - ○ review insurance coverage and procedures
  - ○ Initiate insurance claims
  - ○ maintain and/or complete necessary paperwork
  - ○ adhere to defined procedures

- Minimize risks
  - ○ comply with legal obligations related to the organization and facility
  - ○ review strategies for access control

- Comply with the risk management plan
  - ○ follow the levels of authority for each element of the risk management plan
  - ○ implement policies and procedures
  - ○ implement the contingency plan as related to facilities, labour, attendees, currency, supplies, services, and special needs
  - ○ follow security/emergency policies and procedures
  - ○ review all names and phone numbers
  - ○ review first aid services
  - ○ report all incidents
  - ○ complete necessary paperwork
  - ○ implement risk plan related to service of alcohol
  - ○ implement the medical emergency plan

- Comply with legislation and legal obligations
  - ○ comply with cancellation clauses of contracts

- Implement the contingency plan

- Review the contingency plan
  - ○ review policies and procedures related to contingencies
  - ○ recognize decision making authority related to contingencies

- Respond to unplanned situations as per plan
  - anticipate potential emergencies and challenges
  - identify when to implement the contingency plan
  - implement activities and communications as per plan
  - demonstrate calm, tact, diplomacy, and flexibility

- Follow security and emergency policies and procedures

- Review the list of contact names and services
  - review the list of names and phone numbers to contact in case of an emergency
  - review emergency first aid services and supplies, security staff and emergency service staff available

- Follow the security and emergency procedures plan
  - review and follow security strategies for access control
  - review and follow procedures in case of an emergency
  - use designated communication systems in an emergency

FIRE

The site inspection should cover safety features such as:

- smoke detectors and alarm devices/notification systems, including those for people with disabilities

- location of fire exits and exit signs (consider alternate routes, in case one exit is not useable)

- fire extinguishers

- sprinkler systems

- guestroom evacuation maps

Find out how facility employees are trained to respond to fire and other emergencies (bomb threats, etc.), and have meeting staff prepared for such an event. Consider including a fire safety booklet in the registration materials.

MEDICAL

Identify medical services available in and outside the facility and know the facility's procedure for dealing with medical emergencies. The following information must be available for any event and may be included in the delegate information package:

- availability of house physician or nurse

- nearby doctors

- nearby dentists

- closest hospital and 24-hour clinic

- closest pharmacist (and pharmacy hours)

- how to call for emergency assistance

The meeting professional needs to evaluate the risk for attendees, as some groups have a higher than average incidence of medical emergencies due to age or physical condition. Ensure the facility has access to experienced, licensed medical or paramedical personnel. Consider designating a first aid room for large events.

SEVERE WEATHER

Weather can affect air travel at both departure and arrival points, so be aware of seasonal patterns such as blizzards or hurricanes. Outdoor events should always have an alternative indoor site or the planner should be ready to adjust meeting format if the weather is unsuitable. During negotiations, ask the hotel if guests can keep their rooms at the group rate if they are unable to leave due to weather or other travel restrictions (rooms would probably be available as incoming groups could not arrive either). Be prepared to alter meal guarantees and meeting room setups for a reduced number of attendees.

Events can be interrupted or cancelled due to severe weather. The meeting professional should investigate acquiring insurance against such an occurrence.

LABOUR ISSUES

Labour is necessary to transport and set up booths, complete electrical installations, transport attendees, prepare and serve food, and to clean up. Be aware of any upcoming union contract negotiations in the facility, municipality and with other providers. Facility or service staff should be able to provide this information about their own organization.

DEMONSTRATION

A demonstration is an organized public show of opinion, often protesting against an offending political party or policy. Pickets with placards are usually involved, as is handing out literature, shouting and other activities. Many cities allow demonstrations if the demonstrating group has a permit, does not interfere with normal event activities, and does not come within a specified distance of the event building. If the host organization, attendees, exhibitors, site, or speakers are controversial or have been in the news, you may anticipate a demonstration or confrontation.

When faced with the potential for demonstrations or confrontations, ensure security personnel are present and are equipped with instructions on how to protect the participants or presenters, diffuse the situation and ensure that the meeting objectives may still be achieved. This may require the assistance of a professional service or local law enforcement agencies.

CONFRONTATION

A confrontation is an antagonistic face-to-face interaction with the intent to disrupt the event. Because confrontations are often spontaneous or unpredictable, they are much more difficult to handle than demonstrations. It is desirable to prevent a demonstration from developing into a confrontation though not all confrontations result from demonstrations. Major meeting facilities may hold several group events at the same time, so an event may be disrupted by other meetings that are targets for protest. Shuttle buses may not be able to drive to the pickup point or attendees may be afraid or unwilling to cross a picket line. Officials of the meeting facility and host organization may be required to provide assistance, or the meeting professional may need to hire trained experts such as security personnel, or work with local law enforcement agencies.

MECHANICAL PROBLEMS

Mechanical problems include power outages, loss of heating, ventilation or air conditioning, malfunctioning audio visual equipment, out of service escalators or elevators, and computer system failures. Always have the names and numbers of all suppliers responsible for equipment maintenance and repairs. The venue will have staff on hand or on call to handle emergencies of this type. The meeting professional may even want to pay technicians or engineers to be onsite to handle mechanical emergencies. It is a good idea to give staff members the ability to communicate with each other via walkie-talkies or cellular phones. However, when using these communication devices within the hearing of attendees, remember that comments may be overheard and reacted to by more than the intended receiver of the message.

SPEAKER CANCELLATION

Always have back up speakers available and be prepared to alter the program, as speakers can be delayed in transit, become ill, or not show up due to personal emergencies. The more speakers booked and the greater the distance they must travel, the more likely some will not show up.

Speakers can be requested to arrive at the meeting destination well ahead of their engagement. It is good practice to specify the day before, if the speaker is scheduled for a morning presentation. The meeting professional should reconfirm arrival and departure information in the last few days before the event.

MEETING SUPPLIES DELAYED IN TRANSIT

Meeting programs, registration forms and other materials must be at the event site before the meeting starts. Have a staff member check each item to make sure the entire shipment has arrived and is securely stored on site. Decide well in advance of the event what to do if supplies are lost or delayed. Carry copies of irreplaceable items, such as registration lists and payment records, and consider making duplicates. Consider using technology to send printed materials to the destination for printing.

SYSTEM FAILURE

The meeting professional may want to have a technician onsite for large events. Determine how necessary procedures will be carried out by hand if the computer system cannot be accessed or restored or if there is an electrical failure. In the case of a complete power failure, prepare a contingency plan to include means of light, power, safety, transportation and communication.

TRANSPORTATION BREAKDOWNS

Discuss this with the transportation provider during negotiations and provide for a back up plan. Ensure a radio communication system can be used to bring in backup or spare vehicles, or to rescue a vehicle with mechanical problems.

~ Sample Template ~

RISK MANAGEMENT CHART

Information on
CD Rom

The chart below will enable the meeting professional to anticipate potential risks for an event and assign responsibility for each.

Type of Emergency	Responsible Party	Contact Number	Action Plan
Fire			
Medical			
Severe Weather			
Labour Issues			
Demonstrations and Confrontations			
Other			

RISK MANAGEMENT CHECKLIST

☐ Variety of emergency situations

- fire
- medical
- severe weather
- labour issues
- unexpected occurrences
- demonstrations, protests

☐ Ensure venue

- has policies and procedures in place
- includes copy of risk management plan in your contract

☐ Site features to inspect in the event of fire

- smoke detectors and alarm devices
- location of fire exits and exit signs
- fire extinguishers
- sprinkler systems
- guestroom evacuation plans/maps
- training of staff

☐ Medical emergencies

- check availability and location of
- house physician or nurse
- doctors, dentists
- nearest hospital and clinic
- nearest pharmacist
- include information in delegate information package

☐ Severe weather

- be aware of seasonal patterns in the location you have chosen
- have alternate indoor location when planning outdoor events
- obtain insurance against interruption or cancellation due to severe weather

☐ Labour issues
- be aware of upcoming union contracts that may impact your facility and/or service providers

☐ Demonstrations and confrontations
- ensure security personnel are present and equipped with instructions on how to protect participants

☐ Mechanical problems can include
- power outage
- loss of heating, ventilation or air conditioning
- malfunctioning audio visual equipment
- out of service escalators or elevators
- computer system failures
- ensure you have full contact information to handle such emergencies

☐ Speaker cancellation
- have backup speakers available where possible
- have speakers arrive the day before if travelling from out of town
- reconfirm all travel information a couple of days before

☐ Meeting supplies delayed in transit
- do not ship materials that are irreplaceable such as registration lists and payment records

☐ Technology failure
- contract a technician to be onsite at all times

☐ Transportation breakdowns
- ensure provider has a backup plan in place

☐ Risk management chart
- complete a chart for each event and assign responsibility

CHAPTER REVIEW

The meeting professional should be prepared for a variety of emergency situations, including:

- fire

- medical

- severe weather

- labour issues

- demonstrations and confrontations

- mechanical problems

- technology failure

- transportation breakdowns

- speaker cancellations

- meeting supplies delayed in-transit

It is important to discuss each of these possibilities with the appropriate venue or supplier and agree upon common procedures to manage the situation should they occur. Venues may already have existing emergency policies that you will need to obtain copies of. Policies for each of these emergencies should also be communicated to onsite staff.

For each situation, a responsible party should be assigned and their contact information recorded, along with details of the action plan to be underetaken should the emergency occur. An evaluation of the level of risk for your meeting and its attendees should be part of the planning process.

TEST YOUR KNOWLEDGE

The following self test will indicate the level of understanding and knowledge gained from this chapter. Solutions to all self tests can be found in Appendix A.

1. Venues always have written procedures for what to do in the event of any emergency and you must abide by their policies.

☐ True   ☐ False

2. You can protect yourself against all meeting emergency risk through the purchase of insurance.

☐ True   ☐ False

3. A risk management chart is a useful tool that allows you to anticipate and evaluate the likelihood of emergencies occurring at your event.

☐ True   ☐ False

4. The correct time to ask about the existence of emergency policies at your meeting facility is:

   (a) when you sign the venue contract

   (b) during the site inspection

   (c) during your planning meetings with the program committee

   (d) when you arrive onsite for the meeting

5. During your site inspection of the meeting venue, you should examine safety features such as:

   a) smoke detectors and alarms

   b) fire exits and exit signs

   c) fire extinguishers and sprinkler systems

   d) guestroom evacuation maps

   e) all of the above

6. A medical emergency plan should include:

   a) a detailed medical history of each of your delegates

   b) the setup of a first aid room and hiring of medical personnel for all meetings

   c) gathering information on house physicians, nearby doctors and dentists and the location of the nearest hospital and pharmacy

   d) all of the above

7. To protect against the risk of a weather related emergency, you should:

    (a) be aware of seasonal weather patterns

    (b) arrange for an alternative indoor site for all events scheduled outdoors

    (c) negotiate the continuation of group room rates if attendees are unable to leave due to weather restrictions

    (d) investigate insurance for weather related meeting interruptions

    (e) all of the above

8. Describe the difference between a demonstration and a confrontation.

    _____

    _____

    _____

    _____

    _____

    _____

9. List 3 ways that you can minimize the risk of speaker cancellations.

    _____

    _____

    _____

    _____

    _____

10. List 5 possible mechanical problems that could potentially disrupt your meeting. How would you plan to minimize these risks and deal with them if they do occur?

    _____

    _____

    _____

    _____

    _____

    _____

Speakers

Ensure you understand and can apply the following terms:

- Honorarium
- Keynote speaker
- Ready room
- Speakers bureau
- Speaker release form

Refer to the glossary for further clarification of the key terms for this chapter.

INTRODUCTION

The most important factor in effective education is the speaker. Attendees will find the event meaningful if material is presented by the leaders in their field, great motivators or public figures. A lot of research is required to find and contract the appropriate speaker for an event. For this reason, specialists in speaker selection and management (speakers bureaus) can assist the meeting professional and allow them to concentrate their efforts on other aspects of planning.

LEARNING OBJECTIVES

After completing this chapter, the learner will:

- contact, evaluate and contract speakers

- develop a speaker's manual

- develop speaker protocol

- effectively manage speakers

ROLES AND RESPONSIBILITIES

MEETING MANAGER

○ Research and recommend speakers

- Determine the requirements for speakers
  - ○ recognize the various types and styles of speakers
  - ○ determine the number and type of speakers needed to meet objectives
  - ○ write presentation guidelines
  - ○ establish criteria for speakers
  - ○ establish criteria to evaluate potential speakers
  - ○ establish the compensation package

- Contact potential speakers
  - ○ determine how far in advance to contact speakers
  - ○ research and make use of available resources (e.g., speakers bureaus)

- Evaluate and recommend speakers
  - ○ evaluate potential speakers using defined criteria
  - ○ preview/check references of speakers
  - ○ ensure that meeting site, schedule and events coincide with speaker availability
  - ○ prepare a written agreement/contract

- Manage the requirements of speakers
  - ○ recognize the need to inform and reward speakers
  - ○ discuss tax and immigration considerations
  - ○ provide a profile of the audience and content requirements
  - ○ obtain needed information for promotion introductions
  - ○ meet speakers' needs for information, equipment, services, and accommodation
  - ○ ensure appropriate setup to meet speakers' needs
  - ○ arrange to have speakers properly introduced, thanked and recognized
  - ○ keep speakers well informed
  - ○ determine the necessity for and arrange for a debriefing session with speakers

  - ○ control media access to speakers
  - ○ facilitate speaker briefing and rehearsals
- Evaluate speakers' presentations
  - ○ assess content, presentation and ability to meet audience needs

MEETING COORDINATOR

○ Confirm and co-ordinate speakers

- Arrange and co-ordinate speakers
  - ○ prepare and send out a letter of confirmation for each contract
  - ○ prepare for contingencies related to speakers
  - ○ follow defined policies, procedures and contracts
  - ○ obtain information from speakers
  - ○ obtain needed information/photos from speakers and a description of their presentations

- Determine and attend to speakers' needs
  - ○ determine speakers' needs and special requirements and plan to provide for them
  - ○ process the prescribed government forms for out of country speakers
  - ○ provide briefing, equipment, aids and information required/requested

FINDING SPEAKERS

One of the most effective methods of finding speakers is word of mouth from colleagues. Other meeting professionals may be able to direct you to speakers or speakers bureaus that have been used successfully in the past. Speakers' associations or bureaus, the Internet, industry experts, and learning institutions can also be good sources.

Using a call for presentations is an excellent method of attracting speakers. A call for papers or presentations is a non-profit organization's invitation to its members, and other interested parties, to deliver educational sessions at a conference. The proposals received are usually judged by a committee and accepted or rejected on their own merits.

HOW A SPEAKERS BUREAU WORKS

A speakers bureau reviews and compiles a list of speakers in various fields that are then matched to the host organization's needs. The bureau acts as a representative for a number of speakers. The fee charged by a bureau is paid by the speaker, not the host organization.

Before approaching a speakers bureau, the meeting professional must understand the objectives for the particular session. Every speaker is different, in terms of their willingness, ability and techniques used in customizing their presentations. It is extremely important at the outset, prior to confirming a speaker, that the meeting professional's expectations in terms of customization are clearly set out, and that the speaker and the client are in agreement as to how this will take place.

A questionnaire is completed, which provides background information about the client and their event, and the objectives set out for the presentation. Once this is completed and provided to the speaker, a conference call or face-to-face meeting is arranged to further discuss the objectives and how the speaker will customize their material to most effectively communicate the message that needs to be heard by the audience. Some speakers like to call a handful of delegates who will actually attend the meeting, in order to get the "unofficial" version of where the host/organization stands in their industry/field.

~ Sample Template ~

SAMPLE CALL FOR PRESENTATIONS

Information on
CD Rom

CALL FOR PAPERS OR PRESENTATIONS

Papers or Presentations may address topics relevant to potential attendees including but not limited to *(provide suggestions or examples)*:

DEVELOPING YOUR PAPERS OR PRESENTATION

Presenters are expected to share information and experience but may not use the conference as a platform for commercial sales, self-promotion, or to criticize competitors

Presentations should be approximately 45/60/90 *(identify length of session)* minutes long. A limited number of 2/3 hour sessions will be offered. Please indicate if you would be willing to present in this expanded format. (Conference format needs to be identified prior to the call for presentations)

Presenters of successful submissions will be required to confirm their participation soon after being notified and must adhere to conference regulations

SUBMISSION CRITERIA

Submission Deadline: *(chose deadline based on the critical path)*

Each session proposal must be submitted separately and include a written abstract that describes the presentation in 100 words or less. Each abstract must also include three expected learning outcomes, and indicate whether it would be suitable for a "basic", "intermediate" or "advanced" audience or some combination thereof. A biography of the presenter(s) and the names and contact information of two people who can discuss the presenter's ability to speak on the proposed topic, must accompany the abstract.

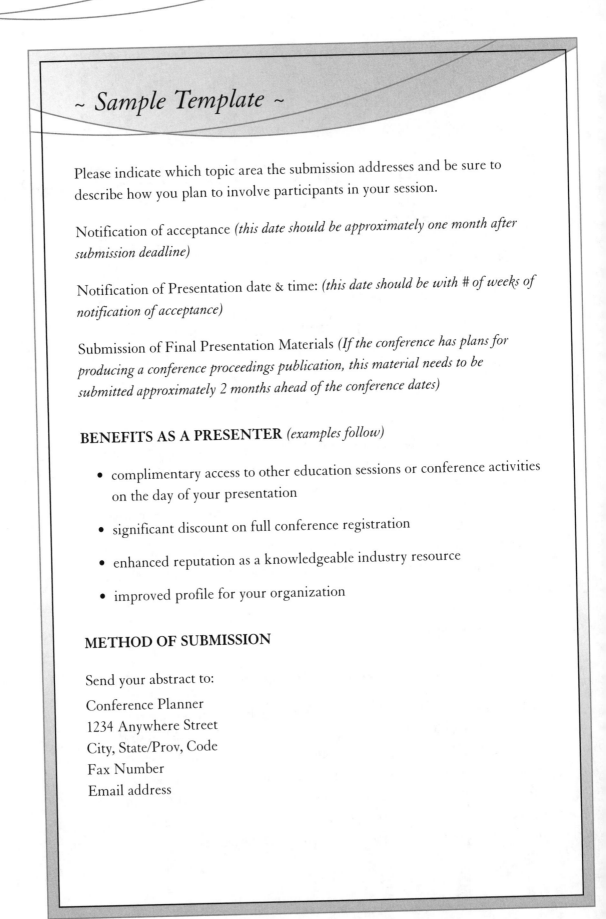

~ *Sample Template* ~

Please indicate which topic area the submission addresses and be sure to describe how you plan to involve participants in your session.

Notification of acceptance *(this date should be approximately one month after submission deadline)*

Notification of Presentation date & time: *(this date should be with # of weeks of notification of acceptance)*

Submission of Final Presentation Materials *(If the conference has plans for producing a conference proceedings publication, this material needs to be submitted approximately 2 months ahead of the conference dates)*

BENEFITS AS A PRESENTER *(examples follow)*

- complimentary access to other education sessions or conference activities on the day of your presentation

- significant discount on full conference registration

- enhanced reputation as a knowledgeable industry resource

- improved profile for your organization

METHOD OF SUBMISSION

Send your abstract to:

Conference Planner
1234 Anywhere Street
City, State/Prov, Code
Fax Number
Email address

SELECTING SPEAKERS

When selecting a speaker for an event, ask for and check references. Listen to a copy of previous speeches made by the speaker or observe the speaker giving a presentation. Pay attention to phone conversations with the speaker to determine if the speaker possesses vibrant and interesting qualities. If the speaker cannot project these over the phone, they may not be able to project these to the group. Large events with many speakers may require a speakers committee to select and work with speakers.

HOT TIP

Thoroughly Brief Outsiders

If you're bringing in an outside speaker or an entertainer, tell them about your industry, association or company. Nothing will turn off an audience faster than someone who shows they know little or nothing about the group. Depending on the situation, a talk or act sprinkled with anecdotes about key people in the audience has real appeal.

CONTRACTING SPEAKERS

The following information should be provided to the speaker:

- date, exact time and duration of the presentation
- location of event
- size and general profile of the group
- purpose of meeting
- specific topic(s) the speaker is to address and the time allotted
- physical layout of the room
- appropriate attire
- other speeches scheduled during the meeting
- honoraria or fees
- expenses
- travel information

The following information should be obtained from the speaker and detailed in the contract:

- biographical data, introduction guidelines and photograph
- audio visual equipment needs
- guest information, if applicable
- guest room requirements
- food and beverage requirements
- transportation needs
- special security requirements
- special needs
- release form granting permission to record presentation
- cancellation/substitution clause

Once the speaker is confirmed, place their name on the mailing list. All speaker arrangements should be confirmed in a written contract with the speaker.

SPEAKER'S MANUAL

A speaker's manual is a document sent to all speakers outlining your basic requirements and expectations for their presentation.

A speaker's manual should contain:

- General speaker information to be completed by the speaker:
  - name, title, affiliation and address
  - title of the presentation
  - one paragraph description of the presentation
  - space for travel arrangement information, arrival and departure times
  - a list of anyone accompanying the speaker (spouse or aide)

- Event information sheet:
  - general overview of the event
  - length of presentations and session format
  - presentation regulations
  - date, time, and place of speaker's briefings or other events they should attend
  - a dress code for event functions
  - information about the speakers' ready room

- Timetable, listing deadlines for submissions of forms

- Biographical form

- Audio visual and room setup request form, indicating equipment that will be provided and standard setups

- Form listing handout materials, with a place to request duplication, if available

- Recording waiver form, if applicable; also have a space to indicate if they want a free tape of their presentation provided

- Copyright waiver form, if applicable; also have a space to indicate if they want to have reprints of their presentations, and how many

- Instructions on preparing visuals; you may provide a presentation template to follow so that all materials are consistent

- Instructions for making presentations

- A copy of the current event program

- Maps, diagrams of the meeting site, including session rooms, and the host city

- Event registration and hotel reservation forms

~ Sample Template ~

Information on CD Rom

SAMPLE SPEAKER'S MANUAL

TABLE OF CONTENTS

~ Sample Template ~

ITEM	DEADLINE

1. Schedule Conference Call

2. Draft Copy of Speaker Presentations

3. Audio Visual / Room Set-Up Requirements

4. Final speaker presentations/handouts

   - Original copy and electronic version

5. Expense Claim Forms

SESSION INFORMATION

DEVELOPING YOUR SESSION

The meeting professional is available to answer any questions and/or provide assistance with developing your session outline, and will work closely with you to provide an understanding of the audience and to ensure a high quality session.

NON-COMMERCIAL NATURE OF SESSIONS

Speakers and facilitators must refrain from the use of brand names or specific product endorsements in their presentation. Under no circumstances is this platform to be used as a place for direct promotion of a speaker's product, service or monetary self-interest.

HANDOUT MATERIAL

Handouts are a vital component to the learning experience. They provide a "touchstone" to help solidify and recall the content and experience. All speakers are required to provide handouts and all handout materials must be approved by the organization.

~ *Sample Template* ~

Handouts must be in Microsoft Word or PowerPoint. Handouts will not be accepted on company letterhead. It is very helpful to use your presentation as a handout – with room for note taking. The final version should look professional and include bullet point outlines, checklists, forms, case studies, reprints, resource bibliographies, etc. as appropriate.

A draft copy of speaker presentations is due on _____. An original copy and an electronic version of final presentations/handouts by email are due no later than _____. **Only handouts received by the deadline will be duplicated.** NO handouts will be copied onsite.

Handouts not available by the deadline must be copied and shipped at the speaker's own expense – after first being approved.

ROOM SET-UP

You must complete and return the Audio Visual / Room Set-Up Requirements form included in this manual by _____.

Please note that the room set-up will ultimately be at the organization's discretion. We will strive to meet your needs but may need to alter your requested set-up to accommodate everyone using the room that day, including our attendees.

SESSION ATTENDANCE

It is estimated that there will be ___ participants in your session.

PARTICIPATING IN A CONFERENCE CALL

In an effort to better assist speakers and to strengthen sessions, all presenters will meet by conference call with the meeting professional and program committee chair, if applicable.

~ Sample Template ~

During the conference call, please be prepared to discuss your outline, handouts, the session's interactive elements, the primary subject matter of your session and your presentation style. We can also provide further audience information and answer any questions you may have.

SPEAKER READY ROOM/SESSION REHEARSAL

There will be no scheduled rehearsal time for your event. We will, however provide a "speaker ready room" onsite for your use. We recommend that you arrive at your session room 30 minutes prior to the start of your session.

SESSION INTRODUCTIONS

You will be introduced at the beginning of your session. Please provide brief biographical information for use in your introduction and in promotional material.

HELP DURING YOUR SESSION

Onsite staff will help distribute handouts, distribute and collect evaluations and assist you in any way.

EVALUATIONS

Attendees will be asked to evaluate each session. Evaluation forms will be available at the beginning of each session. Please remind attendees to complete the evaluations at the end of your session. You will receive the results of your evaluations approximately one month following the conference.

~ *Sample Template* ~

IN CASE OF EMERGENCY – PRIOR TO EVENT

If you are unable to present as the result of a last-minute emergency, please call the meeting professional. We will provide you with the onsite office telephone number closer to the conference date.

EXPENSE REPORTS

Your expenses must be recorded and submitted no later than 30 days after the conference. Please complete and return the form on page ____. Original receipts must be attached.

The following expenses are eligible to be covered:

- transportation from your home to the local airport and back (either mileage or taxi/limo/bus fare)
- transportation from the airport to the hotel and back

The following items will not be covered:

- parking at your home airport
- incidentals in the hotel (e.g., movies, room service, mini bar)
- food and beverage outside of conference functions

DEVELOPING YOUR SESSION

ACTIVELY INVOLVE YOUR ATTENDEES IN YOUR SESSION

A simple question/answer format is not sufficient. Neither are traditional methods such as pop quizzes. Highly interactive methods encourage learning, build learners' confidence and enhance the transfer of learning to the workplace. The success of your session will depend on the degree of involvement of your learners, as well as the content you provide.

~ *Sample Template* ~

Involving your attendees can be done with activities such as peer discussion, small group activities, case studies, role-play, games or other engaging techniques. A question and answer opportunity is vital, and so is vibrant discussion and debate throughout the entire session.

DEVELOPING YOUR SESSION OUTLINE

1. Analyze Your Learner

- Who are they?

- What do they want from you? (Skills? Content?)

- What do they need? (Confidence? Feedback? A paradigm shift?)

- Why would they come to your session to get it?

2. Determine What to Deliver

Once you have analyzed your audience, you are ready to develop the critical subject matter and issues within your session; describe appropriate sub-topics and subjects; and organize it all in an outline.

All topics and subjects you select should be appropriate to one or more of your learning outcomes. This process helps you to focus on your learners' needs. This might not necessarily be what you think they would like to hear or see.

3. Determine Your Instructional Methods

Include how you intend to deliver your information and how you intend to **actively involve** your attendees. These methods depend on your learning outcomes.

For example, **if a case study is to be used**, it is written as a narrative by the presenter or by one or more of the session participants in advance. It typically describes a real situation that is complex or ambiguous and that requires analysis and decision. As your session will be 90 minutes long,

~ *Sample Template* ~

any case study you use should be shorter than two typed pages. The case study method encourages attendees to learn from each other as well as from you and the handout material.

If simulations and role-plays are used, these should be done as group-based activities designed to mirror the organizational dynamics and decision-making realities of real life situations. Teams of participants practice the design, implementation and control of strategies relevant to association executives. Emphasis is placed on the application, rather than the definition, of concepts, principles and methods relevant within the environment.

METHODS TO INCREASE LEARNING AND ENJOYMENT OF YOUR SESSION

- At the beginning of your session, clarify the participants' expectations and needs from the program by asking for feedback. For example, ask "what are you expecting to get out of this session?".

- Identify how the presented information will benefit the participants. Participants need to understand the value of the session.

- Throughout the program, allow time for participants to relate the material and information back to their current work situations and lives.

- Encourage participants to share "war stories" and successes.

- Check for understanding throughout the session.

- Actively involve participants in any way you can.

~ *Sample Template* ~

DEVELOPING YOUR VISUALS

Why Use Visuals? The entire concept of a successful presentation is based on using the visual medium to reinforce, underscore and support your presentation. Since this event is a learning experience, we encourage you to use a visual medium in your presentations.

- **Plan Content** - Your visual presentation should meaningfully support your statements rather than repeat them. Reinforce every major point in your presentation with a title or graphic visual. Dramatize the major conclusions in your presentation with a special effect. Emphasize, support or reinforce points in your presentation with copy, photographs or charts.

- **Be Consistent** - Focus your presentation using a couple of complimentary colours and one graphic and writing style. This will allow your visuals to build on one another and reinforce your verbal presentation. Change colours or combinations only with a purpose to differentiate sections within the presentation, for a multi-speaker presentation, etc.

- **Use Charts and Graphs Effectively** - Use the correct type of chart for your purpose. Be sure that the relationship you are portraying is obvious. Keep charts and graphs simple.

- **Keep Moving** - A well paced presentation should have a visual change at least once every two minutes. Longer intervals may lead to a disinterested audience. Therefore, be sure and read through your outline and script to determine the necessary intervals. Add or subtract materials, charts and/or graphs until your timing is right.

- **Simplify Visuals** - Edit the copy on your visual to a minimum so that you don't reveal more information than needed. You don't want your attendees to read ahead and not hear what you are saying.

~ *Sample Template* ~

PRESENTATION TIPS AND CAUTIONS

- **Begin With Objectives** - Invite everyone to focus.

- **Be Familiar with the Material** - Talk it - don't read it or recite memorized material.

- **Use Specific Ways to Engage Attendees** - Be specific and concrete. Accompany your key points with analogies or real-life examples to get your attendees involved.

- **Make Sure Your Presentation Relates to Your Handouts** - Include the most important points you want your attendees to remember in both your presentation and handouts. Audiences often react negatively if the handouts do not reflect the presentation and overheads.

- **Refrain From Selling** - Sessions must not be utilized as a vehicle for advertising - this results in negative feedback. (Even speakers who simply overemphasize the positive characteristics of their company/product or abilities without overtly selling receive poor evaluations.) This includes the selling of books, tapes, or other products.

- **Be Comfortable and Down-to-Earth** - Use humor if it adds to the program. Remember that there is a broad mix of people in your session, therefore profanity or off-colour humor is prohibited.

- **Speak to Your Audience** - If you want to draw the attendees' attention to the screen, stop speaking, point to the item, then return your eyes to the audience and resume speaking.

- **Know the Order of Your Visuals** - Avoid looking at the screen to determine which one is portrayed. If you need to refer to a previous visual, have an extra copy made and position it where needed.

- **Be Animated** - Avoid standing firmly in one place (e.g. behind a podium). Move your hands, head and arms. Use facial expressions to emphasize the most important points of your presentation. Effective eye contact will enhance comfort, contact and rapport with the attendees.

~ *Sample Template* ~

- **Seek Feedback** - Read nonverbal signals as well as comments.

- **Avoid Overload** - Keep things simple.

- **Use the Audience as a Resource** - Ask questions of attendees to solicit data and problems. List answers on an overhead or flipchart. (Make sure that it can be seen in the back of the room.)

- **Allow Flexibility to Provide for Interaction and Surprises**

- **Watch the Time** - Bring a small alarm clock or set your watch alarm or have someone cue you so you stay on schedule.

ADULT LEARNING INSIGHTS

- Motivation to participate is different from one adult learner to another - a complex combination of what the person brings to the experience and what happens

- Adult learning is more than the transfer of knowledge – it is also being encouraged to think critically and participate in the learning

- Adults **learn best** when their knowledge and experience is acknowledged and utilized

- Adults want to know "what's in it for me?" – both content and application

Retention of information is enhanced when there is:

- An adult learning environment – with consideration for their physical needs

- Active involvement

- Relevant examples and practice of skills

- A feeling of support, understanding

~ Sample Template ~

Information on
CD Rom

SAMPLE SPEAKER REQUIREMENT FORM

FOR OFFICE USE ONLY

Session: _____

Day: _____ Time: _____

Room: _____

SECTION 1: GENERAL INFORMATION

Please return by: _____ [date], _____ [year]

Name: _____ Title: _____

Company: _____

Address: _____

City: _____ Prov/State: _____ Postal/Zip Code: _____

Bus. Phone: _____ Fax: _____ E-mail: _____

Emergency Name: _____ Tel: _____

SPECIAL NEEDS Please indicate any special needs:

_____

_____

For our planning purposes, please check the food and beverage events that you will be attending:

☐ Thursday reception ☐ Friday luncheon ☐ Friday reception ☐ Saturday luncheon

☐ None of the above

BADGE INFORMATION

Name: _____ Title: _____

Organization/office: _____

Do you want your business address and phone number listed in the program? ☐ Yes ☐ No

SECTION 2: BIOGRAPHICAL INFORMATION

In an effort to have consistency in biographical information in the onsite agenda, we have structured the following format. If more space is needed, please use the back of this form. Your listing will be limited to 50 words.

Name as it should appear in the biographical sketch: _____

Title: _____

Educational Background: _____

Special awards or recognition: _____

~ *Sample Template* ~

Field or specialization; include number of years' experience: _____
_____

Key qualifications that will be of interest to attendees at this conference: _____
_____

PLEASE ENCLOSE PHOTO:

☐ Black and white ☐ Colour Size: _____

SECTION 3: SESSION DESCRIPTION

Brief synopsis of topic issues included: _____
_____
_____

Presentation: ☐ **will** include question and answer session

☐ **will not** include question and answer session

AGREEMENTS AND RELEASES

I agree to limit my presentation information and materials to those directly relevant to the session topic, and will not promote in a commercial way, my products or services or the products or services of any organization. I also agree to have my presentation recorded electronically and available for sale during and after the event.

Signature _____ Date _____

SECTION 4: AUDIO VISUAL AND OTHER REQUIREMENTS

EQUIPMENT

☐ Overhead Projector

☐ 35mm slide projector

☐ computer (specify type)

_____

_____

☐ Data Projector

☐ VCR and Monitor

☐ Other (specify)_____

MICROPHONE

☐ Lectern

☐ Standing

☐ Table

☐ Lavaliere (neck)

☐ Handheld

OTHER

☐ Chalkboard/whiteboard

☐ Flip chart

☐ Markers

HANDOUT MATERIAL

Approximate number of pages _____

☐ Distribute prior to presentation

☐ Distribute following presentation

☐ No materials will be provided

MATERIAL INFORMATION

☐ All materials are enclosed and may be distributed to press and registrants

☐ All materials will be submitted by _____

☐ A copy of my presentation will be available for duplication and distribution

~ Sample Template ~

SECTION 5: FINANCIAL ARRANGEMENT

Terms of agreement should be completed by meeting professional prior to mailing.

Name: _____

Session title: _____ Session date: _____

Presentation: _____

( ) _____ Ext. _____ Time: _____ to _____ Room no: _____

It is understood that the honorarium paid for my presentation at the _____

session on _____[date], _____[year] in _____

will be $ _____.

It is also understood that the following expenses will be paid for or reimbursed as shown:

(specify fare class) _____ air fare to be

☐ paid for ☐ reimbursed by_____.

Other provisions (specify airport/hotel transportation, complimentary tickets, spouse accommodation,

etc. (if none, state NONE) _____.

The speaker will be responsible for any other incidental expenses.

These terms are acceptable to me.

Signature _____ Date _____

RETURN TO:

_____ [name]

_____ [street address]

_____ [city, province/state]

_____ [postal/zip code]

( ) _____ Ext. [telephone]

( ) _____ [fax]

_____ [email]

WORKING WITH SPEAKERS

Once the speaker is confirmed, make sure the speaker's audio visual requests are appropriate for the size of group and the layout of the room. Request an advance copy of the presentation. One week before the event, send the speaker a reminder of the event and include any useful information and changes that may affect the presentation. Include name of the presentation room, expected participation, and a note expressing anticipation of the presentation. Consider providing an amenity or an honorarium to speakers who are not being paid.

Identify VIP speakers (e.g., political figures, senior executives, celebrities) and treat them appropriately. Good communication with all speakers can be enhanced by organizing speakers' breakfast briefings, held each morning for that day's sessions. In addition to speakers, invite session chairs, moderators, panelists, and session monitors.

Always plan to have a speakers lounge or "ready room" where speakers can go over their presentations, meet with audio visual staff, review presentation materials, and make last minute notes. In this area, provide light refreshment, such as coffee, tea, ice, water, and even some lemons to clear the throat.

Assist the host organization to select the appropriate person to introduce speakers. The person doing the introduction should be provided with a prepared brief biography or a script. The speaker should provide appropriate introduction information when they provide material for the promotion of the conference. Arrange to have the speaker and the introducer meet before the session to develop rapport prior to the introduction.

After the event, remember to thank all speakers in writing, share event evaluation results, and pay speakers promptly.

~ *A Conference Journal* ~

A great deal of time and effort was put into the development of the session topics. In keeping with their objectives to make this an unprecedented event, the conference committee had to look beyond the ordinary and think outside the box. Since the presentations were designed to be twenty minutes in length, over five days, in five concurrent breakout rooms, plus daily panel discussions in the general sessions, they needed more than 125 speakers.

For this event, they utilized a web-based database to manage over 800 submissions to the technical program from the abstract phase through to the publication of full papers. Approximately 10 - 12 months out from the conference, a Call for Presentations was sent out. By simply visiting the event website, authors were able to log on to the database, submit an abstract for review, and assign themselves a password which enabled them to return and make edits any time prior to the submission deadline. The edit feature significantly reduced the amount of time spent by the meeting coordinator interacting with authors.

Members of the selection committee were also assigned passwords that allowed them to log on via the website, review papers, and accept or reject them, thus eliminating the need for a coordinator to distribute large volumes of files. They developed rating criteria and then reviewed the papers that were submitted online. Session themes were developed and a number of topics and speakers were identified as an appropriate fit within a particular session and added to the roster. Once the adjudication process was completed email confirmations or rejections were sent for each submission with the click of a button.

They did not rely solely on the Call for Presentations process. Since both organizations usually obtained speakers from within their own industry, the newly created conference committee developed a long list of potential speakers as they related to the defined themes. Speakers were selected for their competency within the industry or their knowledge of a specific advancement or technical development in their field. In many brainstorming sessions, the committee also relied on their combined knowledge of an individual or their presentation at a previous conference and they considered both content and delivery.

The committee was so successful in this process, that at one point they had more speakers than available sessions. Once the final program outline was agreed upon, members of the conference committee contacted potential speakers by telephone, email or personal meeting. After a verbal commitment was obtained, standard contracts confirming all speaker arrangements were developed and sent out by the conference coordinator. Forms were developed requesting information from speakers such as biographical information for inclusion in brochures, presentation titles and audio visual equipment needs. They were also sent specific instructions to assist them with the development of their slide or computer presentation, as well as for the preparation of their abstract that was required for publication in a conference proceedings booklet. This information was entered into the same speaker database so that the information could be easily extracted in summary form. The next step was for authors to upload full papers, all done using the initial password on the site. Finally, the uploaded papers were transmitted via email to a multimedia company to be downloaded to a CD-ROM for distribution in delegate kits.

Just prior to the conference, speakers were sent a reminder notice with the date, time and location of their session. For introductory purposes, copies of this information together with biographies of the presenters were sent to session chair(s). A summary chart that included all speakers, session titles, times, and audio visual equipment required was developed and sent to the audio visual company in advance of the conference. With so many speakers, it was helpful to refer to the summary when ordering equipment or documenting changes when they occurred.

Each theme or overall topic was assigned a session chair. This volunteer was often the first onsite contact with the six or eight speakers within their session. Session Chairs introduced the session theme, introduced and thanked each of the speakers in that particular session, and had to ensure that each 20 minute session began and ended on time. It was their responsibility to also make "housekeeping announcements" such as a reminder to visit the exhibits, thank sponsors or remind delegates to attend an upcoming event.

A large room at the convention center was designated as a speaker ready room where speakers were asked to meet their session Chair to receive final instructions, at least one hour prior to the start of their session. The audio visual technician reviewed each speaker's presentation materials to make sure that everything was in good working order prior to entering the session room. Speakers were offered the opportunity to review their presentation and actually perform a practice run with a mock setup that included a podium, screen and the appropriate projection equipment required by the speaker.

It was a rare occurrence when a speaker didn't show. The key to the successful handling of so many speakers was a good database of appropriate information and the ability to remain in constant communication with speakers and chairs alike in the months leading up to the conference. The meeting coordinator responsible for this aspect of the conference, spent most of the time during the convention between the speaker ready room and the various meeting rooms making sure that everyone was in place, Chairs had the required information to make their introductions and announcements and speakers had the appropriate equipment selected for their competency within.

SPEAKER CHECKLIST

☐ Sources of speakers

- colleagues
- industry experts
- call for abstracts/papers
- staff/management
- periodicals/trade publications
- professional speakers bureaus
- local personalities
- organizational membership

- universities and colleges

☐ Screening potential speakers

- obtain references
- view recordings of previous speeches

- attend actual presentation

☐ Information to be provided to speaker

- presentation time
- date
- location (city and facility)
- meeting title and brief description
- meeting objectives
- host organization
- local maps
- facility floor plan
- presentation room layout
- audio visual equipment available
- session description
- specific points/topics to be addressed
- expected audience demographics and special interests

- speaker requirement and release form

☐ Obtain from speaker

- audio visual requirements
- handout material
- duplication
- distribution
- deadline date
- special needs
- travel and accommodation arrangements
- photograph
- biography

☐ Arrangements to be made with speaker

- rehearsal
- presentation introduction
- escort assigned
- badges
- function tickets
- guest programs
- expense submission deadlines
- payment of fees

☐ Amenities

- ready room
- light refreshment
- audio visual equipment
- communication systems

☐ Post-presentation

- recognition
- gift/plaque/certificate
- honorarium
- press coverage
- thank you letter
- speaker evaluation

CHAPTER REVIEW

KEY POINTS

☐ Sources of speakers for an event include:

- colleagues

- call for abstracts

- trade publications

- speakers associations or bureaus

- government agencies

- universities and colleges

☐ Word-of-mouth is still one of the best methods to select a speaker

☐ Screening techniques for speakers include:

- ask for and check references

- listen to copy of previous speech

- pay attention to phone conversation

- observe the speaker giving an actual presentation

- Provide detailed event information to the speaker, and determine speaker needs at the time of negotiation

☐ A speakers' manual can be used to gather information about speakers, while informing them about the event, and should contain:

- general speaker information to be completed by the speaker

- an event information sheet

- a timetable, listing submission deadlines

- biography form

- audio visual and room setup form

- handout materials form

- recording waiver form, if applicable

- copyright waiver form, if applicable

- instructions on preparing visuals, with template if applicable

- presentation instructions

- current event program

- maps of the venue, meeting rooms and host city

- event registration and hotel reservation forms

☐ Provide a speaker ready room where presenters can:

- go over their presentations

- meet audio visual staff

- review presentation materials

- make last minute notes

TEST YOUR KNOWLEDGE

The following self test will indicate the level of understanding and knowledge gained from this chapter. Solutions to all self tests can be found in Appendix A.

1. The best method to select a speaker for an event is word-of-mouth.
    ☐ True ☐ False

2. Asking speakers to provide a copy of their speech at least two weeks prior to the event can be interpreted as a lack of faith in the speaker.
    ☐ True ☐ False

3. Speaker selection should always be handled by the speakers' committee.
    ☐ True ☐ False

4. Speakers bureaus can provide a list of appropriate presenters, but cost the host organization additional fees.
    ☐ True ☐ False

5. If a speaker responds to a call for presentations/call for papers, you must include him/her as part of the conference agenda.
    ☐ True ☐ False

6. The primary purpose of a speakers ready room is to:
    (a) keep speakers away from crowds in a restricted access area
    (b) allow speakers an opportunity to meet each other
    (c) enable speakers to review presentations, meet audio visual staff
    (d) permit speakers to loosen up in a boisterous environment
    (e) provide a place for speaker refreshments

7. Speaker special needs should be determined:
    (a) during the pre-session briefing
    (b) when forming the letter of agreement
    (c) from consultation with industry peers
    (d) during the initial telephone interview
    (e) just prior to the pre-conference meeting

8. You are the meeting professional responsible for the annual meeting of an international professional organization in the dental health care field. Attendees will include general practitioners, specialists, support staff (assistants, receptionists, and office managers), spouses, and children. In your own words, describe how you would go about selecting speakers for this event.

    _____

    _____

    _____

    _____

    _____

9. Describe the information that should be included in a speakers contract.

    _____

    _____

    _____

10. What information should speakers be provided with in a speakers manual?

    _____

    _____

    _____

Marketing and Media

INTRODUCTION

Marketing is the practice of combining, blending, integrating and controlling the factors that have an influence on sales.

Regardless of the type of meeting being planned, or the expectations of the participants, some marketing will have to take place, even if it is only to remind participants of the upcoming event. Often meeting professionals concentrate on communicating with delegates and pay less attention to others such as sponsors, exhibitors, suppliers and guests. Each audience requires a different message; each message may be delivered in a variety of formats.

Media interest in a meeting requires attention to both the message to be delivered and the logistics required for the media to work effectively.

Ensure you understand and can apply the following terms:

- Graphics
- Marketing plan
- Promotion
- Promotional mix
- Publicity
- Sponsorship

Refer to the glossary for further clarification of the key terms for this chapter.

LEARNING OBJECTIVES

After completing this chapter, the learner will:

- define key marketing terms

- understand the applicability of marketing principles and strategies

- appreciate the need to market to various stakeholders

- consider the differences between publicity, promotion and public relations

- understand the various target audiences and assess their needs

- understand the basics of the promotion process and brochure design

- be aware of some basic printing and graphics terminology

- be aware of the planning elements involving the media

ROLES AND RESPONSIBILITIES

MEETING MANAGER

○ Develop a marketing plan

- Set marketing objectives and establish a marketing budget
  - ○ identify methods of measuring the effectiveness of a marketing plan
  - ○ set realistic objectives
  - ○ determine the marketing mix
  - ○ establish an appropriate budget

- Implement marketing strategies
  - ○ define and schedule marketing strategies and promotional activities
  - ○ match marketing objectives with marketing strategies
  - ○ define and execute promotional and publicity activities
  - ○ match marketing strategies with target audience(s)
  - ○ market all elements of the program plan

- Prepare marketing materials
  - determine and design types of marketing materials
  - match marketing materials with the image or identity for the meeting organization and meeting objectives
  - identify the content for promotional pieces
  - maintain consistency in logos, slogans, graphics and content
  - determine timeframes for the distribution of materials
  - determine distribution methods
  - evaluate results and adjust marketing materials as required

MEETING COORDINATOR

○ Implement the marketing plan

- Review the marketing plan
  - schedule all marketing activities and implement the activities of the plan
  - seek direction if necessary
  - monitor and report progress to the manager

- Monitor the production of marketing materials
  - ensure that the supply and quality of materials meet specifications
  - prepare materials for mailing

- Distribute marketing materials
  - adhere to the distribution schedule and target dates

- Implement the media plan
  - review and monitor the progress of the media plan
  - schedule communications activities
  - monitor and report progress to the manager
  - schedule media releases, conferences and interviews
  - adhere to policies related to the media
  - implement and co-ordinate media strategies
  - distribute media kits

- Co-ordinate services for the media
  - provide the media with needed equipment, resources, and supplies

MARKETING AND THE MEETING PROFESSIONAL

The meeting professional is responsible for creating the right program in the right destination at the right time of year for the right price in order to attract not only the right attendees, but also the right sponsors, exhibitors and suppliers. As well, the meeting professional has to satisfy the meeting objectives. That may be to provide meaningful education at a reasonable price or to create a teambuilding environment for senior executives. Before a marketing strategy can be developed to attract these participants, the meeting professional needs to have a good understanding of what elements of the program will appeal to the various attendees. Since there is considerable competition for attendees, exhibitors and sponsors, a careful marketing strategy should be developed.

The type of event being planned will have some impact on how the marketing process will work. As an example, an annual general meeting of a trade organization will take much more marketing to attract the targeted attendance figures than the national sales meeting of a corporation. The reason for this is fairly straightforward. For those people attending the national sales meeting, participation in the meeting would be part of their job, and in effect attendance at the meeting would be mandatory. Marketing for corporate meetings may be a simple reminder of where, when and why it will occur. Conversely, those people attending the annual general meeting of a trade organization are essentially choosing to attend, or may have to convince their superiors of the value of attending. The marketing strategy for each will need to be significantly different.

In addition to delegates, marketing must be aimed towards sponsors and exhibitors. Potential sponsors and exhibitors will need to be shown the value or return on their investment. It is the responsibility of the meeting professional to define the benefits of sponsorship or exhibiting. This can be accomplished by providing a demographic profile of past and expected attendees. As a general rule, meeting professionals prepare a package of benefits to help sell sponsorships or exhibit space. For sponsors, it is no longer enough to market "showing support for the industry" as a benefit. There is strong competition for sponsorship dollars and sponsors are in a position where they can choose the events and activities with which they want to be associated.

The meeting professional should review and monitor the marketing plan to ensure that objectives are being met and adjust accordingly if not.

MARKETING PLAN

A marketing plan is used to co-ordinate all marketing activities and ensure they are consistent with the meeting's objectives.

A basic marketing plan includes the following four elements:

1. Conducting market research

2. Identifying target markets

3. Establishing marketing objectives

4. Developing the action plan

1. CONDUCTING MARKET RESEARCH

Conducting market research is an important first step as it is here that the meeting professional assesses the strengths and weakness of the meeting in order to apply the best promotional mix for the target audience. The meeting professional must also objectively appraise any competing meetings. If the targeted participants are not attending the planned meeting as a condition of their employment conceivably they could be considering other meetings to attend.

In order to best determine how well the planned event measures up to the competition, an unbiased analysis that identifies the strengths and weaknesses should be prepared. Include in this analysis:

- destination chosen

- cost to participate (registration, transportation, accommodation)

- facilities (conference centre and hotels)

- quality of educational program offered

- diversity of food and beverage events

- variety of social and recreational activities

- guest programs available

- pre and post conference tours

Compare all of these aspects of the planned meeting to any similar meetings that may be taking place during the same general time frame.

Consider any external factors that may influence attendance at the planned event. Examples may include:

- a downturn in the economy

- the destination chosen and the time of year

2. IDENTIFYING YOUR TARGET MARKETS

Part of market research is identifying and understanding your ideal audience. Questions to ask include:

- Who do we want to attend?

- Why would they attend?

- What do they need or want?

- What can we offer them that our competitor is not?

- What are the demographics of the ideal attendee?

Answering these questions (and others) will help to determine who the target audience is and help set marketing goals to reach them. Knowing whom your audience is and what they need will help sell your conference.

After the primary audience has been determined the meeting professional can identify additional groups that may have an interest in attending or being involved.

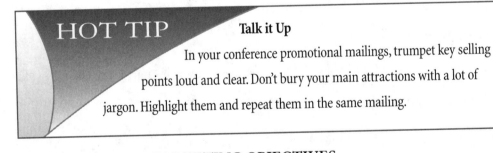

HOT TIP

Talk it Up

In your conference promotional mailings, trumpet key selling points loud and clear. Don't bury your main attractions with a lot of jargon. Highlight them and repeat them in the same mailing.

3. ESTABLISHING MARKETING OBJECTIVES

The meeting professional must then develop marketing objectives that take into consideration the target audience and the market research that has been done. Examples of marketing objectives may be:

- Increase media coverage of event

- Increase stronger presence on the Internet

- Reposition meeting to be top event of the year

Positioning refers to how the customer perceives your product. It is a combination of the reputation of the quality of the meeting and how the meeting differs from other similar meetings. The positioning will be an important factor in the advertising and promotion of the event. For example, if the planned event is 'the largest trade show of its kind' that can be an effective focus for all the advertising. As well, the fact that it is the largest trade show can be turned into benefits to attract exhibitors, sponsors and delegates.

After developing marketing objectives, an action plan needs to be established which accomplishes the set goals. An action plan should consider:

- specific objectives

- a description of the target groups to be solicited.

- action steps to accomplish those objectives (e.g., direct mail campaign)

- allocation of sufficient budget to achieve objectives

A marketing mix is composed of a number of elements such as advertising, sales, product, price, research and planning. The "4 P's" of marketing are:

- Product - the actual meeting or event program

- Place - the location of the meeting

- Promotion - the persuasive technique used to demonstrate to the potential delegate that this event will be worth the time and/or money

- Price - the overall cost of the event

4. DEVELOPING THE ACTION PLAN

The implementation of the action plan is merely identifying the action steps and then determining who will be responsible to complete each step. Your timelines or production schedule should be considered in this process. The meeting professional must also continually review and monitor the action steps being taken.

The action steps used will need to communicate to potential attendees, sponsors and exhibitors information about the meeting or event program - the 4 P's need to be clear and concise. Action steps should be:

- decide which promotional forms to be used and in what manner

- promotional mix (e.g., ongoing website, weekly newspaper advertisements, public relations campaign)

- set the promotional schedule

- craft the promotional material

- graphic design and printing

DECIDING PROMOTIONAL MIX

The promotional mix is a blend of strategies used to achieve your marketing objectives. Four major promotional tools are advertising, public relations, promotions and personal selling. Through your market research, you should have determined the most effective means to reach your target audience. For example, a direct mail promotional piece may not be the best means to reach a group of computer programmers. Conversely, a website might not be the most effective means to reach health care workers who may have limited access to the Internet.

ADVERTISING

Advertising is what you say about your conference. In most instances meetings must be advertised to educate potential attendees, exhibitors or sponsors about the meeting and its benefits.

Advertising can be done in a variety of media formats including television, newspapers, trade magazines, direct mailings, websites and fax and email mailings. For direct mailing activities, mailing lists can be purchased from list brokers. Purchased mailing lists that can be used for direct mail or email are available in a variety of combinations, depending on the demographics being targeted. For example, you could ask for a listing of all the architects in the United States or only those in California.

PUBLIC RELATIONS

Public relations includes publicity, which is often a major portion of public relations and is often the most highly visible part of a public relations program. Properly utilized, public relations can reinforce advertising, expand the distribution of message, add or establish credibility and generate support and excitement.

Since many conferences, events or meetings will gain in attendance by attaining second party endorsements, public relations is an effective low-cost means to consider when planning your promotional activities. The late public relations counsel and journalist Herb Baus, advised, "Everything that the organization can do to improve its public relations will improve its ability to get results and realize the objectives for which it exists" (Herb Baus; The Publicity Kit, 1991, pg 8). When developing a public relations plan, you should consider the following three points:

1. What impression do you want to make on the general public?

2. What is it that you want the public to do?

   (e.g., learn more about the organization or register for the conference or event?)

3. What actions need to be taken by the public in order for the host organization to achieve the objectives?

SALES PROMOTION

Attendance can be promoted to delegates by offering price reductions for early registration. Promotions can also be offered to exhibitors by offering them incentive to reserve their booth space early. Sponsors may be offered more opportunities for exposure of their logo for an early commitment to support the event.

PERSONAL SELLING

Personal selling involves person-to-person contact. It may involve the host organization's president explaining the advantages of attending the annual conference. Or it may involve the president of the corporation informing employees of the purpose and location of the next staff meeting. One of the most effective methods of personal selling can be from past attendees who provide glowing testimonials to potential attendees about the value of the upcoming conference.

SETTING PROMOTIONAL SCHEDULE

Where possible set the dates, locations, venue or facilities a year or more in advance. Again where applicable, disseminate this information to the attendees during the current meeting. Promotions for the next year can take a variety of styles such as presentation of a gavel to next year's chairman, advertisement on the last page of the onsite program, or a promotional item related to the next year's theme.

~ *Sample Template* ~

A typical promotion schedule (depending on available budget) for an upcoming meeting may be as follows:

CRAFTING PROMOTIONAL MATERIAL

Date/Status	Marketing Medium	Target	Purpose	Message
16 months	Exhibitor Prospectus – personally distributed	Current year exhibitors	To sell exhibit space	Value of exhibiting, rental fees, rules and regulations, space applications/ contract
13 months	Exhibitor Prospectus (mailed)	Potential new exhibitors	To sell exhibit space	Value of exhibiting, rental fees, rules and regulations, space applications/ contract
12 months – 1 month	Photo gallery	Visitors to website	To sell the destination	City X is different and special. Don't miss it.
12 months	Postcard(mailed)	Past and potential attendees	To create awareness, profile the dates	Plan to be there, Register now and reserve hotel rooms.
10 - 12 months	Call for Presentations	Potential speakers, past attendees, mailing list	To assist to develop the education program	What can you contribute to the knowledge of your peers?
8 - 10 months	Trade magazine advertisement	All subscribers	Highlight upcoming date and location	City X is different and special. Don't miss it.
8 - 10 months	Sponsor Opportunities Teaser	Past and potential sponsors	To secure sponsorships	Value of sponsoring, opportunities, costs
8 months	Registration material (mailed and on website)	Past attendees and potential new attendees	Early bird registration opportunities	Register now, take advantage of the savings
3 months	Complete Registration Program (mailed and on website)	Past attendees and potential new attendees	To increase registration	Full program information

The promotional materials have a direct specific aim: to generate attendance at the meeting. Material must be upbeat dynamic and enthusiastic. Sentences should be short ad punchy! Emphasize the personal benefits of attendance, rather than a list of features.

Use phrases like:

.....You will learn

.....Gather new insights into

.....She will teach you how to...

Don't be afraid to repeat important information including dates, destination, program benefits and cost. This only helps to reinforce the message.

If budget permits, use colour in the promotional materials to add drama and excitement. Picture captions should suggest attendance benefits. No one needs to be told that they are looking at a picture of the swimming pool but a reference to the wide range of family activities available on site might encourage an undecided attendee to register.

Promotional brochures should have the most important selling message on the cover. Given the volume of mail that most participants receive every day, an eye catching informative brochure is a must if the meeting professional hopes to attract targeted groups in sufficient numbers. The cover of the brochure should include a catchy event title and/or readily identified graphics. As well the host organization should be clearly identified and specific information such as dates and location should be listed. The brochure contents should include complete information on speakers and the program. The conference promotional information or brochure may take several forms. For example, it may be commercially printed, it may become a website, it may be a PDF file that is emailed to all potential attendees, or it could be faxed sheets. The important point is to consider all the potential uses of the promotional pieces in the early design stages.

Basic content of a program brochure should include:

- date and time of program

- title of program

- host organization

- location (destination and facilities)

- who should attend and why

- meeting schedule including social recreational and pre/post activities

- speakers' names, titles and affiliations

- facility information

- fees and what they include

- registration form

- accommodation information

- guest activity and child care information

- special events and functions

- continuing education credits if applicable

- meeting logo/theme

The conference registration form and the hotel reservation form should also be considered marketing tools, as in effect they remind the potential delegate of the upcoming event and urge him/her to take action. In addition to soliciting information and a commitment to participate, they should reinforce the theme.

GRAPHIC DESIGN AND PRINTING

If the meeting professional is involved in the design process some key points should be kept in mind. Consider how the promotional pieces will be used. For example, will you need to email the program material and the registration form? Will you need to fax the information? Encourage the design of the conference logo to be readily used in a variety of forms such as in printed media using a smaller version for nametag card stock to much larger versions for signage.

DESIGNING THE PIECE

Give the graphic artist the final text desired and provide the following information:

- purpose of the piece

- who will receive it

- tone or mood you want to achieve. Describe this by using descriptive terms, such as
  - light
  - serious
  - modern

- multilingual requirements (number of languages)

- desired method of production

- number of colours required

- desired type of layout

- your budget

HOT TIP

Decode the Communication

Airlines do it. The computer crowd does it. Spies do it too. But you shouldn't. In your agenda or conference program, don't date your schedule for June 7 at 06-07-99. (or is that 07-06-99?) Nor should the session that begins at 2:30 p.m. be slated for 14:30 hrs. Why make people work for what you mean?

Each element of the printing process will have an estimated deadline. Work with the printer to determine the deadlines to meet all the requirements for reviewing various drafts and any committee member reviews that have been determined.

Use the following graphic design and printing guideline to assist in the preparation of meeting promotional materials:

ITEMS THAT CAN BE PRINTED

- promotional piece(s) and envelopes

- program

- program-at-a-glance pocket cards

- badge card stock

- folder for registration materials

- event tickets

- registration receipts

- special letterhead
- special-issue newsletter
- evaluation forms
- local information (e.g., restaurants, sightseeing, entertainment)
- registration materials
- exhibitors directory
- exhibit prospectus
- sponsorship prospectus
- teaser postcards

OTHER PROMOTIONAL METHODS

- website for the meeting
- web site for the organization
- web based registration
- web links to/from destination
- sponsor websites
- virtual trade shows
- fax and electronic broadcasts
- electronic newsletters
- promotional items (e.g., key chains, pen)
- PDF copies of printed materials

PUBLICITY AND MEDIA

Often the best promotional message comes not from the brochures that are distributed, but from the publicity that is generated about the event by the media, whether it be trade or consumer. Meeting professionals can encourage positive media messages by providing the media with releases. These releases are often the basis for stories and features and as such they should include the release date in the upper right hand corner, a contact name including the phone number, and answers to the "who, what, where, when, and why" of the event.

Regardless how big or "important" your conference, remember no newspaper, radio or television station owes you publicity. If you want media attention, you have to attract it. The key is to provide a legitimate "news" angle to get them interested.

HOT TIP

Give a Good News Angle

Regardless how big or "important" your conference, remember no newspaper, radio or television station owes you publicity. If you want media attention, you have to attract it. The key is to provide a legitimate "news" angle to get them interested.

WORKING WITH THE MEDIA

When members of the media attend an event, their objective is usually to gain access to VIPs, not necessarily to promote the host organization. The meeting professional may supplement press kits with information, making sure it is correct, newsworthy, and easy to use. A large event may warrant supplying additional computers, telephones, fax machine, small press size notepads with organization logo, and refreshments for members of the media.

If possible, keep a record of how many media representatives attended, what publications or type of publications they represent, and how much coverage the organization received. This information will be useful to exhibitors in post meeting publicity, and to track post event coverage.

PRESS OR MEDIA KIT GENERALLY INCLUDES:

- cover letter

- media release

- fact sheet

- organizational or conference brochure

- graphics and graphic standards

- tickets and/or posters (if applicable)

ELEMENTS OF A MEDIA OR PRESS RELEASE:

- The top of the page should include the date of the release plus the phrase "For Immediate Release".

- A contact name and phone number should be included, "for more information".

- A compelling but short headline or title at the top of the page is needed to help catch the media's attention .

- The format should be a single letter-sized page, double spaced with the event or conference date, time, site or venue, any other event specific information underlined.

- The announcement should not be any longer than three paragraphs in length. The lead paragraph should tell the main part of the story and then the remaining paragraphs give additional information. Here is the opportunity to provide more information about a special keynote speaker or a VIP to be in attendance.

- At the bottom of the page, include the word "more" if you are continuing to another page.

- At the conclusion of the release, use the word "end" or "30".

ELEMENTS OF A FACT SHEET

A fact sheet is a one-page summary that could include the following details:

- statistics about the group involved

- general listing of the attendees home cities, especially if it is a national or international conference

- brief history of the conference or event

- may include information on key speakers or announcements to be made (e.g., scientific discovery or product roll-out)

- any other pertinent facts that may be of interest to the media (e.g., number of attendees in the city hotel rooms and subsequent dollar value to the host city)

SPEAKING TO THE MEDIA

If media representatives are expected to be present at the event, then the host organization should appoint an 'official' spokesperson, who will be available onsite. Representing the host organization, the media spokesperson should, at all times, convey the values, objectives and messages consistent with those of the host organization. To avoid information being misconstrued or miscommunicated at the time of the interview, it is recommended that where possible, media questions are considered and appropriate responses are prepared in advance.

MEDIA CREDENTIALS

Prior to the conference, the meeting professional should have developed a registration policy regarding media representatives. It is generally accepted that trade or industry media representatives are provided complimentary registration. If that is the case, these representatives should be identified with a unique badge or some means of specific media identification. Consideration should be given to any legislation that prohibits the taking of photographs without permission of the subjects. Conference photographers should also be clearly identified and may need an assistant to enable obtaining permission for photographs.

MEDIA ROOM

You may need to plan and prepare for a large number of media to be present at the conference.

If this is the case, consider:

- a meeting room designated as the 'media room' should include access into the Internet and phone lines, tables and chairs for computers and working reporters; it is important that the room is not a "dead zone" for mobile phones.

- a separate room for interviews with celebrities, VIPs, keynotes speakers, and/or organization spokesperson(s). If you do not have a separate room try to set up a separate area with some hard wall display sections to reduce the noise from others and to create a quiet area for the interview

- a volunteer may need to be assigned to be in the media room at scheduled times during the event

MEDIA BRIEFING

Media briefings are arranged to give a quick overview of the entire conference with particular attention to a story idea or "hook" that would be of interest to the media. For example, if a scientific discovery will be discussed, this would be an opportunity to answer specific media questions. The briefing is best scheduled the day before the conference opens. If VIPs are attending over the days of the conference, the meeting professional might arrange a breakfast briefing for media each morning.

MEDIA OR NEWS CONFERENCES

When a conference is hosting a celebrity or a well-known person identified with the conference group, the meeting professional and hosting organization may decide to hold a news conference. If that decision is made, some specific arrangements will need to be in place. It will require extra equipment from the audio visual supplier. A starting and stopping time needs to be announced to the media. Ground rules need to be established and everyone in attendance should know ahead of time whether the person will be reading a prepared statement and whether a question and answer period will be allowed. You may wish to have a moderator manage the question and answer session, if there is to be one.

SCRUMS

On some occasions, when a VIP or celebrity is in attendance, a "scrum" may occur. Scrums are impromptu news conferences. The celebrity or VIP is quickly surrounded by media representatives and usually is asked a barrage of questions. The meeting professional needs to know ahead of time if the person being interviewed will allow a scrum to develop. If not, the meeting organizers may need to provide security or assist the person to move quickly out of the area.

EVENT MEDIA COVERAGE

The extent of the media coverage for your event is, to some degree, contingent on other external factors. Local, national and international news stories of the day will generally take precedence over any content that could be considered discretionary. Try to avoid submitting details about your event during peak times (e.g., on Monday when most print and broadcast media are reporting on previous weekend's events). Newsworthy events are unpredictable and constantly changing. Establishing good communication with media contacts and maintaining an awareness of local national and international news stories may help in determining the most appropriate time to plan coverage of your event.

~ *A Conference Journal* ~

Eighteen months prior to the conference, a team of four people comprised of the manager of communications and a volunteer from each association was asked to develop the marketing plan for this joint meeting.

Their starting point was to review the existing marketing materials from both organizations. This included an early promotional piece announcing the meeting, the program brochure that included the registration form, several ads in industry magazines, onsite materials plus a separate exhibit prospectus and exhibitor directory. Past promotional efforts had been effective but the challenge facing them was how to pull two very different styles together with reasonable costs.

They decided to hold a competition. They invited a number of graphic designers working in tandem with printers to create a concept, together with estimated costs, that would flow through all of the print promotion. The selection process proved to be very difficult because the concepts were exceptional and they were of equal caliber. To help them make their decision, the marketing committee developed criteria that went beyond artistic ability to include financial considerations, location of the printer's office, personality of the key contact and their ability to communicate with committee members and finally, taking into account past experience with either one or both groups. After rating the submissions using these criteria they were able to make their decision.

Once the graphic designer was selected, they set to work developing a comprehensive marketing plan and budget. As conference details were confirmed, the meeting manager became heavily involved in the development of brochures, tickets, onsite program, registration form and all exhibit materials. While the meeting coordinator provided information about speaker presentations, it was the responsibility of the meeting manager to finalize and assemble program details, including sponsor recognition. A complete draft of the brochure was developed and sent to the marketing team at which time it was reworked, a rough layout prepared and then sent to the designer who would then add the creative artwork and present a complete layout for approval.

Marketing materials were distributed to over 50,000 people worldwide, through a combination of their own member and nonmember mailings lists, purchased lists from other relation associations, magazine inserts, and attendance at trade shows. They created a new website that was also linked to each of the associations and of course, all marketing materials were put on the web as soon as they were available. Advertisements were taken out in major industry papers and magazines around the world and key representatives from the conference planning committee attended industry events throughout the year that enabled them to get the word out and distribute conference materials.

About three months prior to the conference, they decided to hire a professional Public Relations (PR) consultant to develop an effective media campaign that included the preparation of media releases, media kits and fact sheets. Although association staff could have managed this function, existing resources were already stretched beyond their means throughout the planning phase of the conference and it was agreed, that the professional had more experience in this specialized area with better access to local media.

During the conference, the consultant was required to brief the media and schedule interviews with several key individuals from the host organization. A media room was setup with a work area for reporters complete with access to Internet, telephone lines, several work stations and a separate area was designated for interviews. The PR consultant managed this area throughout the conference, making sure that interviews were conducted as scheduled, distributed media kits and fact sheets and kept track of the media in attendance.

The results were outstanding. They had more coverage than they had ever received before both in local papers and industry magazines around the world. Articles about the event continued to appear months after the conference had ended.

MARKETING AND MEDIA CHECKLIST

Information on **CD Rom**

MARKETING

- ☐ Market research complete
  - target Markets identified
  - expectations of the audience identified
  - marketing objectives established
    - ○ action steps identified
    - ○ promotional mix identified
    - ○ website
    - ○ direct mail pieces
    - ○ mailing lists complete
    - ○ bulk mail requirements identified
    - ○ advertisements
- ☐ Key information identified
- ☐ Need for advertising agency considered
  - public relations activities
  - testimonials
- ☐ Set promotional schedule
- ☐ Determine graphic design elements
  - logo designed
  - applications of logo use determined
  - website
  - conference products
  - all printed materials
    - ○ stationary
    - ○ program booklets, registration materials
    - ○ onsite materials
    - ○ exhibitor prospectus
    - ○ sponsor prospectus
    - ○ conference products – e.g., pens
    - ○ Photographs
    - ○ need determined
    - ○ obtain permission if needed

PUBLICITY AND MEDIA

☐ Organization spokesperson identified

☐ Targeted media representatives identified
- media or press kit prepared and includes
  - ○ cover letter
  - ○ media release
  - ○ fact sheet
  - ○ organizational or conference brochure
  - ○ graphics and graphics standards
  - ○ tickets and/or posters

- prepare for media
  - ○ policy for media credentials determined
  - ○ media credentials prepared
  - ○ meeting room for media representatives identified
  - ○ arrangements made for media or news conference

CHAPTER REVIEW

Marketing for an event should be geared both towards delegates and towards sponsors, exhibitors and the media. A basic marketing plan includes 4 elements, as follows:

1. conducting market research

2. identifying target markets

3. establishing marketing objectives

4. developing the action plan

The marketing plan will outline what combination of advertising, public relations, sales promotion and personal selling will be used to meet your marketing objectives. A marketing action plan outlines:

- promotional mix to be used

- scheduling of the marketing/promotion plan

- content and message of the promotional materials

- graphic design and printing techniques to be used

Publicity and media can play an important role in a meetings marketing plan. Publicity and media coverage can be maximized by employing the following elements:

- press or media kits – including press releases and fact sheets

- media room

- media briefings

- media or news conferences

- scrums

- event media coverage

TEST YOUR KNOWLEDGE

The following self test will indicate the level of understanding and knowledge gained from this chapter. Solutions to all self tests can be found in Appendix A.

1. If participants are required to attend a meeting as part of their job, no marketing is required.

    ☐ True   ☐ False

2. Media packages are primarily used to emphasize the presence of VIPs and speakers.

    ☐ True   ☐ False

3. The key to effective marketing of a meeting is to focus all marketing efforts on attracting potential delegates.

    ☐ True   ☐ False

4. A properly developed registration package can be an effective marketing tool.

    ☐ True   ☐ False

5. Setting realistic objectives is a critical aspect of effective marketing.

    ☐ True   ☐ False

6. All marketing materials should have a consistent theme and image.

    ☐ True   ☐ False

7. The best time to begin promoting next year's meeting is:

    (a) during the workshops at this year's   meeting

    (b) whenever membership dues notices are sent out

    (c) during a general session or meal function at this year's meeting

    (d) 6 months before the actual meeting dates

8. A media fact sheet should contain:

    (a) statistics about the group involved and a general listing of attendees home cities

    (b) a brief history of the conference or event

    (c) information on key speakers, announcements to be made or other items of media interest

    (d) all of the above

9. Match the promotional category to the appropriate type of tool it uses:

   1) advertising   a) price discounts, special gifts or bonuses

   2) public relations   b) one on one or group meetings, phone calls, testimonials

   3) sales promotion   c) TV, radio, direct mail, web, fax, emails, magazines,
                               newspapers
   4) personal selling

                            d) press releases, fact sheets, news conferences

10. Identify the 4 P's of the marketing mix.

   _____

   _____

   _____

11. What is the purpose of conducting marketing research?

   _____

   _____

   _____

12. What are the 7 basic elements of a media release?

   _____

   _____

   _____

   _____

   _____

   _____

   _____

NOTES

Trade Shows

INTRODUCTION

The term "trade show" is often used interchangeably with terms like "convention", "exhibition" and "exposition". Internationally, the terms "trade event" and "trade fair" are often used. For the purposes of this guide, a trade show is defined as a temporary, face-to-face marketplace where vendors present products and services and build relationships with existing and prospective buyers.

Trade shows are held for two key reasons. First, they can represent a significant source of revenue for the host organization and second, they offer an educational opportunity for those in attendance. In fact, the exhibit or trade show is often viewed as a component of the educational program and serves to supplement the more formal workshops and seminars.

Trade shows are a marketing vehicle for companies to promote their organization, products or service to potential customers and to qualify prospective customers. The face-to-face contact between exhibitors and prospective customers in a trade show setting is a unique and substantial benefit to exhibitors.

Ensure you understand and can apply the following terms:

- Booth space
- Corner booth
- Customs broker
- End-cap booth
- Exclusive contractor
- Exhibition manager
- Exhibitor
- Exhibitor prospectus
- Exhibitor manual
- Fire marshal
- General service contractor
- Horizontal show
- Installation and dismantle
- Island booth
- Linear booth
- Marshaling yard
- Material handling
- Move-in/move-out
- Official contractor
- Peninsula booth
- Perimeter booth
- Show services
- Vertical show

Refer to the glossary for further clarification of the key terms for this chapter.

One of the keys to a successful trade show is to bring together the right combination of buyers and sellers. Trade shows typically fail if the wrong products and services are on display or the wrong attendees are on the floor. Surveying the potential attendees to determine what their needs are is a good first step in determining whether or not a trade show will be effective. Consult both buyers and key suppliers to determine if there is sufficient interest in holding a trade show.

Questions to ask during development might include:

- Is a trade show appropriate as a stand alone event or part of a meeting?

- What products and services are of interest to the attendees?

- What types of companies are likely to exhibit at this trade show?

- Who are the key suppliers to this audience?

- What are the profitability objectives for the trade show?

LEARNING OBJECTIVES

After completing this chapter, the learner will:

- understand the process involved in organizing a trade show

- identify the various types of trade shows

- describe the role of the exhibition manager

- describe the role of the various service contractors

- understand the educational value of holding a trade show

- identify the contents of the exhibitor manual

- understand the profit, partnering and stakeholder value of holding a trade show

ROLES AND RESPONSIBILITIES

EXHIBITION MANAGER

○ Plan, promote and produce a trade show/exhibition program.

- Determine objectives
  - ○ target interests of attendees
  - ○ determine the purpose of a trade show/exhibition

- Design the trade show/exhibition
  - ○ develop a theme
  - ○ select venue based on your stakeholders' preferences, space requirements, facility rental fees, union jurisdictions, facility's exclusive contractors, proximity to conference sessions, meeting rooms, hotels and restaurants for attendees and exhibitors, building regulations including fire and security, insurance and loading dock access
  - ○ create a facility floor plan with the venue, fire marshal and general service contractor's input to maximize traffic flow and space usage
  - ○ plan the show schedule, including move-in/move-out plan, and dovetailing with the conference schedule to create unopposed hours for exhibitors
  - ○ develop an exhibitor prospectus, including all required elements
  - ○ develop an exhibitor manual, including all required elements (e.g., facility regulations and restrictions, exhibitors' policies and guidelines, information on official contractors, all necessary forms)
  - ○ manage distribution of the prospectus
  - ○ determine show requirements, compile Requests for Proposal (RFPs), solicit and review bids, select vendors, and negotiate contracts with the venue, exclusive contractors, a general contractor and subcontractors

- Cultivate, secure and maintain relationships with exhibitors
  - ○ target potential exhibitors
  - ○ prepare attendance marketing plan and implement
  - ○ monitor booth space sales and sponsorship signups
  - ○ evaluate the trade show/exposition program for both Return on Investment (ROI) and Return on Objective (ROO)

ADDITIONAL STAFF

○ Additional staff may be required to manage sales, marketing, operations and administration to produce the trade show.

- Participate in the planning and production of a trade show/exhibition
- Implement the trade show/exposition plan

TYPES OF TRADE SHOWS

B2B AND B2C

Trade shows fall into two main categories: Business to Business and Business to Consumer. Business to Business (B2B) events, like those associated with conferences and meetings, target a very particular audience demographic specific to the industry they represent. The exhibitors at B2B events are generally offering products, services and solutions to enhance the effectiveness and profitability of the businesses represented by the attendees. B2B trade shows may be stand alone or part of a conference program. They may or may not have admission fees for attendees.

Business to Consumer (B2C) events focus on people: the products, services and solutions that are of interest to consumers. Often referred to as consumer shows, Business to Consumer trade shows usually have a central theme, or a particular type of merchandise, and generally include an admission fee for the public to attend. Exhibitors are encouraged to contact consumers and sell their products and services on the floor of the show. There is not usually a substantial education component to a Business to Consumer trade show.

HORIZONAL AND VERTICAL SHOWS

Trade shows are also classified as being either horizontal or vertical, based on their audience profile. A vertical show is one at which the products or services being displayed represent one element of an industry or profession. Horizontal shows showcase products or services that represent all segments of an industry or profession. As an example, a trade show for all types of medical professionals involved in nursing would be considered more horizontal than a show for only operating room surgical nurses, which would be considered a vertical show.

GEOGRAPHY

Trade shows can also be segmented by the geography of the area where they draw their exhibitors and attendees. Some shows are international in scope, drawing many attendees and exhibitors from countries outside that of the venue.

Other shows are domestic, drawing attendees and exhibitors from the entire country where the show is being held, a region of the country (usually considered within an hours's drive of the trade show).

KEY PERSONNEL

EXHIBITION MANAGER

Also known as the show manager or show management, the exhibition manager is the person responsible for all aspects of planning, promoting, and producing an exhibition. The exhibition manager may be on the staff of the sponsoring organization, on the staff of a third-party exhibition management company, or a contracted individual.

EXHIBITS MANAGER

An exhibits manager is part of the exhibition management staff and is in charge of the entire exhibit area.

GENERAL SERVICE CONTRACTOR

The exhibition manager may select an official service company to oversee the physical set-up and dismantle of the show floor, which will work for the sponsoring organization and provide services for the individual exhibitors. This company is known as the general service contractor (GSC), the official general contractor or the decorator. The GSC's contract with the organization sponsoring the trade show may include assisting with venue selection, design of the booth layout and floor plan, production and placement of directional and informational signage and registration counters, rental and laying of aisle carpeting, construction of pipe and drape or system exhibits and basic furnishings such as folding tables and stackable chairs as part of exhibit packages.

The general service contractor will also provide services for the exhibitors including labor for the installation and dismantle of exhibits; rental of exhibits, carpet/pad and furnishings and accessible storage of items exhibitors will need during the show. The GSC also manages material handling (also known as drayage) of exhibitors' freight which generally includes pre-show storage for up to 30 days at no cost in an advance warehouse local to show site, local movement from the advance warehouse to show site, unloading freight at the docks and movement to the exhibitor's booth space, storage of empty crates/cartons/pallets during the trade show, return of crates to the exhibitor's booth space at show close, and movement from the booth to the dock for reloading on the exhibitor's chosen carrier.

EXCLUSIVE CONTRACTORS

An exclusive contractor is a contractor appointed by the show or building management as the sole provider of specified services. Exclusive contractors often include those dealing with the venue's infrastructure and property, such as telecommunications, Internet, plumbing, compressed air, electrical services and in-house catering. A show's general service contractor may also claim some of their services as exclusive, such as material handling and overhead rigging.

SUBCONTRACTORS

The show organizer may contract for services benefiting all exhibitors such as perimeter security and registration. These contractors are also known as specialty subcontractors.

OFFICIAL CONTRACTORS

Official contractors are a select group of companies contracted by the show organizer to provide services for exhibitors. Services provided by the official contractors may include rental of audio-visual, lead-retrieval equipment, computers, flowers and plants, and custom furnishings; hotel rooms; exhibit photography; in-booth security; temporary staffing; shipping via airfreight, van line or common carrier; and travel services such as airline or car rental. Exhibitors are not mandated by show management to use the services of the official contractors whose information is provided in the exhibitor manual as a service to exhibitors who do not have their own contractors for these services.

EXHIBITOR-APPOINTED CONTRACTORS

An exhibitor-appointed contractor (EAC) is any company selected by the exhibitor providing the same services offered by an official contractor, who will need access to an exhibit on the show floor during installation, show dates, and dismantling. The term "EAC" is most often used to refer to an independent contractor who is appointed by an exhibitor to install and dismantle their exhibit. The term EAC can also apply to other contractors chosen by the exhibitor, such as audio-visual rental companies.

Notification by the exhibitor to show management of their intent to use an outside contractor is generally required using a form called the EAC Form, found in the exhibitor manual. This form must be completed by the exhibitor and submitted 30-60 days before show set-up. The EAC will be required to submit a certificate of insurance showing coverage for both general liability and workers compensation.

EACs are also known as independent contractors or non-official contractors.

EXHIBIT MANAGER

An exhibit manager is the person who manages a single exhibit for a company or organization. This person is also sometimes known as a trade show manager within their company or organization.

EXHIBIT HOUSE

An exhibit house, also known as a display company or display builder, designs, fabricates and stores trade show exhibits. Many organizations hire their services to help them design and build a trade show exhibit that reflects their company image and brand. In the event of damage to the exhibit properties, exhibit houses can repair and refurbish them, as well as provide warehouse storage when the exhibit is not in use.

SHIPPING COMPANY

Sometimes referred to as a freight forwarder, specialized exhibit transportation company or carrier, a shipping company will manage the transportation of exhibit properties from each exhibitor's location to the trade show site or an advance warehouse provided by the general service contractor.

CUSTOMS BROKER

If exhibitors from outside the country where the trade show is being held will be shipping exhibit materials across international borders, their materials must clear customs enroute to the trade show. The customs broker, who has specific and detailed knowledge of international shipping regulations, will work closely with your exhibitors and their shipping company in order to ensure that the proper paperwork is completed and enough lead time is allotted to arrange for on-time delivery at show site.

GUIDELINES FOR BOOTH SPACES

The following guidelines for display rules and regulations were established in accordance with those set forth by the International Association for Exhibit Management (IAEM) – a global association that serves as the foremost authority on exhibition management and operations to promote continuity and consistency among North American exhibitions. Many exhibition organizers include a copy of the IAEM document "Guidelines for Display Rules and Regulations" in their rules to exhibitors. The 2005, updated document and the copy reprinted here include compliance with fire, safety, Americans with Disabilities Act (ADA) and other governmental requirements – and IAEM also recommends checking with local exhibition service contractors for local regulations.

IAEM BOOTH SPACE DESIGN, PLACEMENT AND ADVICE

A standard booth space in the United States is 10' (feet) wide by 10' (feet) deep (3.05m x 3.05m). Miltiples of 10' x 10' spaces are connected to configure into one of seven types of booth spaces:

Linear Booth

Linear Booths have only one side exposed to an aisle and are generally arranged in a series along a straight line. They are also called "in-line" booths.

Dimensions

For purposes of consistency and ease of layout and/or reconfiguration, floor plan design in increments of 10ft (3.05m) has become the de facto standard in the United States. Therefore, unless constricted by space or other limitations, Linear Booths are most commonly 10ft (3.05m) wide and 10ft (3.05m) deep, i.e. 10ft by 10ft (3.05m by 3.05m). A maximum back wall height limitation of 8ft (2.44m) is generally specified.

Use of Space

Regardless of the number of Linear Booths utilized, e.g. 10ft by 20ft (3.05m by 6.10m), 10ft by 30ft (3.05m by 9.14m), 10ft by 40ft (3.05m by 12.19m), etc. display materials should be arranged in such a manner so as not to obstruct sight lines of neighboring exhibitors. The maximum height of 8ft (2.44m) is allowed only in the rear half of the booth space, with a 4ft (1.22m) height restriction imposed on all materials in the remaining space forward to the aisle. (See Line-of-Sight exception on page 8.) Note: When three or more Linear Booths are used in combination as a single exhibit space, the 4ft (1.22m) height limitation is applied only to that portion of exhibit space which is within 10ft (3.05m) of an adjoining booth.

Corner Booth

A Corner Booth is a Linear Booth exposed to aisles on two sides.
All other guidelines for Linear Booths apply.

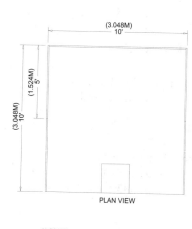
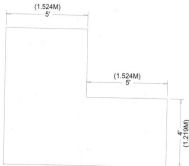

PLAN VIEW

LEFT SIDE VIEW

FRONT VIEW

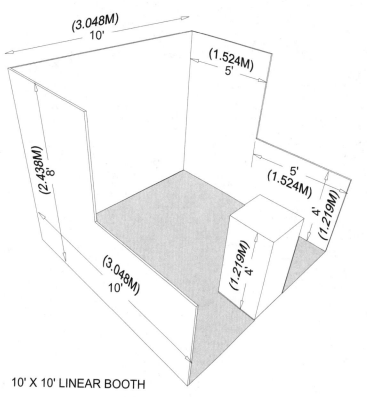

10' X 10' LINEAR BOOTH

Perimeter Booth

A Perimeter Booth is a Linear Booth that backs to an outside wall of the exhibit facility rather than to another exhibit.

Dimensions and Use of Space

All guidelines for Linear Booths apply to Perimeter Booths except that the typical maximum back wall height is 12ft (3.66m).

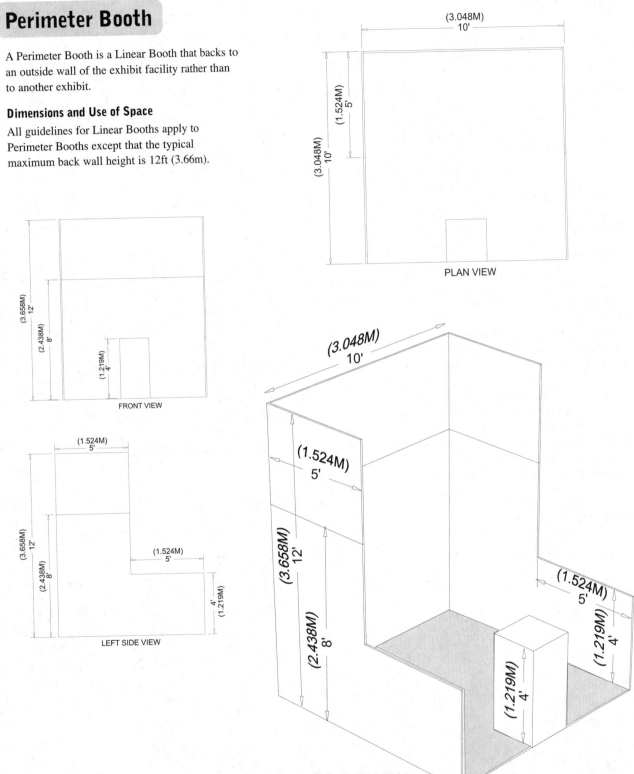

PLAN VIEW

FRONT VIEW

LEFT SIDE VIEW

10' X 10' PERIMETER BOOTH

End-cap Booth

An End-cap Booth is exposed to aisles on three sides and composed of two booths.

Dimensions

End-cap Booths are generally ten feet (10') deep by twenty feet (20') wide. The maximum backwall height of eight feet (8') is allowed only in the rear half of the booth space and within five feet (5') of the two side aisles with a four foot (4') height restriction imposed on all materials in the remaining space forward to the aisle.

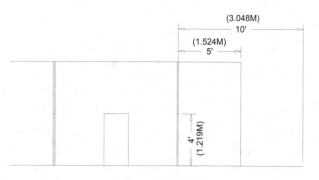

LEFT SIDE VIEW

FRONT VIEW

PLAN VIEW

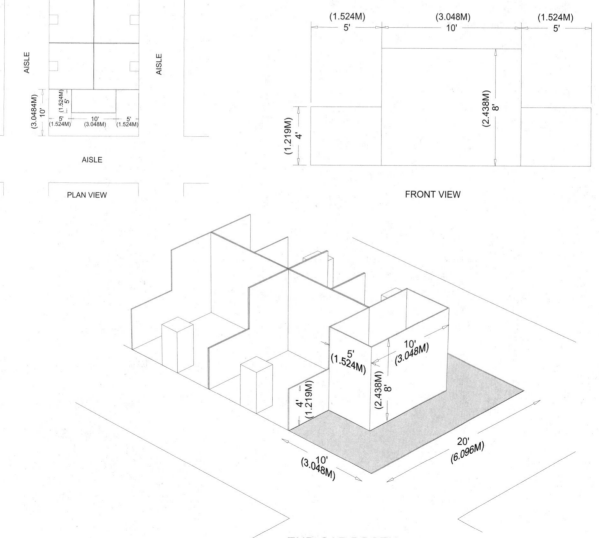

END-CAP BOOTH

Peninsula Booth

A Peninsula Booth is exposed to aisles on three (3) sides and composed of a minimum of four booths. There are two types of Peninsula Booths: (a) one which backs up to Linear Booths, and (b) one which backs to another Peninsula Booth and is referred to as a "Split Island Booth."

Dimensions

A Peninsula Booth is usually 20' x 20' or larger. When a Peninsula Booth backs up to two Linear Booths, the backwall is restricted to four feet (4') high within five feet (5') of each aisle, permitting adequate line of sight for the adjoining Linear Booths. Sixteen feet (16') is a typical maximum height allowance, including signage for the center portion of the backwall.

PLAN VIEW

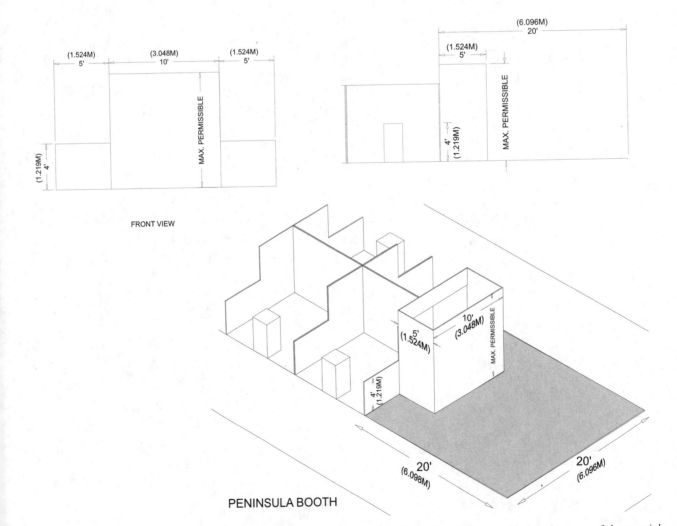

FRONT VIEW

PENINSULA BOOTH

Split Island Booth

A Split Island Booth is a Peninsula Booth which shares a common backwall with another Peninsula Booth. The entire cubic content of this booth may be used, up to the maximum allowable height, without any back wall line of sight restrictions. Sixteen feet (16') is a typical maximum height allowance, including signage. The entire cubic content of the space may be used up to the maximum allowable height.

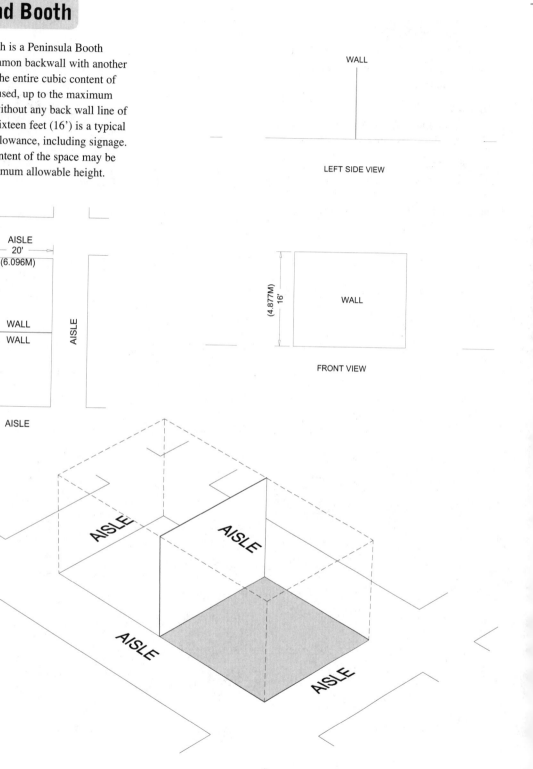

SPLIT ISLAND BOOTH

Island Booth

An Island Booth is any size booth exposed to
aisles on all four sides.

Dimensions
An Island Booth is typically 20' x 20' or larger,
although it may be configured differently.

Use of Space
The entire cubic content of the space may be used
up to the maximum allowable height, which is
usually sixteen feet (16'), including signage.

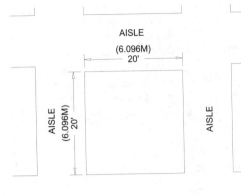

AISLE

(6.096M)
20'

AISLE

AISLE

AISLE

PLAN VIEW

(4.877M)
16'

FRONT VIEW

AISLE AISLE

AISLE AISLE

ISLAND BOOTH

Extended Header Booth 20ft (6.10m) or Longer

An Extended Header Booth is a Linear Booth 20ft (6.10m) or longer with a center extended header.

Dimensions and Use of Space

All guidelines for Linear Booths apply to Extended Header Booths, except that the center extended header has a maximum height of 8ft (2.44m), a maximum width of 20 percent of the length of the booth, and a maximum depth of 9ft (2.7m) from the back wall.

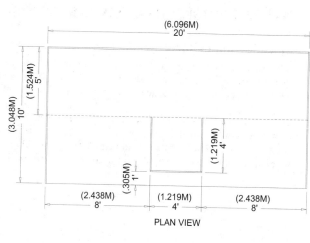

PLAN VIEW

LEFT SIDE VIEW

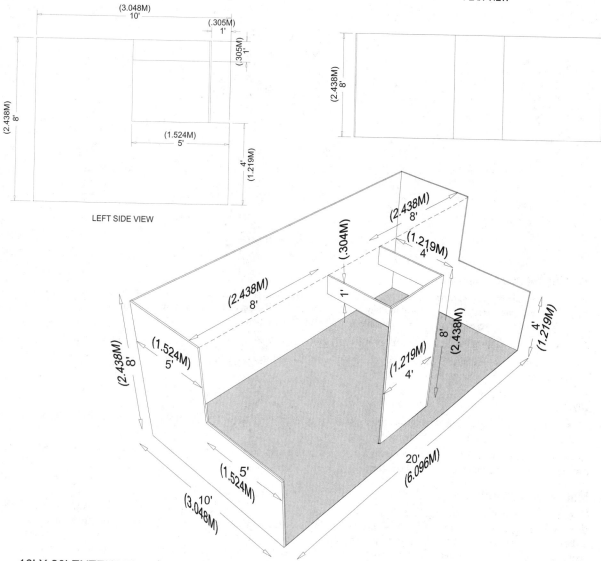

10' X 20' EXTENDED HEADER BOOTH

Other Important Considerations

Canopies and Ceilings

Canopies, including ceilings, umbrellas and canopy frames, can be either decorative or functional (such as to shade computer monitors from ambient light or for hanging products). Canopies for Linear or Perimeter Booths should comply with line of sight requirements (see "Use of Space for Linear or Perimeter Booths").

The base of the Canopy should not be lower than seven feet (7') from the floor within five feet (5') of any aisle. Canopy supports should be no wider than three inches (3"). This applies to any booth configuration that has a sightline restriction, such as a Linear Booth. Fire and safety regulations in many facilities strictly govern the use of canopies, ceilings and other similar coverings. Check with the appropriate local agencies prior to determining specific exhibition rules.

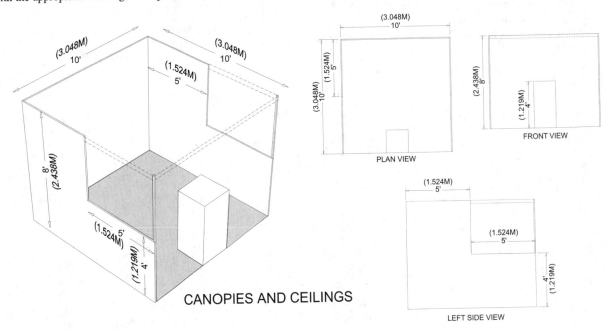

CANOPIES AND CEILINGS

Hanging Signs & Graphics

Hanging signs and graphics are permitted in all standard Peninsula and Island Booths, usually to a maximum height of sixteen feet (16'). Whether suspended from above or supported from below, they should comply with all ordinary use-of-space requirements (for example, the highest point of any sign should not exceed the maximum allowable height for the booth type).

Hanging Signs & Graphics should be set back ten feet (10') from adjacent booths.

Approval for the use of Hanging Signs & Graphics should be received from the exhibition organizer at least 60 days prior to installation. Drawings should be available for inspection.

Towers

A Tower is a freestanding exhibit component separate from the main exhibit fixture. The height restriction is the same as that which applies to the appropriate exhibit configuration being used.

Towers in excess of eight feet (8') should have drawings available for inspection. Fire and safety regulations in many facilities strictly govern the use of towers. A building permit may be required.

Multi-story Exhibit

A Multi-story Exhibit is a booth where the display fixtures exceed twelve feet (12'), including Double-decker and Triple-decker Booths. In many cities, a Multi-storied Exhibit requires prior approval by the exhibit facility and/or relevant local government agency because it is deemed to be a "structure" for building purposes. The city building department generally needs to issue a building permit based on an application and drawings prepared and submitted by a licensed architect or engineer. Exhibitors should obtain local building regulations early on to ensure that all time constraints are met. Exhibition organizers should be prepared to assist exhibitors in this application process.

Reprinted with express written permission of the International Association for Exhibition Management, the sole owner of the copyright, and any publication, reproduction or duplication of them in any form, print or electronic, without their express permission is strictly prohibited.

Issues Common To All Booth Types

Americans with Disabilities Act (ADA)

All exhibiting companies are required to be in compliance with the Americans with Disabilities Act (ADA) and are encouraged to be sensitive, and as reasonably accommodating as possible, to attendees with disabilities. Information regarding ADA compliance is available from the U.S. Department of Justice ADA Information Line (800-514-0301) and from web site **www.usdoj.gov/crt/ada/infoline.htm.**

Structural Integrity

All exhibit displays should be designed and erected in a manner that will withstand normal contact or vibration caused by neighboring exhibitors, hall laborers or installation/dismantling equipment such as fork lifts. Displays should also be able to withstand moderate wind effects that may occur in the exhibit hall when freight doors are open. Refer to local building codes that regulate temporary structures.

Exhibitors should ensure that any display fixtures such as tables, racks or shelves are designed and installed properly to support the product or marketing materials to be displayed upon them.

Flammable and Toxic Materials

All materials used in display construction or decorating should be made of fire retardant materials and be certified as flame retardant. Samples should also be available for testing. Materials that cannot be treated to meet the requirements should not be used. A flameproofing certificate should be available for inspection.

Exhibitors should dispose of any waste products they generate during the exhibition in accordance with guidelines established by the Environmental Protection Agency and the facility.

Electrical

Every exhibit facility has different electrical requirements; however, minimum guidelines are suggested:

All 110-volt wiring should be grounded three-wire.

Wiring that touches the floor should be SO cord (minimum 14-gauge/three-wire) flat cord, which is insulated to qualify for extra hard usage .

Cord wiring above floor level can be SJ which is rated for hard usage .

Using zip cords, two-wire cords, latex cords, plastic cord, lamp cord, open clip sockets, and two-wire clamp-on fixtures is not recommended and is often prohibited. Cube taps are not recommended and are often prohibited.

Power strips (multi-plug connectors) should be UL approved, with built-in over-load protectors.

Lighting

Exhibitors should adhere to the following suggested minimum guidelines when determining booth lighting:

No lighting, fixtures, lighting trusses or overhead lighting are allowed outside the boundaries of the exhibit space. Exhibitors intending to use hanging light systems should submit drawings to exhibition management for approval.

Lighting should be directed to the inner confines of the booth space. Lighting should not project onto other exhibits or show aisles.

Lighting which is potentially harmful, such as lasers or ultraviolet lighting, should comply with facility rules and be approved in writing by exhibition management.

Lighting that spins, rotates, pulsates and other specialized lighting effects should be in good taste and not interfere with neighboring exhibitors or otherwise detract from the general atmosphere of the event.

(continued on next page)

Issues Common To All Booth Types *(continued)*

Storage

Fire regulations in most exhibit facilities prohibit storing product, literature, empty packing containers or packing materials behind back drapes or under draped tables. In most cases, however, exhibitors may store a limited supply of literature or product appropriately within the booth area, so long as these items do not impede access to utility services, create a safety problem or look unsightly.

Demonstrations

As a matter of safety and courtesy to others, exhibitors should conduct sales presentations and product demonstrations in a manner which assures all exhibitor personnel and attendees are within the contracted exhibit space and not encroaching on the aisle or neighboring exhibits. It is the responsibility of each exhibitor to arrange displays, product presentation and demonstration areas to ensure compliance.

Special caution should be taken when demonstrating machinery or equipment that has moving parts, cooking equipment with an open flame, or any product that is otherwise potentially dangerous. Exhibitors should establish a minimum setback of three feet (3') and/or install hazard barriers as necessary to prevent accidental injury to spectators. Sound demonstrations should not exceed 85 decibels. Additionally, demonstrations should only be conducted by qualified personnel.

Sound/Music

In general, exhibitors may use sound equipment in their booths so long as the noise level does not disrupt the activities of neighboring exhibitors. Speakers and other sound devices should be positioned so as to direct sound into the booth rather than into the aisle. Rule of thumb: Sound and noise should not exceed 85 decibels.

Exhibitors should be aware that music played in their booths, whether live or recorded, may be subject to laws governing the use of copyrighted compositions. ASCAP, BMI and SESAC are three authorized licensing organizations that collect copyright fees on behalf of composers and publishers of music.

Advisory Notes To Exhibition Organizers

End-cap Booths: End-cap Booths cause more problems between exhibitors than any other type of booth, because most exhibitors fail to observe backwall height restrictions. Exhibition managers should be alert to exhibitors' reserving End-Cap configurations to ensure they do not violate Linear Booth line-of-sight regulations for neighboring exhibits.

Fire Equipment: Fire hoses and extinguishers should be visible and accessible at all times.

Hanging Signs: Although the Guidelines indicate sixteen feet (16') maximum height, some exhibitions permit eighteen feet (18'), twenty feet (20') or no limit. Caution should be exercised so exhibitors will not compete over air space for hanging signs.

Exhibitors should be advised to install "hanging points" at the time of manufacture of the sign or display.

Hardwall Booths: Expositions that provide Hardwall Booths should specify if these structures can be used for display and attaching products.

Line of Sight: It is common at certain events, such as gift and craft shows, to eliminate the line-of-sight requirement for Linear, End-Cap and Peninsula Booths that back up to Linear Booths. This permits exhibitors to utilize the full cubic content of the booth.

Perimeter Openings: Large peninsulas and islands with long high walls can create a "tunnel-like" effect. Exhibitors may be required to install a minimum six-foot (6') opening every thirty feet (30').

Pipe and Drape: These are commonly used at exhibitions to define exhibits. Exhibition managers often include in their Rules and Regulations that this equipment is not intended as a display fixture. Therefore product and signs should not be attached or affixed.

Product Height: Some exhibitors have products that exceed display height restrictions. Exhibition organizers should establish guidelines for displaying such products. For example, some shows require that these exhibitors reserve only perimeter space. Products exceeding height restrictions for Islands and Peninsulas are usually permitted.

Vehicles: Rules vary depending on the facility, but generally it is required that vehicles on display have no more than a 1/4 tank of gas. The filler cap should be sealed and the batteries disconnected. External chargers are usually recommended for demonstration purposes.

EXHIBIT PACKAGES

Some shows rent exhibitors only space, while others put together a basic exhibit package. A standard exhibit package includes an 8' x 10' or 10' x 10' exhibit space, a 8' tall pipe-and-drape backwall with 3' high side drapes between booth spaces, a 6' table draped on 3 sides, 2 chairs, a wastebasket and a 7" x 44" sign with the exhibitor's name and booth space number. Some show managers include a 500 Watt electrical outlet and a 9' x 10' carpet if the hall is not carpeted.

This type of package allows exhibitors to easily exhibit at a show for a fixed fee.

SPACE REQUIREMENTS

The total amount of space you will need to rent for your exhibit hall is called your Gross Square Feet (GSF). GSF includes space for aisles between your booths, registration areas, show offices, food stations, pillars, lounges, etc.

The Net Square Feet (NSF) is the amount of space you plan to convert into booth spaces for sale to exhibitors and excludes aisles, registration areas, show offices, food stations, pillars, lounges, etc.

The formula for computing how many Gross Square Feet to rent is: NSF x 2 = GSF.

CONVERSION OF BOOTH MEASUREMENTS FROM IMPERIAL TO METRIC

4' = 1.22 metres
5' = 1.52 metres
8' = 2.44 metres
10' = 3.05 metres
12' = 3.66 metres

TYPICAL TRADE SHOW FLOOR

SPACE ALLOCATION

Many exhibition managers hold their booth space selection for the following year's show during the current show. Exhibitors are given the opportunity to come to a sales office near the show floor at a specific time to select their booth space for the following year and sign a space contract at that time. Other show manager's accomplish space sign-up via email, fax or telephone after the current show has closed.

While every show will be guided by its own specific criteria for booth space selection, the following list may serve as a useful guideline:

- First come, first served
  - receive the exhibitor prospectus at the same time, a firm date for receiving - deposits or applications must be set, and an internal system to log signed contracts and payments must be in place

- Point system
  - points are given to potential exhibitors based on a number of factors (participation in previous years, number of consecutive years as an exhibitor, amount of NSF of booth space contracted, sponsorship and advertising spending, etc.) and booth space is selected by exhibitors in order of those with highest points to lowest points

- Lottery
  - considered to be fair, but may offend the large exhibitor who finds themselves in a remote corner. Space is awarded based on numerical order of the lot drawn

- Combination
  - in some cases, a combination of methods described above may be used.

Other considerations may include:

- Preference should be given to any company that has exhibited with the organization in previous trade shows.

- How closely the product or service offered by the applicant corresponds with the particular attendee profile may help determine how interested the participants will be.

- If any exhibitor requires too large a space, a special space or separate from the designated floor plan, this may be used as a criteria for rejection. If the possibility exists that the applicant could dominate the exhibition, to the detriment of others, it may not be a wise decision to accept the application.

- At some trade shows, booth selection priority is given to new exhibitors rather than those returning. This can alienate your loyal long-term exhibitors.

- If the show floor is divided into themed areas, one of the areas may be filled while others are not. In that case, an applicant for the filled area would be declined, though an applicant for another section where there is still space available, would be accepted.

- Consideration should be given to companies for past participation if they have been acquired or merged with another exhibitor. Generally, show management acknowledges the company with the higher number of priority points for future space selection.

ESTABLISHING TRADE SHOW HOURS

Trade shows that are part of a conference should have dedicated show hours that do not compete with keynotes, seminars or workshops. Exhibitors expect a reasonable amount of unopposed time for conference delegates to spend on the trade show floor, as they have invested a substantial amount of money and effort in their participation.

~ Sample Template ~

ESTIMATED TRADE SHOW REVENUE

Booth Space Sales
    Premium Space Sales $_____
    Meeting Room Rental $_____
Sponsorships $_____
Advertising $_____
Revenue Sharing with Official Contractors $_____
Interest from Cash Flow $_____
    Total Revenue $_____

ESTIMATED EXPENSES

Advertising $_____
Aisle Carpet Rental $_____
Audio-Visual Equipment and Staging Labor $_____
Cleaning and Post-Show Trash Removal $_____
Communication (staff radios) $_____
Computer Equipment /Internet/Labor $_____
Decorating (Exhibit Hall Décor i.e.entrance unit, masking drape) $_____
Exhibit Packages (pipe, drape, table, chairs, signage) $_____
Exhibitor Education $_____
Facility Rental $_____
Floral $_____
Food and Beverage (staff, space draw, meals, receptions) $_____
Giveaways (registration bags, etc.) $_____
Ground Transportation (shuttles) $_____
Insurance (event cancellation, general liability) $_____
Legal Fees (contract review, etc.) $_____
Marketing (exhibitor and attendee including list development) $_____
Material Handling (Drayage) $_____
Meeting Room Rental (show offices) $_____
Office Equipment $_____
Printing (prospectus, exhibitor manual) $_____
Registration Kiosks and Labor $_____
Registration System, Staff Expenses and Materials $_____
Research $_____
Risk Management Planning $_____
Security $_____
Shipping and Freight   `$_____

Information on
CD Rom

~ *Sample Template* ~

Information on CD Rom

Signage (directional, aisle)	$_____
Keynote or Speaker Expenses	$_____
Sponsorship Collateral and Fulfillment	$_____
Staff Expenses:	
Administrative Overhead	$_____
Exhibit Sales Commissions	$_____
Staff Salaries/Benefits	$_____
Travel, Lodging, Food and Beverage	$_____
Temporary Staff	$_____
Travel and Entertainment	$_____
Utilities	
Electrical	$_____
Internet (wired or wireless)	$_____
Telephone	$_____
Gas	$_____
Web Site Design and Maintenance	$_____
Total Expenses	$_____
Total possible number of 10' x 10' booth spaces	_____
Divide total cost by total booth spaces	$_____
Add profit per booth	$_____
Total booth rental fee	$_____

The cost of rented booth space is generally calculated by the square foot or in increments of 100 net square feet. This cost may be increased depending on the type of booth space, prime location, the perceived desirability and number of booth spaces available of each type. For example, a premium may be charged for corner linear booths compared to standard linear booths because of the additional access to the aisle. Some show managers charge corner premiums on all booth spaces, including peninsulas and islands.

Complimentary space might be considered for such groups as sponsors or affiliated organizations who will attract additional exhibitors and attendees to your show.

Start-up costs for shows are high due to the preliminary marketing costs to build both an exhibitor and attendee base.

SOURCES OF POTENTIAL EXHIBITORS

Marketing of a trade show's booth space should concentrate on those companies whose products and services relate closely to the attendee's needs and to the theme of the trade show. Show managers often reserve the right in their space contract to exclude those exhibitors who do not match their exhibitor criteria.

PAST EXHIBITORS

If previous exhibitions have been conducted, past exhibitor lists present a solid foundation for potential exhibitors at future trade shows.

COMMERCIAL MAILING LISTS

There are a number of services that assemble and maintain current mailing lists for virtually any type of business or interest. They then sell these lists to other businesses.

OTHER EXHIBITIONS

There are companies who maintain databases of companies who exhibit at trade shows, or you can attend competitive shows to gain access to their exhibitor directory. The World Wide Web is a great source of information on potential exhibitors as some shows list all exhibitor information online.

INDUSTRY ASSOCIATIONS/GROUPS

Member-based organizations, such as industry associations and groups, convention and visitors' bureaus (CVB's) and local chambers of commerce are also good sources from which to acquire potential exhibitors. The members of these organizations generally have a common interest in a specific subject matter, industry or market segment.

INDUSTRY PUBLICATIONS

Purchasing a list of the names of advertisers or subscribers to industry- or market-specific magazines and trade publications that are of interest to your audience is also a good source of exhibitors.

MARKETING TO EXHIBITORS

When the meeting professional is satisfied that the space being considered will suit the needs of the event, the task of marketing the trade show to prospective exhibitors can begin. It is important to realize that potential exhibitors have many trade shows to choose from. The meeting professional must demonstrate why a prospective exhibitor should participate in this particular trade show. If previous trade shows have successfully occurred, then the task of marketing to and attracting potential exhibitors becomes much easier. Consider the following marketing ideas to help attract exhibitors:

- Provide a demographic profile of the attendees at past conferences and trade shows. Be sure to include information on attendees' roles or position titles, interest by product type, size of organizations represented, decision-making authority, budgets, timeframes to purchase, etc.

If your trade show has been audited by an independent third party to verify attendee and exhibitor demographics, publish your audit results and provide summaries of your results to both current and potential exhibitors.

- If possible, offer potential exhibitors the opportunity to showcase or feature any new products or services. This can occur either in trade show attendee brochures, on the show's Web site or in a designated area on the exhibit floor.

- Offer exhibitors a mailing list of the previous year's attendees and current year's pre-registration list of delegates who will be attending the show. If you are reluctant to give out your attendee lists, offer exhibitors the opportunity to submit their promotional materials to be labeled and mailed to your list(s) through an independent mailing house.

- Identify those companies who have previously exhibited. If a potential exhibitor sees that the competition is exhibiting, they may feel the need to participate as well.

EXHIBITOR PROSPECTUS

The primary tool used to attract and inform exhibitors is the exhibitor prospectus. This tool is used to provide interested companies with all the information they need in order to make a decision to exhibit. While each prospectus may be somewhat different, a typical prospectus would include the following information:

- name of conference/trade show

- dates of conference and trade show (which may be different) including move-in and move-out dates

- exhibit hall or facility and location

- show schedule, including total number of unopposed exhibit hall hours

- attendee demographics from prior year and note if these figures were audited by an independent third party

- number of attendees anticipated for next show

- number of exhibitors

- conference/trade show theme

- benefits of exhibiting

- types and sizes of booth spaces and exhibits allowed

- floor plan (printed on a separate sheet as changes will be made a number of times during booth space sales)

- booth space or package fees and payment schedule

- cancellation and refund policy

- sponsorship and speaker opportunities

- education, product promotion and public relations opportunities

- application form/contract with terms and conditions

- exhibit space sales contact person name, telephone, fax and email

NAME OF MEETING

Include name of conference/trade show and also the name of the association or sponsor

DATE(S) OF CONFERENCE AND TRADE SHOW

Exhibitors need to know the exact dates of the conference and trade show, which may not be the same, to determine if it fits into their plans and other commitments.

EXHIBIT FACILITY AND LOCATION

The description should include property, city and country. Most exhibitors will want to know where the exhibit space is located in relation to other activities and facilities. It may affect their request for specific booth locations.

CONFERENCE AND SHOW SCHEDULE SUMMARY

If the trade show is scheduled to start after the conference or end before the conference, the exhibitor must make plans accordingly. Exhibitors need to be able to schedule their staff to work at the trade show and must have exact dates. Exhibition hours should appear in an overview section in a format designed to stand out. The times set aside for attendees to visit the exhibit floor and unopposed hours with no conflicting activities should be spelled out.

DEMOGRAPHICS/NUMBER OF ATTENDEES

The demographics of the attendees will provide the exhibitor with information to adequately assess whether they are potential customers. The presentation of realistic data, in the form of previous year's attendance of delegates minus exhibitor personnel and conference staff, and estimated delegate attendance for the upcoming event are key to helping a potential exhibitor analyze the opportunity and build loyalty among current exhibitors. If you have had your show audited by an independent third-party, provide your exhibitors with a summary of this information in your exhibitor prospectus.

CONFERENCE THEME

The theme is important to the potential exhibitor when deciding if their products fit within the context of the conference, or in limiting those products they choose to display. This is a good place to sell the benefit of the theme to potential exhibitors.

BENEFITS OF EXHIBITING

It is in this area that the arguments can be presented as to why the exhibitor should attend this trade show. Providing information on buying influence of the attendees, market segmentation, demographics and psychographics of the potential attendees should be presented. Hard data, in the form of actual statistics from previous event history and preferably audited by an independent third party, is crucial to help convince the exhibitor to participate.

FLOOR PLAN

Design and include a copy of the current floor plan to give potential exhibitors a reference, enabling them to request a certain booth or area, and to understand the scope of the exhibition. If they have an existing display or exhibit, it will also give them a reasonable estimate for the size of space they require. This is probably one of the more important parts of the prospectus for the corporate exhibit manager, so the floor plan should be accurate and to scale. Ideally, it should include:

- description of standard booth unit

- free form/island space availability

- entrances and exits

- registration and traffic flow from conference sessions

- scientific/poster areas

- show offices

- ceiling height

- aisle width

- obstructions (columns, fire apparatus with set-backs, balconies, pipes, fixtures)

- freight dock and freight elevator locations, dimensions and capacities

- utilities available in booth spaces (water, gas, phone, compressed air, Internet, telecommunications, etc.)

- food and beverage concessions and seating

- rest rooms

- exhibitor lounge

- floor load

- feature areas such as product neighborhoods, new product showcases, international pavilions and start-up company zones

In addition to exhibitor booth spaces, featured areas such as educational theaters, birds-of-a-feather roundtables, food and rest areas, Internet cafés and bookstores can attract show attendees to the exhibit floor and encourage them to linger there.

SPACE FEES/PAYMENTS

The price of each booth space type should be clearly stated in the Exhibitor Prospectus. Be sure to describe what the price includes, (e.g. packages that include pipe and drape, carpet, basic 7" x 44" signage, table, chairs, wastebasket, etc.) or if the cost is for raw space.

All financial information should be presented here. A percentage deposit is commonly requested with the application form. Provide the dates when additional payments are due. Also include guidelines for cancellation and refunds.

SPONSORSHIP OPPORTUNITIES

Sponsorships, also known as marketing promotional opportunities, provide exhibitors with ways to increase their visibility to attendees at the trade show by increasing the number of impressions. Sponsorships can be sold either as packages including a number of items or individually for a flat fee. Before considering the purchase of a sponsorship, the exhibiting company will want some assurance of a good return on their investment. Sponsorships are usually limited in number to ensure exclusivity.

Trade show floor sponsorships might include:

- refreshment breaks or a branded espresso or ice cream cart

- breakfast or lunch

- Internet café

- banners and signage

- educational sessions or speakers

- rest areas and lounges

- bookstore

- badge lanyards

EXHIBIT SPACE APPLICATION FORM/CONTRACT

This form should be simple and concise. It should include all the pertinent information concerning the exhibitor including:

- exhibit, marketing and press contacts' names, telephone numbers and email addresses
- booth space preferences (giving the exhibitor space to request up to 4 choices)
- area to compute cost of their exhibit (package or net square footage) and deposit due
- product or service to be shown (if it is a juried show)
- product listing of 25 to 50 words for the attendee program or show Web site
- requests for proximity to other exhibitors, or competitors that they do not wish to be near
- how the application should be submitted
- any pertinent deadlines

TERMS AND CONDITIONS

List all terms and conditions, referencing rules and regulations that will follow as part of the exhibitor manual, that are related to the use of booth space, exhibitor conduct, show management and facility restrictions.

CONTACT PERSON

When an exhibitor has a question, it must be answered as quickly and accurately as possible to show the professionalism of show management. Promotional materials should include a telephone number, email address and Web site URL for the show.

~ *Sample Template* ~

SAMPLE EXHIBITOR PROSPECTUS

THE EVENT OF THE YEAR

WHAT?

Hundreds of associations will be represented by key decision makers at HOST's National Conference and Showcase October 2-4. For all those who sell products and services to the association market, exhibiting at this event can be a very effective sales call to meet X# of association buyers.

Showcase will feature more than 110 10' x 10' booths. This year we continue to offer great exposure as Showcase will run on Friday afternoon, October 3. Showcase will be open to registered Conference delegates and meetings industry professionals and association staff. We expect to see a busy show floor.

Don't delay! Book today for this significant opportunity to market to an influential group of buyers.

WHEN AND WHERE?

Showcase 2006 will be held in conjunction with HOST's National Conference at the HOTEL in LOCATION, October 2-4.

WHO?

The HOST is …….

HOST members are professionals continually striving to keep pace in a rapidly changing environment while, at the same time, developing and maintaining an effective and cost efficient operation. They rely on events like this to provide their own convenient one-stop shopping experience and to learn about the many new goods and services that are available.

~ *Sample Template* ~

WHY EXHIBIT?

If your company has a product or service that is of use to executives, this show is for you. Key decision-makers from across Canada will attend the show — your best opportunity for direct access to the most important decision-makers in the field.

SCHEDULE OF EVENTS

Thursday, October 2

Morning Intensive Workshops

Afternoon Intensive Workshops

Opening Ceremonies and Plenary Session

Evening Welcome Reception

Showcase Setup

Friday, October 3

Morning Breakfast and Keynote

Concurrent Sessions

Afternoon Honors and Awards Presentation

Lunch

5-Hour Showcase

Evening Discover Victoria

Saturday, October 4

Morning Breakfast

Concurrent Plenary Sessions

Annual General Meeting

Afternoon Concurrent Sessions

Plenary Session and Closing Ceremonies

Evening Reception and Dinner

~ *Sample Template* ~

CONFERENCE PROGRAM

A preliminary conference program and registration form will be forwarded under separate cover. Exhibit prices do not include registration to conference or networking functions.

DRAW PRIZES

Suppliers are encouraged to donate prizes for which attendee names will be drawn throughout the show. Attendees will be asked to deposit business cards into a bowl, hat or box you provide at your display. The prizes will be drawn from the cards left at your display. After the draw, all business cards are yours to keep.

ACCOMMODATIONS

A block of rooms has been reserved at the following hotels. You must contact the hotel individually to book your reservations prior to September 2 in order to receive HOST conference rates. Please ask for the HOST room block.

CONFERENCE HOTELS

NAME OF HOTEL
LIST SINGLE AND DOUBLE RATES, ADDITIONAL PERSON
ADDRESS
TELEPHONE

Note if any of the hotels is the "official show hotel" and the proximity of the block hotels to the conference venue, if not providing a printed map or Web site URL to an online map.

Note if there is a conference code to refer to when making your reservation to get the reduced housing block rate.

~ *Sample Template* ~

SHOW MANAGEMENT

HOST 2006 and Showcase 2006 are managed by HOST.
Questions should be referred to
NAME at TELEPHONE NUMBER or EMAIL

WHAT'S INCLUDED

Included in your Display Fees are one 8' deep by 10' wide booth space, pipe and drape, one black and white 7" x 44" sign with your company name, one listing in the Showcase 2006 Show Guide, one early bird and one final delegate list and two exhibitor badges. The show floor is carpeted.

Display fees do not include access to education or networking events at HOST 2006.

DISPLAY FEES AND REGISTRATION

For each 8' x 10' booth space:

	NONMEMBER	MEMBER
Early Bird (before April 5, 2006)*	$1000	$1495
Regular rate (after April 4, 2006)	$1145	$1795

Purchase 3 or more booths and receive a 10% discount off any rate.

The Early Bird rate only applies to those applications received and paid in full by April 4, 2006.

Please complete the attached "Exhibit Space Application/Contract" and send it together with full payment to:

> Showcase 2006
> c/o HOST
> Address
> City, State or Province, Country
> Postal or ZIP Code

~ *Sample Template* ~

SIGN ME UP!

YES! We are interested in sponsorship opportunities that will increase our exposure and contact with delegates.

☐ Please contact me with more information on sponsorship levels and benefits.

First Name _____ Last Name _____

Title _____ Membership # _____

Organization _____

Address _____

City _____ Prov/State _____ Postal/Zip Code _____

Phone _____ Fax _____

Email _____

PAYMENT INFORMATION

This application must be accompanied by the total amount due. Booth location will not be confirmed until payment is received. The Early Bird rate only applies to those applications received and paid in full by April 4.

Early Bird Booths
Member Rate   _____ @ $1000.00 = $_____
Non-Member Rate   _____ @ $1495.00 = $_____

Regular Rate Booths
Member Rate   _____ @ $1145.00 = $_____
Non-Member Rate   _____ @ $1795.00 = $_____

Multiple Booth Discount (10%) - $_____

Booth Fees Total = $_____

~ Sample Template ~

PAYMENT METHOD

☐ Cheque ☐ VISA ☐ MasterCard ☐ American Express

Card Number_____ Exp. Date_____

Verification Code _____

Billing Address_____

City_____ Prov/State_____ Postal Code/Zip Code _____

Name of Cardholder_____

Signature of Cardholder_____

BOOTH SPACE SELECTIONS

Please note that booth space locations will be assigned on a first-come, first-served basis.

1st Choice _____ 2nd Choice_____ 3rd Choice _____

Please do NOT locate me adjacent to:

_____

If this application is accepted, the Exhibitor agrees to be bound by the terms and conditions on the reverse side of this application and by those set forth in the Showcase 2006 exibitor manual. The undersigned is fully authorized to commit the Exhibitor to all terms and conditions of this contract. An unsigned contract will be returned.

Signature_____

Print Name_____ Date_____

~ *Sample Template* ~

TERMS AND CONDITIONS OF CONTRACT BETWEEN EXHIBITOR AND HOST ("MANAGEMENT")

1. Management reserves the right to alter or change the space assigned to the Exhibitor. Management further reserves the right, at its sole discretion to change the date or dates upon which the show is held, or to cancel the show, and shall not be liable in damages or otherwise by reason of any such change or cancellation, other than to refund in full any amounts paid by the Exhibitor to Management.

2. The Exhibitor shall not assign this contract or sublet the space or any part thereof or permit same to be used by any other person, without the prior written consent of Management. Any attempt to do so is null and void and will result in immediate cancellation of this contract, and the forfeiture of any amounts paid by the Exhibitor to Management.

3. The Exhibitor shall comply with all rules and regulations by Management for the show and agrees that Management's decision to adopt and enforce any such rule or regulation shall be final and binding.

4. The Exhibitor is responsible for compliance with all applicable laws, bylaws, ordinances, regulations, requirements, codes and standards, including those with respect to fire, safety, health and environmental matters and shall ensure that all equipment, materials and goods used by the Exhibitor so comply.

5. The Exhibitor shall indemnify and hold Management harmless from and against any loss, injury or damages whatsoever suffered by Management as a result the Exhibitor's failure to comply with the terms and conditions of this contract or as a result of the Exhibitor's participation in the show, including without limitation, any third party claim against Management with respect to loss, injury or damage sustained or suffered by any other exhibitors, the owner of the building, attendees of the show, and their respective directors, officers, agents and employees.

6. This contract may be cancelled by either party provided written notice is received by the other by August 31, in which case all monies paid by the

Exhibitor will be refunded less an administration fee of $250 per booth. If the Exhibitor cancels after such date, it will be responsible for the full contract price.

7. Management reserves the right at any time to alter or remove exhibits or any part thereof, including printed material, products, signs, lights or sound, and to expel exhibitors or their personnel if, in Management's opinion, their conduct or presentation is objectionable to Management or to other show participants.

8. Exhibitor's display must comply with all requirements of Management and of the owner of the building, including maximum height requirements. The Exhibitor must provide at least one, and not more than two, staff per booth/marketplace to maintain exhibit during show hours. The Exhibitor agrees to confine its presentation and marketing activities to the contracted booth space only.

9. All goods shipped to the show must be clearly marked with the name of the Exhibitor and the number of the booth space. Goods must not be shipped to the show for any shipping charges to be paid on arrival and any such goods will not be accepted by Management. Management assumes no responsibility for loss or damage to the Exhibitor's goods or property either before, during or after the show.

10. In consideration of the Exhibitor's participation in the show, the Exhibitor hereby releases Management, its directors, officers, agents and employees from any and all claims, losses, or damages whatsoever suffered or sustained by the Exhibitor in connection with its participation in the show, including, without limitation, any claims for loss or theft of property, personal injury, or loss of business or profits, whether arising from any act of Management or otherwise.

11. The Exhibitor is responsible for the placement and cost of insurance relating to its participation in the show. The Exhibitor shall carry liability insurance of $2 million, as well as such additional insurance as may be required by Management.

~ *Sample Template* ~

The Exhibitor agrees to furnish immediately to Management upon request certificates of insurance pertaining to policies of insurance carried by the Exhibitor together with satisfactory evidence from the insurers of the continuation of such policies. If the Exhibitor fails to comply with any of the foregoing, in addition to any other rights or remedies available to Management at law or under this contract, Management shall have the right to take possession of the display space for such purposes as it sees fit and the Exhibitor will be held liable for the full contract price for the said space.

12. The Exhibitor agrees that no display may be dismantled or goods removed during the entire run of the show. The Exhibitor agrees to remove the exhibit, equipment and appurtenances from the show building by the final move-out time. In the event of failure to do so, the Exhibitor agrees to pay for such additional costs as may be incurred by Management.

13. The Exhibitor will comply with the rules and regulations of any unionized contractors, which may be selected by Management to service the exhibitors. Any dispute between the Exhibitor and any such contractor or union representative will be referred to Management for resolution, whose decision shall be final and binding on all parties.

14. Management reserves the right to cancel this contract and to withhold possession of the space or to expel the Exhibitor there from if the Exhibitor fails to comply with any terms and conditions of this contract or the show rules and regulation, in which case the Exhibitor shall forfeit as liquidated damages and not as a penalty all payments made pursuant to this contract, all without limiting Management's other rights and remedies at law under this contract as a result of such failure to comply.

15. Processing of payment by Management does not in itself constitute acceptance into Showcase 2006.

Disclaimer: These templates are provided for reference purposes only and are not intended to apply to any specific event. Qualified professional and legal advice should be sought when drafting any contract.

EXHIBITOR MANUAL

It is in the best interest of all trade show stakeholders that clear policies and regulations for exhibits be established and communicated to the exhibiting companies.

After a contract has been signed and deposit or payment made for booth space, show management provides an Exhibitor Manual outlining rules and regulations, timelines and forms for ordering show services and marketing opportunities for the exhibitor. It is the responsibility of show management to see that all information is included in this manual and that the information is accurate and consistent, whether in a hard-copy binder mailed to the exhibitor or online on the show's Web site.

The Exhibitor Manual includes the following:

- Names and contact information of key trade show management personnel

- Fact sheet of basic show information

- Key deadlines

- Current floor plan

- Contractor information from the general service contractor, exclusive contractors, and official contractors and subcontractors with their show service order forms

- Information on naming exhibitor-appointed contractors and the notification form

- Exhibitor badge information and order forms

- Information on hotel accommodations and travel

- Marketing and sponsorship opportunities

- Press and media opportunities

- Shipping information including customs broker information

- Move-in and move-out schedules for exhibitors

- Overview of unions and basic jurisdictions

- Rules and regulations for exhibitors

- Updates

The general service contractor's portion of the Exhibitor Manual provides information, pricing, and order forms for show services. Once an exhibitor is confirmed, the exhibitor manual is sent to the exhibitor by the meeting professional or GSC.

Forms in the Exhibitor Manual will enable exhibitor to contract for:

- accessible on-site storage
- A/V rental and labor
- carpet cleaning and porter service
- carpet/pad rental and labor
- catering
- compressed air
- computer and office equipment rental
- credit card authorization(s)
- customs brokerage
- electrical
- exhibit accessories
- exhibit system or custom design and rental
- exhibitor-appointed contractors
- exhibitor badges
- floral arrangements and plants
- forklift (in-booth)
- furnishings (standard and custom)
- graphics production
- hotel rooms
- installation and dismantle (I & D) labor (by the general service contractor)
- Internet access and equipment rental
- lead retrieval system rental
- material handling (drayage)
- office equipment rental
- photography
- pipe and drape
- plumbing
- promotional opportunities and sponsorships
- rigging
- shipping
- sign production
- security
- telephone and telecommunications
- temporary staff
- third party billing form
- travel (air and car rental)
- water

Exhibitors are responsible for completing the order forms for the products and services they require by the deadline date specified on the form and sending the completed form with payment or credit card information to the contractor named on the form. Costs for all these services are in addition to the expense of the booth space rental unless provided as part of a booth space package to exhibitors. Many of these forms will have early-bird deadlines which can save exhibitors substantial amounts.

It should be noted that some facilities have exclusive contracts with companies to provide some of the services listed above. Exhibitors are not required to use the official vendors whose forms appear in the Exhibitor Manual. Exhibitors should check with Show Management to determine which vendors have the exclusive right to provide products and services in the facility and must be used and which vendors are official and are only recommended vendors for products and services.

SHIPPING AND MATERIAL HANDLING

Coordination of exhibitor shipping and receiving of exhibit materials must be carefully planned and those procedures clearly stated here in the Exhibitor Manual. The shipping information form should include a place to list the name of the carrier being used, if the shipment is being sent to the advance warehouse or direct-to-site, and when it will arrive. If large exhibit properties are anticipated, it is a good idea to ask the size of the largest freight container to assure that adequate forklifts are on available. If materials are being shipped from overseas, a reputable customs broker should be suggested for the use of exhibitors. Information on the costs associated with material handling (drayage) and special handling fees, off target penalties, and overtime costs should be included.

MOVE-IN / MOVE-OUT

The exhibition manager, in conjunction with the general service contractor, will design a schedule that indicates which exhibitors may move in and out of the hall at specific times. There may be financial penalties to those exhibitors whose shipping carriers do not arriving for unloading or loading at the designated times.

For larger trade shows or those with limited dock access, it may be necessary to gather exhibitors' trucks at a nearby location in order to facilitate their orderly arrival at available docks at show site. This location is called a marshaling yard.

FACILITY SELECTION AND REGULATIONS

The exhibition manager should pay particular attention to the facility's rules and regulations. Privately-owned facilities such as hotels and conference centers typically operate quite differently from convention facilities owned and operated by some level of government. Three particular areas to investigate are exclusive contracts, use of union labor and fire regulations.

If the facility has entered in an exclusive contract with providers of services such as A/V or computer rentals, exhibitors lose their ability to control their costs by using their own vendors for these services, which can increase an exhibitor's overall cost to participate.

It is the exhibition manager's responsibility to understand if the facility has entered into contracts with unions that stipulate the jurisdictions covered, work rules and union pay scales. Possible labor disruptions due to contract negotiations during the time period surrounding the trade show should also be considered.

Fire regulations often restrict the floor layout, the types of exhibit materials that can be used and the type of product demonstrations that can take place. The fire marshal will be involved in floor layout and have the final approval of the floor plans, and inspectors will sometimes tour the show floor to insure that both show management and exhibitors are complying with all applicable fire regulations.

EXHIBITOR INSURANCE

The exhibition manager may require each exhibitor to carry third-party insurance in order to participate in the show. The facility will determine a threshold amount, though show management may require a higher amount. Copies of certificates of insurance for both general liability and workers' compensation insurance policies should be supplied by each exhibitor, naming appropriate additional insureds such as the show organizer, show management, the facility and the general service contractor.

EXHIBITOR-APPOINTED CONTRACTORS (EACS)

If exhibitors do not wish to use the products and services provided by the general service contractor and official contractors, they may select to use vendors of their own choice, called Exhibitor-Appointed Contractors (EACs). These exhibitor-chosen vendors are also known as Exhibitor-Designated Contractors (EDCs). Show management provides forms in the exhibitor manual for exhibitors to notify show management of their intent to hire EACs. These forms spell out the responsibilities of both the exhibitor and EAC, including completion of a form stating the exhibitor's intent to hire an EAC and submission of a certificate of insurance in the types and amounts required with specific additionally-named insureds.

SEVEN PLANNING STEPS FOR SUCCESS

1. SELECTING APPROPRIATE FACILITY AND SPACE

When planning trade shows, it is important to match the services, layout and equipment as closely as possible to the profile of the event. Small to medium sized trade shows do not require the same type of facility, space and services as large, complex ones. For example, if the trade show has a number of exhibitors occupying large booth spaces, it probably also has labor-intensive exhibits that require a facility with extensive loading dock access and large freight elevator, if a multi-story facility with upper level exhibit space. For this type of an event, extra time for move-in/move-out and heavy equipment to transport the displays from the loading dock to the booth areas is generally required. In the case of small to medium sized trade shows, in which small displays are used and setups relatively simple, the costs associated with major convention facilities and services can be avoided.

2. CREATING AND MANAGING AN EFFECTIVE TRADE SHOW FLOOR PLAN

The floor plan design is a key element in the overall success of a trade show and should be customized to reflect the needs of the exhibitors. For instance, if the majority of exhibitors prefer 10' by 10' booth spaces, then the floor plan should be designed to accommodate them. Traffic flow around the exhibit hall will be most effective when it optimizes the exhibit hall space, minimizing obstructions such as columns, floor ports for utility access and fire apparatus. A trade show floor plan should be designed to consider related activities such as food and beverage stations and feature areas.

3. CONTRACTING SHOW SERVICES

Trade shows are complex events, involving many different services and suppliers. A clear understanding of the scope of the event, the times allotted for move-in/move-out, and the types of heavy equipment and services that exhibitors may require will help the exhibition manager secure a general service contractor who can properly service the needs of show management, exhibitors and attendees. A good general service contractor works closely with the exhibition manager to design the exhibit floor plan, secure the necessary equipment, arrange utilities and source services and equipment from other suppliers, if required. Be specific in your request for proposal (RFP) to general service contractors as to what services are required and when. Remember to include security services to guard the exhibit hall and other key areas during non-show hours.

4. PLANNING ADEQUATE MOVE-IN / MOVE-OUT TIME

A smooth and effective move-in/move-out process requires careful planning and attention to detail. When contracting with the facility, the exhibition manager will need to provide adequate time for these two key elements. Incorrect planning can cause problems and increased costs for all involved and result in dissatisfied exhibitors. The previous event history and other data pertinent to the event will assist you in booking the time and services that are appropriate for the success of your trade show. Remember that the larger the event, the more complex the scheduling with regard to the move-in and move-out of exhibitor and show freight. You may need to reserve the exhibit space for a number of days before and after a large show to facilitate smooth move-in/move-out.

You will need to schedule all on-site contractors in advance of the event to coordinate when they will be available onsite. Be aware that payment of overtime varies by day, hour, venue, labor source and union jurisdiction. Also, if move-out begins after 4:00 p.m., (16:00), shipping services may not be available until the next day or may be charged at higher overtime rates. Finish the show early on the last day to permit a smooth move-out, if possible.

5. OPTIMIZING ADMINISTRATION AND COMMUNICATION EFFICIENCY

Too few shows reinforce positive exhibitor relations with solid, clear, concise administrative management and ongoing communications throughout the year.

Be clear about the policies and procedures for exhibitors to participate in all show phases and be accurate and consistent about times, dates, schedules, and deadlines. Provide clear requirements for exhibitor action or feedback. Checklists with return dates for securing services and other trade show-related items are excellent tools for exhibitors. Consider all exhibitors' requests for variances to your show policies and procedures, keeping in mind best practices for all exhibitors.

6. EFFECTIVELY MANAGING EXHIBITOR REGISTRATION PROCEDURES

One of the most time-consuming and hard-to-control tasks in preparing for a trade show is compiling exhibitor names and titles to produce final name badges for exhibit staff. Many businesses are unable to finalize their exhibit staff rosters in advance; therefore, lists constantly change prior to the event. Identify a date approximately two weeks prior to show opening when exhibitors must submit their badge request form, either in hard copy or online.

If badges are being mailed to the exhibitors in advance of the event, be specific about when they can expect to receive them. If badges will only be available for pick-up at the event, be specific about when and where they can be claimed onsite. Remember that this is generally not a priority for exhibitors prior to the event, so be prepared by having adequate staff and resources available onsite to efficiently process changes to existing names or titles of exhibitor badges.

7. SECURING THE RIGHT ONSITE TEAM

A well-coordinated show management staff can make move-in / move-out a positive experience for both exhibitors and show management. If the convention includes educational sessions, requires a complicated move-in / move-out or has a large show floor, plan for adequate staffing. Build in the ability to have one or two "floater" staff, known as floor managers, available to respond to requests from exhibitors or suppliers, so that senior show management can oversee the overall event. Having sufficient radios or cell phones for all staff that need to stay in communication will expedite problem resolution. Your ability to deliver outstanding service during this phase of the event can make or break its success. Be prepared with a written plan and staff the plan appropriately.

ATTRACTING ATTENDEES

Once the trade show floor is designed and exhibit sales are underway, the exhibition manager must market the show to prospective attendees.

Features on the show floor will help to draw attendees to the exhibits; knowledgeable and engaging exhibitors will keep them there.

Possible added attractions to promote show floor attendance include:

- food and beverage

- new product area

- opening ceremony

- Internet cafés

- educational sessions

- theater or keynote areas

- raffles with prize drawings

- exhibitor passport programs

- celebrity demonstrations

- rest areas and lounges

- informal birds-of-a-feather area

- poster area

- bookstore or resources area

If the trade show is part of a conference, all marketing pieces should be integrated. If the trade show stands alone, typical marketing methods will apply.

~ A Conference Journal ~

In celebration of the millennium, two associations combined their annual conferences into one full week of educational sessions and social events. They decided not to do the same with their respective trade shows but opted to run them as separate entities, one from Sunday to noon on Wednesday and the second from midday Wednesday to the close of the conference on Friday.

There were several reasons for this decision with the first being space limitations. Once they had determined the site for the conference, they also realized that there was no room for a single combined trade show, since each show needed close to 200,000 sq. ft. It would have been physically impossible to merge the two without losing 50% of the revenue. Additionally, the suppliers and buyers of products and services were very different from one another, although the two organizations represented the same industry. After lengthy consideration, they decided to setup each show independently using their existing managers, while marketing the shows jointly with the conference.

Each show represented a significant source of revenue for the association; however, booth sales were managed very differently between the two. The first show generally sold itself, year after year. Once the exhibitor prospectus was mailed out, prior year exhibitors were given a deadline to renew and an option to have the same booth space back as in the previous year, in return for early renewal. Alternatively, if they wished to move, early renewal ensured that they had first choice on another available prime location. This alone resulted in a 65% sellout rate. Slowly, the remainder of the show would sell until just a few weeks prior to the conference. The reason for this success is that they were well known as one of the largest annual events of its kind in the world. There were approximately 700 10' by 10' booth spaces in this floor plan, with the majority sold as singles, a relatively small number of doubles and about four or five islands.

The second show had a commissionable sales team representing different geographical areas across the country. The sales team attended other trade shows during the year to sell booth space and actively promoted their show. The primary reason for this stepped-up activity was competition. They were not the only exhibition in their industry that provided a showcase for their type of products and services. There were numerous trade shows held around the world annually and the competition was significant. With a lot of hard work, their show sold out and was a great success. Because of the heavy equipment on display, some of the booth spaces were large, open areas approximately the size of 20 or 30 one hundred square foot booth spaces.

With so many differences between these two shows, it is easy to see why they needed to be managed independently from one another. As a result, each show produced their own exhibitor manual and established independent contracts using their preferred contractors for setup, carpeting, exhibit installation and dismantle, furniture rental, signs and graphics, decorating and material handling of exhibits. Both associations responded to the needs of their exhibitors and made special provisions, including reduced booth space fees, for exhibitors who exhibited in both shows.

Traditionally, entry to the shows was limited to industry representatives who were registered for the conference but in this special year, the shows were open to the public. When advertising the conference, promotional pieces included the two trade shows and for the first time, advertisements in trade magazines and journals featured invitations to attend the show only. The industry was so large, it was felt that many individuals who did not register for the conference would attend the shows. One of the organizations also promoted their show to outlying regions and offered complimentary buses to the show site.

To consider a show to be successful, a look from several perspectives is required. The planning committee considered the sold-out show to be a success but the exhibitors had a different viewpoint. Their needs included a guarantee of qualified visitors in large numbers to provide them with the opportunity for face-to-face interaction with prospective clients thereby increasing the potential for current or future sales. The difficulty with running a show within the context of a conference is that both areas compete for the delegates' time. In this case, sessions ran from 9:00 a.m. to 5:00 p.m. (9:00 – 17:00) and the shows had similar timing except that the show floors were open for an hour longer than the conference sessions. This was not enough to lure people to the trade show, since the conferences also included evening social events.

Both organizations knew that they needed to conduct a number of scheduled events on the show floor to entice delegates. The first show organized a raffle drawing for a prize valued at over $15,000. The contest consisted of a passport that required these stamp of at least 15 exhibiting companies spread throughout each of the aisles of the show. This ensured that at least those that entered the draw had to visit every aisle from one end of the hall to the other. Surprisingly, there were quite a number of entries. The winner was drawn at the end of the show and this too became an opportunity for media to cover the story. Overall, this event was considered to be very successful.

The second show had many successful years and they benefited from the manager's expertise in conducting show features throughout the exhibition. They scheduled a trade show opening ceremony; invited VIPs; had media coverage; and followed this with an opening reception hosted by one of their largest sponsors. On the second day, another major sponsor hosted an evening reception. Both organizations also made sure that a hot lunch would be available for sale on the show floor in addition to regular concession booths. Informal seating either with small café tables and chairs or park benches also helped visitors remain on the show floor.

Delegates attended the conference for different reasons, some for education and networking while for others, it presented a global, personal shopping experience. For many, the trade show provided all three, while others rarely visited the show floor, preferring to go to the formal sessions and social events for their networking.

TRADE SHOW CHECKLIST

☐ Types of trade shows and exhibitions

    o business to business (B2B)

    o business to consumer (B2C)

    o vertical

    o horizontal

    o international

    o domestic

    o regional

    o local

☐ Key personnel

    o exhibition manager

    o exhibits manager

    o show contractors

        • general service contractor

        • exclusive contractor

        • subcontractors

        • official contractors

        • exhibitor-appointed contractors

    o exhibit manager

    o exhibit house

    o shipping company

    o customs broker

☐ Types of booth space

    o linear booth

    o corner booth

o inline booth with canopy

o end cap booth

o perimeter booth

o peninsula booth

o island booth

☐ Standard exhibit packages include

o 8' x 10' or 10' x 10' booth space

o 8' tall pipe-and-drape backwall

o 3' high side drapes

o 6' table draped on 3 sides

o 2 chairs

o 1 wastebasket

o 7" x 44" ID sign with exhibitor's name and booth number

o Optional items: 500 Watt electrical drop and carpet

☐ Space requirements

o Formula: Net Square Feet (NSF) x 2 = Gross Square Feet (GSF)

☐ Space allocation

o Types
  • first-come, first-served basis
  • point system
  • lottery
  • combination of above

o Considerations
  • previously exhibited
  • product or service corresponds to attendee profile
  • domination of trade show floor
  • new vs. previous exhibitor
  • use of themed areas or pavilions to allocate space

☐ Establish show floor hours

    o maximize attendance by delegates

    o dedicated, unopposed hours if part of a conference

    o show floor open at food and beverage times

☐ Establish exhibit fees

    o Major revenue generator

- Booth space, premium space and meeting room space sales
- Sponsorships
- Advertising
- Revenue sharing with official contractors
- Interest from cash flow

    o Determine a break-even cost including all expenses

- advertising
- aisle carpet
- audio-visual equipment and labor
- cleaning and post-show trash removal
- communication tools
- computer equipment/Internet/Labor
- decorating
- exhibit packages
- exhibitor education
- facility rental
- floral
- food and beverage
- giveaways
- ground transportation
- insurance
- legal fee
- marketing
- material handling
- meeting room rental

- office equipment
- printing
- registration kiosks and labour
- registration expenses, system, materials, staff
- research
- risk management planning
- security
- shipping and freight management
- signage
- speaker expenses
- sponsorship fulfillment
- staff expenses
- temporary staff
- travel and entertainment
- utilities
- Web design and maintenance

☐ Sources of potential exhibitors

o past exhibitors

o purchased/rented commercial mailing lists

o other exhibitions

o industry associations/groups

o industry publications

☐ Marketing to exhibitors

o provide demographic profile of attendees

o offer potential exhibitors opportunity to showcase new products

o offer exhibitors mailing list of delegates attending

o identify previous exhibitors

o consider third-party audit to verify attendance

☐ Exhibitor prospectus

   o A marketing tool to exhibitors should include:

1. name of conference/trade show
2. dates of conference and trade show
3. exhibition facility and location
4. trade show schedule
5. attendee demographics from prior year
6. number of attendees anticipated for next show
7. number of exhibitors
8. theme of conference/trade show
9. benefits of exhibiting
10. types and sizes of booth spaces or exhibit packages
11. floor plan
12. booth space fees and payment schedule
13. cancellation and refund policy
14. sponsorship and speaker opportunities
15. education, product promotion and public relations opportunities
16. booth space application form with contract including terms and conditions
17. contact person's name, phone, email address

☐ Exhibitor Manual

   o Is sent out to exhibitors after contract signed and deposit received/cleared

   o Should include information on:

- Names and contact information of key trade show management personnel
- Fact sheet of basic show information
- Key deadlines
- Current floor plan
- Contractor information from the general service contractor, exclusive contractors, and official contractors and subcontractors with their show service order forms
- Information on naming exhibitor-appointed contractors and the notification form

- Exhibitor badge information and order forms
- Information on hotel accommodations and travel
- Marketing and sponsorship opportunities
- Press and media opportunities
- Shipping information including customs broker information
- Move-in and move-out schedules for exhibitors
- Overview of unions and basic jurisdictions
- Rules and regulations for exhibitors
- Updates

o Includes information and forms for ordering:

- accessible on-site storage
- A/V rental and labor
- carpet cleaning and porter service
- carpet/pad rental and labor
- catering
- compressed air
- computer and office equipment rental
- credit card authorization(s)
- customs brokerage
- electrical
- exhibit accessories
- exhibit system or custom design and rental
- exhibitor-appointed contractor forms
- exhibitor badges
- floral arrangements and plants
- forklift (in-booth)
- furnishings (standard and custom)
- graphics production
- hotel rooms
- installation and dismantle (I & D) labor (by the general services contractor)
- Internet access and equipment rental
- lead retrieval system rental
- material handling (drayage)

- office equipment rental
- photography
- pipe and drape
- plumbing
- promotional opportunities and sponsorships
- rigging
- shipping
- sign production
- security
- telephone and telecommunications
- temporary staff
- third-party billing form
- travel (air and car rental)
- water

☐ Facility Selection and Regulations

  o Space requirements

  o Facility rental fees

  o Union jurisdictions

  o Exclusive contractors

  o Proximity to conference sessions and meeting rooms

  o Proximity to hotels and restaurants for attendees and exhibitors

  o Building regulations including fire and security

  o Insurance

  o Loading dock access

☐ Attracting attendees

  o Add features that will draw attendees to the show floor

  - food and beverage
  - new product area
  - opening ceremony
  - Internet cafés
  - educational sessions

- theater or keynote areas
- raffles with prize drawings
- exhibitor passport programs
- celebrity demonstrations
- rest areas and lounges
- informal birds-of-a-feather area
- poster area
- bookstore or resources area

CHAPTER REVIEW

KEY POINTS

- Trade shows are face-to-face marketing events, where exhibitors present products and services and build relationships with existing and prospective buyers.

- Professional or scientific exhibitions are associated with meetings of professional groups.

- Public or consumer shows usually have central theme and an admission fee for the public to attend.

- The ideal site for an exhibition has a positive traffic flow through the exhibition area and is located adjacent to meeting rooms, registration areas and food and beverage areas.

- Exhibitors may choose from the following seven types of booth spaces: linear, corner, inline with canopy, end cap, perimeter, peninsula, and island

- Space on the trade show floor may be allocated on a first-come, first-served basis, via a points system, via lottery or by some combination of these systems.

- Sources of potential exhibitors include: past exhibitors, purchased/rented commercial mailing lists, other exhibitions, industry associations/groups, and industry publications.

- Criteria to screen exhibitors include past participation as exhibitor or sponsor, product or service corresponds to attendee profile and amount of space required

- The exhibitor prospectus is the primary tool to attract and inform exhibitors. It typically includes the following elements:
  - name of conference/trade show
  - dates of conference and trade show
  - exhibition facility and location
  - trade show schedule
  - theme of conference/trade show

- benefits of exhibiting

- attendee demographics from prior year

- number of attendees anticipated for next show

- number of exhibitors

- floor plan

- types and sizes of booth spaces or exhibit packages

- booth space fees and payment schedule

- cancellation and refund policy

- sponsorship and speaker opportunities

- education, product promotion and public relations opportunities

- booth space application form with contract including terms and conditions

- contact person's name, phone, email address

- Once an exhibitor has signed a booth space contract, they are provided with an exhibitors manual which will outline information on:

- Features on the trade show floor assist in drawing delegates to the exhibits and include:

  - food and beverage

  - new product area

  - opening ceremony

  - Internet cafés

  - educational sessions

  - theater or keynote areas

  - raffles with prize drawings

  - exhibitor passport programs

  - celebrity demonstrations

  - rest areas and lounges

  - informal birds-of-a-feather area

  - poster area

  - bookstore or resources area

TEST YOUR KNOWLEDGE

The following self test will indicate the level of understanding and knowledge gained from this chapter. Solutions to all self tests can be found in Appendix A.

1. Trade shows bring together buyers and sellers within a particular industry.

   ☐ True   ☐ False

2. It is the sole responsibility of individual exhibitors to market the trade show.

   ☐ True   ☐ False

3. Normally the exhibitor and the facility negotiate booth location and prices.

   ☐ True   ☐ False

4. Trade shows are often used by organizations to generate revenue.

   ☐ True   ☐ False

5. An exhibitor prospectus is used as:

   (a) a record of past exhibitors

   (b) a marketing tool to attract potential exhibitors

   (c) an invoice for billing exhibitors

   (d) a program for delegates to see what products are being exhibited

6. Exhibitions are often offered in conjunction with meetings in order to:

   (a) give delegates something to do in their spare time

   (b) make use of otherwise empty space in the meeting facility

   (c) as a benefit to those industry members who have sponsored some aspect of the meeting

   (d) to supplement the education of the delegates

7. An exhibitors manual typically does NOT include which of the following?

   (a) registration, move-in/out and show hours

   (b) a list of delegates

   (c) shipping instructions

   (d) a list of facility regulations

   (e) show services order forms

8. What is the definition of a trade show?

_____

_____

_____

_____

9. Identify the seven types of exhibit spaces.

_____

_____

_____

10. List 4 questions that should be answered when attempting to determine
    whether to hold a trade show or not.

_____

_____

_____

_____

NOTES

Sponsorship

INTRODUCTION

Cash and goods and services acquired through sponsorship can offset the cost of an event. This saving can be passed along to the attendee in the form of reduced registration costs, or can be used to enhance the event. This chapter will assist the meeting professional in developing procedures for soliciting and securing sponsorships.

LEARNING OBJECTIVES

After completing this chapter, the learner will:

- determine sponsorship/fundraising objectives
- prepare sponsorship benefit packages
- develop sponsorship agreement forms
- prepare information packages for sponsor solicitation
- develop sponsorship recognition packages

Ensure you understand and can apply the following terms:

- Sponsor
- Sponsorship
- Sponsorship agreement
- Sponsorship benefits package
- Sponsorship committee

Refer to the glossary for further clarification of the key terms for this chapter.

ROLES AND RESPONSIBILITIES

MEETING MANAGER

○ Determine financial objectives

- Determine sources of funding
  - ○ identify the types of sponsorships/subsidies/funding available
  - ○ identify if any potential sponsorships conflict with meeting sponsor(s)
  - ○ identify in kind services (e.g., people, skills, equipment, space, services)
  - ○ determine the level of participant funding and other sources of funding
  - ○ write a prospectus and solicit sources of funding

○ Plan for sponsorship and fundraising

- Execute a plan to sell sponsorships
  - ○ determine sponsorship objectives
  - ○ target sponsorship opportunities
  - ○ prepare sponsorship prospectus
  - ○ cultivate, secure and recognize sponsorships
  - ○ adhere to sponsorship agreements
  - ○ evaluate results of sponsorships

- Execute a fundraising plan
  - ○ determine fundraising objectives
  - ○ select appropriate fundraising activities
  - ○ analyze financial and human resource implications
  - ○ source products and services
  - ○ evaluate results of fundraising

- Apply for grants
  - ○ research opportunities
  - ○ prepare and present grant proposals
  - ○ comply with grant requirements
  - ○ follow up

MEETING COORDINATOR

○ Assist in the administration of sponsorship/fundraising programs

- Administer sponsorship agreements
  - ○ review and implement all aspects of sponsorship agreements
  - ○ review and implement the sponsorship recognition plan
  - ○ prepare appropriate communication (e.g., letters, contracts, media releases) and follow up on any inquiries

- Prepare applications for grants
  - ○ research opportunities for grants
  - ○ prepare draft grant submissions
  - ○ follow up on grant applications as required

SPONSOR VERSUS SPONSORSHIP

A sponsor is an individual or organization who contributes money, goods, or services to the event in order to defray expenses, in exchange for recognition.

A sponsorship is the opportunity purchased by the sponsor in order to increase their visibility and/or profile at the event.

Sponsorships can be acquired through financial means or through in kind donations.

Sponsorships for funding, services, and supplies may be solicited from:

- corporations

- not for profit organizations

- government (all levels)

- individuals

SPONSORSHIP OPPORTUNITIES

Sponsorships can be solicited for many meeting components, including :

- Cash
  - grants for entire event
  - attendee travel
  - attendee scholarships
  - speaker travel and expenses
  - youth/student registration
  - meeting room rental costs
  - speakers
  - food and beverage
  - hospitality suites
  - social events

- Goods
  - printed material, signage
  - conference office equipment
  - computer hardware
  - audio visual equipment
  - registration materials
  - badges/lanyards
  - memo pads
  - delegate bag
  - pens/pencils
  - gifts
  - prizes
  - flowers, décor

- Services
  - registration services
  - speakers
  - onsite staff
  - mailing
  - printing

- marketing
- web hosting
- web casting
- transportation
- translation and interpretation

HOST ORGANIZATION OBJECTIVES

The philosophy of the host organization will determine the degree and scope of the sponsorships offered. An entire event may be underwritten by one organization, known as the exclusive event sponsor. If the sponsorship committee is seeking co-sponsorship, approval must be obtained from both potential sponsors, as some sponsors require exclusive sponsorship for an event. In all cases, credit must be given to the sponsoring organization that reflects their contribution.

Sponsorships should be solicited from organizations that are congruent with host organization's policies and values. Determine sponsorship objectives that clearly identify which aspects of the event sponsors will be solicited for.

When writing sponsorship objectives, the host organization should consider:

- objectives for sponsorship
- scope of sponsorship (entire event or individual sessions)
- program elements with potential for sponsorship
- target dollar value
- sponsorship costs (e.g., advertising, exhibit space)
- criteria for sponsors

SOLICITING SPONSORSHIPS

When approaching potential sponsors, keep the following guidelines in mind:

- approach perspective sponsors as early as possible
- understand how sponsoring at your event fits into the sponsor's overall marketing strategy
- identify the financial commitment required for each level of sponsorship
- outline the benefits relevant to each level
- if appropriate, stress community benefits with event sponsors

SPONSOR OPPORTUNITIES PACKAGE

In exchange for their investment in the event, potential sponsors will evaluate sponsorship opportunities that:

- promote product/service
- enhance public image
- increase awareness
- improve sales
- are of an altruistic interest in supporting the host organization

This can be accomplished through the presentation of a sponsor opportunities package.

The potential sponsor should be presented with a clear summary of the benefits of sponsorship from sponsoring the particular event. This package should include:

- detailed and informative outline of the event
- event themes
- confirmed speakers
- attendee profile
- outline program
- anticipated media interest

Typically, sponsorship opportunities are available in a variety of price ranges. For example, Bronze values up to $5,000, Silver from $5,000 - $10,000, Gold from $10,000 to $20,000, etc. The highest profile (and therefore the most expensive) opportunities belong in the highest category, and so on. For example, sponsorship of the closing dinner would be Gold; a refreshment break would be Bronze.

Sponsors will want to know that the event is in line with their corporate philosophy and decide at what level they wish to participate.

Some of the ways the sponsor may be recognized throughout the event include:

- signage

- acknowledgement in event program

- receptions

- hospitality suites

- special function invitations

- exhibit space

- logo on event marketing pieces

- exclusive product sponsorship

- banner advertising or links on websites

- delegate mailing lists

- podium time to address delegates

~ Sample Template ~

Information on CD Rom

SAMPLE SPONSORSHIP OPPORTUNITIES PACKAGE

LEVEL	BENEFITS
Platinum	• promotional piece in delegate package • 2 – 8 X 10 booths • 4 complimentary conference registrations • full page ad in final program • opportunity to speak • logo on all conference signage
Gold	• 1 – 8 X 10 booth • 3 complimentary conference registrations • _ page ad in final program • logo on all conference signage
Silver	• 50% discount on one 8 X 10 booth • 2 complimentary conference registrations • _ page ad in final program • logo on all conference materials
Bronze	• 25% discount on one 8 X 10 booth • 1 complimentary conference registration • name on all conference materials

THE SPONSORSHIP AGREEMENT

Although it is usually best to begin the relationship in an informal way, a written document of the terms and conditions should be prepared and signed before the event is planned, and the sponsor promoted.

To avoid misunderstandings, a sponsorship contract should include provisions for:

- the date and location of the event

- the value to be paid by the sponsor, how it is to be paid (including specifying goods and services in kind) and when it is to be paid

- a description of the event(s) or program(s)

- the way in which the event is to be identified (name or designation)

- the marketing material in which the sponsor's name and logo are to appear (the exact form of the name to be used)

- the use of signage and where it is to be placed

- the size of ads, their placement and frequency. Proximity of ads (or a specific prohibition) to other promotional items from competing companies or brands

- the use of media releases, and the responsibility to track and gather such coverage

- deadlines for placements in printed or electronic materials and the form in which they must be received

- number of people from the sponsoring company who may attend free of charge; number who may attend at a preferential rate; number of guests

- special functions; detail any sponsor costs for these

- guidelines for displaying or serving the company's product(s) or services, if applicable

- access to the host organization's mailing list

- a designated liaison from each party with contact information

- the signature of a representative of each party, to indicate acceptance of the terms

SPONSORSHIP FULFILLMENT AND RECOGNITION

Once a sponsorship agreement has been executed, it is imperative that the host organization deliver what was promised in the agreement. When a number of sponsors support one meeting, it is useful to design a tracking document to ensure deadlines are met, and staff understand who is accountable for what.

At the event, it is important to recognize sponsors publicly. This can be done through a variety of ways.

PROGRAM BOOK

- list sponsors on a separate program page, rather than tying them to a particular session

- acknowledge total event sponsors, partial sponsors, and co-sponsors

- use logo if possible

SPONSOR REPRESENTATIVES

- invite sponsor representatives to attend special functions

- seat sponsor representatives at head tables

- consider VIP designation for total event sponsor representatives

- have event chair acknowledge sponsors and their representatives from the podium at sessions and special functions

SOCIAL FUNCTIONS

- allows sponsor representatives access to event attendees

- provide opportunities for sponsor representatives to have access to event attendees

VISUAL RECOGNITION

- table tent cards at meal functions and social events

- signs outside banquet halls

- signs outside session rooms

- thank you notes in scripts for organization officers

- encourage delegates to do business with sponsors

- web links

- logo on title slide at presentations

ONSITE AND POST EVENT

- have staff member assigned to be sponsor liaison

- personal thank you from senior management

- evaluation (ask for sponsor feedback)

~ A Conference Journal ~

The host organizations of the millennium event soon realized that by planning this unprecedented event, they needed to make expenditures that would not have ordinarily been required. When the first draft of the budget was completed, it was obvious that revenues from conference registration and the trade show could not generate the net profits needed to run their respective associations. This resulted in a decision to combine their sponsorship activities and develop an extensive program that would make up the shortfall.

Their methods of obtaining sponsorship were quite different from one another. One association, fortunate to have several major annual sponsors and a large staff, solicited sponsors through peer-to-peer calls and letters by association volunteers, with support from a staff member. These sponsors made up the majority of the entire sponsorship program with donations in excess of $100,000 each. In this case, the sponsors gave funds to fund a reception or awards gala and the cash was used to provide elements of that particular function such as food and beverage, décor or audio visual support and staging. The event, in some cases, was actually named after the sponsoring company or if not specifically named, had such a high level of sponsor recognition that delegates regularly referred to it as the sponsor's event. Smaller donations of cash offset general expenses and gifts in kind were graciously accepted and for example, used to print the registration brochure, thereby eliminating that expense. Regardless of how or where the sponsorship was used, sponsors were recognized throughout the event, in print materials and signs.

The other organization had only been conducting their sponsorship program for a few years and due to limited volunteer support at the outset and a relatively small staff, had to outsource sponsorship efforts to a consultant. Working very closely with the meeting manager, their goal was to develop an objective driven and structured sponsorship program that established sponsorship targets at all levels. They also wanted to create major sponsorship opportunities to establish new long-term relationships. In this new program, every sponsorship component had detailed benefits for recognition throughout the event. These were also tiered to include greater visibility for larger amounts. In developing the program, sponsor recognition was crucial. They felt they would not succeed within their community without offering exceptional marketing value or corporate exposure in exchange for sponsor contributions.

It was the responsibility of the consultant, once the program was finalized, to go into the field and make contact with interested potential sponsors. Their initial efforts generated approximately 25 investors whose support was added to the general revenue base, although recognition of their contribution was designated to a specific area of the conference or trade show.

In the new combined approach, their objective was to raise one million dollars in sponsorship. They employed various approaches to help them to meet their goal. At least 18 months prior to the conference they began by hiring the same consultant who had worked with one of the organizations and then developed a sponsorship committee comprised of volunteers from both organizations. A sponsorship chair was identified, who was President and CEO of a major firm within their industry and had a significant profile in the industry. This individual, on behalf of his organization, made a corporate contribution of one hundred thousand dollars. It was hoped that this benchmark contribution could be used as leverage to garner other one hundred thousand dollar contributors.

The meeting manager and the consultant developed a new sponsorship program that included many of the new components of the joint conference. A price range was established that took into account major donations from the past and utilized tiered levels of donations. Then they combined their list of past sponsors and prospects to develop a unified list of over 400 prospects. The list was ranked, based on whether support had been received in the past and how likely it was to be received again. Once this was complete, they began with the "A" companies, who were deemed most likely to contribute to this new endeavor because they were past supporters, and worked their way through the list making personal calls, with follow up in writing. In cases, where a volunteer knew a senior individual from a sponsoring company, they were asked to make the initial call to determine interest and the dollar amount of the contribution. Once that was verbally confirmed, the consultant was then sent to meet with the prospect to determine where they would like to assign their donation, perhaps to a social event, or refreshment break or an educational component of the conference. For those prospects that were deemed to be less likely to donate, companies that had never made a contribution and were not directly involved in the same industry but there was a perceived link, a formal letter soliciting sponsorship was sent first as an introduction to the event and the program. Time permitting a call from the consultant was made in follow up.

When combining these two programs, the host organizations had to recognize and agree to maintain existing agreements. For example, not wishing to risk losing the longstanding awards gala sponsor, that sponsor became the major sponsor of the joint awards gala. This required very careful execution because the other association had their awards gala sponsors who were considered to be the major sponsor of that event, although giving significantly smaller donations. Compromise was required between the host organizations and all of the sponsors. It should be noted that while one organization was quite happy to have the sponsor organize and develop the event to their satisfaction, the other maintained strict control over event logistics through the meeting manager and used sponsor contributions to support the event in the form of entertainment, technology or even wine with dinner. This too had to be managed with sensitivity, taking care not to disrupt existing relationships, yet maintain control over conference logistics.

The meeting coordinator recorded confirmed sponsorships into a master chart and allocated corresponding benefits that had been identified by the consultant. As the conference approached, they also make sure that recognition was implemented according to the outline. In some cases a corporate name or logo was included in the preliminary program brochure and then followed up with inclusion on a list of sponsors on the website and then again in all onsite print materials and signs. Acknowledgements from the podium were made daily for major contributors and all sponsors were sent a thank you letter.

Corporate sponsors were very pleased with the level of recognition they received and the host organizers considered the sponsorship program to be a great success from a financial perspective. There were 80 paying sponsors at the conference and an additional seven sponsors provided gifts in kind for a total of $1,045,100. They exceeded their objective and gained a significant number of new sponsors that would continue to partner with each association in the future.

Information on CD Rom

SPONSORSHIP CHECKLIST

○ Sponsorship committee

- organization staff members

- host committee members

- other

○ Sponsorship opportunities

- funds
  - grants for entire event
  - attendee travel
  - attendee expenses
  - speaker fees, travel and expenses
  - youth/scholarships
  - space rental
  - operational costs
  - food and beverage
  - local transportation
  - hospitality suites
  - receptions
  - social events

- equipment
  - office equipment
  - computer hardware
  - audio visual

- event briefcases
  - memo pads/paper
  - conference documents/binder

- pens/pencils

- gifts/awards

- flowers/décor

- refreshments

- products

- services
  - on-line services
  - security staff and equipment
  - organizational staff

○ Sponsorship sources

- corporations

- non-profit organizations/foundations

- government
  - municipal
  - provincial
  - federal

- educational institutions

- individuals

○ Develop sponsorship policy

- review with event chair, organization management

- finalize sponsorship policy

○ Set sponsorship/funding goals

○ Identify potential sponsors

○ Contact sponsors during their annual budget preparation period, if possible

○ Match opportunities to potential sponsors

○ Prepare sponsor benefit packages

- detailed and informative outline of objectives

- event themes

- event speakers

- delegate profile

- draft program

- signage potential

- acknowledgement in event program

- special sponsorship pages

- receptions

- hospitality suites

- special functions invitations

- exhibition space

- logo on event letterhead

- previous conference history

- attendee profile

- exclusive product sponsor

○ Acknowledge sponsors immediately and continuously until the event ends

○ Prepare sponsorship agreement form

○ Invite sponsors to pre-conference event, if possible

○ Send thank you letters to all sponsors

CHAPTER REVIEW

KEY POINTS

- A Sponsor is an individual or organization who contributes funding, goods, or services to an event

- Sponsorship sources include
  - corporations
  - non-profit organizations
  - government
  - individuals

- Sponsorship committee is formed to determine sponsorship/fundraising objectives, seek sponsorships, and donations of goods, services, and equipment

- Sponsoring organization goals include
  - product promotion
  - improve public image
  - increase visibility
  - increase sales by direct marketing to attendees
  - altruistic interest in host organization

- Sponsorship organization expects to receive value for their investment in the event

- Sponsor benefits package should contain
  - outline of event
  - event theme
  - event speakers and presenters
  - delegate profile
  - draft program
  - exhibit exposure
  - community and corporate benefits
  - acknowledgements
  - sponsorship agreement forms

- Contact potential sponsors well in advance of event
  - formal presentation at least one month before sponsor's annual budget deadline
  - 10 or 11 months before event begins
- Sponsorship recognition may include
  - special page in program book
  - invitations to special functions
  - receptions and hospitality suites
  - acknowledgement in table and tent cards
  - signs
  - thank you notes
  - head table seating
  - VIP designation

TEST YOUR KNOWLEDGE

The following self test will indicate the level of understanding and knowledge gained from this chapter. Solutions to all self tests can be found in Appendix A.

1. The event sponsor contributes funding for an aspect of the event in return for some tangible or intangible benefit.

    ☐ True   ☐ False

2. Sponsorship can be solicited for funds, services or supplies.

    ☐ True   ☐ False

3. The following are all potential sponsorship sources: government agencies, community groups, corporations, suppliers, organization members, and non-profit organizations.

    ☐ True   ☐ False

4. Food and beverage, social events, audio visual presentations, and gifts are all types of activities open for sponsorship.

    ☐ True   ☐ False

5. The primary function of a sponsorship committee is:

    (a) reduce the planning load of the meeting professional

    (b) generate new members for the host organization

    (c) ensure sponsorship organization representatives receive VIP treatment

    (d) seek donation of funds, goods, services, and equipment

    (e) all of the above

6   Sponsoring organizations should be acknowledged by:

    (a) table tent cards at meal functions and social events

    (b) signs outside of banquet halls and session rooms

    (c) VIP treatment for total event sponsor representatives

    (d) thank you notes in scripts for organization officers

    (e) all of the above

7. You are the meeting professional chairing the sponsorship committee for the next Recreational Race Car Drivers annual meeting, eleven months from now. List six organizations that you could approach for sponsorship.

_____

_____

_____

_____

_____

_____

8. As you are soliciting funds, services, and equipment for the event in question 7, what recognition elements could you include in your sponsorship benefits package?

_____

_____

_____

_____

_____

_____

Chapter 11

Registration

INTRODUCTION

Registration is a critical part of any event, where first impressions are made and the tone is set. That first impression is made long before delegates travel to the meeting. The easier the registration process before the meeting, the more likely targeted registration levels will be achieved.

Onsite registration considerations involve more logistical elements than design. Planning is required to ensure that event attendees are processed quickly, efficiently, and in a stress free manner.

The aim of this chapter is to assist the meeting professional in developing effective event registration.

Tips on how to create registration forms are followed by sample forms. Many aspects of onsite registration are discussed, including registration packages and badges. Finally, checklists are included to aid the meeting professional in creating successful registration for any event.

Ensure you understand and can apply the following terms:

- Advance registration
- Incentive
- Lanyard
- Onsite registration
- Registration
- Registration policy
- Registration procedure
- Web based registration

Refer to the glossary for further clarification of the key terms for this chapter.

LEARNING OBJECTIVES

After completing this chapter, the learner will:

- develop registration policies

- create a well designed registration form

- determine the requirements of onsite registration

- develop a registration package

- understand the elements of web based registration

ROLES AND RESPONSIBILITIES

MEETING MANAGER

○ Develop registration systems

- Establish registration policies, pre-conference procedures, and timeframes
  ○ write and communicate clear registration policies, including registration cutoff date and pricing structures, registration and records system, procedures for registering persons with special needs and accounting procedures and a plan to secure revenues during registration

- Design registration forms
  ○ determine the need for and use of different forms and formats
  ○ incorporate information needed for various purposes

- Determine the registration layout and service areas required onsite
  ○ plan the setup, physical layout, management and tear down of registration

- Arrange for services, equipment, supplies and staffing
  ○ establish procedures for registration staff
  ○ determine the need for and ensure that required services, equipment and supplies are arranged
  ○ arrange for staff training
  ○ demonstrate flexibility when responding to last minute changes
  ○ prepare a contingency and emergency plan for persons with special needs

  - work with the facility to ensure that needs are met
  - communicate accessibility for persons with special needs

- Determine information required in registration packages
  - design complete registration packages
  - determine the types and numbers of registration packages required, based on registration format

MEETING COORDINATOR

○ Implement registration systems

- Co-ordinate registrations
  - adhere to policies

- Co-ordinate staffing, services, equipment and supplies
  - process registrations as per policy
  - prepare duplicate or multi-part registration forms
  - co-ordinate housing and pre-registration
  - follow planned registration procedures, timeframes, policies, sequence, and schedule
  - use computer software for managing registrations as applicable
  - oversee physical layout, setup and tear down of registration
  - receive payments and maintain the security of revenues
  - train registration staff
  - respond to the needs of delegates
  - implement traffic and crowd control

- Prepare registration materials
  - co-ordinate stuffing of registration kits

- Communicate registration data
  - gather information for registration packages
  - print nametags/nametag holders
  - acknowledge the need to differentiate among registrants
  - prepare and/or purchase other materials
  - communicate "housekeeping" details to attendees as required

- assemble registration packages for distribution
- compile data
- reconcile and analyze data
- prepare summaries and reports

REGISTRATION BASICS

PRE-REGISTRATION

Registration prior to the conference is not always necessary. It can indicate the number of participants so planning and logistical support needs can be arranged. Payments from registrations help cover advance expenses; otherwise, revenue is not generated until the event occurs.

If appropriate, gather information regarding participant interests which can be useful in planning sessions, field trips, offsite events, transportation, and accommodation.

When attendance can be estimated, name badges, room assignments, small group assignments, and materials needed in quantity can be readied for registration.

CONFIRMATION

Confirm registration with a form letter, email, or fax.

EARLY BIRD REGISTRATION

Participants, who register by an established deadline, may be offered a lower registration fee than those who register after that deadline. This is commonly known as the early bird date.

COMPLIMENTARY REGISTRATION

Complimentary registration may be extended to program presenters (depending on the policies of the organization), members of the media, local dignitaries, and VIPs. Determine what activities they will have access to.

ESTABLISHING REGISTRATION POLICIES

A policy is a written instruction that dictates how certain situations will be handled. The meeting professional will try to anticipate every possible scenario and circumstance that may occur. If policies are comprehensive and clearly written, event staff members will be able to reference policies and apply them to any situation.

All registration policies and procedures need to be outlined, including traffic flow management and crisis management. Staff member training can be based upon these written policies and procedures. This is an excellent opportunity to review how conflicts will be solved, individual responsibilities, level of authority, and methods of communication.

It is recommended that the meeting professional write policies that address the following:

- Pre-registration (early bird or other discount deadlines)
  - deadlines
  - handling of mail delays of registration forms
  - handling of lost registration forms

- Multiple registrations from same company
  - discount available
  - amount of discount
  - minimum number of registrations to qualify for a discount
  - cancellations and/or substitutions
  - fee for aid to person with a disability

- Refunds
  - standard refund policy to be stated on form
  - cancellation date/applicable fee
  - exceptions

- Part-time attendance
  - partial registration fee
  - registration offered by day, or to specific events, and fees
  - meal exclusion
  - companion registration

- Function tickets
  - handling of lost function tickets
  - handling of those without tickets to sold out function

REGISTRATION PROCEDURES

Once the meeting professional has set registration policy, procedures will be written that define the method used to carry out those policies. In order to develop efficient procedures, it is necessary to determine all steps involved with each function. The following are considerations when writing registration procedure:

- Cash procedures
  - attendee receipts
  - contracted bonded cashiers onsite
  - schedule for cash pickups for safe storage
  - accounting procedures
  - currency exchange

- Credit
  - acceptable credit/debit cards
  - train registration staff to process credit and debit cards

- Forms
  - distribution of completed forms (hard copies)
  - database management of files
  - computerized system training both pre-registration and onsite

- Function tickets
  - purchase/distribution of function tickets (pre-registration and onsite)
  - ticket exchange procedure
  - posted instructions to attendees on function ticket purchases/exchange/refunds

- Special needs
  - processing of attendees with special needs
  - trained staff available for language and interpretation
  - fully accessible area onsite

REGISTRATION FORM

A registration form is designed to gather information, whether in advance of the meeting or onsite, from all participants who want to attend. The form is brief and easy to understand, allowing for quick and stress free registration.

The potential attendees should have a number of options for providing registration information. Include within these options the following: pre-printed form, form that can be downloaded from a website and faxed or mailed to the registrar, interactive registration form that can be completed online and emailed.

Onsite registration should allow for the most ease of processing registrations. It is recommended that either computers are available for online processing or an area set aside for onsite registration for attendees to complete preprinted registration forms. The method chosen will be a function of the type and size of the event.

A registration form should:

- be clean in appearance

- be easy to read

- be simple and concise

- avoid long blocks of text set in capital letters

- not ask open ended questions, only "yes", "no", or multiple choice

- use boxes for each letter, instead of a blank line

- use a paper finish that is plain, easy to write, or print on

- use colours that photocopy and fax well

ONLINE REGISTRATION

Online registration significantly reduces the time required to register each attendee, and allows for quick analysis of attendee trends. Online registration eliminates many repetitive errors. The cost involved in adaptation to the event may be very small. Registration software packages can:

- generate a mailing list for pre-registration material

- process pre-registration responses, create a registrant data file, and send confirmation

- print badges, including plastic "credit card" type which stores attendee information and can be "swiped" by exhibitors at trade shows for further contact, or for security

- print individual event tickets, tickets for meal functions, and special invitations

- accept payment on secured websites

CHECKLIST FOR MANDATORY VS OPTIONAL REGISTRATION QUESTIONS

Every registration form should provide basic information. Depending on your event, additional optional information may also be necessary. Your registration form should reflect the needs of your organization and the specific event.

MANDATORY	OPTIONAL
First name	Membership/employee number
Last name	Name of guest (if registering)
Preferred name for badge	Designations
Job title	Is this your first conference?
Organization	Guest Fees (and what they include)
Address	Additional tickets (for social functions)
City	Session selections (if applicable)
Province/state	
Postal/zip code	
Country	
Telephone	
Fax	
Email	
Special needs (e.g., accessibility, diet)	
Registration fees (and what they include)	
Currency	
Applicable registration discounts (multiple groups, early bird etc.)	
Payment owing	
Taxes	
Total amount due	
Payment method (cheque, credit card)	
Credit card number (if applicable)	
Expiry date (if applicable)	
Name of cardholder (if applicable)	
Signature (if applicable)	
Address and contact details to forward payment (mail, fax or web based)	
An email address for general enquiries	
The website of the sponsoring organization	

SEE THE APEX
(Accepted Practices Exchange)
section for detailed templates of:

> Event Specifications Guide
> Registration
> Housing
> Rooming
> Post-Event Report

METHODS OF WEB BASED REGISTRATION

Contributed by Bassel Annab, Exposoft Solutions Inc.

ONLINE REGISTRATION

There are three common views in the industry with respect to the Internet and registration. The first is using the Internet as another form of Business to Business (B2B) or Business to Consumer (B2C) communication. The second is the ability to collect and store the information to a file. The third is to use a web-enabled application as your registration software to create intelligent content.

REGISTRATION FORM

This method is by far the most time consuming for capturing information. Typically a PDF form is designed and posted online and can be based on an original hardcopy registration form or invitation. A delegate would print out the form, manually fill it out and submit their registration application via fax or traditional mail. All the information then has to be manually re-entered into a local spreadsheet or database.

FILE METHOD

In this method a form is designed online based on the original registration form or invitation. Once a delegate registers and submits their application the information is captured in a file. This static information is then emailed to an account at which point it is logged in a spreadsheet or entered in a local database. The file may also be downloaded to a local computer on a periodic basis and merged with a local application.

INTERNET APPLICATION

This method allows one to capture the information through a web-enabled online registration form. This method also allows secured users to view and report on the information through online capabilities. The key difference is that this intelligent database captures all information received by any method of registration (fax, mail, phone) online. Reports and information required from the registration process are retrieved through the online application.

HOT TIP

Web Site Tip

If using a web site to promote your conference, build the creative around a registration form. Make the registration form the central focus when navigating the site. Linking program descriptions to the form increases the likelihood people will register online.

REGISTRATION KIT MATERIALS

On completion of the registration process, including payment, the registrant will receive confirmation. Attendees may also receive:

- pre-conference reading material

- receipts

- destination information

- facility/accommodation brochure

Minimize the amount of material sent out with confirmations, as attendees often neglect to bring the package with them and require another onsite. Onsite registration packages will contain the bulk of material required by attendees. Registration kits should be pre-assembled for ease of handing out, along with a name badge, to those who pre-registered. Extra kits and badges need to be available for those registering onsite. The following is a suggested list of items for an onsite registration kit:

- attendee registration list (unless confidential)

- child care services

- program at a glance

- emergency/medical information

- event program/updates (onsite program)

- exhibit/trade show details (hours, location, floor plan)

- function tickets

- future conference registration information

- information about the destination

- information about guest speakers

- information about the guest program

- listing of award recipients

- listing of major sponsors

- lost and found

- meeting headquarters office

- message centre

- name badge

- order forms for purchasing tapes of sessions and other conference material

- other event specific information

- PDA and cell phone policy

- promotional items

- receipt

- smoking policy

- special needs information (barrier-free access to meeting rooms, visual or hearing impairment, translation and interpretation details, dietary concerns)

- transportation services

- writing materials and note pads

~ *Sample Template* ~

PRINTED MATERIALS REQUIREMENTS

Information on **CD Rom**

The chart below will help the meeting professional plan onsite registration requirements.

Item	Quantity at Registration	Location	Delegated to:
Signs/banners _____ _____ _____	_____ _____ _____	_____ _____ _____	
On-site program			
Meal tickets			
Special function tickets			
Registration list			
Registration forms			
Receipts			
Evaluation forms			
Badges			
Ribbons			
Floor plan for Seating at Events			

THE NAME BADGE

The primary function of a badge is to identify the attendee.

Badges may also:

- communicate the attendee's company and location

- aid security

- define registrant categories

- recognize special designations

- store attendee information

- provide sales leads and sources of information

HOW TO DESIGN A BADGE

- The largest type on the badge is used for the attendee's preferred first and last name

- Include the name and location of the attendee's company in smaller lettering

- Colour-coding of badges by registrant categories is easy to understand for attendees and exhibitors

  e.g.,   green – organization members
  yellow – delegates
  blue – suppliers
  red – buyers

- Special designations can be easily accomplished by adding a seal or ribbon to the badge to recognize staff members, students, speakers, VIP's etc.

- If the event is a trade show, consider using a bar-code style badge

- Select a badge type:

Stick On	• least expensive, least desirable
	• frequently falls off, adhesive can damage fabric
Plastic Pin On	• leaves marks/holes in clothing
	• cards tend to fall out of holder
Clip On	• may leave marks
	• considered much better than stick or pin on
Lanyard	• no marks on clothing
	• adjustable
	• can be imprinted with logo
	• badge may turn backwards
Magnetic	• professional looking
	• expensive
	• difficult to make changes to

- Do not let attendees write their own name on the badge, the result would not be uniform, and may be illegible.

- Have extra badges on hand to accommodate changes and onsite registrations.

HOT TIP Clip or pin on badges should be worn on the right side, so that two people shaking hands can read each other's badge. For security reasons, badges should be removed when leaving the venue.

ONSITE REGISTRATION

Determine what equipment is required for onsite registration. Make sure that the necessary tools are available to process all forms of payment accepted. This may include payee stamps for cheques, a cash float, and credit and debit card processing.

The following is a helpful list of supplies needed onsite.

~ *Sample Template* ~

EQUIPMENT AND SUPPLY CHECKLIST

Stock Item	Qty	Location	Ordered
badges	——	——	☐
badge holders	——	——	☐
calculator	——	——	☐
cash box	——	——	☐
cash float	——	——	☐
computer	——	——	☐
credit/debit card processing	——	——	☐
date stamp and pad	——	——	☐
easel	——	——	☐
first aid kit	——	——	☐
flip chart and markers	——	——	☐
key onsite contact list	——	——	☐
lanyards	——	——	☐
maps (venue, city)	——	——	☐
masking tape	——	——	☐
message board	——	——	☐
onsite program	——	——	☐
paper	——	——	☐
paper clips	——	——	☐
pencils	——	——	☐
pens	——	——	☐
printer	——	——	☐
receipt book	——	——	☐
recycling/wastebaskets	——	——	☐
ribbons	——	——	☐
scissors	——	——	☐
stapler	——	——	☐
staple remover	——	——	☐
tacks or pins	——	——	☐
tape	——	——	☐
telephone/Internet connections	——	——	☐

DEVELOPING A FLOOR PLAN

It is necessary to determine all activities that take place during onsite registration so that space can be allocated. The following elements may require floor space at registration. Depending on the event, some may be grouped together, others may require further division alphabetically due to size of event:

- hospitality area

- information

- lost and found

- messages

- onsite registration desk(s)

- pre-registration desk(s)

- publications for display/sale

- registration material storage/distribution

- session/event tickets

- transportation (ground and air)

Next, determine how much floor area is available for registration at the event site. Sketch a floor plan, indicating the space allocation and placement of furniture, equipment, materials, and staff. Do not forget to include:

- signage

- tables

- stanchions

- kiosks

- chairs

- easels

- telephones/Internet connection

- computers and printers

- entrances and exits

TYPICAL REGISTRATION SYSTEMS

SIMPLE REGISTRATION SYSTEM

A simple registration system that can be used by both small and large groups typically places the registration counters along one or more walls, and behind these counters tables can be lined up to be used as work surfaces, while the area underneath can be used as storage space. Counters are preferred to table surfaces as they provide more space and appear more professional. Signage can be used to subdivide the registrants. The number of divisions a system uses depends on the total number of attendees and the complexity of the system. Most systems designate areas by alphabetic grouping, pre-registered attendees, VIP/guests, and individual ticket sales.

REGISTRATION SYSTEM WITH QUEUE

Regardless of how the registration area is delineated, queues are a basic requirement that permits lines to move in an orderly fashion and to remain relatively straight, avoiding intermingling and chaos.

The meeting professional must consider the type of queue (straight or serpentine) and determine whether a single processing station or multiple stations will be required. A single processing station can have rows of stanchions in front of the registration counter. For multiple station processing, a single or a serpentine line can be used, with the registrant at the front of the line going to the next available clerk.

REGISTRATION SYSTEM WITH STRAIGHT QUEUE

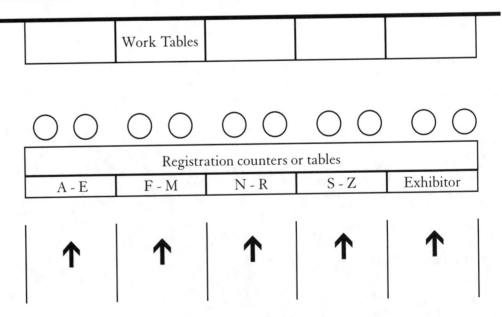

The serpentine queue will hold a larger number of people in the same space as a straight queue, and gives the impression of moving faster than a straight line. In a serpentine queue, all registration staff must be able to provide identical services. Multiple stations will prevent the line from stalling behind a particular attendee who takes extra time to process.

REGISTRATION SYSTEM WITH SERPENTINE QUEUE

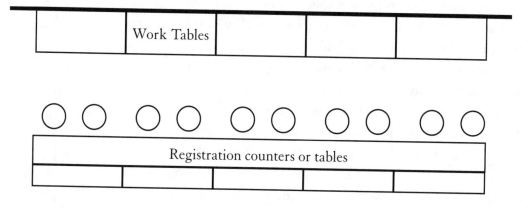

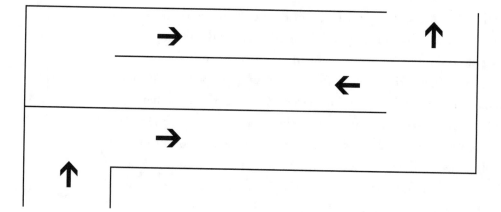

~ *A Conference Journal* ~

As the joint planning committee progressed with the overall conference strategy, the meeting manager and coordinators from both organizations tackled the requirements for registration. They began with a sharing of information as to the method of registration used by each association. The national association handled all registration in-house, using their own customized computerized registration system, while the international organization used a very different computerized registration system belonging to an external supplier. Due to the extraordinary size of this conference, they agreed to outsource the millennium conference registration requirements. In an effort to be transparent and unbiased in the selection of a registration company, they prepared a joint request for proposal, combining the needs of both organizations and obtained responses from three registration companies.

Once they had made their decision, they defined registration policies such as fees, early bird discounts, refunds, cancellations, and whether or not they would offer one day passes. As with many other components of this joint venture, their pricing of conference fees was completely different from one another. One association charged $450 for members that included daily coffee breaks while the other charged $175 for members and no refreshments were provided, unless sponsored. A compromise was difficult to determine because one group felt that a significant increase to the fees, given the financial circumstances of their members, might have resulted in a loss of registrations. Similarly, the second group felt that if their members received large discounts, it would be difficult to justify putting the fees back to the regular rates the following year.

They also had to review whether or not to sell one-day passes since this new registration category could, it was argued, increase attendance at both the conference and the trade shows if some individuals had an interest in portions of the event but not enough to attend for the week. However, once they looked at the logistics of adding yet another category of registration to an already varied list that required different coloured name badges, they saw that it was becoming an unwieldy process. Delegate badges were used to gain or restrict access to some areas of the conference, such as exhibits only, tours only, full conference, etc. This required monitors or security personnel at the entrance to each session to ensure that delegates wore the correct badge for admission to that particular area. This had the potential to slow down access to the sessions and the combinations of one-day passes over the full week were endless. After much consideration and debate, they reached a compromise that they felt they could live with that kept the overall conference rate low to promote attendance and restricted one-day passes to exhibits only. The meeting manager submitted a conference fee framework for approval by the joint planning committee and subsequently, to each association's respective board of directors.

Their next steps included reviewing the various conference components to determine events that required separate ticketing from those that could be attended by general admission with a name badge only. Once this task was completed, they were able to collaborate with the registration company to develop a workable registration form. The form had to take into account all of the elements of the conference that required a separate fee and registration such as general admission, social events, trade show one-day passes, tours and separate pre-conference seminars. It was also important to ensure that the form was user friendly for delegates and was designed in such a manner for ease of use by the individuals who were going to process the registrations into the database.

The registration form was included in the main conference brochure and distributed by direct mail, magazine inserts and a copy posted on the website with the registration form. Delegates were asked to complete the form, print it out and then submit their registration by fax or mail, together with full payment.

As the registration process began, the registration company was required to keep track of sales by event and submit a weekly summary to the meeting manager who would analyze the data to determine whether or not they were on track. In the case of lagging registrations after the early bird deadline, they decided to implement an additional advertising campaign in several industry magazines to boost registrations. By analyzing the data regularly, they were also able to make projections to determine whether or not they would meet their budget expectations. Within two months of the conference, they also discussed whether or not to cancel some of the more costly components of the conference, such as the audience response technology. They decided then, once and for all, that whether or not registrations met their expectations, it was imperative that they do everything necessary to meet their conference objectives.

This analysis was also used to determine seating availability and cutoff limits for event sales. For example, they printed 500 tickets for one of the luncheons because that was the room capacity, however, after holding back tickets for sponsors, speakers and special guests they restricted the registration company from selling any more than a maximum of 480 tickets.

Name badges not only identified the delegate with their name and company, they also showed the various conference elements in which the delegate had registered, at the bottom of the badge. Receipts reflected the same information together with the cost and the full amount paid. Tickets, in addition to sequential numbering, also contained the name, date and location of the event and, where appropriate, included the name of the event sponsors.

They had decided early on that all badges and tickets were to be distributed onsite, although the past experience of one of the associations was to mail out badges and tickets ahead of time. This necessitated the development of floor plans for onsite registration desks that enabled pre-registered delegates to pick up their registration kits arranged in alphabetical order by the delegate's surname, at separate counters. All registrations received in the two weeks prior to the conference were considered onsite. These plus walk-ins during the conference were required to go to counters in a different area and identified as onsite registrations. These registrations would take more time because a registration form had to be filled out, cash transaction completed and a new name badge printed, before giving the delegate a registration kit. They also identified a separate counter for the sale of individual event tickets, and another area for admission to the trade shows which required a badge for easy identification for the exhibitor. Registration utilized the entire lobby area of the convention centre but was well designed to ensure adequate traffic flow. They had sufficient registration equipment and staff onsite to ensure that delegates did not have a long wait. This was an issue with the international organization, as their group had a 40% onsite registration rate compared to the national group's standard 5% - 10%.

The location of the millennium event was quite unique in that it encompassed two separate buildings. This required the setup of two identical registration areas, one in each building. Registration was setup in the north building on Saturday and remained operational until Wednesday at noon. After the last session in the morning, delegates were instructed to leave the building and follow the directional signs to the facility's internal walkway leading to the south building. Once they arrived, they were directed to the grand opening reception of the second trade show or to the scheduled luncheon. To handle new registrations and ticket sales for the second half of the conference, duplicate registrations counters, signs and equipment were set up the night before and tested. A second crew of registration staff was available first thing in the morning.

Back at the north building, exhibitors moved out while conference rooms and existing registration areas were dismantled. Unbelievably, everyone made their way to the south building and enjoyed the remainder of the conference for the next two and a half days.

Information on CD Rom

REGISTRATION CHECKLIST

☐ Assign responsibility for developing registration form

☐ Prepare registration form

- identify information to be sent to participants
- event title
- event objectives
- format
- date
- duration
- time
- location
- facility
- address
- registration fees
- pre-registration fees
- special pre-registration fee schedule and dates
- accepted methods of payment
- cancellation fee
- housing options
- meals included in registration fee
- other meals available
- provided child care services and cost
- return address

☐ Information needed from registrants

- name
- title
- organization
- mailing address
- program elements of interest
- housing preference
- name of person(s) room will be shared with
- meals

- event specific information
- special needs
- method of payment
- emergency contact

☐ Prior to developing event registration procedures, the meeting professional should determine

- necessity of pre-registration for the event
- availability of accommodation arrangements with event pre-registration, or if attendees are to make their own accommodation arrangements
- implementation of guest programs
- provision for child care
- if activities within the event require special sign up procedures or ticket sales
- dates for the various stages of pre-registration
- if confirmations will be sent to pre-registered participants
- if a computer was used for pre-registration, will the data be available at the event
- if exhibitors will be provided with a pre-registration mailing list

☐ Registration procedures

- determine location and availability of the registration area
- signage requirements of the registration area
- traffic flow in the registration area
- provisions for pre-registered participants
- adequate writing space available
- writing implements available
- sufficient ventilation in registration area
- adequate lighting in registration area
- other traffic in registration area
- order sufficient supply of all registration forms
- online registration
- storage of registration materials and equipment
- communication methods for registration personnel

☐ Registration desk

- identify person responsible for registration desk
- prepare participant packets
- content on badges
- availability of badges
- special provisions for group registrations
- placement of bulletin board
- location for special event ticket sales

☐ Hospitality and information desk

- determine necessity of hospitality desk
- procedure for problem solving
- procedure if no record of advance registration
- accepted methods of payment
- sponsor information to be provided
- verification procedure for membership status
- procedure for collection of membership dues
- identify publications available for sale
- replacement of lost badges and function tickets
- policy for onsite requests for media and other special privilege passes
- policy for dealing with unauthorized persons

☐ Personal needs of participants

- available lodging information
- special hospitality
- tours and sightseeing arrangements
- shopping services
- translation and simultaneous interpretations
- accessibility

☐ Financial aspects

- identify personnel responsible for financial activity
- identify personnel responsible for cash count
- accepted methods of payment
- type of cheques (personal and/or business)

- type of credit cards
- purchase order
- billing, identify terms and conditions
- refund policy and procedures
- partial payment for individual events
- receipt procedure
- staffing
- volunteers
- types of personnel needed
- supervisory staff
- training of registration staff
- operational dry run
- staff policy manual
- supplies and services
- condition of site equipment
- determine supplies and equipment needed

☐ Onsite office

- location
- floor plan
- hours of operation
- staffing schedule
- equipment
- computers
- copying machines
- fax machines
- other
- furniture
- chairs
- desks
- cabinets
- other

CHAPTER REVIEW

KEY POINTS

- Set registration policy for advance registration, group bookings, refunds, partial attendance, and function tickets

- Develop registration procedures for forms, payment, information desk, and function tickets

- An effectively designed registration form:

- appears clean, easy to read, simple and concise

- asks only "yes", "no", or multiple choice questions

- forces registrant to print information by using boxes, not blank lines

- easily folded or inserted into printer

- finish is plain, easy to write or print on

- uses colours that photocopy well

- In preparation for site registration, the meeting professional will:

- determine all activities involved

- develop a floor plan

- include equipment, staff requirements

- write registration procedures

- provide supplies

- implement cash control measures

- consider online registration to save time

- Registration package will include:

- program

- function tickets

- registration list

- writing material

- information on local area, speakers, child care, guest program

- receipt form

- evaluation form

- badge

- Badges are necessary to:

- communicate attendee name, company, and location

- facilitate security

- identify registrant categories

- recognize special designations

- store attendee information and provide sales leads (electronic or bar coded badges)

- An onsite office provides a location for the meeting professional and staff members to communicate with event facility personnel, suppliers, host organization officers, and VIPs, to provide information, and to solve problems before they develop into crises.

TEST YOUR KNOWLEDGE

The following self test will indicate the level of understanding and knowledge gained from this chapter. Solutions to all self tests can be found in Appendix A.

1. A floor plan of the registration site will include floor area, equipment, staff placement, and traffic flow.

    ☐ True   ☐ False

2. Registration forms are a good opportunity to gather detailed information about event attendees.

    ☐ True   ☐ False

3. A registration form can ask questions in a variety of ways, as long as the form appears clean and easy to read.

    ☐ True   ☐ False

4. A web based registration form should ask different questions then a hard copy (printed and mailed) registration form.

    ☐ True   ☐ False

5. Registration forms should be:

    (a) printed on glossy paper

    (b) in bright colours such as blue

    (c) detailed for gathering extensive data on attendees

    (d) allow sufficient space for filling in detailed handwritten responses

    (e) utilize multiple choice or yes/no formats whenever possible

6. The onsite registration area will:

    (a) accommodate the maximum number of people expected at any given time

    (b) have one table for both pre-registered and registering attendees for simplicity

    (c) be prominently located in close proximity to many other activities for convenience

    (d) include a lost & found, information, and hospitality table

7. An early bird registration fee is:

    (a) a form of advance registration incentive

    (b) when fees decrease after a cutoff date

    (c) used to allow some registrants access to all events, while others attend only those selected

    (d) implemented when a guest program is available

    (e) a method of discounting fees for members versus non members

8. A meeting professional can encourage pre-registration by:

    (a) offering a lower registration fee up to a cutoff date

    (b) discounting fees for guest programs

    (c) issuing commemorative gifts

    (d) including reduced membership fees for new members

    (e) all of the above

9. Registration policies should be written to dictate how all of the following situations will be handled except:

    (a) advance registration

    (b) multiple reservations

    (c) refunds

    (d) final staffing requirements

    (e) part time attendance

10. How can a computer-based program aid in the registration process?

    _____

    _____

11. What is normally included in a registration package?

    _____

    _____

12. What information will a meeting professional seek before beginning the registration planning process?

    _____

    _____

NOTES

Chapter 12

Meeting Logistics

INTRODUCTION

Meeting logistics refers to the tasks undertaken to ensure the effective management of materials, information and people for the implementation of an event. Logistics occur at both pre-event and onsite stages of the event. Planning is required to ensure that attendees can derive the most benefit by moving through all aspects of the event quickly, efficiently, and in a stress free manner.

Ensure you understand and can apply the following terms:

- APEX
- Barrier-free design
- Cash bar
- Destination management company
- Host bar
- Operations manual
- Post conference meeting
- Pre conference meeting
- Printing and electronic distribution methods
- Rooming list
- Registration materials
- Signage
- Simultaneous interpretation
- Traffic flow
- Translator

Refer to the glossary for further clarification of the key terms for this chapter.

LEARNING OBJECTIVES

After completing this chapter, the learner will:

- construct a working operations manual

- develop a transportation plan

- co-ordinate pre and post conference meetings

- determine traffic flow patterns

- determine need for translation and simultaneous interpretation services

- determine food and beverage requirements

ROLES AND RESPONSIBILITIES

MEETING MANAGER

○ Plan to meet food and beverage requirements

- Determine food and beverage requirements
  - ○ determine food and beverage requirements including dietary and special requirements, given the budget and meeting objectives
  - ○ research and select menus, price, and service styles
  - ○ identify food and beverage options
  - ○ schedule food and beverage requirements
  - ○ work with the facility's catering staff
  - ○ determine and use the operation's overset policy
  - ○ plan nutritionally balanced and appealing menus, incorporating known tastes, allergies, religions and cultural requirements of the attendees
  - ○ determine reception and hospitality suite requirements
  - ○ plan for the amount of time and space needed for food and beverage breaks
  - ○ plan for service styles as required
  - ○ plan for décor
  - ○ plan for special dietary requirements including allergies

- Determine food and beverage related policies
  - ○ determine service charge, setup fee, overage and guarantee policies

- ○ plan controls over food and beverage quality and quantity
- ○ plan to provide responsible service of alcohol
- ○ apply knowledge of relevant legislation and liability related to the service of alcohol
- ○ determine policies related to alcohol consumption and service

○ Develop a critical path/timelines

- Determine tasks
  - ○ identify and prioritize all tasks
  - ○ sequence tasks and activities
  - ○ determine accountability for tasks

- Determine timeframes
  - ○ incorporate all components of the meeting plan
  - ○ incorporate all contractual arrangements

- Develop system(s) for monitoring progress
  - ○ prepare checklists for tracking purposes

○ Develop a conference résumé

- Produce and distribute a conference résumé
  - ○ gather and compile all information needed by suppliers
  - ○ develop the format and content requirements
  - ○ produce a detailed résumé

- Compare function sheets to the conference résumé and correct discrepancies

- Determine and communicate signing authority and allowable charges for each master account

- Develop and distribute an operations manual
  - ○ gather and compile all necessary information for staff
  - ○ incorporate a list of key contacts
  - ○ determine the distribution of the manual
  - ○ approve changes to the operations manual
  - ○ use the operations manual to make pre-meeting adjustments in a cost-effective manner
  - ○ communicate adjustments to all involved

○ Plan and conduct pre and post conference meetings

- Prepare for the meetings
  - ○ identify the number of meetings and their participants
  - ○ identify the objectives of the meetings
  - ○ prepare support materials
  - ○ schedule meetings
  - ○ set and distribute the agenda for each meeting
  - ○ distribute an operations manual sheets in advance of the pre-conference meeting(s)

- Conduct pre and post conference meetings
  - ○ completely preview and communicate all plans with appropriate persons
  - ○ review and confirm function sheets and make changes as required
  - ○ review specifications
  - ○ facilitate communications among staff and the facilities
  - ○ resolve any discrepancies
  - ○ prepare an action plan

○ Plan traffic flow and crowd control

- Plan for crowd control and traffic flow
  - ○ determine appropriate entry and exit points, considering safety and traffic flow
  - ○ use creative strategies for crowd control
  - ○ plan traffic flows for all components of the program
  - ○ communicate the traffic plan to appropriate personnel

MEETING COORDINATOR

○ Implement the food and beverage plan

- Communicate food and beverage requirements
  - ○ communicate dietary and special food and beverage requirements in writing
  - ○ communicate the number of people, number of meals, theme events, receptions, refreshment breaks, cocktail parties, seasonal and local food usage, and special meals required
  - ○ advise service staff of the location and identity of persons with special needs and special requests

- Implement food and beverage arrangements
  - implement and monitor pricing, service style, service level, and portion sizes
  - implement and monitor hospitality suite food and beverage policy and requirements

- Monitor food and beverage quality and quantity as per guarantee and contract
  - monitor attendance
  - adjust food and beverage requirements according to the guarantee
  - observe patterns related to food consumption and make corrections as required
  - monitor number of meals served and compare to billing
  - check food and beverage inventory
  - monitor the menu and service styles as per contract
  - review guarantees and adjustments

- Monitor the responsible service of alcohol
  - monitor beverage consumption
  - demonstrate an awareness of legal liability related to service of alcohol

○ Participate in pre and post conference meetings

- Attend meetings
  - review function sheets, plans, and specifications
  - prepare and/or distribute documentation
  - prepare support materials
  - record concerns and outcomes
  - distribute the necessary documentation

○ Implement meeting space and setup requirements

- Design floor plans
  - use charts to scale and planning aids to match room size and attendees, and to indicate room arrangements: position of furniture, seating arrangements
  - demonstrate awareness of the number of attendees who can be seated, given room size and other considerations such as number of aisles, seating style, head table, lectern, fire regulations, exits, etc.
  - recognize various room setups, seating arrangements, their advantages and disadvantages, to make the best use of space available

- Arrange for needs of delegates
  - arrange seating to meet the needs of delegates
  - arrange for meeting room amenities and services
  - provide aids and services for speakers
  - arrange for configured tables for the distribution of refreshments, print materials, nametags, etc.

○ Implement printing requirements

- Participate in production of print materials
  - enforce deadlines and monitor delivery schedules
  - follow specifications and policies
  - produce copy and artwork for approval

- Plan for the distribution, shipping and/or storage of printed materials
  - inspect completed samples before distribution
  - plan for the distribution and/or storage of printed materials
  - choose shipping arrangements for printed materials
  - adhere to the critical path

○ Implement the transportation plan

- Arrange transportation services
  - adhere to contractual arrangements
  - communicate transportation arrangements
  - process confirmed transportation arrangements
  - address any accessibility challenges

- Monitor transportation arrangements and access controls
  - monitor the use of access controls
  - identify and solve problems related to transportation

○ Set up and control signage

- Implement the signage plan
  - produce signage
  - place and adjust signage
  - monitor signage to ensure that needs are met
  - adhere to facility restrictions
  - remove and store signage

- ○ Arrange for shipping, receiving, and storage

  - Determine the need for subcontractors
    - ○ determine the roles of transportation coordinators, customs brokers, and drayage companies

  - Meet shipping and storage needs
    - ○ establish shipping and storage needs
    - ○ identify and choose shipping options
    - ○ schedule and arrange shipping
    - ○ block a room to meet storage requirements
    - ○ develop an inventory procedure
    - ○ recognize restrictions related to space, time, labour, and other resources
    - ○ communicate arrangements
    - ○ co-ordinate customs administration

- ○ Implement interpretation and translation services

  - Co-ordinate translation and interpretation services
    - ○ arrange for services, equipment and supplies to meet requirements
    - ○ ensure that delegates' and speakers' needs are met
    - ○ co-ordinate security
    - ○ adhere to service contracts
    - ○ identify and solve problems related to translation and interpretation

- ○ Plan and set up an onsite office

  - Plan an office
    - ○ determine equipment, supplies and services, which will be required
    - ○ determine the availability and accessing of onsite supplies and services
    - ○ communicate services available to delegates
    - ○ arrange for security and utilities
    - ○ arrange delivery and inventory of supplies and equipment

  - Set up an office
    - ○ receive, control and return an inventory of supplies and materials
    - ○ co-ordinate pickups, disconnections, and service

  - Arrange onsite communications
    - ○ arrange for equipment, services and supplies

- adhere to policies and procedures
- co-ordinate and maintain onsite communications

○ Implement meeting setup requirements

- Monitor meeting room setups
  - compare room setups with function sheets
  - monitor utilities
  - maintain contact with key personnel within the facility
  - solve problems related to meeting room setups

○ Implement traffic flow and crowd control

- Implement traffic flow
  - review the contingency plan
  - follow and monitor defined procedures
  - demonstrate an understanding of safety, legislative, contingency and emergency considerations

- Implement crowd control
  - review the contingency plan
  - follow and monitor defined procedures
  - demonstrate an understanding of safety, legislative, contingency and emergency considerations

○ Implement and monitor a housing plan

- Manage accommodations
  - recognize the interdependence of the Meeting Coordinator and facility staff
  - provide the facility needed information
  - develop a service relationship with facility staff
  - adhere to defined systems for registering delegates, guests, speakers, VIPs.
  - prepare and update a rooming list

- Monitor the room block
  - adhere to the policies of the accommodation facility
  - identify and solve problems related to accommodation
  - work closely with the appropriate key personnel
  - monitor housing requests and ensure that requirements are met

○ Adhere to contracts onsite

- Review contracted prices, products, and services
  - ○ review all relevant contracted agreements
  - ○ demonstrate an understanding of contract details and expectations
  - ○ ensure contract compliance

- Maintain two way communication with facilities and suppliers
  - ○ provide information and updates
  - ○ exchange information and monitor services

LOGISTICS CONSIDERATIONS

The meeting professional should ensure the following actions are taken in preparation for any conference.

- Develop a timeline or critical path

- Meet with and make arrangements with needed suppliers. This could be as follows:
  - Destination Management Company (DMC)
  - transportation companies
    - air
    - ground
  - florists
  - photographers
  - special security
  - website designer
  - décor
  - entertainment
  - childcare

- Plan all food and beverage functions

- Investigate the need and arrange for translation and simultaneous interpretation

- Determine signage needs and place order for all required signs

- Plan the onsite office layout, equipment and communication needs

- Prepare rooming lists for hotel properties

- Prepare an onsite operations manual. It should include:
  - banquet event orders (final version)
  - contact phone numbers of all suppliers
  - committee and staff telephone numbers

- Arrange for and conduct a pre-conference meeting

TIMELINES OR CRITICAL PATH

Determining the internal and external factors which will impact the overall planning process is critical to determining the anticipated timeline. The timeline includes each task to be accomplished and is the core of the program plan. The timeline should be specific to the meeting and follow the meeting process from the conception of the meeting to completion and afterward.

A good organizational program forms the basis of all planned activities that will follow. Formalizing the process by constructing a schedule of activities necessary to complete a stimulating program within the available timeframes is essential.

A fully developed schedule is especially helpful when a committee is involved in program planning. The process is most successful when members of the programming group know what is expected of them from the start. Giving the group timeframes and deadlines assures a rational planning process.

Effectively managing a critical path includes adjusting tasks and deadlines as planning requires.

The following is an outline of a typical schedule for a large annual meeting of an educational organization.

~ *Sample Template* ~

SAMPLE TIME LINE

Tasks	Who?	When?	Done?
PRIOR TO 13 MONTHS			
Prepare preliminary budget	Manager	February	
Develop deposit schedule	Manager	March	
Determine appropriate tier (A, B or C) for meeting 3 years out	Manager	May	
Send RFP to CVBs (copy Chapter Presidents)		May	
Review proposals from responding suppliers and select potential sites		July	
Conduct site inspections as required		August/September	
Select site for meeting 3 years out		September	
Negotiate hotel rates and blocks; sign contracts		November/December	
Negotiate with convention centre for meeting space; sign contracts		November/December	
AUGUST (13 MONTHS)			
Appoint Host Committee co-chairs (typically CVB rep and Chapter member)			
Review, update and circulate terms of reference to Host Committee co-chairs			
Design meeting icon			
Design exhibitor prospectus (for distribution at current meeting)			
Establish registration, exhibit fees			
Produce first draft of exhibit floorplan			
Design call for submissions (for distribution at current meeting)			
Draft communications plan			
SEPTEMBER (12 MONTHS)			
Review critical path for adjustments and update as required		Ongoing	
Select sub-committee chairs (Education, Networking) with advice from Host Co-chairs			
Review, update and circulate terms of reference to Sub-committee chairs			
Print next year's exhibitor prospectus (for distribution at current conference)			

~ *Sample Template* ~

Tasks	Who?	When?	Done?
Draft program flow (include opening ceremonies/keynote, welcome reception, Discover reception, closing reception/ dinner, board and/or committee meetings, showcase, keynote and concurrent sessions, meals and breaks, honours & awards, AGM)			
Recruit committee members	Sub-committee chairs		
Schedule Host Committee debrief meeting at conclusion of current conference			
Review, update and circulate terms of reference to Sub-committee members			
Update and print Call for Submissions			
OCTOBER (11 MONTHS)			
Review critical path for adjustments and update as required		Ongoing	
Confirm sponsorships as required – send out agreement letters, manage fulfillment		Ongoing	
Review and update preliminary budget		Ongoing	
Confirm with exhibitors as they register		Ongoing	
Confirm with delegates as they register		Ongoing	
Host committee meeting - select logo/theme, confirm sub-committee chairs, finalize program flow			
Education committee meeting – distribute program flow, discuss keynotes and concurrent sessions, review terms of reference, establish meeting schedule			
Update and print Sponsorship Opportunities			
Distribute Call for Submissions			
NOVEMBER (10 MONTHS)			
Review critical path for adjustments and update as required		Ongoing	
Confirm sponsorships as required – send out agreement letters, manage fulfillment		Ongoing	
Confirm with exhibitors as they register		Ongoing	
Confirm with delegates as they register		Ongoing	

~ Sample Template ~

Tasks	Who?	When?	Done?
Education committee meeting – add content to program flow; brainstorm concurrent session topics/speakers, potential keynote speakers, call for submissions response update			
Networking committee meeting – review terms of reference, gala reception/dinner, fun night, welcome reception, networking, meet & greet; transportation and tours			
Distribute Sponsorship Opportunities			
Host committee meeting – committee updates, new business			
Update and print File Folder and preliminary registration form			
Establish convention number with airline(s)			
Call for Submissions deadline			
DECEMBER (9 MONTHS)			
Review critical path for adjustments and update as required		Ongoing	
Confirm sponsorships as required – send out agreement letters, manage fulfillment		Ongoing	
Confirm with exhibitors as they register		Ongoing	
Confirm with delegates as they register		Ongoing	
Education committee meeting – update keynotes, review call for submissions proposals, concurrent session topics/ speakers - fill holes where necessary			
Host committee meeting – committee updates, new business			
Networking committee meeting			
Deadline for Call for Submission responses			
Education committee meeting – finalize keynotes and concurrent sessions			
Distribute File Folder and preliminary registration form			
JANUARY (8 MONTHS)			
Review critical path for adjustments and update as required		Ongoing	

~ *Sample Template* ~

Tasks	Who?	When?	Done?
Confirm sponsorships as required – send out agreement letters, manage fulfillment	.	Ongoing	
Confirm with exhibitors as they register		Ongoing	
Confirm with delegates as they register		Ongoing	
Host committee meeting – committee updates, new business			
Networking committee meeting			
Education committee meeting – finalize anything not covered			
Update Registration Brochure and registration form			
Confirm speakers – send agreements to chosen speakers, include special reg form with speaker rates			
Update ad for magazine (Feb/Mar issue)			
FEBRUARY (7 MONTHS)			
Review critical path for adjustments and update as required		Ongoing	
Confirm sponsorships as required – send out agreement letters, manage fulfillment		Ongoing	
Confirm with exhibitors as they register		Ongoing	
Confirm with delegates as they register		Ongoing	
Networking committee meeting			
Host committee meeting			
Update speaker manual – releases, travel, housing, audio visual, room set-up, handouts, expense claim form, deadlines			
Update ad for magazine (March/April issue)			
Follow up on outstanding speaker agreements			
Distribute speaker manual			
Print and distribute Registration Brochure and registration form			
Select and order delegate bags			
MARCH (6 MONTHS)			
Review critical path for adjustments and update as required		Ongoing	
Confirm sponsorships as required – send out agreement letters, manage fulfillment		Ongoing	
Confirm with exhibitors as they register		Ongoing	

~ Sample Template ~

Tasks	Who?	When?	Done?
Confirm with delegates as they register		Ongoing	
Update exhibitor manual, obtain all inserts			
Arrange insurance coverage			
Networking committee meeting			
Host committee meeting			
Determine and book staff, speaker and VIP room requirements			
Distribute exhibitor manual			
Schedule speaker/panel conference calls			
APRIL (5 MONTHS)			
Review critical path for adjustments and update as required		Ongoing	
Confirm sponsorships as required – send out agreement letters, manage fulfillment		Ongoing	
Confirm with exhibitors as they register		Ongoing	
Confirm with delegates as they register		Ongoing	
Prepare first draft of meeting resumé			
Networking committee meeting			
Host committee meeting			
Draft of speaker presentations due			
MAY (4 MONTHS)			
Review critical path for adjustments and update as required		Ongoing	
Confirm sponsorships as required – send out agreement letters, manage fulfillment		Ongoing	
Confirm with exhibitors as they register		Ongoing	
Confirm with delegates as they register		Ongoing	
Update meeting resumé as required		Ongoing	
Update showcase invitations			
Book audio visual requirements for keynotes			
Volunteer recruitment session with Chapter			
Networking committee meeting			
Host committee meeting			
Determine mailing list for showcase invitations			
Book preliminary concurrent session audio visual			
Networking committee meeting			
Draft F & B requirements for all related functions			

~ *Sample Template* ~

Tasks	Who?	When?	Done?
Send letter from President to last year's delegates and previous year's delegates			
Order name badge stock, name badge holders, special ribbons/buttons			
Confirm photographer			
Room set-up and A/V forms due			
JUNE (3 MONTHS)			
Review critical path for adjustments and update as required		Ongoing	
Confirm sponsorships as required – send out agreement letters, manage fulfillment		Ongoing	
Confirm with exhibitors as they register		Ongoing	
Confirm with delegates as they register		Ongoing	
Update meeting resumé as required		Ongoing	
Networking committee meeting			
Host committee meeting			
Determine session introducers/thankers			
Develop security schedule and training notes			
Confirm requirements and contract security for tradeshow			
Write and distribute scripts for plenary sessions			
Final speaker presentations due			
Networking committee meeting			
Host committee meeting			
Write scripts for meal functions			
Distribute showcase registration form			
Write concurrent session scripts			
JULY (2 MONTHS)			
Review critical path for adjustments and update as required		Ongoing	
Confirm sponsorships as required – send out agreement letters, manage fulfillment		Ongoing	
Confirm with exhibitors as they register		Ongoing	
Confirm with delegates as they register		Ongoing	
Update meeting resumé as required		Ongoing	
Obtain necessary insurance documents for facility			
Compose transportation routes and schedule for events			

~ Sample Template ~

Tasks	Who?	When?	Done?
Obtain maps and city information and permits, if required			
Finalize meeting room set-ups and room allocations for sessions			
Source and purchase and wrap speakers gifts/thank you cards			
Letter to sponsors with early bird reg list			
Letter to exhibitors with early bird reg list			
Order awards			
Confirm staging design			
Networking committee meeting			
Host committee meeting			
Determine staff / volunteer requirements and schedule – prepare training notes			
Determine on-site registration staffing requirements			
AUGUST (1 MONTH)			
Review critical path for adjustments and update as required		Ongoing	
Confirm sponsorships as required – send out agreement letters, manage fulfillment		Ongoing	
Confirm with exhibitors as they register		Ongoing	
Confirm with delegates as they register		Ongoing	
Update meeting resumé as required		Ongoing	
Send updated registration list (August 30) to sponsors			
Arrange tie-down meetings with facilities			
Host committee meeting			
Networking committee meeting			
Send reception invitations to first-timers			
Send reception invitations to exhibitors			
Send lunch invitations to sponsors			
Reconfirm speakers and their requirements			
Determine and order keynote and concurrent session signage			
Update on-site program			
Determine on-site office equipment requirements and order			
Finalize concurrent session audio visual			
Design and order sponsor recognition signage			
Update on-site program/show guide			

~ *Sample Template* ~

Tasks	Who?	When?	Done?
Design next year's exhibitor prospectus			
Send meeting resumé to convention centre, hotels, other suppliers			
Confirm all F & B requirements and provide preliminary guarantees			
Exhibitor names for booths to signage company			
SEPTEMBER (0 MONTHS)			
Review critical path for adjustments and update as required		Ongoing	
Confirm sponsorships as required – send out agreement letters, manage fulfillment		Ongoing	
Confirm with exhibitors as they register		Ongoing	
Confirm with delegates as they register		Ongoing	
Update meeting resumé as required		Ongoing	
Determine on-site communications requirements and order (walkies)			
Develop on-site cash handling procedures			
Develop on-site registration procedures			
Print on-site program/show guide			
Confirm location and accessibility for deliveries (book loading dock)			
Inventory and order any remaining signage			
Develop on-site registration packages			
Draft and copy conference evaluation forms – concurrent and overall			
Draft showcase evaluation forms			
Prepare on-site registration forms			
Gala Night - assign tables for VIP guests			
Prepare badges for registered attendees			
Order VIP amenities			
Order staff amenities			
Copy cash sheets for on-site (pack in box)			
Prepare list of delegates for registration kit			
Prepare registration file for on-site			
Finalize and print all speaker handouts			
Verify VIP arrivals			
Finalize and print menus/floorplans for gala night			
Pack and send all conference materials			
Determine meal/transportation guarantees and provide to facility			

~ *Sample Template* ~

Tasks	Who?	When?	Done?
Travel to conference – manager and planner			
Travel to conference – staff			
Arrange daily invoice review with hotels, convention centre			
ON-SITE			
Set up conference offices			
Receive and inventory all shipments, equipment, supplies			
Review VIP arrangements			
Conduct individual tie-down meetings with suppliers and facility departments			
Prepare registration kits onsite			
Set up on-site registration/information area			
Conduct personnel instructional briefings for registration staff, volunteers, etc.			
Post gala dinner table sign-up sheet at registration (if necessary)			
Security staff briefing			
Distribute on-site registration/ information packages			
Disbribute Call for Submissions (for next year's conference)			
Distribute exhibitor prospectus (for next year's conference)			
Hold exhibitor recognition event (at close of Showcase)			
Arrange for return shipment of all materials			
Board meeting			
Deposit registration fees/ process credit card payments			
Hold sponsor recognition event			
Hold post-conference meetings			
POST-CONFERENCE			
Conduct post-conference and wrap-up meeting with facility departments and suppliers as needed.			
Meet to debrief conference (final day or day after)	Host Committee		
Send thank you letters and Showcase evaluation forms to exhibitors			

~ *Sample Template* ~

Tasks	Who?	When?	Done?
Send thank you letters to sponsors, facilities and volunteers			
Send thank you letters to speakers (include reimbursement cheques for expenses, as appropriate)			
Submit expense report; ensure other staff do same			
Send final delegate list to exhibitors and sponsors			
Prepare summary of all evaluations			
Prepare final accounting			
Review invoices for payment and code			
Ensure sponsor recognition ad in magazine September/October issue			
Select photos for website gallery			
Send expense reimbursements to speakers			

DESTINATION MANAGEMENT COMPANIES (DMC)

According to the Association of Destination Management Executives (ADME),

the definition of a DMC is "a professional services company possessing extensive local knowledge, expertise and resources, specializing in the design and implementation of events, activities, tours, transportation and program logistics".

The list of services provided by a DMC may vary from one company to another. However, a full service DMC provides: site inspections; negotiates hotel room rates; airport meet and greet services; shuttle transportation; customized tours and guest programs; pre and post conference tours; youth programs; dine arounds; team building programs; sports activities; event design, production and execution; gifts; and amenities. Clients rely on DMCs for their local expertise, contacts, facilities and volume buying power. The DMC becomes the eyes and ears of the client in the destination where the program is taking place.

Destination Management Companies (DMC) can be very helpful to the meeting professional, especially when planning a meeting/event in a new city or country. Destination Management Companies are specialists with an understanding of local venues, culture, protocol, costs, suppliers, etc. The DMC can be very helpful in planning part or all of the meeting professional's pre/post programs, offsite events, onsite registration.

Be sure to obtain and check references for the DMC you plan on contracting.

TRANSPORTATION

Selecting a location and facility for an event must be followed by a means of transporting attendees. This aspect of meeting planning may not be necessary if the event is geared to a local audience, residing less than 150 km or miles from the event site, or if attendees are expected to make their own arrangements. There are two main modes of travel to consider: air and ground transportation. Air travel is used to bring the attendees from various locations to the event, while ground transportation is used to bring attendees from the airport, to their accommodations, to the event facility, on excursions both event and nonevent related, and finally back to the airport.

A transportation plan must be developed for the event. A review of the event itinerary is useful to determine locations and times when ground transportation will be needed. As the following discussion will indicate, transportation vendors may provide planning aid including optimized routes, but it remains important for the meeting professional to understand and be able to communicate the transportation needs for the event.

AIR TRAVEL

Making air travel arrangements for event attendees, speakers, planning staff members, and VIPs is complicated by regulations, merged carriers, routing changes, airline special rates, and frequent flyer rewards. It may seem easier to the meeting professional to have event attendees make their own travel arrangements, but doing so may be passing up an opportunity to promote the event, increase attendance and save money because group fares would no longer apply.

Many attendees prefer to book their travel directly via the Internet. This method is generally more convenient for the attendee and facilitates attendees being able to make changes to their travel relatively easily. In many cases attendees who book their own travel may be able to secure less expensive fares by utilizing their frequent flyer points and other incentives offered at the time of booking.

Professional travel agents, some who specialize in group travel, can be utilized. It is a good idea to get a referral and ask for and check references.

A professional travel agent should be able to provide the meeting professional and attendees with a toll-free telephone number providing after hours assistance with travel needs.

Major airlines will have staff available to help make travel arrangements. Airlines will usually provide the following:

- Convention desk
  The carrier may have convention reservation desks with toll-free numbers for event attendees to make air and car rental arrangements. The meeting professional may organize a dedicated convention number that attendees can use to identify themselves as part of the group. Various discounts can be negotiated.

- Negotiated air fares
  Depending on the size of the event, a prearranged discount for volume or by zone may be possible

- Staff travel
  Complimentary or reduced rates for authorized member of the meeting professional's staff. Negotiation for air travel is similar to how complimentary

rooms are agreed upon (e.g., one complimentary air ticket for every 50 air tickets sold).

- Air cargo
Cargo specialists can advise for efficient onsite delivery of event displays and materials.

- Arrival and departure
A carrier may provide complete arrival/departure manifests to aid in accommodating VIPs, planning hotel check-ins, coordinating ground transport, and staffing registration desk.

- Cost analysis for site selection
An airline may consider the location of event attendees to determine an event site with the least air costs. An analysis of usually 10 to 15 cities is performed, with the specified class travel (economy, business, etc.)

- Promotional assistance
The carrier may provide the meeting professional with destination promotional brochures. While the pamphlets are free, the meeting professional must budget for the postage cost of mailing.

- Advertising
The airline may be willing to take out an ad in an organization magazine or newsletter to help promote the event.

GROUND TRANSPORTATION

When selecting a ground operator, it is important to consider the following criteria:

- cost

- operator's reputation

- number, condition, type and availability of vehicles

- special services provided

- security and safety concerns

- whether drivers are from the local area

Most operators have minimum booking restrictions, usually 4 or 5 hours, after which the cost reduces dramatically. Price schedule is important, as it may be more economical to pay for all day transport, rather than two 4 hour minimums.

Cost components may include fuel, equipment maintenance, union requirements , pay scales, and others. Surcharges may be in place to allow the carrier to pass the increasing cost of oil, fuel and insurance on to the client. Ensure all surcharges are listed in the contract

HOW TO ARRANGE GROUND TRANSPORTATION

To ensure that ground transportation will effectively meet the needs of event attendees, the meeting professional should start as far in advance as possible. It is advisable to get at least three proposals, and ask for and check references. Asking the potential carrier the following 10 questions can ensure a smooth ride.

1. Does the vendor have any corporate accounts?
    - experience with similar events
    - offer special services
    - VIP treatment

2. What is the condition and age of the vehicles?
    - air conditioning
    - public address system
    - restroom facilities
    - latest inspection for safety and other compliance

3. What are the minimum contract periods and costs?
    - surcharges, tolls, or taxes
    - minimum period
    - second driver
    - cost of dispatcher on per hour basis
    - waiting time/driving time costs
    - discounts available
        - volume
        - season
        - prepayment
        - youth/seniors

4. How big are the vehicles? Are they accessible to people with disabilities?
   - size of units
   - number of passengers legally allowed per unit
   - wheel chair accessible ramps
   - grip bars
   - special needs requested in advance

5. Are all vehicles insured?
   - liability coverage
   - request to see insurance documentation
   - include indemnification clause in the event of an accident

6. Ask for a contact person who is accessible on a 24-hour basis

7. Will the vendor work out a contingency plan with you?
   - length of time the vehicles wait for the attendees
   - extra pay for overtime

8. How are the vehicles dispatched?
   - for volume (e.g., 10 or more), for time (e.g., every 30 minutes)
   - onsite communication during the event to co-ordinate loading and unloading of passengers
   - backup vehicles or maintenance available in case of breakdown
   - spare vehicle available for the event

9. Does the vendor have enough vehicles to handle your group?
   - vendor owns and operates all vehicles, or sub contracts
   - vendor's responsibility to deal with the subcontractor

10. What duties can the driver/operator be expected to perform?
    - uniformed staff
    - provide assistance with storing or retrieving luggage
    - trained as a tour guide
    - speak other languages
    - drug/alcohol testing
    - familiarity with location
    - licensed to cross state/provincial/country lines

Industry Insight

WORLD YOUTH DAY 2002 TRANSPORTATION (WYD)

Contributed by Roger Halfacre, MTS, CTC, Director of World Youth Day Transportation. Ann Corbitt, Manager of Fleet Acquisition.

Mega events and global congresses add several more layers of planning and complexities in the development process. These types of events usually have a longer time frame in the planning and implementation; however, world events such as economic downturns and armed conflicts can cause several revisions and rethinking of the original plan.

World Youth Day 2002, held in Toronto, Ontario and area from July 23-28, 2002, was such an event. The original mandate given to the planners by the Canadian Conference of Catholic Bishops and the Vatican's Pontifical Council for the Laity was to plan for 750,000 participants from 170 countries. The world events in September, 2001 radically changed projections and final attendance. Final numbers were 183,000 registered attendees from 150 countries and over 800,000 people who attended the Papal Mass at Downsview Park on July 28, 2002.

The key to planning transportation for special events; irregardless of the attendance numbers lies with communication skills. Of course the more attendees and the larger the event, the more stakeholders will surface and need to be included in the communications plan. Examples of such are local communities and businesses impacted by road closures; health care system access; existing ridership using public transportation; the trucking associations; and the WYD in-house needs for moving 650 Cardinals and bishops, 3500 media members, thousands of volunteers and security personnel as well as the delegates.

Key partners in this transportation planning were the City of Toronto Transportation Department, as well as the Toronto Transit Commission. Dedicated personnel were identified and daily communications resulted in a high level of collaboration and trust that developed over twenty months of planning. Numerous other public agencies and private associations came to the planning table as needed during this period. An important aspect we learned in transportation planning was that every day things changed and we were faced with numerous variables, including many unforeseen. Open and frequent communications were a must and we actively engaged a process of relationship building.

The end result of WYD's successful transportation plan was a focus on safety, respect for all stakeholders and participants and a commitment for open and frequent communications. Final accounting shows that WYD chartered 3,946 motor coaches and school buses, 165 wheelchair accessible vehicles, the complete fleets of ten transit agencies, and cooperation with 43 airlines. In addition, there were numerous lane and road closures, signage and wayfinding, and community consultations.

FOOD AND BEVERAGE

In spite of all the efforts of the meeting professional to provide an educational and informative program, often the success of a meeting will be measured by the quality of the food and beverage events. It is also in the area of food and beverage that there is great potential to exceed budget allotments. Therefore a great deal of time and attention must be given to planning food and beverage functions for meetings.

As a first step the meeting professional should determine how many functions will take place during the meeting, what the anticipated attendance at each function will be and any special dietary requirements of the meeting participants. Some of this information can be gathered from records of past meetings. It is necessary to survey participants to determine any special dietary requirements. The meeting professional should sit down with the food and beverage manager of the facilities being considered to review requirements and options.

It is imperative to plan a menu that will be balanced nutritionally and appealing to a variety of people. Cultural requirements and known tastes of participants will also help dictate menus. The facility should be able to offer a variety of alternatives in order to meet the required elements of the functions. Most facilities and caterers will have policies governing guarantees, service charges, setup fees and overset allowances. While many of these items are negotiable the meeting professional should have an appreciation of their impact on the bottom line.

Meeting professionals do not have to include all meals for the conference in the planning process. Nor, for that matter do they have to include three meals per day. Often delegates will welcome a free evening or lunch in order to explore the destination or to socialize with a smaller group of colleagues.

BREAKFAST

Typically breakfast is one of the most difficult meals to plan, due to people's eating habits. While some attendees prefer to skip breakfast, others will expect a well balanced, nutritional meal. Meeting professionals seem to have found the most success through the provision of a continental breakfast, served buffet style. Often meeting professionals will allot a longer timeframe for breakfast then they will to other meals. This accommodates most participants as it allows them to choose when they want to eat. As well, it suits the needs of both the early risers and those participants who sleep longer in the morning. Some professionals will even add a more extensive selection of food to the first refreshment break of the morning to accommodate those participants who don't normally eat until mid-morning.

LUNCH

Lunch is the one meal that most meeting professionals prefer to have as an organized meal function, particularly when there is a program scheduled in the afternoon. Free time for lunch normally proves to be somewhat chaotic as one of two things happen:

- Many participants leave the facility and are either late returning for afternoon sessions or don't return at all, or

- Other participants may feel that they do not have the time to leave the facility and as a result create long lines in the facility's food and beverage outlets.

A well organized lunch can help keep meeting schedules on track as most delegates are gathered in one room and it is relatively easy to pass on instructions or to adjust schedules and times.

REFRESHMENT BREAKS

Mid-morning and mid-afternoon refreshment breaks mean much more to participants than a chance to grab a quick cup of coffee. These breaks are considered essential to re-energize participants and to allow them enough time to move to other seminars or to make use of the restrooms and phones. If at all possible try to arrange for the food and beverage service to take place outside of the meeting room, as participants will appreciate the opportunity to clear their minds from the subject matter being discussed.

Don't fall into the trap of merely serving coffee, tea and soft drinks. There is much room for creativity when planning refreshment breaks. Consider offering an assortment of fruit juices, or perhaps an ice cream stand to add variety.

~ *Sample Template* ~

Information on CD Rom

Refreshment Break Allowances
Adapted from Patti J. Shock, Professor & Department Chair
Tourism & Convention Administration, Harrah College of Hotel Administration
University of Nevada, Las Vegas

NOTE: 1 Gallon of coffee = 20 - 6 oz cups.
   In Europe, coffee is ordered by the cup or by the litre.

Morning Breaks

Drink	Attendance #	All Male	All Female	50/50
Regular coffee	Attendance	x60%	x50%	x55%
Decaf coffee	Attendance	x20%	x25%	x25%
Tea	Attendance	x10%	x15%	x10%
Soft Drinks/Water	Attendance	x25%	x25%	x35%

Afternoon Breaks

Drink	Attendance #	All Male	All Female	50/50
Regular coffee	Attendance	x35%	x30%	x35%
Decaf coffee	Attendance	x20%	x20%	x20%
Tea	Attendance	x10%	x15%	x10%
Soft Drinks/Water	Attendance	x70%	x70%	x70%

Hot Drinks Only

Drink	Attendance #	All Male	All Female	50/50
Regular Coffee	Attendance	x70%	x55%	x65%
Decaf Coffee	Attendance	x25%	x30%	x30%
Tea	Attendance	x10%	x20%	x10%

For Example: 50/50 group, 625 people, Afternoon Break. Required:

Regular Coffee	= 35% x 625 = 218 cups = 10.9 gallons = 11 gallons
Decaf Coffee	= 20% x625 = 125 cups = 7.8 gallons = 8 gallons
Tea	= 10% x 625 = 62 cups = 3.1 gallons = 3 gallons
Soft Drinks/Water	= 70% x 628 = soft drinks/water
	(ensure about 50% diet soft drinks included)

TYPES OF ROOM/FOOD PACKAGE PLANS

FAP — Full American Plan: facility rate includes three full meals each day and a sleeping room

MAP — Modified American Plan: facility rate includes breakfast, dinner and a sleeping room

EP — European Plan: no meals included in rate – only sleeping room.

CMP — Complete Meeting Package: 3 meals, continuous breaks, guest room, meeting room standard audio visual

DINNER

Typically, meeting professionals save the most elaborate themed meal functions for dinner. Often this meal is combined with awards presentations or entertainment. Wherever possible, if dietary concerns allow, try to incorporate some regional cuisine into the dinner menus. The catering director of the facility should be able to offer suggestions.

RECEPTIONS

Receptions are often offered as a pre-dinner function or in lieu of a more formal meal. These functions provide a good opportunity for participants to socialize and are often a welcome break from the more formal aspects of the program. The service of alcohol at these functions has become a significant issue for meeting professionals both from a cost and a liability perspective. Meeting professionals are looking at creative means of reducing consumption and thereby reducing costs and risk at receptions where alcohol is being served. The least expensive method of arranging for the service of alcohol is through a cash bar, whereby the participants pay for their own drinks. This also transfers some of the responsibility of consumption to the consumer.

While this is the most cost efficient method of serving alcohol, many groups would prefer to have some sort of hosted bar where the drinks are prepaid. This can be accomplished through one of the following three methods. There can be a "per person" fee where a flat rate is charged per participant, a "per drink" fee can be arranged for each drink served, or "per bottle" where the meeting professional pays only for those bottles opened. Beverage costs can be reduced by providing participants with a predetermined number of tickets. In this manner the meeting professional knows exactly how much the event will cost. A combination of complimentary drink tickets and a cash bar will also help reduce costs and consumption.

Even limiting the variety of alcohol served (e.g., beer and wine only) or the number of serving stations have been proven as effective ways to reduce costs, although some participants may feel that these methods are less than first class. Whatever method is chosen, ensure that participants have the option of choosing nonalcoholic drinks at a reduced cost or no cost to them.

In order to reduce food costs at a reception, ask for the food to be displayed on round tables rather than long buffet style tables. Also remember, the more crowded the room the less food will be consumed. Keep this in mind when selecting rooms to use for various functions. Napkins rather than plates will also reduce food consumption. Decisions that are made with regard to these measures will all hinge on the theme of the event, the budget for the event, and the expectations of the participants. When considering food and beverage consumption and room layout, do not overlook audience demographics. Ensure adequate seating for elderly, participants with physical challenges and health conditions.

SERVICE STYLES

Adapted from Patti J. Shock, Professor & Department Chair
Tourism & Convention Administration, Harrah College of Hotel Administration
University of Nevada, Las Vegas

Style of Service	Description
Buffet	Food is arranged on tables. Guests serve themselves, then take plates to a table. Beverages are usually served on the table. Buffets are generally more expensive than plated served meals, because there is no portion control and surpluses must be built in to assure adequate supplies. Be sure to allow adequate space around the buffet table for lines. Provide 1 buffet line for 100 guests
Action Stations	Sometimes referred to as Performance Stations or Exhibition Cooking. Action stations are similar to a buffet, except food is being freshly prepared as guests wait and watch. Common action stations: grilled meats, pastas, omelets, crepes, sushi, Belgian waffles
Reception	Light foods are served buffet style or passed on trays by servers (butlered). Guests usually stand and serve themselves. Receptions are often referred to as "walk and talks". Receptions can serve only finger foods, or only fork foods or a combination. By adding plates, the cost increases approximately 1/3.

Style of Service	Description
English Service/ Family Style	Guests are seated and large serving platters and bowls of food are placed on the dining room table by servers. Guests pass the food around the table. A Host often will carve the meat. This is an expensive style of service. Surpluses must be built in.
Plated/American Style Service	Guests are seated and served food which as been proportioned and plated in the kitchen. Food is served from the left. The meat or entrée is placed directly in front of the guest at 6 o'clock position. Beverages are served from the right. When guest has finished, both plates and glassware are removed from the right. American service is most functional, most common, most economical, most controllable and most efficient type of service.
Preset	Some foods are already on the table when guests arrive. The most common items to preset are water, butter, bread, appetizer/salad. At luncheons, where time is of the essence, the dessert is often preset as well.
Butlered	At receptions, butlered refers to having hors d'oeuvres passed on trays and the guest helps himself or herself.
French Service	Guests are seated, foods are cooked tableside on a portable cooking cart. Servers place the food on platters (usually silver) then pass the platters at tableside. Guests help themselves from the platters.
Russian Service	Guests are seated. Platters of food are assembled in the kitchen. Servers take the platters to the tables and serve from the left, placing the food on the guest's plate using two large silver forks or one fork and one spoon.
White Glove	Guests are seated. There is one server for every two guests. Servers wear white gloves. Foods are preplated. Each server carries two plates from the kitchen and stands behind the two guests assigned to the wait staff. At a signal from the banquet captain, all servings are set in from of all the guests at the same time.

FOOD AND BEVERAGE FORMULAS

Staffing Requirements

Breakfast	Russian Service	One server for every 15 participants
	Plated Service	One server for every 16-20 participants
	Buffet Service	One server per four tables
Lunch	Same ratios as breakfast	
Dinner	French Service	One server for 8-10 participants
	Plated Service	One server for 16-20 participants
	Buffet Service	One server for four tables
Buffet		One buffet table for 75-100 participants
Bar Staffing		One bar for each 100-125 participants

Alcohol Allowances per person

The following allowances are general guidelines for individual consumption and subject to regional, cultural and demographic variation. No complex math is required for cash bar setup, only budgeting for bar costs if minimum sales are not met.

Hour 1	1.5 drinks
Hour 2	additional 1.0 drinks
2 hour reception	3-4 glasses of wine
Wine with dinner	1.5 to 2.0 – 4 oz. glasses (3-4 bottles of wine for 10 people) or 1 glass per course if a new wine is introduced

Beverage service

First Hour:	50% men/50% women	2.25 drinks

Variables:
- number of attendees
- consumption per participant
- length of function
- size of alcohol bottles

number of attendees x drinks per participant = total drinks needed

total drinks needed / drinks per bottle = no. of bottles

1 - 26 oz bottle – 21-24 drinks

1 bottle of wine serves 5 drinks

Round up to nearest bottle when ordering. Since all bottles opened will be billed including those that are mostly full, the meeting professional may make a specific request for small bottle sizes. Multiple bar setups will provide better service for attendees, but will also result in a larger number of partial bottles left over.

ESTIMATING FOOD AND BEVERAGE

Formulas are guidelines for estimating consumption, order amounts, guarantees, and costs. There are as many formulas in existence as there are different types of events. Personal experience, good judgment, and knowledge of the attendee profile and the event program will enable the meeting professional to adapt formulas to individual events.

Variables:
- taxation rates
- gratuity and/or service rates
- determine whether gratuity is figured before or after taxes
- number of attendees
- attendance percentages
- facility percent overset

Find total food and beverage cost:

number of people x cost per person

+ (number of people x cost per person) x % gratuity

+ (number of people x cost per person) x % sales tax

+ (number of people x cost per person) x % other applicable

Total Food and Beverage cost = ??

Determine the number of servings (covers) that can be safely guaranteed:

Most facilities will require meal guarantees, so the meeting professional will need to know how many event attendees will go to each food and beverage function. The facility will usually provide the guaranteed number, plus a small additional percentage (overset). The standard lead-time on guarantees is 48 to 72 hours before your meal function. The venue will charge for the number guaranteed or the number of covers served, whichever is higher.

number of attendees x % guarantee = number guaranteed

number guaranteed x % overset = total room set

Note: if room is set in round tables, the facility will most likely round up the numbers to the nearest full table.

Be sure to have your staff count and confirm the numbers with the facility banquet manager on duty during the function, particularly in the event you have more people than guaranteed.

TRANSLATION AND SIMULTANEOUS INTERPRETATION

Simultaneous interpreters can be sourced through the local convention and visitor bureau, audio visual providers, local directories and the Internet.

There may be need for print and electronic materials in more than one language. Accurate translation is very important. Avoid using all self-appointed translators and interpreters including professors, teachers, and committee or organization members.

Determine the appropriate individual to grant final approval on all translated material before going to print.

Simultaneous interpretation may be desired during the event. When interpreters are required, ask for and check professional references from other clients they have served in the past. Check their setup requirements (extra space, equipment, etc.), as it may be necessary to book meeting rooms a day in advance. Provide copies of speeches in advance to interpreters if possible.

EVENT SIGNAGE

Signs are an important means of communication with attendees during the event, used to give directions and program information. Signs are also used as motivational tools, to greet attendees with a welcome, or recognize a corporation or association. Signage is a meetings industry term that encompasses signs and the psychological impact of sign design and placement.

Venues typically place restrictions on the locations in which signage may be displayed. Be sure to gain authorization for any signage to be placed in public areas of the venue.

The signage requirements for most events can be categorized into six areas:

1. office and service areas

2. directional assistance

3. function room identification

4. ground transportation vehicle and stops

5. sponsorship related, and

6. general event information

OFFICE AND SERVICE AREAS

- uniform, same size, colour, and typeface

- organization's logo for quick identification

- simple wording

- standard format 55 cm x 70 cm (22" x 28")

- to reuse, omit room names and numbers

DIRECTIONAL ASSISTANCE

- mark locations of supplementary directional signs on floor plan

- determine placement, size, and copy that works best in area provided

- do not select very small size to save money

- place a minimum of 2m (6') from the floor for visibility

- hang from ceiling if practical

FUNCTION ROOM IDENTIFICATION

- signs may list meeting topics as well

- uniform colour and format

- size depends on mounting method used (sign holders built into room entrances, weighted stanchion with or without holders, or tripod easels)

GROUND TRANSPORTATION VEHICLES AND STOPS

Vehicles

- window signs identify route number of vehicle

- front and side window

- most efficient for large operation may be letter sized signs that can be photocopied and taped to windows

Stops

- large displays or tent signs on the curb to identify bus route numbers, and hotels on each route

- minimum 55 cm x 70 cm (22" x 28")

- mount on heavy sign standards suitable for outdoors

- water resistant

SPONSORSHIP RELATED

- sponsor recognition

- size, content, and placement should be included in sponsorship agreement

GENERAL EVENT INFORMATION

- can announce special meetings or promote functions

- avoid crowding with too much copy

TEMPORARY SIGNS

- make sure local fire regulations are adhered to

Material	Available sizes	Features
Showcard stock	up to 100 cm x 150 cm (40" x 60")	widest selection of colour low price
Coroplast	up to 120 cm x 240 cm (4' x 8')	white more rigid than showcard stock slightly more expensive
Foamcore	up to 120 cm x 240 cm (4' x 8')	used for double sided signage short life span
Sail cloth	any size available	used for large signs and banners usually fitted with grommets for hanging
Vinyl	any size available	good for outdoor use

PERMANENT SIGNS

Permanent signs can be custom made out of durable materials for repeated use. Plexiglas, masonite, veneer plywood, metal, and plastics all are available in a variety of colours and sizes.

ELECTRONIC SIGNS

Some conference facilities have electronic signs that can be programmed for each meeting room, or will have monitors throughout the facility that can be preprogrammed with daily meeting details.

SIGN SPECIFICATIONS

When placing or pricing a sign order, be sure to include the following

- size

- colour of background

- font size and colour of lettering

- type of material

- format (landscape or portrait)

- typed copy, not handwritten

- number of signs required

- placement (hanging, attached to wall, placed in existing holder, etc.; determine and include rules for where signs can be placed within the facility)

- floor plan designating positions of each sign

- date and time for completion of placement

- any sponsor related requests for sign placement

Industry Insight

DELEGATES RECEIVE FINISHED PROCEEDINGS BEFORE LEAVING SITE

Contributed by Mitchell Beer, InfoLink: The Conference Publishers

In December 1997, three Canadian government departments hosted an international conference in Ottawa to ban a weapon that has killed more civilians than all the weapons of mass destruction combined. At the end of the two-day Landmine Treaty Conference, Canada's foreign affairs minister held up an inch-thick, bilingual, desktop published document and presented it to attendees as their agenda for action. Within 45 minutes, copies of the finished report began arriving onsite for international delegates to bring home.

The report was the work of an independent team of writers, editors, translators and production artists who joined together in a tightly organized effort to give attendees the resources they needed to create practical, life-saving results in the days and weeks following their event. The report was unprecedented in the history of international treaty making, and highlighted the role of conference proceedings in helping attendees and organizers get the most out of their meetings.

MESSAGE CENTRES

The event message centre can be combined with the information desk and/or lost and found to save space and for added convenience. The message/info centre should be equipped with the following: telephone(s), fax machines, computer with online service, message pads, pens, local maps, restaurant guides, general tourist information, and general conference information. The major consideration for locating a message centre is to have the physical location central to attendee traffic flow, perhaps near the registration area.

ONSITE OFFICE

An onsite office is needed to provide a headquarters for meeting professionals and staff during the event. The meeting professional and staff members can communicate with event facility personnel, suppliers, host organization officers, and speakers. This space must function as a control point, where knowledgeable staff can be contacted quickly to provide information and solve problems.

The individual event will dictate the hours and number of staff needed to provide adequate coverage. Most facilities will provide office space or draped tables in a designated area. Anticipate functions that will be performed in the onsite office. By having the right equipment on hand, such as computers, photocopiers, fax machines, typewriters, etc., the meeting professional can more efficiently deal with issues, preventing wasted time, frustration and potentially avoiding crisis situations.

EQUIPMENT

The meeting professional can rent business equipment or use their own. If renting, look for a rental firm that is a member of the local convention bureau, as this generally indicates the firm has an understanding of the meetings industry and its needs. Remember, once a firm is familiar with the meeting professional's needs, this information can be reused for subsequent events, or sent to branches in other cities.

The supplier of business equipment will:

- provide a full price list

- deliver, setup, test, and pick up equipment

- give a discounted rate for backup equipment

- provide an emergency contact telephone number

When ordering, the meeting professional will specify the type of machines required. If computers are necessary, indicate memory capacity, frequency, operating system, full size or laptop, and peripheral equipment (mice, printers, modems, etc.) needed. Determine if paper is included or must be ordered separately. Include a backup source of power for computers to save information in the case of a power outage, and access to technical support, which is very important when renting computers.

Photocopiers are very important for the onsite office. Having this equipment on hand can save time and money. Determine the specifications of the equipment required. The order will include supplies such as paper and toner.

Make sure electrical outlets are available in the onsite office where equipment is to be installed, and be aware that installation of equipment usually must occur on a business day, not a weekend. Having equipment installed at least a day before the event to reduce the confusion at the event opening. Make sure all equipment is functional before the installer leaves, and that staff know how to operate the equipment, and whom to contact in case of an emergency.

FURNITURE

Draw a scale floor plan of the office or area where furniture and equipment will be needed. Depending on the event, the onsite office may require chairs, desks, and cabinets. When ordering furniture, be specific: secretarial or executive chairs; number of drawers and size of cabinets; locking desks and cabinets. Include a copy of the floor plan with furniture placement.

COMMUNICATION SYSTEMS

The meeting professional will ensure that methods of communicating with staff, suppliers, host organization, participants, VIPs and guests are present. These may include:

- telephone(s)
- fax machine(s)
- online services
- pagers for staff
- walkie-talkies

Many companies provide "one stop shopping", and will strive to meet all of the equipment and service needs for an event, looking after the program, speaker, communications, and onsite office. Audio visual providers can supply highly technical equipment and the technicians to operate it.

Be sure to inform the facility management of intended physical layout of the onsite office, and all requirements (spatial and electrical).

ROOMING LISTS

Rooming lists are lists provided to the hotel for bedroom accommodations. Rooming lists are created when the host organization is making the reservations for the guests. This list is usually required 21 days prior to the event. It should include the following information:

- name of guest(s)

- arrival date

- departure date

- smoking/nonsmoking

- single/double/kingsize

- payment (personal credit card or master bill)

- what is included if master billed

- room and taxes only

- room, taxes and incidentals

- any limitations on incidentals

- identify VIPs

- if special room amenities are required

If guests are making their own hotel reservations, a rooming list is not required, and the guests become a part of the accommodation block booked by the host organization. The meeting professional must ensure that all guests at the event are included in the guestroom block as this affects attrition and/or meeting room costs. The meeting professional can combine both methods by providing a rooming list for a portion of the block (e.g., staff, speakers) and allowing attendees to make their own accommodation arrangements.

OPERATIONS MANUAL

An operations manual lists the step-by-step procedures and logistical details that, together, make up the meeting. It is also known as a conference manual, meeting procedural guide, or résumé. It will include:

- banquet event orders

- names and contact information including suppliers, committee members and staff

- program at a glance

This is a very important aspect of meeting logistics. If event procedures are explicitly and clearly defined, the meeting professional will increase the effectiveness of staff members in executing an event.

Procedures should be reviewed and revised after each event, so that subsequent events benefit from the meeting professional's experience.

PRE CONFERENCE MEETING

A pre conference meeting is:

> A meeting at the convention centre/hotel/conference centre just before the show begins move-in. The meeting planning staff, department heads, other facility staff as appropriate and contractors review the purpose and details of the event and make last minute adjustments. Also called pre-convention briefing or pre event (function) meeting.

The pre conference meeting is generally held a day or two before the start of the event. Attendees at the meeting vary. The following individuals are likely to be in attendance for a large event with a number of banquets, meetings, and complex setups:

- meeting professional and staff members

- director of convention services and the convention service manager responsible for servicing the group

- salesperson who secured the group and perhaps the director of sales

- food and beverage manager, catering/banquet manager and the chef

- facility's general manager and accounting department representative

- director of exhibit service, floor manager, and a convention service secretary

- representatives from the following departments

- housekeeping

- telecommunication services

- recreational facilities

- audio visual supplier

- front office

- security

- reservations

- concierge

- other major suppliers (e.g., décor, transportation)

POST CONFERENCE MEETING

A post conference meeting or telephone interview follows the conclusion of the event. This meeting provides a forum for reviewing services levels, reviewing billing and resolving any billing issues. The same people meet for an after the fact review of the conference.

SEE THE APEX (Accepted Practices Exchange) section for detailed templates of:Event Specifications Guide

> **Registration**
>
> **Housing**
>
> **Rooming**
>
> **Post-Event Report**

NOTES

~ A Conference Journal ~

Approximately 18 months prior to the actual event, conference time lines were determined and a critical path prepared. This formed the basis of the work schedule for both the meeting manager and meeting coordinators.

Early on in the process, they obtained enlarged floor plans from the venue and assigned meetings and events to the various rooms and open areas, making sure that it was the best use of the space while ensuring reasonable traffic flow. From this perspective, they were able to transfer the information to another document that would become the basis for their meeting résumé. As details of events were confirmed, information was incorporated into the résumé. This document was their guide for pre-planning and onsite management. It included the date, time, name of the event, room number, setup requirements, audio visual support, food and beverage, if any, and also noted any special details. For example, if there was a gift for a luncheon speaker, the time and the person making the presentation was identified while a separate note served as a reminder to place the gift at the podium. This was done for every single detail of the conference, no matter how small, so that everything was contained in one place. When they were done, they had 67 legal size pages of text in chart form detailing the conference from move-in to move-out.

Communication was paramount to the success of the implementation of this joint conference. The résumé was distributed to the facility coordinator, audio visual supplier, food and beverage coordinator, trade show contractor, registration company and, of course, all association staff so that everyone knew the details of the event. Key individuals from each area were asked to review the document and advise the meeting manager of any omissions or suggestions for improvement. These were incorporated, and a final document re-submitted to everyone. Several days prior to move in, these individuals came together at a pre-conference meeting and went over last minute details, to ensure that everyone was working within the same framework. With the logistics documented and distributed well in advance, the meeting was generally used more for introduction of all onsite personnel and an opportunity to go over last minute details such a delegate arrivals, final attendance, or changes to food and beverage guarantees.

A week prior to the event, operations manuals were created for the meeting manager and each of the coordinators. These binders, included the telephone numbers of key personnel of various suppliers as well as all onsite staff, a section for room layouts and floor plans, a list of sponsors and fulfillment requirements at each event, the meeting résumé in chronological order, and all special requirements by various additional suppliers used for special events such as the décor details, stage requirements, audio visual support and entertainment details. The operations manual contained a detailed security and room monitor schedule as well as all scripts that had been prepared for the master of ceremonies or chairs for all functions.

Good communication didn't stop at pre-planning but continued all the way through the conference. Walkie-talkies were distributed to the individuals responsible for onsite implementation from the suppliers mentioned above as well as the meeting manager, meeting coordinators and a number of association staff. This enabled the meeting manager to stay in touch with everyone at all times during the conference. The meeting manager and meeting coordinators were also issued cellphones to ensure that communication was possible, even in remote areas of the building or when using other venues.

Delegates required a different means of communication. Signs using a consistent format and colour for identification were used to provide direction, program information, sponsor recognition and to welcome delegates. Signs were placed outside every room to identify the function and time, if applicable. Large coloured banners were hung from the ceiling in the covered walkway to assist delegates in moving from one facility to the other, while six foot high, double sided directional signs stood front and centre in the main hallways that identified major conference areas. In addition, floor plans of each level, for each facility, were incorporated into the onsite program and a staff person responsible for providing information about the facility and the location of sessions or events was situated at an information booth located in the main registration area. Finally, a message centre with ample seating was created on the trade show floor to provide a meeting place for delegates or enabled delegates to leave messages for one another.

This particular conference was more complicated than most in terms of logistics, in part because of the fact that it was a joint conference with two associations used to different methodologies, combined with the need for multiple venues due to the size of the conference. Sessions were conducted in two separate buildings of the convention centre. A nearby hotel and the south building of the convention centre were used for social functions while the two trade shows carried on separately in both buildings of the convention centre. This single factor created the need to move all participants from the north building to the south building midweek. There was also a spouses program that required a hospitality suite for daily presentations and a gathering point for tours. This was held at the hotel together with the pre-conference seminar program and a large number of corporate hospitality suites.

Not mentioned previously, the meeting manager was asked to identify space in the south building in which to conduct a second conference over the last two and a half days of the main conference. This group needed several breakouts, a plenary session and social events for approximately 500 government officials from around the world. Although planned by a different group of volunteers, it was integrated into the main conference by registration in that these officials, who represented the same industry, were encouraged to attend the main conference for a reduced registration fee. The planning committee for this event provided progress reports to the joint conference planning committee and the budget was integrated into the main conference budget. To maintain control over logistics and to provide consistency with all suppliers, the meeting manager and meeting coordinators organized the logistics for this conference and carried out the onsite management, at the same time as the joint millennium event.

Social events, while never small in number, ranged from a simple sponsored welcome reception for 2,500 people to a full production awards night and millennium celebration gala, each with over 1,000 participants. The receptions generally required the setup of a host bar and in some cases food stations with pre dinner snacks while the awards function and gala required full décor, an up-scale elaborate dinner menu, entertainment that was staged and produced and an awards ceremony with more than 25 awards that were acknowledged and distributed. The setup for these two events required two full days to test lighting, sound, setup the décor and rehearse the routines.

Managing the logistics for this event was a challenge for everyone concerned but it also offered great rewards. When the sessions were over, the exhibits had moved out and the delegates had left, there was tremendous relief as well as an overwhelming sense of accomplishment and teamwork.

MEETING LOGISTICS CHECKLIST

Information on
CD Rom

☐ Air Travel

- arrangements made with
  - travel agents
  - airlines
  - internet
- tickets
  - paper
  - electronic
- provided information
- expected attendance
- past attendance (if applicable)
- cargo opportunities
- appoint an official carrier
- publicize air travel information in event promotion materials
- kinds of fares
  - group
  - promotional
  - excursion
  - other

☐ Ground Transportation

- if using an airline, do they provide
  - complimentary staff travel
  - cost analysis
  - promotional assistance
  - convention desk
  - rental car assistance
  - arrival/departure manifests
  - VIP lounge
  - special baggage centre
  - pre-boarding privileges
  - electronic ticketing
  - complimentary ticket ratio

- determine
  - minimum rental period for vehicles
  - overtime availability
  - capacity
  - dispatch method
  - accessibility
  - condition of vehicles
  - back up vehicles
  - air conditioning/heating
  - distance from event
  - pick up/drop off and parking at event departure points
  - hours of use
  - route
  - insurance
  - driver contract status
  - price

☐ Function Room Selection

- detail nature of each function with facility staff; inspect possible sites for
  - sufficient space
  - adequate electrical outlets, voltage capabilities
  - good acoustics, lighting, ventilation
  - columns or other obstructions
  - accessibility of exits, restrooms, dressing rooms
  - mobility easements

☐ Room Set-Ups

- work with a scaled diagram and be sure to consider
  - type of activities
  - expected attendance
  - number, dimensions of tables
  - type of food service
  - best table placement

- possible items for head tables include
  - platform
  - additional two feet of space for lectern or podium
  - place cards
  - special services, decorations, beverages, gifts

☐ Pre-event Arrangements

- assign staff members to:
  - serve as ticket collectors, ushers, escorts for special guests
  - co-ordinate attendance, consumption revisions with catering department
  - inventory beverages before and after function
  - make/ distribute seating plans, place cards, programs, gifts
  - attend to entertainers or special guests needs
- provide system for notifying attendees of any changes in function location; instruct staff and attendees on:
  - seating procedures
  - assignment of alternative locations
  - handling admission, tickets cash collection
- check periodically that all instructions to facility on menu, table, seating arrangements, etc., are being carried out; co-ordinate the exact schedule for:
  - room setups
  - ticket sales
  - cocktails
  - when doors open
  - seating of head table guests
  - special opening ceremonies
  - food service
  - tables cleared
  - speakers
  - entertainment, music, dancing

☐ Signage Requirements

- signs needed
  - office and service areas
  - directional assistance
  - function room identification
  - ground transportation vehicles and stops
  - general event information

- sign specifications
  - size
  - colour of background
  - colour of lettering
  - type of material
  - format
  - copy
  - number of signs required
  - placement
  - floor plan
  - date and time

☐ Pre convention meeting

- set up schedule of onsite briefings involving:
  - convention service manager
  - onsite meeting manager
  - outside suppliers
  - convention bureau representative
  - others as required
  - organization staff members

- well in advance of meeting, send function sheets to:
  - convention service manager
  - appropriate outside suppliers

- include in function sheets:
  - organization name and date for each function
  - room for each

- time function begins and ends
- scheduled setup time
- expected attendance at each
- staff member in charge
- room set up diagrams
- special services, facilities required
- billing instructions

- review details regarding:
  - food/beverage
  - entertainment
  - audio visual equipment
  - engineering/special utilities
  - accommodation reservations

☐ Translation and Simultaneous Interpretation

- registration
- onsite cash management
- transportation
- parking
- receiving/shipping
- telephone/Internet connections
- sign
- working language of destination
- other languages according to need

☐ Housekeeping

☐ Special tours

☐ Security

☐ Other

☐ Printed materials

- working language of destination
- other languages according to need

☐ Traffic Flow and Crowd Control

- registration
  - number of stations
  - pre-registered attendees separate
  - duration
  - expected peak
  - method of crowd control

- function rooms
  - location and number of signs
  - location and number of staff members
  - staggered breaks
  - adequate restroom facilities
  - expected peak
  - method of crowd control

- to ground transportation/accommodation
  - location and number of signs
  - location and number of staff members
  - expected peak
  - method of crowd control

CHAPTER REVIEW

KEY POINTS

- A timeline or critical path will assist in organizing meeting logistics and provide a tool for assigning responsibility and setting deadlines. Critical paths should be organized by deadline date and are particularly useful when dealing with committees.

- Destination management companies (DMC's) can assist the meeting professional by providing extensive local expertise of the host city regarding transportation, pre/post event tours, activities, offsite events, program logistics and event design and implementation. DMC's are particularly helpful when the meeting professional is operating in a new city or country.

- Air travel arrangements can be made by professional travel advisors, travel agents, or airlines, who must be provided with information on group demographics, expected attendance, past attendance and cargo opportunities. These travel professionals can assist by providing convention desk services, negotiated group fares, promotional assistance and discounted staff travel.

- Select a ground transportation operator based on

  - cost
  - reputation
  - number, condition, and availability   of vehicles
  - special services.

- Food and beverage plays a key role in the overall success of the meeting. Food and beverage costs are often a large part of the meeting budget and food and beverage formulas and guidelines can assist in managing these costs, and ensuring appropriate service levels.

- Signage plays an important part in providing direction to delegates, communicating program information and recognizing sponsors. Signage is most commonly used for

- office and service areas

  - directional assistance
  - function room identification
  - ground transportation vehicle and stops
  - sponsorship related
  - general event information

- A rooming list is generally provided to the meeting venue 21 days prior to the event and included detailed information on delegate accommodation requirements.

- The operations manual lists the step by step procedures and logistical details that make an event run smoothly. The operations manual includes banquet event orders, names and contact information of supplies, committee members and staff and a program at a glance.

- Pre convention meetings

- are essential to the success of any well organized event

- will be held in the days immediately preceding the event

- may be attended by all hotel staff with responsibility to the event

- require accurate function sheets completed by the meeting professional several weeks in advance of the pre-convention meeting

- will not be used to make major changes to the event program

- When translation of printed materials is necessary, send advance copies for final approval before going to print. Language or sign interpreters may have special setup requirements that may include having access to the meeting rooms a day in advance.

- Traffic flow and crowd control are necessary for all aspects of the event, will be a driving force in event site selection, and must be incorporated into event scheduling.

TEST YOUR KNOWLEDGE

The following self test will indicate the level of understanding and knowledge gained from this chapter. Solutions to all self tests can be found in Appendix A.

1. Policies are written specifications of how certain situations will be handled, and procedures are written instructions that describe the methods used to carry out the policy.

    ☐ True   ☐ False

2. Pre-convention meetings are not always necessary before the start of a convention.

    ☐ True   ☐ False

3. Volunteer translators, including professors, teachers, and committee or organization members are always a valuable and inexpensive resource for translating printed materials.

    ☐ True   ☐ False

4. The majority of traffic flow and crowd control problems can be avoided by careful site selection, and by staggered event starting times, breaks and ending times.

    ☐ True   ☐ False

5. A pre-convention meeting will be held:

    (a) several months in advance of any event

    (b) a few days before an event begins

    (c) only if the meeting professional believes the pre-convention meeting is necessary

    (d) only if the host facility believes the pre-convention meeting is necessary

    (e) only if more than 500 participants are registered for the event

6. Which of the following would best describe the meeting professional's role at the pre-convention meeting?

    (a) should keep a low profile and say very little

    (b) should use the meeting to introduce several recent changes to the event program

    (c) should clearly outline the group's goals, objectives, needs, and expectations

    (d) should strive for power and control over others attending the meeting

    (e) none of the above are correct roles for the meeting professional

7. A destination management company can be used to:

   (a) plan the educational content of the meeting

   (b) replace the meeting professional in the planning role

   (c) provide local expertise on transportation and offsite venues and assist in planning tours

   (d) choose the destination city only

   (e) all of the above

8. What are four services that most airlines usually provide to meeting professionals?

   _____

   _____

   _____

   _____

   _____

9. Give examples of traffic flow and crowd control measures commonly used at large meetings.

   _____

   _____

   _____

   _____

   _____

10. Describe 4 different food and beverage service style and suggest when each would be most appropriately used.

   _____

   _____

   _____

   _____

   _____

NOTES

Chapter 13

Technology

INTRODUCTION

Audio describes something that can be heard. Visual describes what can be seen. Each can be used separately but elements of both are usually used together in a presentation. Audio visual aids can enhance or replace a live presentation.

AUDIO VISUAL IN MEETINGS

- Almost all conferences use some kind of audio visual (AV) aids

- AV equipment may be as simple as a flip chart or as sophisticated as multi-site satellite linked communication

- Selecting of appropriate equipment is critical to a meeting's success

- Presenters are becoming more sophisticated in AV delivery techniques. As a result, the meeting professional must understand the available options and the benefits and limitation of each.

Selecting a knowledgeable AV supplier will enable both the meeting professional and the presenter to feel confident in the choice of and comfortable with the use of the appropriate equipment.

Ensure you understand and can apply the following terms:

- Front screen projection
- Plasma screens
- Rear screen
- PDA
- Teleconferencing
- Teleprompter
- Video conferencing
- Wireless audio response system

Refer to the glossary for further clarification of the key terms for this chapter.

LEARNING OBJECTIVES

After completing this chapter, the learner will:

- understand the basic audio visual equipment

- select appropriate technology for all elements of an event

ROLES AND RESPONSIBILITIES

MEETING MANAGER

○ Incorporate current technologies

- Demonstrate an awareness of emerging technologies
  - ○ research emerging technologies
  - ○ use current terminology related to computer applications, communication systems, audio visual equipment and printing
  - ○ anticipate the impact of technologies (e.g., financial, suitability, logistical)
  - ○ demonstrate an understanding of communication systems
  - ○ demonstrate an understanding of audio visual technology

- Use appropriate computer applications
  - ○ identify software programs available and their applications
  - ○ assess the compatibility of a technological solution
  - ○ outsource appropriate products and services related to technology
  - ○ incorporate the use of technologies in all planning stages

MEETING COORDINATOR

○ Demonstrate an understanding of current technologies in the meeting industry

- Demonstrate an awareness of developing technologies
  - ○ identify how to access information about technological applications in the meeting industry
  - ○ research emerging technologies

- Use computer applications
  - identify software programs available and their applications
  - use computer components and current software applications

- Demonstrate an understanding of communication systems
  - use systems currently available in the meeting industry
  - implement interpretation and translation requirements as per plan
  - implement audio visual plan with service providers

AUDIO VISUAL BASICS AND APPLICATIONS

The following audio visual equipment is commonly used by presenters in small and large meeting formats. The meeting professional should be familiar with this equipment at a minimum.

DESCRIPTION

Audio Recordings	Cassette tape or Compact Disc recordings of presentations that can be sold to the attendees, at or after the meeting
Data Projector	Unit used to drive the image from a laptop computer to the screen
Flipchart	Large pad of paper placed on an easel and used by a speaker for illustrative purposes. Requires markers
Front Screen Projection	Projection equipment is visible in the room. Usually at the back or in the centre aisle. Projection onto the front of a screen
Microphones	Converts sound into electronic signals for amplification Can be wireless, lavalier (clip on), hand-held, table, floor stand,or attached to a podium (stationary)
Opaque Projector (Document Projection)	Designed to project the image of an opaque object, such as a sheet of paper
Overhead Transparency Projector	AV equipment designed to project and magnify an image on a transparent sheet of acetate

PowerPoint	A Microsoft software program that uses design templates to build computer-driven slide presentations. Includes graphics and special animation features.
Projection Stands	Platform or area from which AV presentations are controlled
Rear Screen Projection	Projection equipment hidden behind a curtain at the front of the room, behind the presenter. Projection onto the back of a screen
Screens	Surface on which images are displayed. Portable screens usually on a tri-pod (3 legs and a supporting rod). Available in sized ranging from 4' to 8'. Larger (non-portable) screens available up to 30'. May be built into the meeting room
Simultaneous Interpretation	Process of translating one language into another while the speaker is presenting
Sound System	Audio speaker system used to project sound
Teleconferencing	Type of meeting which brings together three or more people in two or more locations through telecommunication – either audio or visual
Video	Visual tape used to record a presentation. In large venues, may use I-Mag (Image Magnification) to enable audience to see presenter more clearly on a large screen, such as concerts.
Video Cassette Recorder (VCR)	Visual playback and recording equipment. Available in multiple formats such as VHS or PAL.

HOT TIP

Podium Pointer

Check mic heights against the speaker's height. A speaker who is especially short will find the typical level for the podium a barrier and probably an embarrassment. People over 6 ft. 3 in can be similarly embarrassed if they have to stoop into the mic. Experienced speakers can quickly make an adjustment while laughing off the situation. The best bet, however, is to avoid such awkward moments by planning ahead. Have someone ready to adjust equipment heights for each speaker.

BEYOND THE BASICS

The equipment described below may be useful in enhancing presentations. The meeting professional should be familiar enough with these technologies to discuss their appropriate use with presenters and audio visual suppliers.

TELEPROMPTERS®

TelePrompTers® can enhance the quality of an event by improving the speaker's delivery. Transparent screen(s) at the speaker's eye level scroll the script from which the speaker reads. The audience cannot see the script and barely notices the screens. The presenter appears to be looking at the audience. The meeting professional should encourage speakers to familiarize themselves and practice with the TelePrompTer®. The presenter should be speaking at a normal pace and cadence. It is the operator's job to have the text scrolling at the proper speed.

Type should be large and easy to read, with clear stops/starts at the end/beginning of sentences. All words should be spelled, no abbreviations. Include cues such as pauses, gestures, ad lib references, all in parenthesis so the speaker does not read them out loud.

Insist there be an onsite rehearsal with the TelePrompTer® to check equipment and display panel height. Give the speaker an exact duplicate hard copy for preparation and fallback in case of equipment failure.

SMARTBOARD©

Interactive SMARTboards© are digital white boards. It is touch screen electronic technology. Touch any projected image on the SMARTboard© to help demonstrate a point and change projected data immediately. The SMARTboard© interactive whiteboard turns your computer and projector into a powerful tool for teaching, collaborating and presenting. With a computer image projected onto the board, you can simply press on its large, touch-sensitive surface to access and control any application. Using a pen from the SMART© Pen Tray, you can work naturally at the board to take notes and highlight important information. The user can write notes, draw diagrams, illustrate ideas or highlight key information with electronic ink. The information can also be saved, emailed or printed out.

WEBCASTING

Webcasting is the delivery of audio or video content, via the Internet to a group of online participants. Since the audio and video is one way only (from presenter to audience), webcasting is best suited for situations where the message has to be broadcast to a large and geographically diverse audience.

A webcast can be held live, or archived for on demand viewing. Webcasts that are conducted live include events such as Annual General Meetings, analyst or investor conferences, or generally any event where dissemination of the information is time sensitive. Sales training sessions and membership education are typically recorded as archive only webcasts so viewers can access the information at a time most convenient for them.

Webcasting technology has progressed to the point where most users' computers already have the hardware and software necessary to view a webcast. Whether live or archived, webcasting offers an excellent opportunity to increase the reach of a message to a worldwide audience at minimal incremental cost per viewer.

PLASMA SCREENS

Plasma flat screen technology performs extraordinarily well under most ambient light conditions. The bright lights of the facility do not wash out the image on the screen as they do in data projection. The advantage of this technology is that, unlike front view projection screens, you do not have to turn off the lights to see an image clearly and easily.

With 160 degrees viewing angle, people sitting off to one side of the plasma screen will still be able to see the image without losing any of it. In addition, plasma flat screen technology tends to be very lightweight in comparison to similar sized stand display monitors and television screens.

The thinness of these systems allows for the monitor to be placed virtually anywhere. Plasma flat screens can be used in a variety of environments including network control rooms, meeting rooms, executive offices, corporate lobbies, signage, and tradeshows. Another characteristic of a plasma panel is the extreme viewing angles possible both vertically and horizontally. They typically accept inputs for both data and video sources.

WIRELESS AUDIENCE RESPONSE SYSTEM

The audience response system is a tool that provides two way communication between the presenter and the entire audience. Audiences know this system by various names: electronic polling/voting system, reply system, group response system, and classroom polling system or touch pads. Keypads can be used either by a single participant or shared by two. The audience response system can be used for product launches, sales meetings, scientific meetings, medical training, training sessions, team building, voting or delegate resolutions.

Questions are fed into a Windows based computer system and displayed on a large video screen for all participants to view. Participants can then respond using a handheld keypad when prompted by the presenter. A computer collects, stores and analyzes the gathered information. The responses are instantly displayed in graphical format using bar chart, pie chart or cylinder chart form. Anonymity is ensured.

VIDEO CONFERENCING

Video conferencing can reduce the travel costs of event participants, while increasing education and training opportunities by giving wider access to a variety of speakers. Video conferencing refers to the real-time and typically interactive transmission of image and sound (usually in digital format) between two or more sites. Although video conferences are primarily two way exchanges, they can be one way audio or video only.

Dial-up video conferencing systems allow participants to call each other as if they were dialing a telephone call. There are national and international firms capable of providing full outsourcing services in this area, on a one time or an extended lease basis. Hotels, universities, movie theaters, conference centres, convention centres, and other venues may have rooms equipped for video conferencing, which can be used for a fee. As network costs and transmission bandwidths have declined, so have the size of video conferencing systems. At the time of publication, more and more desktop systems are being installed.

POINT-TO-MULTIPOINT BROADCASTING

Data is transmitted via satellite from the source location to anywhere on the globe. Lease of a broadcast studio and production crew is required, as is set up of a satellite dish and equipment at the receiving site, a monitor, and finally, renting time on a satellite for transmission. Broadcast programs generally last two hours. Permanent down links can be installed for regularly broadcast sessions, weekly, monthly, or quarterly.

Industry Insight

THE ELECTRONIC EVENT GUIDE GOES MOBILE

What PDAs, Tablet PCs and the latest phones can do for your meeting info

Contributed by Tiffany Devitt, NearSpace Inc.

Before 1998, most meetings didn't have a dedicated website for delivering event information to attendees. Today, virtually all of them do. Typically, attendees use the event website to register, to peruse exhibitor lists, and to study the agenda. Unlike the printed catalog, it's available well in advance of the show, and is updated often. Moreover, it usually includes helpful planning tools such as an itinerary builder, personal checklists, links to exhibitor websites, and downloadable abstracts.

With the proliferation of Personal Digital Assistants (PDAs) such as those made by Palm, Sony, Handspring, and Dell, the advent of "Tablet" PCs (which are a cross between a PDA and laptop) and PDA-phone hybrids, event producers have an opportunity to take these digital strengths and go mobile with them.

PDA event guides in particular, are gaining popularity today. For the meeting manager they offer an engaging and cost effective way of delivering information. Exhibitors can be listed by product, sponsorship level and alphabetically; sessions can be listed by day, time and program - without impacting the cost. The PDA Guide can also be updated continuously throughout the event - in stark contrast to the printed catalog, which is often sent into production several weeks in advance.

For attendees, PDA Guides offer a far superior experience to paper based guides. Meeting participants can tap on an exhibitor name to find its location on an interactive map of the exhibition floor instead of looking up the booth number in a hardcopy catalog and then trying to find it on a hard to read foldout map. Attendees can use the PDA Guide to read up on a session's participants and then add it to the calendar on their PDA. Or, they can view a time-synchronized list of sessions going on at that very moment. They can look up an exhibitor using a keyword search, add those exhibitors to a personal checklist, and even create a custom map showing where they're all located.

The mobile electronic event guide can also usually offer features not available on the web, features which assist attendees in managing their time onsite. For instance, suppose that an attendee has a particularly fruitful encounter with an exhibitor or participant. They can look up the company's entry in the PDA Guide, attach a free-form note indicating what they discussed and what follow-up is required. They can then export the exhibitor's contact information - along with the company description and their personal notes - to the address book on their PDA. When they get back to the office and synchronize their device, this information is then available via their desktop contact manager, such as Microsoft Outlook. Attendees can also chose to export their notes and/or checklist as an electronic "Trip Report," which they can then email to colleagues.

The initial response to the PDA Event Guide has been extraordinary. At NearSpace, attendees have emailed us to say: "The PDA Guide was a fantastic asset."; "The coolest thing since sliced bread."; and "An excellent planning tool."

PDA Guides can also be quite helpful in facilitating interaction between participants. They can be used to collect feedback via digital questionnaires and surveys. Attendees can tap a button within the PDA Guide to rate a session or send a meeting request to a vendor. With a growing number of handheld devices offering wireless access, they can support real-time chat and messaging among participants.

Because a professional PDA Guide is so useful and well regarded, it provides a high value opportunity for a sponsor or sponsors to showcase their message - not just during the event - but afterwards. Unlike a hefty printed catalog which is usually left at the event venue or in the hotel room, the PDA Guide is likely to go home with attendees where it is available to reference long after the meeting is over.

In summary, mobile electronic event guides help attendees maximize the time and money they spend at an event. They also enhance communication between exhibitors, attendees and the event producer. And, they are often self-funding. As such, they're almost certain to become a "must-have" for events in the not to distant future.

> ## HOT TIP
>
> **Avoid Voices in the Dark**
>
> "Whoops, wrong switch. Try the dimmer by the door. Can we turn the rear lights down too?" The worst interruption to a good presentation is an ill-prepared light dimming. If a presenter has a PowerPoint presentation or video to use, work out the lighting in advance. Avoid killing the lights altogether. Use dimmer switches. A blackened room creates a "voice in the dark" and temporarily kills the mood of communication.

TECHNOLOGY CHECKLIST

☐ Meeting coordination

- demonstrate an awareness of current technologies in the meeting industry

- demonstrate an awareness of developing technologies

- use computer applications

- demonstrate an understanding of communication systems

☐ Audio visual basics and applications

- audio recording

- data projection

- flipcharts

- front or rear screen projection

- microphones

- opaque projectors

- overhead transparency projector

- Power Point software

- projection stands

- projection screens

- simultaneous interpretation

- teleconferencing

- video

- video cassette recorder (VCR)

- podium height consideration

☐ Beyond the basics

- TelePrompTers©

- SMARTboards©

- webcasting

- plasma screens

- wireless audience response system

- video conferencing

- point-to-multipoint broadcasting

- Personal Digital Assistant (PDA)

☐ Presentation room lighting

- benefit of using dimmers to control house lighting

CHAPTER REVIEW

It is the responsibility of the meeting professional to understand the benefits and uses of today's sophisticated audio visual equipment and to be able to talk knowledgeably to speakers to guide them in the selection of the most appropriate technology for their presentations.

The meeting planner should be thoroughly familiar with the following basic audio visual equipment and applications:

- microphones
- sound systems
- front screen and rear screen projection
- screens
- audio recording
- data projectors, document projection, overhead transparency projectors
- video and video cassette recorders
- simultaneous interpretation
- flip charts
- Powerpoint
- projection stands

In addition, an understanding of the following advanced technology will prove very useful:

- TelePrompTers© – a transparent electronic screen that allows the speaker to read from a script which is unnoticable to the audience.
- SMARTboard© – an interactive digital white board that allows you to share, save, email or print out recorded information
- Webcasting – the delivery of audio or video content via the Web

- Plasma screens – Leading edge flat screen technology that allows for clear projection under adverse lighting conditions – used as a substitute for regular monitors or tv screens

- Wireless audience response systems – an electronic tool that allows for real time two way communication between the presenter and the audience – most commonly used for polling and anonymous data collection

- Video conferencing – real time interactive transmission of data and sound between two or more sites

- point-to-multipoint broadcasting – data transmission via satellite from one source location to any number of remote locations

- Mobile electronic event guide – an interactive electronic conference guide, accessed via attendees PDA's, incorporating exhibitor listings, conference sessions and other relevant information, customizable to meet the attendees needs

TEST YOUR KNOWLEDGE

The following **self-test** will indicate the level of understanding and knowledge gained from this chapter. Solutions to all self-tests can be found in **Appendix A**.

1. Audio refers to things that you see and video to things that you hear.

   ☐ True   ☐ False

2. Some speakers find it difficult or embarrassing to adjust their microphone height, so someone else should be assigned to do it for them.

   ☐ True   ☐ False

3. Rehearsals are not required when a speaker uses a TelePrompTer©, due to their advanced technology and ease of use.

   ☐ True   ☐ False

4. An advantage of a SMARTboard© is that information can be easily saved, emailed or printed out automatically.

   ☐ True   ☐ False

5. Wireless audience response systems do not allow peoples responses to remain anonymous.

   ☐ True   ☐ False

6. Webcasting technology allows you to:

   (a) deliver one way audio or video content via the Web

   (b) broadcast live or archive for on-demand viewing

   (c) immediately broadcast time sensitive events such as AGM's, analyst or investor conferences

   d) get your message out to a large and geographically diverse audience

   (e) all of the above

7. The advantages of plasma screens are:

    (a) They perform well under poor lighting conditions and accept both video and data sources

    (b) People can sit off to the far side of the screen and still see an image clearly

    (c) They are lighter than most other display screens and can be used most anywhere

    (d) They are cheaper than other types of screens

    (e) All of the above

    (f) All of the above, except (d)

8. Compare the benefits and costs of video conferencing vs point-to-multipoint broadcasting.

    _____

    _____

    _____

    _____

    _____

9. Name 5 different types of microphones – what type of purpose is each type best suited for?

    _____

    _____

    _____

    _____

    _____

10. When might you use front vs rear screen projection?

    _____

    _____

    _____

    _____

    _____

NOTES

VIPs

INTRODUCTION

The term VIP (very important person) indicates an entitlement to special or preferential treatment. Important people participating in an event should receive recognition for their contribution. The aim of this chapter is to guide the meeting professional in developing procedures for VIP protocol, security, transportation, accommodation, amenities, and gifts.

LEARNING OBJECTIVES

After completing this chapter, the learner will:

- establish protocol guidelines

- identify VIPs

- develop guidelines for meeting VIP needs

- plan transportation, accommodation, amenities and gifts for VIPs

Ensure you understand and can apply the following terms:

Amenities

- Honored guests
- Protocol
- VIP
- VIP host

Refer to the glossary for further clarification of the key terms for this chapter.

ROLES AND RESPONSIBILITIES

MEETING MANAGER

○ Develop VIP guidelines

- Identify VIPs and how they will be acknowledged
  - ○ identify and plan for amenities and gifts that will be provided to VIPs
  - ○ establish communication protocol for VIPs
  - ○ plan for safety and security requirements

- Develop protocol guidelines
  - ○ investigate proper protocol considerations
  - ○ research sources of protocol information
  - ○ determine situations where protocol may be required
  - ○ co-ordinate entry, speaking order, seating arrangements

MEETING COORDINATOR

○ Prepare for VIPs

- Review the list of designated VIPs
  - ○ identify VIPs by name and title
  - ○ communicate VIP details to appropriate personnel
  - ○ review the characteristics of individual VIPs

- Arrange for amenities and gifts
  - ○ purchase gifts as required
  - ○ arrange distribution of gifts/recognition

- Meet the needs of VIPs
  - ○ arrange VIP accommodation, travel, food and beverage service
  - ○ adhere to policies related to VIPs

- Ensure compliance with protocol
  - Monitor compliance with protocol
    - ○ demonstrate knowledge of appropriate protocol procedures
    - ○ review and communicate protocol guidelines

VERY IMPORTANT PEOPLE

WHO IS A VIP?

A very important person (VIP) can be anyone the meeting professional or the host organization wants to recognize as special. This may include:

- political or public figures

- someone of remarkable accomplishment or birthright

- officers of the host organization

- board of directors of the host organization

- high ranking officials of sponsoring companies

- visiting dignitaries

There is the special case of an event where all participants are VIPs, such as an employer-sponsored conference, but usually VIPs are presenters, or make up a small fraction of event attendees. Extraordinary people can be invited to an event to speak to attendees about personal experience, achievement, motivation, or specific knowledge. The meeting professional should confirm all VIP designations with the host organization

WORKING WITH VIPS

Many VIPs may have staff in place to book engagements and make travel arrangements who will prefer to deal with one member of the planning staff. Depending on the magnitude of the event and VIP status, the meeting professional may be able to assign one staff member as VIP liaison. A VIP host can be a staff member or local committee member, someone who will greet the VIP upon arrival and quickly solve any problems. The host must be familiar with the local area, the event program and the role of the VIP.

HOT TIP

Special Guest Registration

Handling special guests at your general registration desk can present problems if you're not careful. If guests show up without normal "credentials" they can feel awkward if the registration desk is not anticipating his or her arrival. To avoid such situations, send guests a colour-coded card or a letter in advance for them to present at the registration desk. Also, provide registration personnel with a list of specially invited guests. A quick check against the master list can earn your guest their badge and materials without delay.

SECURITY

Not every VIP will require special security. The staff of those who do should be able to articulate security needs when committing to the event. The meeting professional should consider:

- political unrest or controversy
- public image of VIP
- security personnel or procedures available at the event site
- police involvement
- other agencies (VIP staff will indicate involvement)
- security consultants
- room sweep (may require reserving a day in advance)

When in doubt, the meeting professional should consult with a security specialist, especially if political figures are involved.

VIP TRANSPORTATION

Transportation of VIPs can be handled by a convention bureau member, professional coordinator or meeting professional staff member. Special arrangements can be made with most airlines for VIPs to proceed to a special VIP room or lounge on arrival. Airline personnel can expedite the check in procedure, including special baggage tags or other markings, and allow late boarding to avoid lineups. Flight staff is informed of names and/or titles of VIPs. Always have a staff member officially greet VIPs on arrival. They need to know:

- airline flight numbers

- arrival and departure times

- availability and location of airport VIP lounge

- customs and immigration procedures

- location at airport to best greet VIPs

- where to park for incoming flights

- drop off points for VIPs

- routes and travel times

For ground transportation, arrangements may be needed for limousines or executive coaches for VIPs, in addition to attendee ground transportation arrangements. Provide the VIP with a personalized greeting in the limousine. A personal letter from the event chair will acknowledge how important their presence is to the event. All VIPs travelling by air should be met at the airport and accompanied by a host to their accommodations, or for those travelling by car, have a host in the hotel lobby to greet the guest and make sure that parking fees are covered.

The VIP program does not end after the presentation but should extend to the arrival of the VIP at their next destination. The VIP host should escort the VIP to the airport and ensure travel arrangements are in place. The final trip to the airport is an occasion to provide small or disposable amenities for the trip. Offer to mail any items too cumbersome for the VIP to carry as personal luggage. Know when the VIP is due at the next or final destination and confirm safe arrival.

ACCOMMODATION

VIP accommodation is usually a suite or room with special significance, able to meet the particular needs of VIP and staff, including amenities, communication requirements and security. Arrange to have VIPs escorted directly to their hotel room if possible. The registration signature card can be placed in the room along with a letter of greeting from the hotel manager, and the host can return the card to front desk once the VIP is settled. Before VIPs arrive, have the following ready in each room:

- event program

- schedule of key events

- map of facilities

- traditional amenities such beverages, fruit baskets, and flowers or items specific to VIP likes

Amenities should be rotated or freshened throughout the VIP's stay, saving perishable items until the second day in case the VIP is delayed. Be aware that incidental expenses incurred by a VIP will be billed to a Master Account.

HOT TIP

Special Assignment

If special accommodation is reserved for your executive members, board members, exhibitors or speakers, make sure the hotel has an exact list. This is crucial if a local housing committee is handling accommodation, since its staff may not be as familiar with the names and status.

AMENITIES AND GIFTS

The following is a summary of what amenities and gifts should be considered for VIPs and where they should be distributed.

LIMOUSINE SERVICE

- personalized greeting from event chair

- small or disposable amenities

HOTEL ROOM

- amenity reflecting local culture
- amenity specific to VIP likes or hobbies
- event information
- letter of greeting

DURING EVENT

- access to communication equipment
- small dinner for VIP and guests

POST EVENT

- gift
- plaque
- certificate

Once the event is over, don't forget to send...

- personalized thank you
- commemorative photos
- attendee list
- speaker list
- offer to mail cumbersome items

ONSITE VIP PROTOCOL

SEATING

Ready rooms should be available for VIP presenters. Special seating arrangements must be made when VIPs attend event sessions or functions.

Have special seats reserved for VIPs who wish to attend event sessions, with appropriate markings or barricade tapes. Have a staff member personally seat VIPs in this reserved area and restrict access to the area.

Have reserved seating for VIPs, and advise VIP or staff member of their table prior to the opening of the event. Mark VIP tables clearly on the floor plan. Locate tables to accommodate any special security measures necessary.

Seating arrangements for VIPs may require consultation with VIPs' staff or host organization members. Personality conflicts, language barriers, security needs, and entourage seating must all be considered.

POST PRESENTATION

At the conclusion of the event, acknowledge the VIPs contribution by presenting a token of recognition such as a gift, plaque or certificate. A short recognition ceremony or a private acknowledgement by key members of the program committee with media coverage may be preferred.

VIP PROTOCOL CHECKLIST

☐ Host organization member responsible for VIP designation

☐ Meeting professional staff member responsible for VIP designation

☐ Invited VIPs
- political figures
- public figures
- officers of host organization
- officials of sponsoring organization
- visiting dignitaries

☐ Meeting professional staff assigned to co-ordinate VIP liaison

☐ Assigned VIP host(s)
- meeting professional staff member
- local convention bureau member
- host organization member

☐ VIP host information package
- airline flight numbers
- arrival and departure times
- availability of airport VIP lounge
- potential customs and immigration problems
- location at airport to best greet VIPs
- where to park for incoming flights
- drop off points for VIPs
- routes and travel times

☐ Local area information

☐ Event program

☐ Role of VIP

☐ Personalized letter from event chair to VIP to be delivered upon arrival

☐ VIP Security

- special security measures necessary
  - political unrest or controversy
  - public image of VIP
  - onsite security personnel or procedures
  - police involvement/other agencies
  - security consultants
  - room sweep
  - restricted access
- method of transportation of VIP to event
  - air travel
  - car
  - train
  - other

☐ VIP Accommodation

- greeted upon arrival by host
- accompanied by host to accommodations
- escorted directly to hotel room
- VIP package placed in room before arrival
  - event program
  - schedule of key events
  - map of facilities
  - traditional amenities
  - items specific to VIP likes

☐ Arrange express checkout

☐ Accompanied by host to return travel arrangements

☐ Arrange transportation for cumbersome items

☐ Confirm safe arrival at destination

☐ Pre-presentation functions

- visit with event chair and/or local members

- pre-session luncheon

- banquet

- reception

- speakers' breakfast

☐ VIP seating

- event session rooms

- special functions

- post presentation functions

- recognition ceremony

- key members of program committee

- event chair

- gift and/or plaque

- certificate

☐ Amenities and Gifts

- limousine from airport to accommodations
  - personalized greeting from event chair
  - small or disposable amenities

- hotel room
  - beverages
  - fruit basket
  - flowers
  - items specific to VIP likes or hobbies
  - local items

- ready room
  - light refreshment
  - audio visual equipment
  - communication systems
- post presentation
  - gift
  - plaque
  - certificate
- limousine to airport from accommodations
  - post-meeting survival kit
  - small or disposable amenities
- post event
  - personalized thank you letter
  - commemorative photos
  - attendee list

☐ International Delegates

- identify all international delegates
  - VIPs
  - speakers
  - attendees
- identify all countries participating in event
- special planning considerations
  - international time differences
  - language translations and interpretation requirements
  - participant's fees and travelling costs
  - compatibility of audio visual and other equipment
  - official language for program book
  - currency requirements and exchange procedures
  - customs office procedures
  - customs limits and restrictions

CHAPTER REVIEW

- A VIP is anyone participating in an event that the meeting professional or the host organization wants to recognize as special, and can be

  - political figures

  - officers of host organization

  - officials of sponsoring organizations

  - public figures

  - visiting dignitaries

- Assign a host to each VIP who is familiar with

  - arrival and departure times, flight numbers

  - local area

  - event program

  - role of VIP

  - special security needs

- VIPs should be seated at event sessions and special functions in reserved seating in a restricted access area
- VIPs could receive a post-presentation recognition gift, plaque, or certificate in a small ceremony from the program committee
- VIPs should receive various amenities during the event, and a personalized thank-you letter

TEST YOUR KNOWLEDGE

The following **self test** will indicate the level of understanding and knowledge gained from this chapter. Solutions to all self tests can be found in **Appendix A**.

1. A VIP host can be a member of the meeting professional's staff, member of the host organization, or local convention bureau member.

   ☐ True   ☐ False

2. All VIP treatment concludes immediately after the speaker has completed the presentation, with a short recognition ceremony attended by key members of the program committee.

   ☐ True   ☐ False

3. VIP arrangements would typically involve:

   (a) transportation

   (b) accommodations

   (c) security

   (d) amenities and gifts

   (e) all of the above

4. VIPs may have staff to make travel and security arrangements. The VIP's staff would most effectively liaison with:

   (a) the meeting professional

   (b) the event chair

   (c) a staff member designated as the VIP liaison

   (d) the designated VIP host

   (e) officials from the sponsoring organization

5. The primary purpose of a Ready Room is to:

   (a) keep VIPs away from crowds in a restricted access area

   (b) allow different VIPs an opportunity to meet

   (c) enable VIP speakers to review presentations and meet multimedia staff

   (d) permit speakers to loosen up in a boisterous environment

   (e) provide a secure area for speakers to rest, eat and drink

6. You are the meeting professional responsible for the annual meeting of an international professional organization in the dental health care field. Attendees will include general practitioners, specialists, support staff (assistants, receptionists, and office managers), spouses, and children. Identify potential VIP categories (and their special needs) that may be invited to participate.

_____

_____

_____

7. One of the VIP presenters selected by the international dental association event committee is at the top of the cosmetic dentistry field, and has treated many famous political and public figures. The committee would like to have this industry leader give an informative presentation, and also have a famous former patient be the keynote speaker. Outline how the meeting professional would accommodate these two very different VIPs.

_____

_____

_____

8. What amenities and gifts would you recommend for each of the VIP's noted in the question above?

_____

_____

_____

NOTES

Chapter
15

International Meetings

INTRODUCTION

An international meeting is defined as a meeting comprised of attendees from two or more countries meeting for mutual reasons. An international meeting may be held outside the national borders of both countries or within the borders of one of the participant nations.

There are countless reasons for an organization to hold a meeting at an international location. Many businesses and organizations have expanded into foreign countries, opening up new markets. Access to many countries has become easier. An international destination may also be perceived to have more appeal to attendees; therefore they are often used for corporate incentive reward programs.

For the meeting professional, an international meeting can add a new element of complexity and challenge to the meeting planning process. It can, in many cases, be more rewarding as well. Unlike domestic meetings, in which customs and practices are likely to be familiar, international meetings require special attention during the pre event and onsite planning process.

Ensure you understand and can apply the following terms:

- Customs broker
- Entry requirements
- International meeting
- Rate of exchange
- Value added tax

Refer to the glossary for further clarification of the key terms for this chapter.

LEARNING OBJECTIVES

After completing this chapter, the learner will:

- define an international meeting

- understand the factors to consider in selecting an international meeting destination

- understand the characteristics of an international contract

- explain the importance of developing business relationships with suppliers

- prepare a checklist for pre event communication

- understand how to arrange for shipping and customs clearance

ROLES AND RESPONSIBILITIES

MEETING MANAGER

○ Develop international meeting strategy

- identify attendees and countries represented at the meeting

- determine the geographical location of the meeting

○ Conduct site selection analysis

- establish site selection criteria

- research potential destinations

- research the cultural and political considerations of potential destinations

- conduct a destination and facility site inspection

- recommend a meeting destination and facility

○ Negotiate international meeting contract

○ Manage the international meeting logistics

- source suppliers

- determine and communicate entry requirements

- research customs and shipping regulations

○ Develop all pre event communication

- entry requirement details

- travel arrangements

- safety and security guidelines

- destination and program information

MEETING COORDINATOR

- Assist with research for potential locations

  - assist with arrangement for site inspection

- Research all necessary documentation for delegates

  - prepare materials for pre event and onsite information package

SELECTING AN INTERNATIONAL MEETING DESTINATION

Conducting in depth research on potential destinations and venues for an international meeting is integral to the success of the event. The International Association of Convention and Visitor Bureaus (IACVB) is a good source of information when gathering preliminary data on international meeting destinations and venues. When researching destinations, consider:

ACCESSIBILITY

- How accessible is the location for attendees?
- Is the destination serviced by major airlines worldwide?

CULTURAL CONSIDERATIONS

- Do any gender or other restrictions exist?
- What traditions, customs, opinions or beliefs prevail?

- What is the general culture of the destination?
- Is it considered a more open or more reserved society? (e.g., some countries do not allow photographs of public or government buildings to be taken. In some countries, covering of arms, head and legs is required.)

DESTINATION

- Are there any laws or restrictions that will prevent attendees from entering the country?

ENTRY REQUIREMENTS

- Are passports, visitor's visas or business permits required to enter the country?

HEALTH CARE

- Are any inoculations or other precautions suggested when traveling to the destinations?

HOLIDAYS AND BUSINESS HOURS

- What religious/statutory holidays are observed over the potential dates of the meeting?
- This applies to both the meeting attendee and the potential destination.
- When might services/facilities be closed?

LANGUAGE

- What is the local language of business?
- Are English speaking personnel and services readily available or for hire?

POLITICAL/SOCIOECONOMIC CLIMATE

- Have government agencies issued any warnings, travel advisories etc. for the destination being considered?

SEASONS AND CLIMATE

- What, if any, are the seasonal weather conditions of the destination? (consider hurricanes, rainy seasons, extreme temperatures)

TOURIST SAFETY

- How safe and secure is the country for tourists?
- What is the level of crime?
- Contact the local authorities and get the details of the English speaking hospitals, doctors and emergency services

WORK ETHIC

- When might services/facilities be closed?

SITE INSPECTION

Once a meeting destination has been determined, the meeting professional should plan a pre event site visit to the destination and all facilities being considered. The site visit also provides an opportunity to meet with key stakeholders and potential suppliers. An in person site inspection should always be conducted prior to signing a facility contract.

CONTRACT NEGOTIATION

When negotiating international venue and supplier contracts, the meeting professional should be prepared for differences in style and procedure. Contracts in some countries will be more formal, others less so. The degree to which a contract can be negotiated will vary from country to country, but as a general rule, the meeting professional should expect fewer negotiables when working with contracts outside of North America. Also, many international contracts charge for items separately (e.g., meeting room by the hour, food and beverage, porterage fees, etc.). The meeting professional should always verify what services and facilities are included in the prices quoted and never assume they are the same as in their native country.

International contracts may also use different terminology. The meeting professional should always clarify terms and ensure the contract reflects, in writing, everything requested. Where possible, the services of a national sales office can help in the negotiation process. Because they are fluent in English as well as in the local language, and familiar with the business practices and procedures of both countries, many national sales office personnel can help to expedite the contract negotiation process for the meeting professional.

Prior to signing a contract for an international meeting, the meeting professional should clarify:

- any unfamiliar terminology (e.g., value-added tax, delegate rate)

- applicable taxes and how they are calculated (and whether refunds are available)

- the contract law that will apply (local or foreign country)

- the types of 'meal plans' available/recommended for the group

- the expected percentage for gratuities, service charges

- when payments should be made and in what currency

Budgets for international meetings should allow for:

- applicable taxes, gratuities, services charges and duties (do not hesitate to use a local tax broker for this as, very often, you can claim part of the taxes back)

- the current rate of exchange (to avoid the exchange rate risk, try to match your income [sponsorship, registration fees, etc.], with your expenses, as this will limit the amount of money that you will need to convert. Also, enquire with your bank to have a guaranteed exchange rate at the time of payment [forward term contract])

- increased travel costs

LEVERAGING SUPPLIER RELATIONSHIPS

From the early planning stages of an international meeting, through to the conclusion of the event, it is essential to solicit and maintain the cooperation of a network of local suppliers. Organizations like the convention and visitors bureau, destination management companies, interpreters, audio visual companies, and others (such as local members of your association, if you belong to one), are local experts who can provide great insight into unfamiliar territory and serve as an onsite 'partner' for the meeting professional.

Local suppliers can help the meeting professional understand how business is conducted in the country; perhaps open doors to other services required; help promote the event; and assist in dealing with local bureaucracy.

An early and open dialogue with suppliers will ensure the meeting professional acquires the products and services needed for a successful meeting.

PROGRAMMING INTERNATIONALLY

When developing the program for an international meeting, remember that attendees will require an increased amount of travel and travel recovery time before they are ready to attend sessions.

This also applies to speakers, whose fees and travelling costs may be increased for an international meeting.

Use your imagination to incorporate the flavors and culture of the local country into your international meeting program by:

- displaying multinational flags

- playing national anthems

- recognizing significant religious or cultural events

- offering menus that feature local cuisine

- providing multilingual staff

- featuring international speakers

- incorporating historical or locally significant venues

PREPARING INTERNATIONAL MEETING ATTENDEES

Adequate preparation of the attendees for an international meeting cannot be overstated. A communication strategy should be developed well in advance to ensure that attendees are properly advised, not only about documentation required for entry into the country, but also what to expect upon arrival and during their stay.

Travel consultants and government websites can provide the most current information in terms of immigration, customs, passport, visa, and other documentation required for entry. Most countries have customs limitations, duties and taxes on certain items, and even items that are deemed unacceptable to bring into or out of the country.

CUSTOMS AND SHIPPING

Every country in the world has its own laws, known as customs laws, governing the import/export of goods. When shipping goods and materials into international destinations it is important for the meeting professional to work closely with a professional shipping company and a customs broker who can find the right type of service. Depending on the type, weight and required delivery time of the goods, the meeting professional will generally utilize the services of a carrier or freight forwarder to move the goods internationally.

A customs broker is an expert in the nuances of customs rules and can act as an agent to ensure the goods enter the country legally and with minimal delay. The customs broker should:

- secure all required forms

- assist in determining the declared value of the items

- complete the required documentation accurately

A professional shipping company and customs broker should establish ongoing communication in order to monitor and track the forwarding and arrival of the freight until it reaches its final destination.

The meeting professional should investigate and understand the insurance coverage maintained by the host organization for lost/stolen equipment. Expensive items should be insured separately with the freight carrier.

Exercise caution with regard to hand carried items. These should be limited in quantity and accompanied by appropriate customs documentation.

SHIPPING GOODS AND MATERIALS

- Research items before ordering to ensure they are exportable from the country of manufacture.
- Where possible, purchase promotional items in the country where the meeting will take place.
- ALWAYS purchase food items locally.
- Hand carried promotional items will require duties paid upon entry into the country; therefore, these are best shipped in advance.

- What items are being shipped? Necessary details must be provided on export documents.

- Pack and seal goods in sturdy containers.

- Brace and pack goods in such a way that weight is evenly distributed.

- Package filter should be made of moisture resistant material. Avoid non-recyclable materials.

- Label all boxes legibly and uniformly in permanent ink and number them.

- Do not list contents or brand names on packages.

- Know your goods, including the 'classification' and 'country of origin'. Be prepared to answer any questions about the goods or materials being shipped.

- Use international symbols for hazardous and fragile materials. A list of international symbols can be obtained from the freight forwarder.

- Make and keep a master list of items shipped and number of boxes. A master list is also essential when settling any claim with your freight forwarder and/or insurance company.

SELECTING A SHIPPING COMPANY

Consider the following points when deciding which company will ship your meeting:

- Do they specialize in a particular area of the world, or a certain type of freight?

- What is their experience shipping and/or clearing meeting materials?

- Are they bonded and insured?

- Are the quoted shipping rates inclusive of document preparation charges?

- Are they a member of a professional industry-recognized association?

- Do they offer 24-hour service? (goods may be crossing borders weekends and after regular business hours due to time differences)

- How do they charge?

COMMUNICATIONS TECHNOLOGY

The costs of email, Internet and telephone communications for international meetings can substantially impact meeting budget and attendee expenses if they are not properly researched and understood by the meeting professional. It is important to determine the most cost effective way of making long distance telephone calls, and accessing Internet and email onsite.

Enquire about:

- in room Internet/email access and how it is billed

- telephone jacks (type needed for laptop computers)

- standard voltage and types of adapters required for electronics and personal appliances

- cell phones (international dialing capabilities, costs)

- availability of international 'calling cards'

- cyber cafés - are there any in the area?

- cost and time necessary to install high speed connection (if you will need it for your meeting)

- use and cost of business centre

The meeting professional should enquire as to whether in-room Internet/email access is available and, if so, how usage is charged.

10 TIPS FOR PLANNING INTERNATIONAL MEETINGS

1. Allow extra time to plan everything.
2. Don't make assumptions.
3. Understand and respect differences in culture, etiquette, body language, and business practices.
4. Be flexible.
5. Develop partnerships with local suppliers.
6. Use technology to save time and money.
7. Conduct extensive research.
8. Ask for help.
9. Have a good travel agent who is accessible from different time zones.
10. Develop a strategy for dealing with crisis situations.
11. Communicate, Communicate, and Communicate!

INTERNATIONAL CHECKLIST

Advise registered attendees to check their passports to ensure they are valid during meeting and travel dates and six months after return to their home country.

☐ Accommodation

- name, address, telephone and fax number of hotel/facility
- amenities included in the hotel guest room charge
- hotel services available and hours of operation
- check-in/check-out times
- voltage, current and type of adapters required for personal items, laptops, etc.

☐ Attire (appropriate for the destination and planned functions)

- day/business
- dining
- touring
- casual
- business casual

☐ Climate

- average temperature during the time of the event
- precipitation
- seasonal variations

☐ Customs

- language(s) spoken in the foreign country
- protocol regarding tipping
- official introductions
- proper use of titles
- pronunciation of names
- seating order

- local business protocol

- cultural taboos

- tipping habits

☐ Destination

- history

- points of interest

☐ Gift Giving

- what

- when

- how to present

☐ Ground Transportation

- what, if any, arrangements have been made

- distance from airport to hotel/facility

- cost of a one-way trip from the airport to the facility (in their local currency and that of the visiting country)

- is an airport shuttle available to the hotel/facility? Cost of a one-way trip?

- Where can tickets be purchased, and where does the shuttle depart from the airport

☐ Holidays

- local

- national

- religious

- political

☐ Insurance

- medical

- what coverage is provided

- where to obtain additional medical insurance if required

- [ ] Key contacts

  - travel agent

  - hotel

  - event staff (if appropriate)

- [ ] Lifestyle

  - days/hours local businesses are open

  - customary dining hours

  - response time to service requests

- [ ] Local laws

- [ ] Local/political climate

- [ ] Monetary

  - local currency of the country, including rate of exchange to country of origin

  - location of closest bank and automated teller machines (if available)

  - restrictions on import/export of currencies

  - where valuables such as jewellery, money, etc. can be stored at the hotel/facility

- [ ] Religious practices

  - days of worship and holidays

  - restrictions on use of alcohol

  - specific food preparation

  - appropriate invocations

- [ ] Travel/entry requirements
- what is required for entry into the country
- inoculations/vaccinations required
- safe and proper procedures for carrying laptops, cameras and film through airport and security checkpoints

CHAPTER REVIEW

When selecting an international meeting destination, the following items should be considered

- accessibility

- cultural considerations

- destination

- entry requirements

- health care

- holidays and business hours

- language

- political and socioeconomic climate

- seasons and climate

- tourist safety

- work ethic

International contracts will present new challenges to the meeting planner because of differences in standards, terminology, style, currency, procedures and pricing. Before signing the contract, these items should be thoroughly discussed and understood.

Budgets for international meetings should allow for

- applicable foreign taxes, gratuities, service charges and duties

- current rate of currency exchange

- increased travel costs

Meeting attendees should be thoroughly briefed on what to expect from the international meeting and destination, including information on visas and required documentation, cultural norms and what to expect during their stay.

It is important for the meeting professional to work closely with a professional shipping company and a customs brokers to ensure that all required items are received at the host destination in a timely manner and to avoid customs delays or extra costs. Special attention should be paid to packing and monitoring packages correctly. A customs broker can assist by

- securing required forms

- assisting in determining declared values for shipments

- completing required documentation

Before confirming an international destination, confirm the availability and costs of communications technology, including

- Internet/email access, availability of high speed access and cyber cafés

- voltage, phone jack and adapter requirements for computers and other electronic devices

- access via cell phone and calling cards

- availability of business centre services

International meetings will require additional research and planning time, as well as flexibility and good relationships with local suppliers.

TEST YOUR KNOWLEDGE

The following **self-test** will indicate the level of understanding and knowledge gained from this chapter. Solutions to all self-tests can be found in **Appendix A**.

1. An international meeting is defined as a meeting at which international delegates are in attendance.

   ☐ True   ☐ False

2. Using local suppliers, DMC's and the convention and visitors bureau as your partners in the event will help to ensure success for an international meeting

   ☐ True   ☐ False

3. It is best not to provide meeting attendees with information about the international destination in advance – they should have the chance to discover and experience it for themselves.

   ☐ True   ☐ False

4. You should not plan to hold a meeting in a destination where government agencies have issued warning or travel advisories.

   ☐ True   ☐ False

5. When evaluating an international contract you should look for:

   (a) unfamiliar terminology

   (b) currency and payment information

   (c) applicable local/national tax rates and expected gratuities and service charge rates

   (d) information on which country's contract law will apply

   (e) all of the above

6. When selecting a shipping company for an international meeting, you should look for:

   (a) the lowest price

   (b) extensive experience in shipping nationally

   (c) membership in local voluntary or service organizations

   (d) shipping rates that include document preparation charges

   (e) extended business hours of up to 18 hours per day

7. The following are all items to consider when choosing an international destination, except:

   (a) cultural considerations

   (b) visas and entry requirements

   (c) seasons and climate

   (d) hotel amenities

   (e) language

8. List 5 ways that you can incorporate the culture of the host country into your meeting program:

   _____

   _____

   _____

   _____

   _____

9. Discuss specific items that you would need to incorporate into the budget for an international meeting that would not be applicable if it were held locally.

   _____

   _____

   _____

10. List 5 items that you would need to research or consider when selecting an international meeting destination.

   _____

   _____

   _____

   _____

   _____

Chapter 16

Post Event Activities

INTRODUCTION

Although there may be a tendency to relax after the official program is complete, there is still much work to be accomplished. This chapter will examine such post meeting activities as evaluating the success of the event in meeting predetermined objectives, measuring the return on investment (ROI) and the value of conducting an attendee post meeting evaluation.

Measuring the success of the event will enable the meeting professional to determine the return on investment and whether objectives have been met.

Ensure you understand and can apply the following terms:

- Evaluation
- Post conference meeting
- Post conference report

Refer to the glossary for further clarification of the key terms for this chapter.

LEARNING OBJECTIVES

After completing this chapter, the learner will:

- understand the value of conducting a thorough meeting evaluation.

- understand the need for a post event meeting with suppliers.

- appreciate the complexities of measuring ROI.

- prepare a post conference report

ROLES AND RESPONSIBILITIES

MEETING MANAGER

○ Design an evaluation process

- Determine the purposes and components of the evaluation
    - ○ recognize various methods used to evaluate meetings, their advantages and disadvantages
    - ○ determine the components of impact which need to be evaluated
    - ○ assess the effectiveness of previous evaluation methods

- Develop evaluation tools
    - ○ identify how information assimilated from an evaluation form will be used
    - ○ develop a simple, non-judgmental evaluation tool
    - ○ determine the format for distribution of evaluation forms
    - ○ communicate the importance of completing forms
    - ○ plan to maximize response rates

- Report results and recommendations
    - ○ determine the criteria for the report
    - ○ analyze data collected
    - ○ prepare a report that outlines changes and trends, results, evaluations and recommendations
    - ○ distribute report to appropriate persons
    - ○ distribute an action plan for planning future meetings

MEETING COORDINATOR

○ Participate in meeting follow up

- Prepare letters, notes and other forms of communication
  - ○ distribute materials as planned
  - ○ adhere to policies related to follow up
  - ○ write and/or send thank you letters, post meeting publicity, special information, and certificates/diplomas as appropriate

- Collect and record data
  - ○ adhere to the plan for collection, production, and distribution of data
  - ○ maintain accurate records and statistics for meeting follow up and evaluation

○ Implement evaluation procedures

- Implement evaluations
  - ○ distribute evaluation tools
  - ○ participate in other forms of evaluation
  - ○ keep records of evaluative comments

- Prepare reports
  - ○ compile data
  - ○ prepare, present, and distribute reports

MEETING EVALUATION

Meeting evaluation is essential to determine if the event was a success, any weaknesses, or improvements necessary in terms of planning a future event. The meeting professional needs to know what should be evaluated and why, in order to develop a system to measure it. The following questions should be asked:

- What specific information does the organization need to know?

- How does the organization plan to use this information?

DESIGNING AN EVALUATION TOOL

Evaluation typically occurs after an event has happened. However, over the course of a three-day meeting the meeting professional may want more comprehensive evaluations on each program component. Evaluations administered immediately after a session usually yields fresher opinions and criticisms. Response rate is typically higher when evaluations are conducted immediately following a session, as staff can be physically present to remind and collect evaluations. If evaluation takes place after the delegates have returned home, consider using a web based format for ease of completion by attendees.

TYPES OF INFORMATION TO GATHER

- dates, locations, hotels, attendance, and room figures of past meetings
- past budgets, financial reports, attendee lists, evaluations, programs
- records of hotels and other suppliers
- current data needs

SOURCES OF EVALUATION INFORMATION

- attendees
- hotel and suppliers
- onsite staff
- internal planning staff
- exhibitors
- sponsors
- speakers

The following six aspects of a meeting should be evaluated. Respondents should be asked for specific information in a format that includes distinct sections, allowing room for detailed answers.

PROGRAM/ATTENDEES

- How soon after the first mailing did phone calls and registration forms start coming in?

- Is attendance growing each year?

- Is the percentage in the various categories changing?

- Was attendance consistent with similar meetings?

- Were there more people in the sessions or the pre-function, or were they attending social events?

- Were the breaks noisy?

- Did attendees arrive on time? Stay to the end?

- Were speakers interesting and informative?

- What have attendees learned from the program?

- Were all topics considered relevant?

- Was the food well received?

- Was there a lot of garbage on the exhibit hall floor at the end of the day?

- Was there enough time to view exhibits?

- At what times did attendees visit the exhibition? Did visits coincide with promotional activities?

- Was the location of the exhibition convenient with respect to other meeting locales?

- Were exhibits educational and/or pertinent to attendees?

STAFF

- Was the staff well briefed on their assignments?

- Were staff encouraged to talk to and/or listen to attendees for feedback and note comments?

- Was a post conference meeting held with members of the hotel staff to collect their evaluations?

- Did attendees have problems unrelated to the program?

- Were staff members calm during mishaps or emergencies?

EXHIBITORS

- What was attendance/traffic on each day of exhibition?

- What was their perception of attendee interest?

- What was the worth of attendee inquiries (e.g., was the attendee a qualified buyer)?

- Were giveaways and promotional items well received?

- What was exhibitor perception of services furnished by hall or show management?

THE MEETING SITE

Meeting site evaluation is an analysis of the meeting facility, the hotel and the general destination. While the meeting professional may choose the meeting site primarily from the standpoint of meeting related services, the attendees may have been looking for something else. Assessing attendees' perception can assist in the planning of future meetings and destinations. For example, consider:

- Were meal guarantees accurate and served on time?

- Was signage anticipated and well placed?

- Were the room sets correct and on time?

- Was the guest room block filled?

SPECIAL ACTIVITIES

Social events, meal functions, recreational activities and transportation may require evaluation as well. Much of this information may be obtained by personal observation of the activities and analysis of information collected onsite (e.g., number of tickets sold for the final evening banquet). While the educational program is usually the primary motivator for delegates to attend, often it is the special activities that make a difference whether or not the attendee will return or not. For example, consider:

- Did the flowers/decorations appear as expected?

- Did the speakers appear at the right time and place?

- Were transportation arrangements adequate?

MARKETING

Evaluation of promotional efforts should be conducted through an analysis of registration records. Monitoring response to mailouts will help determine the effectiveness of the contents and offer future direction.

GUIDELINES FOR DESIGNING PARTICIPANT EVALUATION FORMS

ASK SPECIFIC QUESTIONS

Questions should be worded to assess a single concept. For example asking delegates to rate all the sessions and meals in a single question will result in data that is essentially unusable.

Avoid asking questions that are too general, such as: "Were you satisfied with the educational content of the seminars?" If an individual attended a variety of seminars over three days this may prove to be a difficult question to answer. Instead, ask: "Were you satisfied with the educational content of the negotiation seminar?"

MAKE IT EASY FOR PARTICIPANTS TO COMPLETE EVALUATIONS

When evaluating individual workshops or sessions, keep the questionnaire short. Ask only the most pertinent questions. Attendees may be pressed for time and may not complete or even ignore the questionnaire if they think it will take too long to complete.

Directions, questions and options should be clear and concise. The respondent should not have to interpret anything.

If pencils are required to complete the questionnaire, make sure they are available.

PROVIDE FOR CONVENIENT COLLECTION OF EVALUATIONS

If evaluations are to be collected onsite, receptacles should be clearly marked and readily available. If possible, have staff or volunteers collect evaluations as attendees exit the meeting room.

If evaluations are to be mailed to a central location, provide a self-addressed, postage paid envelope or consider using a postcard. Always include the sponsoring organization's name, address, phone and fax number, and a contact person.

DESIGN THE EVALUATION INSTRUMENT CAREFULLY

- Limit the number of questions on a page, leaving ample blank space between questions, particularly if using open ended questions.

- Use a clear typeface and be consistent throughout the questionnaire. Using coloured paper to distinguish between types of events (e.g., white for food and beverage, green for seminars) will help those people collating and analyzing the data, as well as the delegates to quickly separate the questionnaires from other printed information.

- Minimize the type of response options provided. Once participants understand how to respond to questions such as rating 1 = excellent, 2 = good, 3 = fair, and 4 = poor, then don't confuse them by switching the values in subsequent questions.

- Depending on the type of information required, keep open ended questions to a minimum. Open-ended questions can be difficult to code and often participants won't take the time to respond.

- Format the evaluation to capture the necessary session, time, date and speaker name.

- Include questions that capture demographic information about the participants.

- Use the same survey questions from meeting to meeting so that comparisons over time can be made. This will allow for the tracking from year to year or meeting to meeting to discover trends.

- On rating scales, provide an even number of response choices to reduce error (when five choices are provided, most respondents will choose choice three).

~ Sample Template ~

SAMPLE EVALUATION FORM

INDIVIDUAL SESSION EVALUATION

Session: Using the Internet to market your event   Date: Sept. 18 (a.m.)

Presenter: Jane Smith

Rate the following areas regarding this session using the following rating scale:

	1 = excellent	2 = very good	3 = good	4 = poor
1. Length of session	1	2	3	4
2. Use of audio visual	1	2	3	4
3. Subject Coverage	1	2	3	4
4. Reference materials	1	2	3	4
5. Applicability of content	1	2	3	4

6. What are your suggestions for improving this session?

_____

_____

_____

_____

_____

_____

_____

_____

Information on CD Rom

~ *Sample Template* ~

CONFERENCE EVALUATION

Registration information

Affiliation: ☐ Corporate   ☐ Member   ☐ Non-profit association
             ☐ Academia   ☐ Government ☐ Other_____

Was this your first conference?   ☐ Yes ☐ No

Registration fee: ☐ paid by attendee, not reimbursable
                      ☐ paid by attendee, reimbursable by employer
                      ☐ complimentary/sponsored

Using the following rating scale circle the appropriate response:

1 = excellent   2 = very good   3 = good   4 = poor

Hotel

Check in	1	2	3	4
Guest/sleeping rooms	1	2	3	4
Meeting rooms	1	2	3	4
Food	1	2	3	4

Conference Location

City	1	2	3	4
Facilities	1	2	3	4
Transportation	1	2	3	4

Program content and speakers

Favorite sessions were:

1. _____

2. _____

3. _____

~ Sample Template ~

Least favored sessions were:

1. _____

2. _____

3. _____

The most valuable part of the conference was:

☐ Educational programs   ☐ Cultural programs

☐ Social/meal events   ☐ Exhibit program

☐ Corporate tours   ☐ Other attendees

☐ Recruiting/employment opportunities

Additional comments

_____

_____

_____

_____

_____

_____

_____

_____

POST EVENT MEETING

The post event meeting is held once the meeting concludes. The meeting planning staff, convention service manager, catering manager, other facility staff as appropriate (such as general manager) and contractors review the event, review what went well, as well as opportunities for improvement. Often includes a final review of bills with accounts payable.

MEASURING RETURN ON INVESTMENT (ROI)

The evaluation process will enable the meeting professional to determine if the ROI has been met. The meeting professional should analyze all evaluation data and refer to the original objectives. This comparison of objectives and evaluation will show what objectives were met, to what degree and which were not met. The reasons ROI were not met will be revealed in the analysis.

POST EVENT REPORT

A Post Event Report (PER) is a report of the details and activities of an event. A collection of PERs over time will provide the complete history of a recurring event. A PER is completed by the primary event organizer of an event, in conjunction with the suppliers for that event, and filed with each venue and facility that was utilized. (APEX, 2003)

SEE THE APEX (Accepted Practices Exchange) section for detailed templates of:
    Event Specifications Guide
    Registration
    Housing
    Rooming
    Post-Event Report

HOT TIP

For the History Books

If you hold a conference or meeting at roughly the same time every year, do yourself a favor and develop a historical record. Keep a conference book containing all deadlines, dates and invoices from previous years. Add your comments and notes as you plan and execute each aspect of the conference. You'll thank yourself next year.

~ A Conference Journal ~

Although the meeting was over, there was still work to be done.

Thank you letters were sent to speakers, sponsors and suppliers and a post conference wrap up luncheon was organized to thank the support staff and volunteers of both organizations.

Within a month following the conference, a detailed analysis of the delegate evaluations provided by a professional marketing company was obtained. The results of this formal survey that polled over 600 representatives from exhibitors, delegates and sponsors onsite helped determine the value of the conference from their perspective and provided details of the demographics of the visitors to the conference. All individual remarks were included verbatim and the result was a very comprehensive report. The analysis indicated the conference was an overall success and everyone was very pleased to have been a part of the millennium celebration.

Once all of the evaluations were compiled, each association conducted their own internal meeting with their staff, to share the information provided and obtain input from the support staff as well. This joint venture affected all staff, with an increased workload during the final months leading up to the conference, and post conference as well; particularly in the case of the bookkeepers, whose job it was to reconcile the cash contributions and expenses.

The chairs of each subcommittee of the planning committee were asked to submit their final reports that included their comments on the area they had managed. The meeting manager and coordinators provided reports from a logistics perspective on various aspects of the conference; including such areas as registration, food and beverage, entertainment, and the general flow of the event. All of these comments were shared at one final planning committee meeting.

Finances had to be reconciled against onsite registrations, invoices had to be reviewed in detail and compared to the original order, followed by payments sent to suppliers. Generally invoices were paid within 30 days of receipt. The meeting manager and the treasurer, once all payments had been made and revenues calculated, provided a detailed analysis of the statement of revenues over expenses.

Overall, the conference was deemed to be a great success. It took the combined effort of many volunteers, staff and suppliers to make it happen but it was worth the effort. When asked whether or not they were prepared to do it again, the decision was deferred to some time in the future.

POST EVENT CHECKLIST

Information on CD Rom

☐ Post conference meeting scheduled

☐ Evaluation procedures identified

- evaluation form prepared and duplicated
- evaluation forms distributed
- other areas of evaluation identified
- interviews of participants
- exhibitors and/or sponsors
- anecdotal information recorded
- assimilate all evaluation ratings and comments

☐ Thank you letters prepared

- sponsors
- speakers
- volunteers
- venue

☐ Post Event report prepared

☐ Review return on investment (ROI)

CHAPTER REVIEW

A post event evaluation tool should examine the following 6 meeting aspects:

1. program/attendees

2. staff

3. exhibitors

4. meeting site

5. special activities

6. marketing

Evaluations should be solicited from attendees, hotel and suppliers, onsite staff, internal planning staff, exhibitors, sponsors and speakers. When designing the participant evaluation form, be sure to:

- ask specific questions

- make it easy for participants to complete the evaluation

- provide for convenient collection of evaluations

- design the evaluation instrument carefully

A post event meeting will assist in gathering meeting feedback on what went well and opportunities for improvement.

Feedback received from the evaluation tool and post event meeting will enable the meeting professional to determine if the ROI has been met. By comparing the results of these against the original objectives, any gaps will be identified, as well as highlighting objectives achieved.

A post conference report is a useful tool to capture meeting history and suggestions for future meetings.

TEST YOUR KNOWLEDGE

The following self test will indicate the level of understanding and knowledge gained from this chapter. Solutions to all self tests can be found in Appendix A.

1. Evaluation of a meeting is not necessary if there are no obvious problems.
   ☐ True   ☐ False

2. Post-event meetings should only include facility and sponsoring organization staff.
   ☐ True   ☐ False

3. Asking delegates to evaluate the convention while still onsite is NOT a recommended method of gathering valid data.
   ☐ True   ☐ False

4. Observation of delegates reaction to a speaker is a valid evaluation tool.
   ☐ True   ☐ False

5. The most commonly used method of collecting quantitative data is:
   (a) observation
   (b) questionnaires
   (c) counting number of registrants
   (d) focus groups

6. The advantages of closed ended questions include:
   (a) responses are easy to tabulate
   (b) the questions are shorter to write
   (c) responses can cover a broad range of responses
   (d) all of the above

7. The following stakeholders should not be included in post-meeting evaluations
   (a) delegates
   (b) staff
   (c) suppliers
   (d) none of the above

8. What is the difference between open-ended and closed-ended questions?
    Give an example of each.

    _____

    _____

    _____

9. What is qualitative data?
    Give an example of how you might go about collecting it.

    _____

    _____

    _____

10. While the educational program is essential to evaluate, what other aspects of the
    meeting should also be evaluated?

    _____

    _____

    _____

Chapter 17

Human Resources and Professionalism

INTRODUCTION

Human resource management is a complex subject when planning conferences. Many people are required to ensure success. The meeting professional must be prepared to determine how many people are required, understand the core competencies of each role, design a job description for each, and schedule each person. The meeting professional must also manage people onsite, in a diplomatic, tactful and fair way, understanding that each person must have his or her needs met as well.

Within the meetings industry, there are many disciplines and many people may move from one to another over their careers. This chapter will help you understand the need to stay current, to improve your skills, and to act in a professional and ethical manner in all negotiations and dealings with all stakeholders.

Ensure you understand and can apply the following terms:

- CMP
- CMM
- Room monitor
- Volunteer

Refer to the glossary for further clarification of the key terms for this chapter.

LEARNING OBJECTIVES

After completing this chapter, the learner will:

- forecast and manage human resource needs

- understand the professional conduct appropriate to a practising meeting professional

- understand the role of the volunteer

ROLES AND RESPONSIBILITIES

MEETING MANAGER

○ Human Resources - work with committees

- Clarify roles
  - ○ recognize limitations and challenges inherent in the use of committees
  - ○ recognize roles and responsibilities of committees and their members
  - ○ define the role of each committee and its relation to the level of authority

- Facilitate committees
  - ○ establish a plan for communication among committees
  - ○ establish a system for documenting committee activities

- Support and guide committee members
  - ○ act as group leader as required
  - ○ recognize the efforts of committee members
  - ○ monitor committee functioning and follow up as required

○ Plan to meet human resource needs

- Forecast human resource needs
  - ○ identify numbers and type of staff needed
  - ○ define criteria and terms of reference for volunteers and paid staff
  - ○ assess the need for volunteers
  - ○ identify all available resources for staffing
  - ○ adhere to the HR budget and policies

- respect organizational/internal hiring practices
- develop a volunteer replacement contingency plan

- Determine an appropriate organization of staff
  - determine allocation of staff to match defined roles and responsibilities
  - determine how to blend volunteers and paid employees
  - determine staff identification

- Establish compensation policies and procedures
  - identify appropriate compensation levels and arrangements
  - plan to recognize contribution of all concerned

- Prepare and communicate work descriptions
  - determine the skill, knowledge and experience requirements for each position being filled
  - write job descriptions

- Recruit and select appropriate personnel
  - identify and use various recruitment sources
  - prepare recruitment documents
  - organize recruitment activities
  - conduct interviews and select appropriate personnel
  - adhere to legal, labour and insurance requirements as well as internal/organizational hiring policies
  - provide and request needed information during the hiring process
  - prepare and maintain documents and files

- Develop training activities
  - assess orientation and training requirements
  - produce an orientation and training manual

○ Demonstrate an understanding of the meeting profession

- Maintain up to date information about the meeting industry
  - recognize the complexity, diversity, size and scope of the industry (locally, regionally, nationally, and globally)
  - recognize the economic impact of the industry
  - read industry trade magazines and recognize their contribution
  - use networking opportunities to maintain current information

- ○ participate in professional activities for the meeting industry
- ○ participate in professional trade associations
- ○ participate in ongoing educational opportunities for the industry
- ○ recognize the value of lifelong learning
- ○ recognize the value of professional designations (e.g., CMP [Certified Meeting Professional], CMM [Certified Meeting Professional], CITE [Certified Incentive Travel Executive], etc.)

○ Maintain professional integrity

- • Develop and maintain professional relationships
  - ○ negotiate in good faith
  - ○ build partnerships and alliances
  - ○ demonstrate honesty, openness and integrity
  - ○ apply knowledge of cultural differences
  - ○ adhere to an accepted industry code of ethics (e.g., MPI's Principles of Professionalism)

- • Communicate in a professional manner
  - ○ communicate clearly and effectively in person and in writing
  - ○ demonstrate competency in developing and presenting reports
  - ○ demonstrate calm, diplomacy and tact, especially when handling conflict and stress
  - ○ demonstrate active listening skills
  - ○ distinguish between assertive and aggressive behaviour

- • Apply business administration skills
  - ○ demonstrate an understanding of the planning cycle
  - ○ demonstrate an understanding of the economics of a meeting

- • Demonstrate leadership
  - ○ mentor and coach others in the industry
  - ○ apply time management skills
  - ○ apply group facilitation skills and knowledge
  - ○ respect personal limitations
  - ○ apply team management skills and knowledge
  - ○ use various strategies to resolve tension and conflict
  - ○ apply motivational strategies

- accept responsibility when performing a leadership role
- use authority appropriately
- maintain communication at all levels
- apply knowledge of leadership styles and their applications to various audiences
- use organizational skills
- demonstrate creativity

○ Solve problems

- Apply problem solving skills
  - define problems
  - analyze situations
  - negotiate in good faith
  - use questioning skills and critical thinking skills
  - prioritize
  - recognize and apply solutions to defined problems

- Demonstrate a positive approach to problem solving
  - accept problems as challenges/opportunities
  - demonstrate flexibility
  - demonstrate creativity and resourcefulness
  - demonstrate confidence in personal judgments

MEETING COORDINATOR

○ Work with committees

- Maintain two-way communication
  - advise committee members of procedures and/or changes
  - co-ordinate communication between committees and management

- Act as a resource to committees
  - participate in committee meetings
  - provide information to committees

- ○ Supervise volunteers and staff
  - Direct staff and volunteers
    - ○ participate in recruitment, hiring, training, and placement of staff
    - ○ monitor the HR schedule to satisfy staffing needs
    - ○ orient and train staff and volunteers
    - ○ maintain necessary records and reporting procedures
    - ○ apply terms of contracts and HR policies
    - ○ adhere to the level of authority
    - ○ determine who has signing authority and is able to make decisions
  - Maintain staff visibility
    - ○ use identification for staff visibility
    - ○ educate facility personnel/suppliers about the responsibility/authority of staff members
    - ○ communicate emergency and safety procedures
  - Evaluate the performance of volunteers and staff
    - ○ evaluate performance and report evaluations to management
- ○ Demonstrate an understanding of the meeting profession
  - Maintain up to date information about the meeting industry
    - ○ recognize the complexity, diversity, size and scope of the industry (locally, regionally, nationally, and globally)
    - ○ recognize the economic impact of the industry
    - ○ read industry trade magazines and recognize their contribution
    - ○ use networking opportunities to maintain current information
  - Participate in professional activities for the meeting industry
    - ○ participate in professional trade associations
    - ○ participate in ongoing educational opportunities for the industry
    - ○ recognize the value of lifelong learning
    - ○ recognize opportunities for professional designations

○ Maintain professional integrity

- Develop and maintain professional relationships
  - ○ demonstrate sensitivity and empathy
  - ○ build partnerships and alliances
  - ○ demonstrate honesty, openness and integrity
  - ○ apply knowledge of cultural differences
  - ○ adhere to an accepted industry code of ethics (e.g., MPI's Principles of Professionalism)

- Communicate in a professional manner
  - ○ communicate clearly and effectively in person and in writing
  - ○ demonstrate competency in developing and presenting reports
  - ○ demonstrate calm, diplomacy, and tact, especially when handling conflict and stress
  - ○ demonstrate active-listening skills
  - ○ distinguish between assertive and aggressive behaviour

- Apply business administration skills
  - ○ maintain necessary numerical data
  - ○ demonstrate an understanding of the planning cycle
  - ○ demonstrate an understanding of the economics of a meeting
  - ○ develop business acumen
  - ○ demonstrate leadership
  - ○ demonstrate organizational skills
  - ○ apply time management skills
  - ○ apply group facilitation skills and knowledge
  - ○ respect personal limitations
  - ○ apply team management skills and knowledge
  - ○ use various strategies to resolve tension and conflict
  - ○ apply motivational strategies
  - ○ accept responsibility when performing a leadership role
  - ○ use authority appropriately
  - ○ maintain communication at all levels
  - ○ apply knowledge of leadership styles and their applications to various audiences

- Participate in information gathering and assist in decision making
  - provide details of previous histories
  - perform as a member of a team
  - provide evaluative information
- Solve problems

- Apply problem solving skills
  - analyze situations
  - define problems
  - negotiate
  - use questioning skills and critical thinking skills
  - manage multiple priorities
  - recognize and apply solutions to defined problems
  - Demonstrate a positive approach to problem solving
  - accept problems as challenges
  - demonstrate flexibility
  - demonstrate creativity and resourcefulness
  - demonstrate confidence in personal judgments

FORECASTING YOUR HUMAN RESOURCES NEEDS

Each conference, special event, or trade show requires a number of people onsite to provide assistance to attendees, exhibitors, and speakers.

- Factors that will assist in determining the human resource needs are:
- size of meeting
- complexity of meeting (e.g., trade show, multiple concurrent sessions, guest program, children's program)
- availability of a strong resource pool of talent
- Areas where assistance is generally needed:
- meet and greet at the airport
- greeting or information desks at hotels and meeting facility
- registration desk staff (plan to have several shifts over each day of the conference)

DETERMINING ONSITE STAFF NEEDS

Once the majority of attendees are registered, the registration desk often serves as an information desk and/or message centre. You can estimate the number of staff you will need as follows: assume one minute for every pre-registered attendee to check in at the registration desk at a simple event. 80% of the pre-registered attendees will check in prior to the beginning of the event or conference. Any activity that is added to the process, such as printing of tickets, increases the amount of time that each attendee will require. For instance, you may only be able to process one attendee every five minutes. If that is the case, you will need to increase the number of persons working at the registration desk.

Consider the following roles for onsite support

- Meeting room assistants or room monitors

  It is helpful to have volunteers serve as assistants in the concurrent session meeting rooms. They can provide assistance to the speaker and/or moderator by contacting the audio visual technician for assistance, taking tickets, distribute handouts, etc.)

- Moderators
  Most organization will use an industry related person to introduce and thank concurrent session speakers.

- Trade show assistants
  Sometimes during set up and tear down, volunteers may provide any and all other assistance as required.

- Assisting with directions and traffic flow

- Registration kit assembly

WORKING WITH COMMITTEES

Most conferences are planned by at least one committee, usually because so much work is involved that no one person can do it all. Organizations may have several committees depending on the complexity of the organization and the conference. Each committee should have terms of reference that are clearly understood by all members of the committee. Included in these terms of reference should be the role that the meeting professional will play within each committee.

The following list is a general list of committees that may be part of the conference planning process:

- Steering Committee: overall responsibility and accountability for the conference. Subcommittees report to this committee.

- Social: is responsible for any "social" events during the course of the conference (e.g., awards dinner, VIP reception).

- Trade Show: sets the policies for the trade show, reviews applications, assists with the set up and tear down.

- Program: Determines the content of the education component. (Reviews calls for presentations, researches and contracts keynote speakers.)

- Marketing: Responsible for the development and distribution of the promotional material for the conference (includes graphic and website design, and production of materials).

- Publicity and Media: one person in this committee may be appointed as the official spokesperson for the conference or the conference chairperson may be the designated spokesperson. This committee is responsible for developing the rapport with the related media contacts and preparing the press releases.

- Finance: may be a one person committee; responsible for the banking, bill paying and financial reporting for the conference.

- Sponsorship: responsible for raising both cash and inkind support to defray operating expenses.

HOT TIP

Ask an Advisor

You can appoint an advisory board for your next conference or seminar. Get good people in your industry or company. Pick those who are knowledgeable and preferably well known. You want their ideas. If you can bring them together, so much the better, but you can also talk to them individually, by telephone if necessary. Be open-minded - you may hear suggestions you think are unworkable or impractical but listen carefully. "Outsiders" can usually offer fresh new ideas and approaches.

JOB DESCRIPTIONS

Job descriptions should clearly outline the responsibilities and accountability for each position.

VOLUNTEER COORDINATOR

- Research where to recruit volunteers for the event

- Determine the range of volunteers needed and the specific tasks needed

- Arrange for and conduct a training session for volunteers

- Arrange for and conduct an orientation session at the venue

- Schedule volunteers and notify all stakeholders of the schedule

- Manage volunteers during the conference

- Research and recommend a reward and recognition program

- Evaluate the process

ROOM MONITOR

The following is a sample job description:

- Arrive at the conference venue at least 30 minutes prior to your scheduled shift. Be ready to work, there may not be time to go for coffee, etc.

- Know where you are to be and to whom you should report to

- Be at your assigned meeting room approximately 15 minutes prior to the start of the session. However, do not interrupt a session that may be currently operating

- Once in the meeting room, check the following:
  - water for the speakers
  - speaker gift
  - moderator for the session
  - if there are handouts, assist in distribution when required
  - take tickets at the door and provide the tickets to the moderator for the prize draw
  - monitor the entrance door, check badges, and assist to find seats for latecomers

- collect the evaluations at the end of the session

- report any problems (e.g., no seats left, audio visual problems to the conference office)

- return any necessary items to the conference office (e.g., completed evaluation forms, tickets, speaker gifts not distributed, etc.)

FINDING THE RIGHT PEOPLE FOR THE RIGHT JOB

Where can volunteers and/or support staff be found?

- In most organizations, corporate or not for profit, there will be volunteers who will come forward when the request is made.

- Another source of volunteers is local colleges and universities. Usually students in related disciplines to the host organization are quite willing to assist. It provides an ideal opportunity for networking with potential employers and also gives them access to educational programs within their area of interest. If you are considering recruiting from a college or university, be sure to contact the faculty members with as much lead time as possible. If the faculty feels the conference will serve as a strong educational opportunity for their students, they may suspend classes or allow extra latitude for attendance at the conference.

- Other sources of temporary staff may be local industry related associations, service clubs, fraternities, etc. These groups may expect some compensation in return for their time commitment. For example, service clubs may work areas such as coat check (if the facility will allow it) in return for a cash payment or donation to the service club for the members who give up their time.

- Temporary staffing agencies - if budgets allow, you may consider hiring staff from a staffing agency, preferably one that specializes in the meetings and events industry. This will save time in orientation and training.

VOLUNTEER COORDINATION AND TRAINING

In order to provide a rewarding experience to your staff, it is wise to have one person designated as the staff coordinator. This person can be responsible for scheduling the staff, should be involved in the training or orientation, and onsite during the conference to answer any questions and solve any problems. Coordination of the staff requires coaching and mentoring.

All staff require some training. This training or orientation need not be complex or time consuming but should be comprehensive. One way to simplify this process is to produce a handbook for the event. The handbook should be easily carried by the staff during a shift. It includes such things as key personnel phone numbers and responsibilities, answers to frequently asked questions (e.g., "Where are the public telephones?") and any other pertinent information to the conference, such as the schedule at a glance with the assigned meeting rooms or a facility floor plan.

Schedule your training or orientation at the conference venue. This provides the staff an opportunity to see the facility, the area in which they will be working, and clarify any transportation and/or parking issues.

Be sure to budget to feed staff. Depending on the conference and the venue, you may be able to set up a separate room for the volunteers as "home base". If this is a viable option, include a coffee station, cold drinks, as well as sandwiches and snacks if this is to serve as their location for meals. If the staff are from the industry and or from a related college program, try to budget dollars and space to include them into the scheduled conference meals and related programs.

RECOGNITION

Remember to thank your volunteers early and often. Giving volunteers early, frequent and constant recognition will help to build a strong team who will be loyal and go above and beyond the call of duty. Providing an article of clothing for each volunteer to wear during the conference can serve two purposes: to provide a thank you gift and also to provide visibility of the volunteers to the attendees.

The orientation event can serve also as a thank you party.

> **HOT TIP**
>
> **Thanks at the End of the Day**
> Don't fall prey to the inevitable post conference letdown. Immediately after the conference, one of your "must" responsibilities is to write personal letters of thanks. Write anyone who participated in your sessions, and everyone who helped plan and run the conference.

PROFESSIONALISM

According to the National Directory of Occupational Titles and Codes, a meeting professional is an individual whose job is to "organize, plan and execute activities for individuals who meet for a common cause, whether educational, motivational, or as an incentive to achieve objectives".

A meeting professional is a key member of the management team with challenging responsibilities directly affecting the performance, effectiveness, financial success, and public image of the corporation or association they represent. There are numerous opportunities to acquire successive levels of education in the meeting industry. Ethical business practices are also an important aspect of this professional status.

EDUCATION AND PROFESSIONAL DEVELOPMENT

The tasks and responsibilities of a meeting professional are broad yet specific. You may find yourself serving as a negotiator, accountant, arbitrator, communicator, logistics specialist, program planner, marketer, and crisis manager. You may be responsible for making decisions concerning site selection, the meeting agenda, objectives, content, budgets, entertainment, social functions, transportation, and trade show/exhibit management. You may be hosting important dignitaries where international protocol is essential or you may be providing assistance to a major entertainer. Skills that are essential in ensuring your success as a meeting professional are attention to detail, the ability to multitask and respond to changing priorities.

There are many opportunities available to acquire the necessary education to equip the meeting professional with the necessary skills.

Formal Education
The growth of the industry has been supported by the development of degree granting programs in colleges and universities. Check the educational opportunities in your area for a list of these programs. Distance learning and continuing education opportunities are also available.

Certified Meeting Professional (CMP)
This professional designation is administered by the CIC (Convention Industry Council) and is available through most meeting industry associations. The CMP is a designation that embraces and fosters development in the areas of logistics and tactical operations as they relate to the meeting profession. Individuals who have acquired their CMP are required to re-certify every five years, in order to maintain leading edge knowledge and skills.

Certification in Meeting Management (CMM)

This is a management designation offered to senior industry professionals. This certification focuses on the strategic, business skills of the industry. The CMP is not a prerequisite to acquiring the CMM designation; rather, the objective of this designation is to learn how to determine the meeting management objectives, financial impact, and human resources. Strategies to develop effective event business plans on a global and national level, as well as general business acumen, are key components of the CMM. The CMM designation is offered through Meeting Professionals International and consists of an extended university study experience, followed by a business case study.

ETHICAL BUSINESS PRACTICES

The role of the meeting professional, within an organization, is often a very visible, high profile position. With this come expected behaviours that reflect on the individual, the organization and the meeting profession as a whole. It is the responsibility of every meeting professional to conduct themselves in a professional manner, exercise good judgment and maintain ethical business practices in order to ensure the meeting profession is viewed in the highest possible regard.

Meeting Professionals International (MPI) has developed the following Principles of Professionalism to guide meeting professionals in their role as "ambassadors" for the meetings industry. Adhering to these principles will ensure that we remain honorable, competent, and nondiscriminatory professionals with great integrity.

PRINCIPLES OF PROFESSIONALISM

Meeting Professionals International's (MPI) Principles of Professionalism provides guidelines recommended for all the business behaviour of its members that impacts their perceived character and thus the overall image of MPI. Commitment of these principles is implicit to membership and is essential to instilling public confidence, engaging in fair and equitable practices and building professional relationships with meeting industry colleagues. As members of Meeting Professionals International, we are responsible for ensuring that the meeting industry is held in the highest public* regard throughout the world. Our conduct directly impacts this result.

Maintaining Professional Integrity:

- Honestly REPRESENT AND ACT within one's areas of professional competency and authority without exaggeration, misrepresentation or concealment.

- AVOID actions which are or could be perceived as a conflict of interest or for individual gain.

- OFFER OR ACCEPT only appropriate incentives, goods and services in business transactions.

Utilizing Professional Business Practices:

- HONOR written and oral contracts, striving for clarity and mutual understanding through complete, accurate and timely communications, while respecting legal and contractual rights of others.

- ENSURE rights to privacy and protect confidentiality of privileged information received verbally, in writing or electronically.

- REFRAIN from misusing solicited information, proposals or concepts.

- COMMIT to the protection of the environment by responsible use of resources in the production of meetings.

- ACTIVELY PURSUE educational growth through training, sharing of knowledge, expertise and skills, to advance the meeting industry.

Respecting Diversity:

- EMBRACE AND FOSTER an inclusive business climate of respect for all peoples regardless of national origin, race, religion, sex, marital status, age, sexual orientation, physical or mental impairment.

Adherence to these Principles of Professionalism signifies professionalism, competence, fair dealings and high integrity. Failure to abide by these principles may subject a member to disciplinary action, as set forth by the Bylaws of Meeting Professionals International.

* Encompasses oneself, the association, fellow members, meeting attendees, clients and customers, suppliers and planners, employers and the general public.

HUMAN RESOURCES AND PROFESSIONALISM CHECKLIST

☐ Forecasting your human resources needs

- keep in mind:
  - size of meeting
  - complexity of meeting
  - availability of pool of talent
- where needed:
  - meet and greet at airport
  - greeting at hotel and meeting facility
  - information desk
  - registration desk staff

☐ Volunteer roles

- meeting room assistants or room monitors
- moderators
- trade show assistants

☐ Working with committees

- training
- coordination
- recognition
- o Professional education and development
- formal education
- certification
- principles of professionalism

CHAPTER REVIEW

Many people are required to complete all of the tasks involved in running a meeting. The number and type of people required will be affected by the size and complexity of the meeting and the availability of qualified talent.

Assistance is typically required to fulfill the following roles:

- airport meet and greet

- information desks/greeters

- registration desk personnel

- meeting room assistants or monitors

- moderators

- trade show assistants

- traffic flow facilitators

- registration kit assembly personnel

- volunteer coordinator

Job descriptions should be developed for all roles that clearly outline the responsibilities and accountability for each position.

In many cases, committees are used to complete key planning and pre-event logistical functions. Most committees are made up of volunteers from within the industry that the conference serves. The following committees may have a role to play in the conference planning process:

- steering committee

- social committee

- trade show committee

- program committee

- marketing, media and publicity committees

- finance committee

- sponsorship committee

Volunteers and support staff can be found by:

- communicating that volunteers are required

- seeking out university and college students

- approaching industry related associations, service clubs and fraternities

- using a temporary staffing agency

One person should be designated as the staff coordinator and be responsible for scheduling, training, orientation and onsite management, as well as coaching and mentoring.

Give your volunteers constant thanks and recognition as well as tangible rewards such as an article of clothing if possible.

Education and professional development are crucial to success in the role of the meeting professional. This can be obtained through:

- formal education

- CMP

- CMM

The behaviour and ethics of the meeting professional reflect on the individual, their organization and the meeting profession as a whole. Meeting Professionals International has developed Principles of Professionalism that guide the meeting professional in maintaining the integrity of their role. These principles include:

- maintaining professional integrity

- utilizing professional business practices

- respecting diversity

TEST YOUR KNOWLEDGE

The following self test will indicate the level of understanding and knowledge gained from this chapter. Solutions to all self tests can be found in Appendix A.

1. Volunteers can be recruited to fulfill every human resources need that your meeting may have.

    ☐ True   ☐ False

2. You should plan on 100% of your delegates to check in prior to the beginning of the event or conference.

    ☐ True   ☐ False

3. Job descriptions are only necessary for staff positions.

    ☐ True   ☐ False

4. Volunteers do not require thank you's if they receive a gift for their participation.

    ☐ True   ☐ False

5. The meeting professional will be called upon to fulfill which of the following roles:

    (a) negotiator and arbitrator

    (b) logistics specialist

    (c) program planner

    (d) marketer

    (e) crisis manager

    (f) accountant

    (g) all of the above

5. Which of the following are not acceptable conduct, according the MPI Principles of Professionalism?

    (a) protecting the environment

    (b) accepting appropriate incentives, goods and services in business transactions

    (c) respecting all people regardless of race, religion, sex or national origin

    (d) honoring only written contracts

    (e) avoiding actions that could be perceived as a conflict of interest

6. Committees should not be used as part of the planning process for:

   (a) educational program

   (b) conference finances

   (c) sponsorship

   (d) supplier selection

   (e) marketing

7. Describe the role of the volunteer coordinator and the characteristics of the person you would choose to fulfill this role.

   _____

   _____

   _____

   _____

   _____

8. Suggest 5 ways that you could thank, motivate and reward meeting or event volunteers.

   _____

   _____

   _____

   _____

   _____

I

A C C E P T E D

P R A C T I C E S

E X C H A N G E

The APEX Event Specifications Guide Template

Approved by the Convention Industry Council on September 30, 2004
Updated June 2005

Report Section Contents

Accepted Practices
Instructions for Use
Part I Narrative
Part II Function Schedule
Part III a Function Set-up Order
Part III b Function Set-up Order (Exhibitor Version)

INTRODUCTION

APEX is... The **A**ccepted **P**ractices **Ex**change. **APEX** is an initiative of the Convention Industry Council (CIC) that is bringing together all stakeholders in the development and implementation of industry-wide accepted practices to create and enhance efficiencies throughout the meetings, conventions and exhibitions industry.

Some of the results of accepted practices implementation:

- Time & Cost Savings
- Eased Communication and Sharing of Data
- Enhanced Customer Service
- Streamlined Systems and Processes
- Less Duplication of Effort and Increased Operational Efficiencies
- Better Educated, More Professional Employees

In short, accepted practices will make the industry more efficient, freeing up valuable time to devote collaborative energies to broader, more pressing industry issues. Can you imagine what you would do with more time to think creatively, less repetitive work to complete, and better relationships with your customers and suppliers?

The following sections are printed in 2006 with permission of the Convention Industry Council and include the following information and templates:

Section I – **APEX Event Specifications Guide Template**
Section II – **APEX Housing & Registration Accepted Practices**
Section III –**APEX Post-Event Report Template**

ACCEPTED PRACTICES

1. The term *Event Specifications Guide* or *ESG (acronym)* should be the industry's official term for the document used by an event organizer to convey information clearly and accurately to appropriate venue(s) and/or suppliers regarding all requirements for an event. This is a four-part document which includes:
   - Part I: The Narrative – general overview of the event.
   - Part II: Function Schedule – timetable outlining all functions that compose the overall event.
   - Part IIIa: Function Set-up Order – specifications for each function that is part of the overall event (each function of the event will have its own Function Set-up Order).
   - Part IIIb: Function Set-up Order (Exhibitor Version) – specifications for each booth/stand that is part of an exhibition.

   This is based on accepted terminology defined in the *APEX Industry Glossary*. The *Glossary* defines an event as "an organized occasion such as a meeting, convention, exhibition, special event, gala dinner, etc. An event is often composed of several different yet related functions." The *Glossary* also defines a function as "any of a group of related organized occasions that contribute to a larger event" (e.g. registration area, coat check, rehearsal, outside display, seating area, office, poster session, green room, emergency information area, breakout session, etc.).

2. The *APEX ESG* should be the industry's accepted format for the conveyance of information regarding the requirements of an event.

3. The following fields in the *Narrative* portion of the *ESG* require information input and are designated by *. An acceptable input is "Not Applicable" or "NA":
   Date Originated
   Date Revised
   Event Profile
   - Event Name
   - Event Organizer/Host Organization Mailing Address Line 1
   - Event Organizer/Host Organization City
   - Event Organizer/Host Organization State/Province
   - Event Organizer/Host Organization Postal/Zip Code
   - Event Organizer/Host Organization Country
   - Event Organizer/Host Organization Phone
   - Event Type
   Dates & Times
   - Published Event Start Date
   - Published Event End Date
   - Pre-Event Meeting
     - Day & Date
     - Time
     - Location
     - Attendees
   - Post-Event Meeting
     - Day & Date
     - Time
     - Location
     - Attendees
   Key Event Contacts
   - Complete information for a minimum of one (1) key event contact person
   Attendee Profile
   - Accessibility/Special Needs
   Housing
   - Room Block(s) - Complete information for a minimum of one (1) Hotel or Housing Facility
   - Reservation method
   - Accessibility/Special Needs Rooms
   Safety & Security
   - Medical/Emergency Instructions

- Key Event Organizer/Host Organization Contact in Case of Emergency/Crisis
- Crisis & Emergency Instructions
- On-site Communications
- Hours of surveillance
- Areas for surveillance

Food & Beverage
- Special Requirements
- Catered Food & Beverage Total Expected Attendance Chart

Transportation
- Attendee Shuttle Provided

Shipping/Receiving
- One line of the Shipping Grid
- Expected Outbound Shipping Requirements

Billing Instructions
- Group is tax-exempt
- Room & Tax to Master
- Incidentals to Master
- Guests Pay on Own
- Negotiated Items/Services
- Final Bill to Be Provided to (contact name)
- Final Bill to Be Sent to (mailing address)

Authorized Signatories
- Complete information for a minimum of one (1) authorized signatory

4. There should be various stages in the evolution of the *APEX ESG* and the processes used to complete it:

Stage I - The form will be a word processing file and be completed manually. It will be shared by event organizers and venues/suppliers in electronic and/or hard copy form.
- Every facility and vendor involved in an event should receive a complete copy of the final ESG.
- Each ESG will include dates for pre- and post-event meetings to review and revise information.
- The ESG should be shared in a way that, when changes are made, they can be properly tracked and identified. Specifically, when a change is made from the original published document, a revised date should be inserted, and any change should be highlighted and dated within the document.
- The Function Set-up Order (Exhibitor Version) should be used by exhibitors to communicate booth/stand needs to show management and other vendors. Additionally, show managers can use the form to guide exhibitors through the process of determining and relaying their set-up requirements.
- The suggested timetable for the completion and sharing of the information contained in this document is dependent upon the size and complexity of the meeting, convention, or exhibition.
  - *At a minimum,* an event organizer should send the ESG to all facilities and vendors four weeks prior to the start of the event.
  - *Also, at a minimum,* facilities and vendors should respond with completed orders [production schedules, Banquet Event Orders (BEOs), etc.] no later than two weeks prior to the event.

  While these are recommended guidelines, the needs of each facility and vendor will vary. Event organizers should confer with suppliers to determine the timeline and deadlines for this information. Also, all parties should consult the relevant contract because that could override any recommendation in this document.

Stage II - When industry-related software is updated and new software is developed, programmers will ensure that the APEX data map is referenced so that all data fields are defined correctly and are able to efficiently capture, store, and share information from the APEX ESG. This will allow for more automated sharing and updating of the report.

5. The Convention Industry Council will annually convene a special committee of professionals from across the meetings, conventions, and exhibitions industry to review all recommendations to the contents of the APEX Event Specifications Guide that have been be received in the preceding year. This special committee will consult and confirm that changes to the report are required. It will then make a formal recommendation to the Convention Industry Council for action.

APEX EVENT SPECIFICATIONS GUIDE (ESG) TEMPLATE

Instructions for Use

The *ESG* is a written document that is all inclusive of event details. It includes three sections: 1) Narrative 2) Function Schedule and 3) Function Set-up Order. The following templates will assist event organizers in compiling complete information for a venue partner and contractor/supplier partners. Note the following:

1. Required Information: Several fields require information input. These items are designated by *.

2. Every function must have its own Function Set-up Order.

3. Every function must have a number. All diagrams, photos, sign copy, etc. refer to the function number at all times. When a new function is added, it is at the discretion of the planner whether to order in sequence, or to use "intermediate numbers." Anything other than whole numbers must be formatted as 1a, 1b, 1c, etc. When a function in sequence is cancelled, the function number should not be reassigned.

4. Every section may not apply for every event.

5. Changes & Revisions: ESGs should be shared in a way that, when changes are made, they can be properly tracked and identified. Specifically, when a change is made from the original published document, a revised date should be inserted, and any change should be highlighted and dated within the document.

6. The Function Set-up Order (Exhibitor Version) should be used by exhibitors to communicate booth/stand needs to show management and other vendors. Additionally, show managers can use the form to guide exhibitors through the process of determining and relaying their set-up requirements.

PART I – Narrative

Date Originated*: _____

Date Revised*: _____
Repeat for additional revisions as necessary.

A. EVENT PROFILE

Event Name*: _____

Event Organizer/Host Organization: _____

Event Organizer/Host Organization Phone*: _____

Event Organizer/Host Organization Mailing Address Line 1*: _____

Event Organizer/Host Organization Mailing Address Line 2: _____

Event Organizer/Host Organization City*: _____

Event Organizer/Host Organization State/Province*: _____

Event Organizer/Host Organization Postal/Zip Code*: _____

Event Organizer/Host Organization Country*: _____

Event Organizer/Host Organization Web Address: _____

Event Web Address: _____

Event Organizer/Host Organization Overview *(mission, philosophy, etc.)*: _____

Event Objectives: _____

Event Scope:

Drop Down Options:
❑ Citywide
❑ Single Venue
❑ Multiple Venue
❑ Other: _____

Event Type*:

Drop Down Options:
❑ Board Meeting
❑ Committee Meeting
❑ Customer Event
❑ Educational Meeting
❑ General Business Meeting
❑ Incentive Travel
❑ Local Employee Gathering
❑ Product Launch
❑ Public/Consumer Show

❑ Sales Meeting
❑ Shareholders Meeting
❑ Special Event
❑ Team-Building Event
❑ Training Meeting
❑ Trade Show
❑ Video Conference
❑ Other: _____

Event Frequency:

Drop Down Options:
❑ One Time Only
❑ Biennial
❑ Annual
❑ Semi-Annual
❑ Quarterly

☐ Monthly
☐ Other: _____

Event is mandatory for attendees: ☐ Yes   ☐ No

Spouses & Guests are invited to attend: ☐ Yes   ☐ No

Children are invited to attend: ☐ Yes   ☐ No

Other Event Profile Comments: _____

B. KEY DATES, TIMES, & LOCATIONS

Refer to the complete Schedule of Events (Part II of the ESG) for complete details on all functions and scheduled activities.

Primary Event Facility Name: _____   Event Location City: _____

State/Province: _____   Country: _____

Published Event Start Date*: _____

Published Event End Date*: _____

Pre-Event Meeting
    Day & Date*: _____
    Time* (US & Military via auto calc): _____
    Location*: _____
    Attendees*: _____

Post-Event Meeting
    Day & Date*: _____
    Time* (US & Military via auto calc): _____
    Location*: _____
    Attendees*: _____

Pre-Event Move-in & Set-up Required: ☐ Yes   ☐ No
    If Yes, Specific Schedule Will Be Provided By: _____ *(e.g. name of contractor)*

Other Dates & Times Comments: _____
    e.g. registration desk hours, daily review meetings

C. KEY EVENT CONTACTS

Use this section to list all key personnel for the event (e.g. staff, exhibits manager, general services contractor, A/V company, security company, preferred shipper).

Event Organizer/Host Organization Contacts

Name Title Company	Address Telephone Fax Email Mobile Phone	Description of Responsibilities	Location During Event	Emergency Contact?
Contact1 Name* Contact1 Title* Contact1 Company*	Contact1 Address* Contact1 Telephone* Contact1 Fax* Contact1 Email* Contact1 Mobile Phone*	Contact1 Responsibilities*	☐ On-Site* ☐ Off-site*	☐ Yes ☐ No
Repeat for additional Contacts as necessary.				

Supplier Partner Contacts

Name Title Company	Address Telephone Fax Email Mobile Phone	Description of Responsibilities	Location During Event
Contact1 Name* Contact1 Title* Contact1 Company*	Contact1 Address* Contact1 Telephone* Contact1 Fax* Contact1 Email* Contact1 Mobile Phone*	Contact1 Responsibilities*	❑ On-Site* ❑ Off-site*
Repeat for additional Contacts as necessary.			

Other Event Contacts Comments: _____

D. ATTENDEE PROFILE

See Section E for the Exhibitor Profile.

Expected Total Event Attendance: _____

Number of Pre-Registered Attendees: _____

Number of Domestic Attendees: _____
  Note: Domestic Attendees live in the same country where the event is held

Number of International Attendees: _____

Demographics Profile (Attendees Only): _____

Accessibility/Special Needs*: _____
  Note: Use this section to outline any special needs the group has.

Other Attendee Profile Comments: _____

E. EXHIBITOR PROFILE

Number of Exhibitors Attending: _____

Number of Domestic Exhibitors: _____
  Note: Domestic Exhibitors live in the same country where the event is held

Number of International Exhibitors: _____

Demographics Profile (Exhibitors Only): _____

Number of Exhibiting Companies/Organizations Represented: _____

Accessibility/Special Needs*: _____
  Note: Use this section to outline any special needs the group has.

Other Exhibitor Profile Comments: _____

F. ARRIVAL/DEPARTURE INFORMATION

Major Arrivals: _____

Major Departures: _____

Group Arrivals/Departures: _____

Porterage/Luggage Delivery Requirements: _____

Luggage Storage Requirements: _____

Drive-in and Parking Instructions: _____

Fly-in Instructions: _____

Other Arrival/Departure Comments: _____

G. HOUSING

Room Block(s)*:
For a multi-hotel/housing facility event, name all housing facilities and specify the headquarters

Facility Name	HQ Hotel?	Day 1	Day 2	Day 3	Additional days as necessary
Facility Name1	☐ Yes ☐ No	Final Room Block #	Final Room Block #	Final Room Block #	
Additional facilities as necessary					

Reservation method*:_____

Third-Party Housing Provider Used: ☐ Yes   ☐ No
If Yes, Housing Provider Company Name: _____
Suites: _____

Double/Single Occupancy: _____

Accessibility/Special Needs Rooms*: _____

Amenities: _____

In-room deliveries: _____

Room Drops (outside doors): _____

Other Housing Comments: _____
Note: *See Section D for VIP information*

H. VIPs – VERY IMPORTANT PERSONS

Name	Title	Employer	Arrival Date & Time	Departure Date & Time	Amenities	Upgrades	Relationship to the Event	Comments e.g. special billing, airport transfers
VIP1								
VIP2								
Repeat for additional VIPs as necessary.								

I. FUNCTION SPACE

Use this section to address any special issues or situations that apply to the event.

Off-site Venue(s): _____

Function Rooms: _____

Message Center: _____

Office(s): _____

Registration Area(s): _____

Lounge(s): _____

Speaker Ready Room(s): _____

Press Room: _____

Storage: _____

General Reader Board Information: _____

Other Function Space Comments: _____

J. EXHIBITS

Location(s) of Exhibits: _____

Exhibitor Registration Location(s) : _____

Number of Exhibits: _____

Gross Square Feet Used: _____   Gross Square Meters Used: _____

Net Square Feet Used: _____   Net Square Meters Used: _____

Exhibit Rules & Regulations Attached: ❑ Yes   ❑ No

Show Dates and Times:

Day/Date	Show Hours	Show Hours	Show Hours

Storage Needs: _____

Anticipated POV (Privately Owned Vehicle) Deliveries (#): _____

Exhibitor Schedule

Move-in Begin Date: _____   Move-in End Date: _____
Move-in Begin Time: _____

Move-out Begin Date: _____   Move-out End Date: _____
Move-out End Time: _____

Service Contractor Schedule

Move-in Begin Date: _____   Move-in End Date: _____
Move-in Begin Time: _____

Move-out Begin Date: _____   Move-out End Date: _____
Move-out End Time: _____

See Section B: Dates & Times for Targeted Move-in Information

Other Exhibits Comments: _____

K. UTILITIES

Use this section to describe any special situations in regard to Engineering, Rigging, Electrical, Water, Telecommunications, etc.

L. SAFETY, SECURITY & FIRST-AID

Medical/Emergency Instructions*: _____

Key Event Organizer/Host Organization Contact in Case of Emergency/Crisis*: _____

Crisis & Emergency Instructions*: _____

On-site Communications Protocol*: _____

General Security/Surveillance: ❑ Not Required   ❑ Group To Provide   ❑ Venue To Provide
                                   ❑ Outside Vendor To Provide: _____ (company name)

Day/Date	Location	Hours (start & end)	Hours (start & end)	Hours (start & end)

First-Aid Services: ❑ Not Required   ❑ Group To Provide   ❑ Venue To Provide
                        ❑ Outside Vendor To Provide: _____ (company name)

Day/Date	Location	Hours (start & end)

Keys

Location	Function Name	Start Day & Time	End Day & Time	# of Keys Required	Key Type
					❑ House/Standard ❑ Re-Keyed

VIP and/or Police Escorted Movements: _____

Other Security Comments: _____

M. FOOD & BEVERAGE

Special Requirements*: _____

Catered Food & Beverage Total Expected Attendance*

	Day 1	Day 2	Day 3	Day 4	*Repeat for additional days as necessary.*
Breakfast(s)	#	#	#	#	
AM Break(s)	#	#	#	#	
Lunch(s)	#	#	#	#	
PM Break(s)	#	#	#	#	
Reception(s)	#	#	#	#	
Dinner(s)	#	#	#	#	

On-Site F&B Description: _____

Off-Site F&B Description: _____

Anticipated Outlet/Concession Usage: _____

Other Food & Beverage Comments: _____

N. SPECIAL ACTIVITIES

Recreational Activities: _____

Guest Programs: _____

Tours: _____

Pre- & Post-Event Programs: _____

Entertainment: _____

Children's Programs: _____

Other Special Activities Comments: _____

O. AUDIO/VISUAL REQUIREMENTS
Use this section to address any special issues or situations that apply to the event.

P. TRANSPORTATION

Attendee Shuttle Provided*: ❑ Yes ❑ No
If Yes, complete the following:

Day & Date (i.e., Monday, mm/dd/yyyy)	Route Name	Start Time	End Time	Frequency
Repeat for additional occurrences as necessary.				

Transportation Provider: _____

Shuttle(s) Provided for Off-Site Events: ❑ Yes ❑ No
If Yes, complete the following:

	Off-Site Function 1	Off-Site Function 2	Off-Site Function 3	Off-Site Function 4	Additional Off-Site Functions as Necessary
Departure Location					
Departure Date/Time					
Drop-off Location					
Drop-off Date/Time					
Return Location					
Return Date/time					
Transportation Provider					

Other Transportation Comments: _____

Q. IN CONJUNCTION WITH (ICW) GROUPS

Use this section to list and describe any In Conjunction With (ICW) groups of which suppliers for this event should be aware. Full contact information for the main point of contact should also be included. Additionally, note any important rules and regulations regarding these groups.

R. MEDIA/PRESS

Use this section to address any special issues or situations that apply to the event (e.g. contact information for the person to whom all media inquiries should be sent).

S. SHIPPING/RECEIVING

From:	To:	Shipper:	# of Items:	Expected Delivery Date
(contact and address)	(contact and address)			

Expected Outbound Shipping Requirements*: _____

Dock Usage: _____

Freight Elevator Usage: _____

Drayage to Be Handled By: _____
Other Shipping/Receiving Comments: _____

T. HOUSEKEEPING INSTRUCTIONS
Use this section to address any special issues or situations that apply to the event.

U. FRONT DESK INSTRUCTIONS
Use this section to address any special issues or situations that apply to the event.

V. OTHER REQUIREMENTS

W. BILLING INSTRUCTIONS

Final Bill to Be Provided to*: _____ (contact name)

Final Bill to Be Sent to*: _____ (mailing address)

Special Concessions and Negotiated Items/Services*

Description
Item/Service1
Item/Service2
Repeat for additional items/services as necessary.

On-Site Bill Review Instructions: _____

Third-Party Billing Instructions: _____
Use this section to give specific instructions for goods & services that the event organizer is not responsible for (e.g. contractors expenses, etc.)

Group is tax-exempt*: ❏ Yes   ❏ No
　　If yes, Tax Exempt ID #: _____

Room & Tax to Master*: ❏ Yes   ❏ No

Incidentals to Master*: ❏ Yes   ❏ No

Guests Pay on Own*: ❏ Yes   ❏ No

X. AUTHORIZED SIGNATORIES

Full Name	Title	Approval Authority
Signatory1 Full Name*	Signatory1 Title*	Indicate Approval Authority Instructions*
Repeat for additional Signatories as necessary.		

PART II – Function Schedule

Date Originated: _____

Date Revised*: _____
Repeat for additional revisions as necessary.

Event Name: _____

Event Organizer/Host Organization: _____

Contact Name: _____

Contact Phone: _____

Day & Date	Function Start Time (US & Military via auto calc)	Function End Time (US & Military via auto calc)	Function Name	Facility	Room Name	Set-up	Set For	Function #	Posting Instructions	24-Hour Hold?
						^			❑ Post ❑ Do Not Post	❑ Yes ❑ No

Function Schedule Comments: _____

^enter primary set-up designated on the function's function order.

513

PART IIIa – Function Set-up Order

Date Originated: _____

Date Revised*: _____
Repeat for additional revisions as necessary.

A. EVENT DETAILS

Event Name: _____

Event Organizer/Host Organization: _____

Contact Name: _____

Contact Phone: _____

B. FUNCTION DETAILS

Function #: _____

Function Name: _____

Function Type: *Drop Down Options:*
                                         ❑ Break Out
     ❑ Coat Check
     ❑ Dressing/Green Room
     ❑ Exhibit
     ❑ General Session
     ❑ Meeting
     ❑ Office
     ❑ Photo Room
     ❑ Poster Session
     ❑ Registration
     ❑ Speaker Room
     ❑ Storage
     ❑ Workshop
     ❑ Other

Post to Reader Board? ❑ Post   ❑ Do Not Post
     If Post, Post As: _____

Function Location: _____

Key Event Personnel for this Function: _____

Attendance: _____

Function Start Day/Date: _____
Function Start Time (US & Military via auto calc): _____

Function End Day/Date: _____
Function End Time (US & Military via auto calc): _____

Set Up By (US & Military via auto calc): _____

Dismantle No Later than (US & Military via auto calc): _____

Catered Function: ❑ Yes   ❑ No

C. ROOM SET-UP

Room Set-up Diagram Attached: ❑ Yes ❑ No
    Note: The set-up diagram should indicate A/V placement and electrical needs.
Room Set Room For: _____ (qty.)

Primary Room Set-up: *Drop Down Options:*
❑ 10x10 exhibits
❑ 8x10 exhibits
❑ Island Exhibit
❑ Peninsula Exhibit
❑ Perimeter Exhibit
❑ Tabletop exhibits
❑ Banquet Rounds for 10
❑ Banquet Rounds for 12
❑ Banquet Rounds for 8
❑ Board Room (Conference)
❑ Classroom - 2 per 6 ft. tables
❑ Classroom - 3 per 6 ft. tables
❑ Classroom - 3 per 8 ft. tables
❑ Classroom - 4 per 8 ft. tables
❑ Classroom (Chevron) - 2 per 6 ft. tables
❑ Classroom (Chevron) - 3 per 6 ft. tables
❑ Classroom (Chevron) - 3 per 8 ft. tables
❑ Classroom (Chevron) - 4 per 8 ft. tables
❑ Cocktail Rounds
❑ Crescent Rounds of 5
❑ Crescent Rounds of 6
❑ Crescent Rounds
❑ E-shaped
❑ Existing
❑ Flow (no tables or chairs)
❑ Hollow square
❑ Perimeter Seating
❑ Registration
❑ Royal conference
❑ Talk Show
❑ Theater
❑ Theater - Semi-circle
❑ Theater - Chevron
❑ T-shaped
❑ U-shaped
❑ Other: _____

Secondary Room Set-up: *Choose all that apply:*
❑ Perimeter Seating set for _____ (qty.)
❑ Talk Show Set-up set for _____ (qty.)
❑ Head Table for _____ (qty.)
❑ Lectern *[see Section D (A/V) for style & quantity]*
❑ Rear Screen Projection *[see Section D (A/V) for details]*
❑ Riser
    If yes,
        Riser Height: _____ in. (_____ cm)
        Riser Width: _____ in. (_____ cm)
        Riser Depth: _____ in. (_____ cm)
❑ Dance Floor
    If yes,
        Dance Floor Length: _____ in. (_____ cm)
        Dance Floor Width: _____ in. (_____ cm)
❑ Other: _____

Other Set-up Requirements *(choose all that apply)*:

- ❑ Water Service for Speaker(s)/Moderator(s)
- ❑ Water Service for table(s)
- ❑ Water Service for back of room
- ❑ Pads/Pens for tables
- ❑ Candy for tables
- ❑ VIP Set-up   *If yes,* Describe: _____
- ❑ Table(s) in back of room (for literature, etc.)   *If yes,* Quantity: _____
- ❑ Other: _____

Special Requirements: _____

Room Set-up Comments: _____

D. AUDIO/VISUAL (A/V)

- ❑ Not Required   ❑ Group To Provide
- ❑ Venue To Provide ❑ Outside Vendor To Provide
     If Not Required, go to Section E. Otherwise, complete the following:

A/V Company Name: _____

A/V Equipment/Services Needed *(choose all that apply)*:

Item	Quantity	Item Price	Item Detail/Comments
❑ 35mm Projector w/ Remote	_____	_____	_____
❑ Audio Recording	_____	_____	_____
❑ Background Music	_____	_____	_____
❑ Blackboard w/ Eraser & Chalk	_____	_____	_____
❑ Closed Circuit Video	_____	_____	_____
❑ Data Projector	_____	_____	_____
❑ Dry Erase Board w/ Eraser & Markers	_____	_____	_____
❑ DVD Player	_____	_____	_____
❑ Easel	_____	_____	_____
❑ Electric Pointer	_____	_____	_____
❑ Flipchart & Markers	_____	_____	_____
❑ Lectern (standing)	_____	_____	_____
❑ Lectern (table)	_____	_____	_____
❑ Microphone – Wired Lavaliere	_____	_____	_____
❑ Microphone – Wired Lectern	_____	_____	_____
❑ Microphone – Wired Standing	_____	_____	_____
❑ Microphone – Wired Table	_____	_____	_____
❑ Microphone – Wireless Lavaliere	_____	_____	_____
❑ Microphone – Wireless Lectern	_____	_____	_____
❑ Microphone – Wireless Standing	_____	_____	_____
❑ Microphone – Wireless Table	_____	_____	_____
❑ Monitor Cart	_____	_____	_____
❑ Overhead Projector	_____	_____	_____
❑ Personal Computer – Desktop	_____	_____	_____
❑ Personal Computer - Laptop	_____	_____	_____
❑ Personal Computer - Mac	_____	_____	_____
❑ Powered Speaker	_____	_____	_____
❑ Projection Stand	_____	_____	_____
❑ Screen (indicate size in comments)	_____	_____	_____
❑ Television	_____	_____	_____
❑ VHS Player	_____	_____	_____
❑ Video Camera	_____	_____	_____
❑ Video Monitor	_____	_____	_____
❑ Video Recording	_____	_____	_____
❑ Other: _____	_____	_____	_____

A/V Comments: _____*Include special information such as lighting needs or labor needs (e.g. AV technician).*

E. FOOD & BEVERAGE (F&B)

❑ Not Required   ❑ Group To Provide
❑ Venue To Provide ❑ Outside Vendor To Provide
    If Not Required, go to Section F. Otherwise, complete the following:

F&B Service Time (US & Military via auto calc): _____

Anticipated Attendance: _____

F&B Guarantee: _____

Set for: _____

Meal Type:	*Drop Down Options:*
	❑ Continental Breakfast
	❑ Breakfast
	❑ Brunch
	❑ Lunch
	❑ Dinner
	❑ Break
	❑ Reception
	❑ Hospitality
	❑ Other: _____

Service Type:	*Drop Down Options:*
	❑ Boxed
	❑ Buffet
	❑ Plated
	❑ Other: _____

F&B Menu

Description	Quantity	Price	Per
			Person, gallon, tray, etc.

F&B Comments: _____
    Note: This can address dietary requirements, alcohol policies, and other special issues.

F. DÉCOR

❑ Not Required   ❑ Group To Provide
❑ Venue To Provide ❑ Outside Vendor To Provide
    If Not Required, go to Section G. Otherwise, complete the following:

Decorator Company Name: _____

Décor Instructions/Requests: _____

G. SECURITY

\# of Keys Required: _____

Key(s) should be: ❑ House/Standard Key   ❑ Re-keyed

Security Required: ❑ Not Required   ❑ Group To Provide
                        ❑ Venue To Provide   ❑ Outside Vendor To Provide
If Not Required, go to Section H. Otherwise, complete the following:

Security Company Name: _____

Security Start Time (US & Military via auto calc): _____

Security End Time (US & Military via auto calc): _____

Security Instructions/Requests: _____

H. ACCESSIBILITY

Accessibility/Special Needs Instructions:

I. ENTERTAINMENT/SPEAKER

Entertainment/Speaker: ❑ Yes   ❑ No
If No, go to Section J. If Yes, complete the following:

Speaker Name(s) : _____

Entertainment/Speaker Company: _____

Entertainment/Speaker Instructions/Requests: _____

J. SIGNAGE

❑ Not Required   ❑ Group To Provide
❑ Venue To Provide ❑ Outside Vendor To Provide
If Not Required, go to Section K. Otherwise, complete the following:

Signage Company: _____

Easel Required: ❑ Yes   ❑ No

Signage Instructions/Requests: _____

K. TRANSPORTATION

Transportation Required: ❑ Yes   ❑ No
If No, go to Section L. If Yes, complete the following:

Transportation Company: _____

Transportation Instructions/Requests: _____

L. SHIPPING/RECEIVING

Shipping/Receiving Required: ❑ Yes   ❑ No
  If No, go to Section M. If Yes, complete the following:

Shipping/Receiving/Mail Instructions/Requests: _____

M. UTILITIES

Electrical Connections: ❑ Not Required   ❑ Group To Provide
              ❑ Venue To Provide ❑ Outside Vendor To Provide

Optional:

Connection Type	Quantity	Price

Connection types can include specific service type such as 120 volt (10 amp) service or power strip quad box etc.

Electrical Notes:

Include Electrical needs, description of use and quantity.

Telecommunications Connections: ❑ Not Required   ❑ Group To Provide
                    ❑ Venue To Provide   ❑ Outside Vendor To Provide

Voice Services

Item	Quantity	Price	Comments
❑ Analog Phone Line	_____	_____	❑ Long distance
			❑ Restricted
			❑ Other_____
❑ Multi-Line Phone Set	_____	_____	_____
❑ Single Line Phone Set	_____	_____	_____
❑ Speaker Phone	_____	_____	_____
❑ Voice Mail Box	_____	_____	_____
❑ Other: _____	_____	_____	_____

Data Services

Item	Quantity	Price
❑ Internet Connection – Ethernet	_____	_____
❑ Internet Connection – Wireless	_____	_____
❑ ISDN Line	_____	_____
❑ T-1 Line	_____	_____
❑ Other: _____	_____	_____

Telecommunications Notes:

Include placement information and other requirements here.

Cleaning Services: ❑ Not Required   ❑ Group To Provide
                      ❑ Venue To Provide   ❑ Outside Vendor To Provide

Cleaning Contractor: _____

Cleaning Refresh Times and Instructions:

> *Specify multiple cleaning and refresh times as needed. Also indicated trash removal times if different from refresh times*

Other Utilities: ❑ Not Required   ❑ Group To Provide
                 ❑ Venue To Provide   ❑ Outside Vendor To Provide

Item	Quantity	Price
❑ Air (indicate PSI/Pascal: _____)	_____	_____
❑ Drain	_____	_____
❑ Natural Gas/Propane	_____	_____
❑ Water (indicate minimum pressure: _____)	_____	_____
❑ Fill & Drain (indicate gallons: _____)	_____	_____
❑ Steam	_____	_____
❑ Other: _____	_____	

Other Utilities Notes:

N. BILLING INSTRUCTIONS

Billing Instructions: _____
> *Note any instructions that are unique to this function and not covered by information in the narrative.*

Organizer Cost Center: _____

PART IIIb – Function Set-up Order (Exhibitor Version)

Date Originated: _____

Date Revised*: _____
Repeat for additional revisions as necessary.

A. EVENT DETAILS

Event Name: _____

Event Organizer/Host Organization: _____

Contact Name: _____

Contact Phone: _____

B. BOOTH DETAILS

Booth #: _____

Booth Location: _____

Booth Type:
- ❑ 8'x10'
- ❑ 10'x10'
- ❑ Island
- ❑ Peninsula
- ❑ Perimeter
- ❑ Table Top
- ❑ Other: _____

Booth Name: _____

Company Name: _____

Key Contact Person for Booth: _____

Booth Start Day/Date: _____
Booth Start Time (US & Military via auto calc): _____

Booth End Day/Date: _____
Booth End Time (US & Military via auto calc): _____

Set Up By (US & Military via auto calc): _____

Tear Down No Later than (US & Military via auto calc): _____

C. BOOTH SET-UP

Booth Set-up Diagram Attached: ❑ Yes   ❑ No
   Note: The set-up diagram should indicate A/V placement and electrical needs.

Inventory Needed *(list all that apply)*:

Description	Quantity	Price/Per	Comments
	_____	_____	_____
	_____	_____	_____
	_____	_____	_____

Special Requirements: _____ *e.g. double-decker, floor load*
Booth Set-up Comments: _____

D. AUDIO/VISUAL (A/V)

❑ Not Required ❑ Booth To Provide
❑ Venue To Provide ❑ Outside Vendor To Provide
  If Not Required, go to Section E. Otherwise, complete the following:

A/V Equipment/Services Needed *(choose all that apply)*:

Item	Quantity	Item Price	Item Detail/Comments
❑ 35mm Projector w/ Remote	_____	_____	_____
❑ Audio Recording	_____	_____	_____
❑ Background Music	_____	_____	_____
❑ Blackboard w/ Eraser & Chalk	_____	_____	_____
❑ Closed Circuit Video	_____	_____	_____
❑ Data Projector	_____	_____	_____
❑ Dry Erase Board w/ Eraser & Markers	_____	_____	_____
❑ DVD Player	_____	_____	_____
❑ Easel	_____	_____	_____
❑ Electric Pointer	_____	_____	_____
❑ Flipchart & Markers	_____	_____	_____
❑ Lectern (standing)	_____	_____	_____
❑ Lectern (table)	_____	_____	_____
❑ Microphone – Wired Lavaliere	_____	_____	_____
❑ Microphone – Wired Lectern	_____	_____	_____
❑ Microphone – Wired Standing	_____	_____	_____
❑ Microphone – Wired Table	_____	_____	_____
❑ Microphone – Wireless Lavaliere	_____	_____	_____
❑ Microphone – Wireless Lectern	_____	_____	_____
❑ Microphone – Wireless Standing	_____	_____	_____
❑ Microphone – Wireless Table	_____	_____	_____
❑ Monitor Cart	_____	_____	_____
❑ Overhead Projector	_____	_____	_____
❑ Personal Computer – Desktop	_____	_____	_____
❑ Personal Computer - Laptop	_____	_____	_____
❑ Personal Computer - Mac	_____	_____	_____
❑ Powered Speaker	_____	_____	_____
❑ Projection Stand	_____	_____	_____
❑ Screen (indicate size in comments)	_____	_____	_____
❑ Television	_____	_____	_____
❑ VHS Player	_____	_____	_____
❑ Video Camera	_____	_____	_____
❑ Video Monitor	_____	_____	_____
❑ Video Recording	_____	_____	_____
❑ Other: _____	_____	_____	_____

A/V Comments: _____

E. FOOD & BEVERAGE (F&B)

❑ Not Required   ❑ Booth To Provide
❑ Venue To Provide ❑ Outside Vendor To Provide
   If Not Required, go to Section F. Otherwise, complete the following:

F&B Service Time (US & Military via auto calc): _____

Anticipated Attendance: _____

F&B Guarantee: _____

Set for: _____

Meal Type: *Drop Down Options:*
                              ❑ Continental Breakfast
                              ❑ Breakfast
                              ❑ Brunch
                              ❑ Lunch
                              ❑ Dinner
                              ❑ Break
                              ❑ Reception
                              ❑ Hospitality
                              ❑ Other: _____

Service Type: *Drop Down Options:*
                              ❑ Boxed
                              ❑ Buffet
                              ❑ Plated
                              ❑ Other: _____

F&B Menu

Description	Quantity	Price	Per
			Person, gallon, tray, etc.

F&B Comments: _____
   Note: This can address dietary requirements, alcohol policies, and other special issues.

F. DÉCOR

❑ Not Required   ❑ Booth To Provide
❑ Venue To Provide ❑ Outside Vendor To Provide
   If Not Required, go to Section G. Otherwise, complete the following:

Exhibitor Appointed Contractor: _____ (include company name and contact information)

Décor Instructions/Requests: _____

G. SECURITY

of Keys Required: _____

Key(s) should be: ❑ House/Standard Key   ❑ Re-keyed

Security Required: ❑ Not Required   ❑ Booth To Provide
                      ❑ Venue To Provide   ❑ Outside Vendor To Provide
   If Not Required, go to Section H. Otherwise, complete the following:

Security Company Name: _____

Security Start Time (US & Military via auto calc): _____

Security End Time (US & Military via auto calc): _____

Security Instructions/Requests: _____

H. ACCESSIBILITY

Accessibility/Special Needs Instructions:

I. ENTERTAINMENT/SPEAKER

Entertainment/Speaker: ❑ Yes   ❑ No
If No, go to Section J. If Yes, complete the following:

Speaker Name(s) : _____

Entertainment/Speaker Company: _____

Entertainment/Speaker Instructions/Requests: _____

J. SIGNAGE

Signage Instructions/Requests: _____

K. MATERIAL HANDLING

Shipping/Receiving Required: ❑ Yes   ❑ No

Customs/Brokerage: ❑ Yes   ❑ No

Shipping Information:

To	From	Sender	Venue

Shipping to Show Carrier: _____
   (Include Company name, address, contact, phone, fax and e-mail.)

Shipping from Show Carrier: _____
   (Include Company name, address, contact, phone, fax and e-mail.)

Material Handling Instructions: _____
   (Specify fragile, oversized etc.)

L. UTILITIES

Electrical Connections:
- ❑ Not Required
- ❑ Venue To Provide
- ❑ Group To Provide
- ❑ Outside Vendor To Provide

Optional:

Connection Type	Quantity	Price

Connection types can include specific service type such as 120 volt (10 amp) service or power strip quad box etc.

Electrical Notes:

Include Electrical needs, description of use and quantity.

Telecommunications Connections:
- ❑ Not Required
- ❑ Venue To Provide
- ❑ Group To Provide
- ❑ Outside Vendor To Provide

Voice Services

Item	Quantity	Price	Comments
❑ Analog Phone Line	_____	_____	❑ Long distance
			❑ Restricted
			❑ Other_____
❑ Multi-Line Phone Set	_____	_____	_____
❑ Single Line Phone Set	_____	_____	_____
❑ Speaker Phone	_____	_____	_____
❑ Voice Mail Box	_____	_____	_____
❑ Other: _____	_____	_____	_____

Data Services

Item	Quantity	Price
❑ Internet Connection – Ethernet	_____	_____
❑ Internet Connection – Wireless	_____	_____
❑ ISDN Line	_____	_____
❑ T-1 Line	_____	_____
❑ Other: _____	_____	_____

Telecommunications Notes:

Include placement information and other requirements here.

Cleaning Services:
- ❑ Not Required
- ❑ Venue To Provide
- ❑ Group To Provide
- ❑ Outside Vendor To Provide

Cleaning Contractor: _____

Cleaning Refresh Times and Instructions:

Specify multiple cleaning and refresh times as needed. Also indicated trash removal times if different from refresh times

Other Utilities: ❑ Not Required ❑ Group To Provide
❑ Venue To Provide ❑ Outside Vendor To Provide

Item	Quantity	Price
❑ Air (indicate PSI/Pascal: _____)	_____	_____
❑ Drain	_____	_____
❑ Natural Gas/Propane	_____	_____
❑ Water (indicate minimum pressure: _____)	_____	_____
❑ Fill & Drain (indicate gallons: _____)	_____	_____
❑ Steam	_____	_____
❑ Other: _____	_____	

Other Utilities Notes:

N. BILLING INSTRUCTIONS

Booth is tax-exempt: ❑ Yes ❑ No

Tax-Exempt ID#: _____

Authorized Signatories: _____

Booth Cost Center: _____

Send Final Bill To:

Company Name: _____
Address: _____
City, State, Postal Code, Country: _____
Contact Person: _____
Title: _____
Phone: _____
Fax: _____
Email: _____

Method of Payment:

Purchase Order, Credit Card Type, Master Account, etc.

Method of Payment #:

PO #, Credit Card # with expiration date, Master Account #

Billing Instructions: _____
Note if any aspect of the function is complimentary and the responsible party.

II

APEX Housing & Registration Accepted Practices

Approved by the Convention Industry Council on August 10, 2005

Report Section Contents

***Special Note**: The term Housing Facility, which is used throughout this report, refers to any establishment that offers lodging to transient travelers and/or groups. Examples of housing facilities are hotels, resorts, conference centers, motels, inns, and bed & breakfasts.*

PREFACE

APEX (Accepted Practices Exchange), an initiative of the Convention Industry Council (CIC), is uniting the entire meetings, conventions and exhibitions industry in the development and implementation of voluntary standards, called *accepted practices*.

This report outlines the accepted practices in the areas of Housing and Registration as defined by the APEX Housing & Registration Panel. This panel was charged with developing industry accepted practices for collecting, reporting, and retrieving complete housing and registration data for meetings, conventions, and other events. A secondary charge was to recommend industry accepted practices around housing issues such as housing providers, Internet issues, international housing, and disclosure.

In its work, the Housing & Registration Panel considered a number of existing accepted practices (including APEX Post-Event Reporting accepted practices*) and identified other best practices throughout the industry (including those summarized in the Convention Industry Council's *Project Attrition Final Report**). The result is the following report.

See www.conventionindustry.org for these resources.

PART I: FORMS

A. APEX Event Registration Form

1.   ACCEPTED PRACTICES

   a.   The APEX Event Registration Form is the industry accepted structure for forms by which attendees can register to attend events of all types. The form can be produced on paper or electronically, and may be designed by event organizers to reflect the "look and feel" of the event or the host organization. All design should be clear, concise, and, if printed, include enough room to hand-write information.

   b.   On the APEX Event Registration Form template, any information enclosed in [brackets] is instruction to the person developing the form and should be deleted once the form has been developed and is ready for public distribution. The event organizer may also add event-specific information that is required for the effective planning and implementation of each event.

   c.   The $ symbol is a currency placeholder only. There is no requirement that all funds be in dollars.

   d.   When an event organizer provides the option of downloading a printed form from a website, the form should be a PDF file in order to prevent editing of key information or layout.

   e.   Procedures and instructions for attendees should be included on the same page as the form to be completed. If this is not possible, the procedures and instructions should be on the page facing or immediately preceding the actual form (for printed materials).

   f.   All sections of the APEX Event Registration Form will not apply to every event. Any section that does not apply should not be included.

   g.   Each event organizer must identify on the form the required information that is specific to each event. Required information should be designated with an asterisk (*) and a notation should be made on the form that "*These fields are required in order for this form to be processed."

   h.   The APEX Event Registration Form will be regularly updated based on the industry's collaborative feedback.

   i.   An event's housing and registration forms should be combined if the processes are not too complex. This is at the discretion of the event organizer.

2.   PROCEDURES & INSTRUCTIONS

   Procedures and instructions for attendees should be included on the same page as the form to be completed. If space does not allow, place this instructional information on a facing page in the registration brochure. The following sections should be used and tailored to the specific event. Information enclosed in [brackets] is instruction to the person developing the form and should be deleted once the form has been developed and is ready for public distribution. The event organizer may also add event-specific information that is required for the effective planning and implementation of each event.

   Event Registration Can Be Completed By:
   Please use only one method to complete your event registration:
   [Indicate all methods that are applicable to the event including, but not limited to:]
   - Telephone: *[Note if the attendee should call the event organizer, or other entity. Include 1) the name of the person/company to call, 2) days and hours of operation, and 3) the telephone number(s) with appropriate country/city/area codes. Note if there are different procedures for international attendees.]*
   - Fax: Complete this form and send it via fax to *[fax number(s) with appropriate country/city/area codes]. [If appropriate, add instructions to include "ATTN: Person or Department" so that the form is efficiently delivered.]*

- Internet: Complete this form on a secure connection at *[URL]*. *[Note what should be expected in the way of confirmation in order to ensure completion of the on-line form.]*
- Mail: Complete this form and mail it with payment to: *[Note mailing instructions including 1) Event Name, 2) Mailing Address, 3) City, 4) State/Province, 5) Postal/Zip Code, and 6) Country. If appropriate, add instructions to include "ATTN: Person or Department" so that the form is efficiently delivered.]*

Acknowledgement of Event Registration:
[Note whether or not acknowledgements of registrations will be sent to attendees, and if they will be, indicate the procedure (for example, The XYZ Conference will send an acknowledgement of your registration via email within one day of your reservation being received. Your badge and credentials will be sent by mail three weeks prior to the start of the event). If you require attendees to provide an email address, or other contact information, in order to receive their acknowledgements, state so here and indicate that requirement on the Event Registration Form with an asterisk (*).]

Fees & Deadlines:
[Describe all types and categories of registration fees offered, indicating the time frame during which they are offered, and the functions and services (for example, shuttle service) that are included in each fee. This section should describe any discounts offered for multiple attendees from the same company or organization. Additionally make note of: 1) any functions that are NOT included in the general registration fee, indicating the fee for each of these items; 2) the type of currency in which all fees must be paid; 3) the final deadline for registration; and, 4) whether or not registration will be available on-site at the event. Disclose any information the attendee should know about the registration fees (for example, $10 is included in the registration fees to offset direct costs including shuttle service).]

Payment Methods Accepted:
[Include event-specific payment instructions (for example, Any registration form received without a valid payment will not be processed. Another example is Selection of an incorrect registration category may require rate adjustment). Indicate all acceptable methods of payment and any related fees that are applicable such as check, money order, credit card (indicate types), wire transfer (indicate associated fees charged), or purchase order. Specify the name of the merchant that will be noted on credit card statements for all charges.]

Changes, Cancellations, & Refunds:
[Clearly state the applicable policies and dates regarding the making, modifying or canceling of an event registration. Note: 1) any fees charged for canceling, and when they will be charged; 2) if the cancellation fee increases the closer a cancellation is made to the event start date; 3) how and when refunds will be made; 4) if refunds will not be given on cancellations made after a specific date, the process for substituting attendees (for example, if a company can pay one registration fee and a different person comes each day, or if one person registers and another comes in his or her place; and, 5) exactly how requests for changes, cancellations, and/or refunds should be made (for example, requests must be made in writing and received by the Event Organizer by <<Date>>)]

Deadlines & Reminders:
[Include event-specific information and reminders here (for example, "Don't forget to fill out your Housing Form!" or state how and when badges/tickets will be distributed). Additional examples of information to be included here are the deadline dates for: cancellation with full refund; making housing reservations at the discounted event rate; making changes and cancellations to registration; receiving discounted registration fees; being listed in the registration directory; and/or cancellation with partial refund.]

[Add Additional Event-Specific Sections to the Registration Procedures as Required.]

APEX EVENT REGISTRATION FORM TEMPLATE

[HEADER]

[At a minimum, the following information should be included in this area:
- *Event Name*
- *Event Dates in <<MonthName StartDate-EndDate, Year>> Format*
- *Name of Primary Event Facility*
- *Event City, State/Province, Country*
- *Deadline for Submitting the Event Registration Form & Receiving Event-Specific Rates*

Additional form header content may include:
- *Event Logo*
- *Event Organizer Logo*
- *Other pertinent information determined by the event organizer]*

ATTENDEE INFORMATION
*These fields are required in order for this form to be processed.

Prefix *(Mr., Ms., Dr., etc.):* _____   Given Name/First Name: _____   MiddleName/Initial: _____

Family Name *(as appears on passport):* _____   Suffix(s) *(Jr., MD, CPA, etc.):* _____

Preferred Name *(for badge):* _____

Employer/Organization: _____   Job Title: _____

Preferred Mailing Address:
   Address1:_____   Address2:_____
   City: _____   State/Province: _____   Zip/Postal Code: _____   Country: _____

Employer/Organization Mailing Address: ❑ Same As Preferred Mailing Address
   If different from preferred address, complete the following:
   Address1:_____   Address2:_____
   City: _____   State/Province: _____   Zip/Postal Code: _____   Country: _____

Preferred Phone: _____ *(Include appropriate country, city, and area codes)*
Mobile Phone: _____ *(Include appropriate country, city, and area codes)*
Fax: _____ *(Include appropriate country, city, and area codes)*

Email: _____

Preferred Method for Receiving Acknowledgement of Registration: ❑ Email   ❑ Fax   ❑ Mail

Would you like to be contacted by event sponsors and exhibitors prior to the event? ❑ Yes By Email   ❑ Yes By Fax   ❑ Yes By Mail   ❑ No

Attendee Type *[List all attendee categories the Event Organizer desires to track, for example, Member, Speaker, Exhibitor, Guest]:*
   ❑ [Attendee Type 1]
   ❑ [Attendee Type 2]
   ❑ *Additional Attendee Types As Necessary*

Do you have any special physical ♿, dietary *(for example, vegetarian, kosher),* or other needs: ❑ Yes ❑ No
   If yes, please describe: _____

[Event-Specific Attendee Information - Use this section to add additional questions that are specific to this event. For example: Are you a first-time attendee for the XYZ Conference? ❑ Yes ❑ No and, If No, How many times have you attended? _____]

ON-SITE EMERGENCY INFORMATION

Where you are staying during the event? _____ *(for example, name of hotel, with a family member, at home)*

In Case of Emergency:
   Name of Person to Contact: _____
   Phone: _____ *(Include appropriate country, city, and area codes)*
   Relationship to You: _____

REGISTRATION FEES

All fees are in *[note type of currency].* *[Note if any functions are limited by space or other requirements]*

	Before [Date]	After [Date]	Additional Date Categories As Necessary
[AttendeeType1]			
[FeeType1]	❏ <<$Amount>>	❏ <<$Amount>>	
[FeeType2]	❏ <<$Amount>>	❏ <<$Amount>>	
Additional Fee Types As Necessary			
[AttendeeType2]			
[FeeType1]	❏ <<$Amount>>	❏ <<$Amount>>	
[FeeType2]	❏ <<$Amount>>	❏ <<$Amount>>	
Additional Fee Types As Necessary			

Additional Attendee Types as Necessary

Note any discounts that are available

Total Cost – Payment Due $_____ $_____

[An event's Fee Types could be Full Registration, One-Day Registration, Special Session/Event #1, etc.]

PAYMENT INFORMATION

Please…only one form of payment per registration!

[Include any special event-specific instructions (for example, Any registration form received without a valid deposit will not be processed). Indicate all methods of payment that are applicable to the event including, but not limited to:]

❏ Check   ❏ Money Order

If paying by check or money order, make it payable to <<Payee>> and mail with this form to: <<Payee>>, <<MailingAddress>>, <<City>>, <<State/Province>>, <<Postal/Zip Code>>, <<Country>>.

❏ <<CardTypeAccepted1>>   ❏ <<CardTypeAccepted2>>   ❏ <<CardTypeAccepted3>>   ❏ *Additional card types as necessary*

    Credit Card Number: _____
    Expiration Date: _____ *NOTE: All credit cards must be valid through the dates of the event.*
    Card's Security Code: _____
    Cardholder's Name: _____
    Cardholder's Signature: _____
    Today's Date: _____
    Billing Address *(If Different from Preferred Mailing Address):*
       Address1: _____   Address2: _____
       City: _____   State/Province: _____   Zip/Postal Code: _____   Country: _____

❏ *Additional Forms of Payment As Necessary (such as wire transfers or purchase orders)*

ACKNOWLEDGEMENTS

[Reiterate all policies outlined in the Registration Procedures regarding acknowledgements.]

SEND COMPLETED REGISTRATION FORMS TO:

[Reiterate all methods by which reservations can be made outlined in the Registration Procedures.]

B. APEX Housing Form

1. ACCEPTED PRACTICES

a. The APEX Housing Form is the industry accepted structure for forms by which attendees can make housing reservations through an event organizer. The form can be produced on paper or electronically, and may be designed by event organizers to reflect the "look and feel" of the event or the host organization. All design should be clear, concise, and, if printed, include enough room to hand-write information.

b. On the APEX Housing Form template, any information enclosed in [brackets] is instruction to the person developing the form and should be deleted once the form has been developed and is ready for public distribution. The event organizer may also add event-specific information that is required for the effective planning and implementation of each event.

c. The $ symbol is a currency placeholder only. There is no requirement that all funds be in dollars.

d. When an event organizer provides the option of downloading a printed form from a website, the form should be a PDF file in order to prevent editing of key information or layout.

e. Procedures and instructions for attendees should be included on the same page as the form to be completed. If this is not possible, the instructions should be on the page facing or immediately preceding the actual form (for printed materials).

f. All sections of the APEX Housing Form will not apply to every event. Any section that does not apply should not be included.

g. Each event organizer must identify on the form the required information that is specific to each event. Required information should be designated with an asterisk (*) and a notation should be made on the form that "*These fields are required in order for this form to be processed."

h. An event organizer should share each housing form with the event-specific housing facility(s) prior to public release in order to ensure that all information needed to service guests is being collected.

i. Event organizers and/or their housing providers should respond to reservation requests within a reasonable timeframe and advise guests when to expect a response and by what methods.

j. The APEX Housing Form will be regularly updated based on the industry's collaborative feedback.

k. An event's housing and registration forms should be combined if the processes are not too complex. This is at the discretion of the event organizer.

l. Event organizers should make event attendees aware of and knowledgeable about the housing process and the official housing facility. With knowledge, attendees may be more likely to book within the event's room block. Communication is key to success in this area. *See also Part II, Section A-2-k.*

m. If the event organizer or a designated housing bureau is controlling the housing process, the organizer or housing bureau should share preliminary pick-up information with the housing facility. This information should be shared as reservations begin to materialize. For example, room pick-up should be shared at pre-designated "benchmark" dates such as 120 days, 90 days, 60 days and 45 days from the start of the event. Also, registration numbers (not names) should be shared by the organizer, if requested by the housing facility. If the organizer and/or housing bureau has the technology available, real-time housing and registration data should be accessible on-line on a "view only" basis. Conversely, if the housing facility is controlling the housing process, the organizer should have access to real time reservations and room pick-up data, including names and confirmation numbers on a "view only," password-protected basis.

2. PROCEDURES & INSTRUCTIONS

Procedures and instructions for attendees should be included on the same page as the form to be completed. The following sections should be used and tailored to the specific event. Information enclosed in [brackets] is instruction to the person developing the form and should be deleted once the form has been developed and is ready for public distribution. The event organizer may also add event-specific information that is required for the effective planning and implementation of each event.

Housing Reservations Can Be Made By:
Please use only one method to make your housing reservation:
[Indicate all methods that are applicable to the event including, but not limited to:]
- Telephone: *[Note if the attendee should call the event organizer, housing bureau or housing facility directly. Include 1) the name of the company/property to call, 2) days and hours of operation, 3) the telephone number(s) with appropriate country/city/area codes, and 4) any reference code for the event. Note if there are different procedures for international attendees.]*
- Fax: Complete this form and send it via fax to *[fax number(s) with appropriate country/city/area codes]. [If appropriate, add instructions to include "ATTN: Person or Department" so that the form is efficiently delivered.]*
- Internet: Complete this form on a secure connection at *[URL]. [Note what should be expected in the way of confirmation in order to ensure completion of the on-line form.]*
- Mail: Complete this form and mail it with payment to: *[Note mailing instructions including 1) Event Name, 2) Mailing Address, 3) City, 4) State/Province, 5) Postal/Zip Code, and 6) Country. If appropriate, add instructions to include "ATTN: Person or Department" so that the form is efficiently delivered.]*

Acknowledgement of Reservations:
[Note whether or not acknowledgements of reservations will be sent to attendees, and if they will be, indicate the procedure (for example, The XYZ Conference will send an acknowledgement of your reservation via email within 10 days of your reservation being received.). Also note whether or not this acknowledgement will include a confirmation number from the housing facility. If you require attendees to provide an email address, or other contact information, in order to receive their acknowledgements, state so here and indicate that requirement on the Housing Form with an asterisk (*). An example of language for this section is: The XYZ Conference Housing Bureau will send you an acknowledgement of your reservation. Please review all information for accuracy. E-mail confirmations will be sent within <<NumberOfDays>> of your reservation being processed. If you do not receive an acknowledgement in this time frame, please contact the XYZ Conference Housing Bureau. You may also check your reservation via the internet at www.xyz.net, regardless of how you booked your reservation. You will not receive a confirmation directly from the housing facility.]

Rates & Taxes:
[Indicate the rate(s) offered for each housing facility where rooms for the event are available. Include the dates that the special rate(s) will be honored. Include information on any applicable taxes (for example, tax per room per night in dollars and percentage of room rate) or fees (like resort fees). Disclose any information the attendee should know about the housing rates (for example, $10 is included in the daily housing rate to offset direct costs including shuttle service, registration technology use, etc.). An example of language for this section is: To take advantage of the special <<Event>> rates, make your reservation by <<Date>>. After this date the official <<Event>> room block(s) will be released and the hotel may charge higher rates. All rates are per room per night and are subject to a <<%>> tax. Rates also include <<$Amount>> to offset event-related housing costs including <<shuttle service, etc.>>. The hotel may charge additional fees for rooms with more than one occupant.]

[For all options available, this section should include the housing facility name(s), address(es), and rates, and locations.]

Payment Methods Accepted:
[Include any special event-specific payment instructions (for example, Any form received without a valid payment will not be processed). Indicate all methods of payment and any related fees that are applicable to the event including, but not limited to: check; money order; credit card (indicate types); wire transfer (indicate associated fees charged); or purchase order. Specify the name of the merchant that will be noted on credit card statements for all charges.]

Special Requests:
Special requests for specific room types cannot be guaranteed. Requests will be honored based on availability.

Deposits:
[Indicate any required deposit amounts and applicable rules (for example, All reservations requests must be accompanied by a deposit in the amount of $XX. Housing Forms received without a valid deposit will not be processed.). Note whether deposits are non-refundable, identify when credit cards will be charged, and any other event-specific rules and regulations regarding deposits. See the complete accepted practices for the areas of Housing & Registration for recommendations about deposits (Part II).]

Changes, Cancellations, Refunds & Early Departures:
[Clearly state the applicable policies and dates regarding the making, modifying or canceling of a room reservation. Note any fees charged for canceling, and when they will be charged. Indicate if the cancellation fee increases the closer a cancellation is made to the planned arrival date. Also, clearly outline any fees that will be charged if an attendee departs earlier than a reservation ends. State any policy regarding refunds if rooms are resold. Note any applicable housing facility cancellation policy. An example of language for this section is: Reservations may be changed or cancelled until <<Date>> without penalty. Changes, including shortened stays and substitutions, and cancellations received after <<Date>> will be assessed a <$Amount>> processing fee. Your deposit will be forfeited if you do not cancel by <<Date>>. Use the XYZ Conference Housing Bureau for all changes and cancellation until <<Date>> by calling <<Phone>>. Do not contact the hotel directly until after <<Date>>.]

Deadlines & Reminders:
[Include event-specific information and reminders here (for example, "Don't forget to fill out your Event Registration Form!"). This section could include information on special air or car rental rates that have been negotiated for the even and how to get them, or a privacy statement here.]

[Add Additional Event-Specific Sections to the Housing Procedures as Required.]

APEX HOUSING FORM TEMPLATE

[HEADER]

[At a minimum, the following information should be included at the top of every housing form:
- *Event Name*
- *Event Dates in <<MonthName StartDate-EndDate, Year>> Format*
- *Name of Primary Event Facility*
- *Event City, State/Province, Country*
- *Deadline for Submitting the Housing Form & Receiving Event-Specific Rates*

Additional form header content may include:
- *Event Logo*
- *Event Organizer Logo*
- *Other pertinent information determined by the event organizer]*

CONTACT INFORMATION
*These fields are required in order for this form to be processed.

Prefix *(Mr., Ms., Dr., etc.)*: _____   Given Name/First Name: _____   MiddleName/Initial: _____

Family Name *(as appears on passport)*: _____   Suffix(s) *(Jr., MD, CPA, etc.)*: _____

Employer/Organization: _____

Preferred Mailing Address:
     Address1:_____   Address2:_____
     City: _____ State/Province: _____ Zip/Postal Code: _____   Country: _____

Employer/Organization Mailing Address: ❑ Same As Preferred Mailing Address
     If different from preferred address, complete the following:
     Address1:_____   Address2:_____
     City: _____ State/Province: _____ Zip/Postal Code: _____   Country: _____

Preferred Phone: _____ *(Include appropriate country, city, and area codes)*
Mobile Phone:_____ *(Include appropriate country, city, and area codes)*
Fax: _____ *(Include appropriate country, city, and area codes)*

Email: _____

Preferred Method for Receiving Acknowledgement of Reservation Request: ❑ Email   ❑ Fax   ❑ Mail

[Event-Specific Attendee Information - Use this section to add additional questions of attendees that are specific to this event.]

RESERVATION INFORMATION

Arrival (Day & Date): _____ _____ *(for example, Monday 12/31/2006)*   Departure (Day & Date): _____ _____

Guest Type: ❑ Attendee   ❑ Exhibitor   ❑ *Additional Guest Types As Necessary*

Housing Facility: *[If only one option is available, the housing facility name, address and rates should be included directly on the Housing Form. If more than one option is available, all housing facility names, addresses, rates, and locations should be included in the Housing Procedures under the "Rates & Taxes" section. In this instance, this section should direct the attendee to list a specified number of housing facility choices in order of preference (entering the name of the preferred housing facility). A note should be made that preferences will be accommodated based on availability. The event organizer may want to include a question that asks "If hotel preferences are not available, do you prefer location or rate?"]*

Room Type Requested: ❑ Single   ❑ Double   ❑ Double/Double   ❑ Triple   ❑ Quad
     If you would like to request a suite, please contact <<name, phone number, fax number, email>> for more information.

                              ❑ Smoking   ❑ Non-Smoking

Bed Type Requested: ❑ Bed Type 1 *(defined by event organizer)*   ❑ Bed Type 2 *(defined by event organizer)*
                              ❑ *Additional Bed Types as Necessary*

Do you have any special needs or requests: ❑ Yes ❑ No

     If yes, please describe: _____ *(for example, accessible accommodations*   *, early/late arrival, non-feather pillows, bed size)*

Please note:
- Room types and special requests are not guaranteed.
- The housing facility will assign specific room types at check in, based upon availability.
- Some requests such as rollaway beds, cribs or extra refrigerators may incur additional charges.

Rewards Program: _____ Rewards Program Number: _____

Are You Sharing Your Room With Other Occupants? ❑ Yes ❑No
If Yes, list all room occupants. Individuals listed here should not submit their own Housing Forms :
1. Prefix: _____ Given Name/First Name: _____ MiddleName/Initial: _____ Family Name: _____ Suffix(s): _____
Arrival Date: _____ Departure Date: _____
2. Prefix: _____ Given Name/First Name: _____ MiddleName/Initial: _____ Family Name: _____ Suffix(s): _____ Arrival
Date: _____ Departure Date: _____
3. *Additional Shares as Necessary*

*PAYMENT INFORMATION
Please…only one form of payment per reservation!

[Include any special event-specific instructions (for example, A deposit in the amount of $ must accompany a reservations request, Any housing form received without a valid deposit will not be processed). Indicate all methods of payment that are applicable to the event including, but not limited to:]

❑ Check   ❑ Money Order

If paying by check or money order, make it payable to <<Payee>> and mail with this form to: <<Payee>>, <<MailingAddress>>, <<City>>, <<State/Province>>, <<Postal/Zip Code>>, <<Country>>.

❑ <<CardTypeAccepted1>>   ❑ <<CardTypeAccepted2>>   ❑ <<CardTypeAccepted3>>   ❑ *Additional card types as necessary*

Credit Card Number: _____
Expiration Date: _____ *NOTE: All credit cards must be valid through the dates of the event.*
Card's Security Code: _____
Cardholder's Name: _____
Cardholder's Signature: _____
Today's Date: _____
Billing Address *(If Different from Preferred Mailing Address)*:
   Address1: _____ Address2: _____
   City: _____   State/Province: _____   Zip/Postal Code: _____   Country: _____

❑ *Additional Forms of Payment As Necessary (such as wire transfers or purchase orders)*

CHANGES,CANCELLATIONS, REFUNDS
[Reiterate all policies outlined in the Housing Procedures regarding payments, deposits, changes, cancellations, refunds, etc.]

ACKNOWLEDGEMENTS
[Reiterate all policies outlined in the Housing Procedures regarding acknowledgements.]

SEND COMPLETE HOUSING FORMS TO:
[Reiterate all methods by which reservations can be made outlined in the Housing Procedures.]

C. APEX Rooming List

1. ACCEPTED PRACTICES

   a. The APEX Rooming List is the industry accepted format by which event organizers and/or their designates should deliver multiple reservations to a housing facility.

   b. On the APEX Rooming List, any information enclosed in [brackets] is instruction to the person developing the form and should be deleted once the form has been developed and is ready for distribution.

   c. **The $ symbol is a currency placeholder only. There is no requirement that all funds be in dollars.**

   d. The APEX Rooming List will be regularly updated based on the industry's collaborative feedback.

2. INSTRUCTIONS FOR EVENT ORGANIZERS

   The APEX Rooming List is designed to simplify and standardize the process of assembling rooming lists for guest rooms within the Event-Contracted Block (ECB) *See also Part II, Section A-1.* Because items unique to individual events must be accounted for, the event organizer (or designate) using the form must initially perform a series of easy set-up steps so that the form reflects the event's particular character and needs.

   a. Advise the contract housing facility(s) that the APEX Rooming List format will be used for this event.
   b. Enter the event name in the space provided.
   c. Enter the event's earliest contracted arrival date and latest departure date in the spaces provided.
   d. Enter the event organizer/host name and contact information in the spaces provided.
   e. Enter the facility name in the area provided. If rooms are contracted at more than one facility, in automated versions of the APEX Rooming List, all facility names should be included in a drop-down list and the user should be able to select a facility from that list.
   f. Enter the currency type to be used. In automated versions of the APEX Rooming List, the event organizer should be able to select from a drop-down list of currency types.
   g. In the area provided, list all event-specific rate types (for example, Staff, Exhibitor, Speaker) by facility if there is more than one. In automated versions of the APEX Rooming List, this will populate a drop-down list for use as entries are made.
   h. In the areas provided, enter the room types that have been contracted for the event.
   i. FOR THE ORIGINAL ROOMING LIST: Upon completing the original rooming list, submit it to the housing facility according to the agreed upon method (for example, email, fax). Once the facility has entered the reservations, the facility's staff is responsible for reporting back according to the agreement (for example, confirmations back to the event organizer, to the individual attendees, a complete/updated rooming list back to the event organizer).
   j. SUBSEQUENT CHANGES AND CANCELLATIONS TO LIST: After the original rooming list has been sent, all additional reservations, changes and cancellations must be sent in a separate list and dated. If confirmation codes or numbers have been provided by the facility, include the confirmation codes with all reservations that are changing or being cancelled. All other reservations on the original list have not changed and do not need to be sent. Once the facility has entered the changes, the facility's staff is responsible for reporting back according to the contract for the event (for example, confirmations back to the event organizer, to the individual attendees, a complete/updated rooming list back to the event organizer, etc.).

   When preparing subsequent lists for submission, the event organizer should select "Addition," "Modification" or "Cancellation" for each reservation on the list as appropriate. The "Date/Time" field should be completed. In automated versions of the APEX Rooming List, this field should automatically update to reflect the latest date/time the list was saved.

   k. See Part I, Section C-4 for Best Practices when working with Rooming Lists.

3. INSTRUCTIONS FOR HOUSING FACILITIES

    a. Recognize that the Rooming List process will follow APEX Rooming List accepted practices.
    b. Validate that data fields provided by the event organizer match contracted arrangements and actual inventory.
    c. Once the original rooming list is received, review for compliance with contractual terms including room block by room type and date. Adjust as necessary and advise event organizer.
    d. After initial list is received, expect additions, modifications and cancellations in separate dated lists.
    e. The facility will need to provide individual reservation confirmations back to the event organizer for each list received in date and time order.
    f. Rooming lists with credit cards are not secure. Lists should be secured properly.
    g. See Part I, Section C-4 for Best Practices when working with Rooming Lists.

4. BEST PRACTICES FOR EVENT ORGANIZERS AND HOUSING FACILITIES

    a. Always save every rooming list as a separate file. Do not overwrite lists so that historic information is preserved.
    b. Event organizers should date every rooming list that is sent to a housing facility. It helps with the reservation reconciliation process.
    c. Ensure that the rooming list has multiple sort conditions (for example, room type, arrival date).
    d. Shares (roommates) should only be associated with a primary guest reservation. It is not necessary to create individual reservations for shares, however, names should be captured and recorded for reference.
    e. Additions, modifications and cancellations should be compiled into daily lists and submitted in bulk (as opposed to delivering individual changes).
    f. Event organizers should always reconcile the rooming lists sent to a housing facility with the facility's actual manifest to ensure all data was entered correctly. This greatly reduces problems at check-in.
    g. For modified reservations, always identify the original data and what is changed. For example:
        • Guest Name Was: John Smith
        • Guest Name Now: Bill Miller
    h. Event organizers should not resend an entire original rooming list to a property with changes. Only send the additions, modifications and cancellations since the last time a list was sent.

APEX ROOMING LIST TEMPLATE

<<Event Name>>

<<Event Organizer/Host>>

Dates:
<<Earliest Arrival Date>>
<<Latest Departure Date>>

Key Housing Contact:
<<Prefix>> <<GivenName/Initial>> <<MiddleName/Initial>>
<<FamilyName>> <<Suffix(s)>>

<<Address1>>
<<Address2>>
<<City>>, <<State/Province>> <<Postal/Zip Code>>
<<Country>>

<<Phone>>
<<Fax>>
<<Email>>

Rooming List For: <<FacilityName>>

Report Created: <<Date/Time>>

Report Status:	Drop Down Options:
	❏ Original Rooming List
	❏ Additions
	❏ Modifications
	❏ Cancellations
	❏ Other: _____

Currency Type:	Drop Down Options:
	$ (Default)
	❏ Currency
	❏ Currency
	❏ Currency
	❏ Etc.

Group Code: _____

Contact & Share-with Information

<<FamilyName>>, <<Prefix>> <<GivenName/Initial>>,
<<MiddleName/Initial>>, <<Suffix(s)>>
<<Organization>> (Optional)
<<Address1>>
<<Address2>>
<<City>>, <<State/Province>> <<Postal/Zip Code>>
<<Country>>
<<Email>>
<<Phone with appropriate country, city, and area codes >>
<<Fax with appropriate country, city, and area codes >>

Share With:
1. <<FamilyName>>, <<Prefix>> <<GivenName/Initial>>,
   <<MiddleName/Initial>>, <<Suffix(s)>>:
   <<ArrivalDate>> - <<DepartureDate>>
2. <<FamilyName>>, <<Prefix>> <<GivenName/Initial>>,
   <<MiddleName/Initial>>, <<Suffix(s)>>:
   <<ArrivalDate>> - <<DepartureDate>>
3. Repeat as needed for additional roommates

Reservation Information

Stay Dates: <<Arrival Day>> <<ArrivalDate>> -
<<DepartureDay>> <<DepartureDate>>

Nights: <<NumberOfNights>> (should be auto-calc
based on stay dates)

Room   Drop Down Options:
Type: *to be defined by event organizer
              ❏ Room Type
              ❏ Room Type
              ❏ Etc.

Bed Type: Drop Down Options:
              *to be defined by event organizer
              ❏ Bed Type
              ❏ Bed Type
              ❏ Etc.

Special Needs & Requests: ❏ Yes   ❏ No
If Yes, Specify in Comments (This information can
be pulled from the APEX Housing Form).

❏ Smoking Requested
❏ Non-Smoking Requested
❏ No Preference

Guest Status: ❏ VIP

Confirmation Number: _____

Comments & Guarantee

Comments: _____
(indicate upgrades, early or late arrival,
early or late departure, and other special
notes)

Rewards Program/#: _____

Deposit: $_____

Guarantee*: Payment Type

Rate Type:
❏ Rate Type 1
❏ Rate Type 2
❏ Additional Rate Types as Necessary
❏ Staff: _____(#) nights
❏ Comp: _____(#) nights

*Note that to comply with credit card company requirements, the initial APEX rooming list will not require credit card guarantees.

PART II: ACCEPTED PRACTICES

A. Room Blocks

1. Definitions

a. Room Block: Total number of sleeping rooms that are utilized and attributable to one event.

b. Event-Contracted Block (ECB): The rooms that are contracted for by an event organizer with a housing facility(s) for a particular event (the Main Event).

c. Sub-Block: Any group of rooms that is classified or separated differently than the general attendee block within the Event-Contracted Block (ECB).

d. Peripheral Block: A group of rooms that is reserved by a party outside of the ECB but is present in the city as a result of the Main Event (for example, some exhibitors, some international tour groups).
   - A Peripheral Block's consumed room nights should be credited to the Main Event's total room nights for historical tracking purposes.
   - A Peripheral Block may be used to help offset attrition charges against the ECB.
   - A Peripheral Block usually negotiates its own terms (for example, 1/50, staff rate, etc.).

How do you identify Peripheral Blocks? *Event organizers should require each contracted housing facility to report (to the event organizer) what groups are in-house at the same time as the Main Event. Each housing facility should include tour and travel, and wholesalers' reservations which were booked individually over the dates of the Main Event.*

e. Diagram of Block Structure

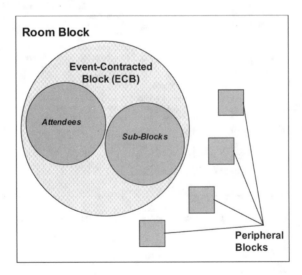

2. Managing Room Blocks

a. Housing Facility/Event Communication
- Conduct pre-event meetings in advance of opening housing with the contracted facility(s) to ensure understanding of and support for established housing procedures. Use these meetings to build relationships and promote the event organizer's support of the facility through its housing policies.

b. Opening Housing Early
   (1) Keep in mind the nature of the event and its attendees when setting the opening date for accepting housing reservations.
   (2) Make housing available early to capture the sub-blocks that want to make housing arrangements well in advance of the event. Without this alternative, sub-blocks might book directly with housing facilities. Make the process easy and convenient for sub-block contacts.
   (3) For annual events, offer sub-blocks the opportunity to make future housing requests on-site at the current year's event.

c. Deposits
   (1) A system of guarantees and, if necessary, deposits, (for example, a first-night deposit) may be required to reserve rooms. *See also Part II, Section B-1.*
   (2) If deposit (or other) policies are stricter for sub-blocks than for general attendees, the event organizer can provide some benefit or additional service to the sub-block in order to offset and justify the additional restriction.

d. Cancellation Policies
   (1) For cancellations made after the contracted cut-off date, deposits may be non-refundable or guarantees forfeited.
   (2) Any non-refundable deposits that are collected should be credited to the event organizer's room block when determining actual pick-up, and to offset attrition liabilities, if applicable. The total deposit amount divided by the group room rate equals the number of rooms nights to be credited.

e. Linking Housing and Registration
   If housing and registration are handled by separate entities, connect them using technology as much as possible. For example, link housing and registration websites and pre-populate an event attendee's data from one site to the other to create a seamless effect (for example, have a link so that an attendee has to enter name, address, telephone number, etc. only once). This can:
   - Allow for easier comparison of housing and registration data.
   - Make it easier to identify people who have registered but not booked housing (and vice versa).
   - Require important data fields to be completed (for example, where attendees are staying).
   - Make the registration and housing processes easier for attendees by reducing required typing.
   - Be used to identify people who register, but do not go onto the official housing website. This can facilitate communications encouraging the use of the official room block.

f. Giving Sub-Blocks On-Line Rooms Management Access
   Allowing individual sub-blocks to manage their rooms via secure Internet access can:
   - Give sub-blocks more control over their rooms.
   - Give sub-blocks the ability to make reservations, changes and cancellations on-line.
   - Allocate inventory to the sub-block and provide secure access.
   - Eliminate the "middleman" and potential errors.

g. Allowing Sub-Blocks to Contract Directly with a Housing Facility
   (1) Consider allowing sub-blocks the option of booking rooms directly with the housing facility, but require that the housing facility report this activity to the event organizer and/or housing bureau.
   (2) Specify in housing facility contracts that the facility should report the sub-block pick-up figures to the event organizer and/or housing bureau.

h. Managing Peripheral Blocks
    (1) Through the event registration process, require that all Peripheral Blocks provide information about where they have housing reservations. This is important because Peripheral Block information can be useful if attrition becomes an issue. Additionally, Peripheral Block pick-up may be important to overall room block performance relative to the cost of convention center use, subsidies, etc.
    (2) Consider specifying in housing facility contracts that peripheral block reservations taken over and above the ECB must be counted toward the ECB pick-up if there is any attrition liability to the event organizer at that housing facility.

i. Contracting
    (1) Event organizers should block and contract for rooms accurately, based on room block history.
    (2) Include verbiage in housing facility contracts regarding reservations taken directly through the housing facility. Sample verbiage is:
        Hotel will not book organization affiliate or attendee housing directly, but will refer those requests to the Official Housing Bureau. If an affiliate or attendee has booked housing directly with the Hotel, appropriate credit for that assignment will be given to the event organizer as if it were part of the event contracted block, or an extension of that block, if the block is eventually filled.
    (3) Include verbiage in housing facility contracts regarding rooms audits. An audit should compare the attendee registration list with the housing reservation list in order to identify attendees that went around the block. These should count in the final pick-up number reported. *See also Tracking Sub-Blocks in Part II, Section A-3.*
    (4) Include verbiage in housing facility contracts to specify pre- and post-event block requests such as "group room rates to apply 3 days prior and 3 days following the contracted event dates based upon group block availability."
    (5) Include verbiage in housing facility contracts that clearly specifies procedures for the booking of hospitality suites, and the event organizer's role in disallowing or approving such bookings.
    (6) Include verbiage in housing facility contracts that addresses whether individual deposits are refunded in the event the organization cancels.
    (7) Specify in housing facility contracts whether or not reservations taken over and above the ECB must be counted toward the ECB pick-up if there is any attrition liability to the event organizer at that housing facility.
    (8) Event organizers should provide a list of readily identifiable sub-blocks to each contracted housing facility.
    (9) Allow the review and adjustment of room blocks at designated benchmark dates in long-term contracts.

j. Continued Service After Cut-Off Date
    At the official cut-off date (for example, 45-, 30-, or 21-days), rooms remaining in unused inventory should be returned to the housing facility for re-sale.
    (1) The housing facility and the event organizer and/or housing bureau should manage the remaining rooms in the ECB, processing and assigning reservations within the existing room block, based on rate availability. This should be done in order to provide service and track pick-up. This will include all changes, substitutions, cancellations and new reservations.
    (2) Any new reservations, cancellations, changes or substitutions for an event that are inadvertently accepted by a contracted housing facility, should be assigned/credited to the official ECB based on availability.
    (3) If possible, establish a wait list in order to fulfill room requests after cut-off.

k. Education & Marketing
    Event organizers should make event attendees aware and knowledgeable of the housing process and the official, contracted housing facility(s). With knowledge, attendees may be more likely to book within the room block. Communication is key to success in this area and some recommended actions follow:

    - Inform attendees that the event organizer has contractual obligations with specific housing facilities. Advise them that the organizer and its attendees have an obligation to fill the room block. Failure to do so may result in financial liabilities. Direct them to book through the official housing channels. This can be communicated in the promotional brochure, through correspondence accompanying housing forms and exhibitor manuals, and on event-related websites.
    - Educate sub-blocks and individual attendees of the importance of providing accurate information about where they are staying during the event. The information is often needed in the event of an

emergency, and to plan for shuttle transportation. Inaccurate shuttle estimates result in delayed transit and poor service levels.

- Inform attendees, along with sub-block and peripheral block contacts, that if they do not book in the ECB, the event organizer is less able to assist them should they need help with any housing issues. This can be communicated through correspondence accompanying housing forms and exhibitor manuals, and on any event-related websites. See additional information on incentives in Part II, Section A-2-I.
- Involve members, exhibitor advisory boards, etc. in supporting and encouraging booking within the ECB.
- Develop an exhibitor, or sub-block, focus group to identify concerns regarding established housing procedures, to develop solutions to those concerns, and incentives to book within the overall room block.
- Conduct surveys of individuals as well as sub-block and peripheral block contacts to determine where they have reserved accommodations, how they made their reservations, and, if they went around the block, the reasons for doing so.
  - Surveys may be done on-site at event registration or by email soon after the event concludes.
  - If the event organizer provides on-site Internet access for attendees, the completion of a housing survey could be required in order to gain access to that service.
- Encourage individuals and sub-blocks to use established housing procedures through:
  - Email – Send email notices to sub-block contacts leading up to the event.
    - ➤ Provide a direct link to the official housing and registration website(s).
    - ➤ Announce the opening of housing.
    - ➤ Contact individuals and sub-blocks that have registered and have not yet booked rooms.
    - ➤ Promote the event by targeting past sub-block contacts.
  - Telemarketing Prior to the Opening of Housing – Make phone calls to key sub-block and peripheral block contacts that have a history of booking outside of the block.
  - Telemarketing During Housing – Once housing has been open for a period of time, contact sub-blocks that have not yet made accommodations reservations within the block. Encourage them to make their reservations via the official housing procedures. If they have made reservations outside of the block, ask them the reasons for doing so, and where they have reserved accommodations.

I. Incentives to Book within the Block

Incentives can be offered to encourage attendees as well as sub-blocks and peripheral blocks to make reservations within the ECB. Some *recommended* incentives are:

- Offer a special "early-bird" rate. Consider negotiating an early-bird rate in the event contract (for example, rooms booked and pre-paid 60 days prior to the event will have a lower rate than all other rooms in the ECB). A discounted rate on housing and/or registration can be implemented to attract attendees and sub-blocks into the ECB and encourage them to book early.
- Offer sub-blocks complimentary rooms/suites and/or upgrades that would otherwise go to the main event organizer.
- Give sub-block contacts a free event registration, or discounted registration rate, for booking though the official housing procedures.
- Offer "value adds" (for example, free breakfast, complimentary fitness center access) for early-bird housing, or for anyone who books though the official housing procedures at any time.
- Provide positive incentives for sub-block pickup (for example, higher housing priority points for picking up a high percentage of the sub-block). Provide a post-event sub-block pick-up report so that sub-block contacts know their blocking activity is accurate and is being monitored by the event organizer.
- Require participation in the ECB in order to have access to shuttle transportation. This will help the event organizer gain control over room block pick-up and manage shuttle arrangements and costs.
  - Require peripheral blocks to pay a fee to the event organizer in order to use shuttle service. This may be effectively monitored through registration.
  - Provide a special badge or shuttle pass to the attendees who book within the ECB.

3. Tracking Sub-Blocks

    a. Avoiding Over-Blocking Sub-Blocks

        (1) To avoid over-blocking and the resulting wash, room utilization by sub-blocks of 20 or more rooms should be tracked from year to year. Identify sub-blocks on the rooming list so that the housing facility can track actual pick-up figures.

        (2) Actual pick-up figures should be used for future reference in allocating rooms to sub-blocks. Requests for rooms exceeding 10% over the prior year's pick-up should be thoroughly reviewed. The decision to grant or withhold approval should be made after consultation with the sub-block's contact, and take into account any special needs unique to the current year event (for example, an exhibitor launching a new product).

    b. Identifying Sub-Blocks

        (1) When different policies are established for sub-blocks than for individual attendees, some sub-blocks may choose to book as individuals to avoid the policies. To stay informed of sub-block activity, monitor the registration lists by sorting the registrants by company, address, or credit card number rather than by individual name. It can help identify this type of booking activity.

        (2) Clearly state in all housing materials that if such activity is identified, the offending group will be contacted and will be required to follow official housing policies for sub-blocks.

B. Technology & the Internet

1. Credit Card and Deposit Guarantees

    a. Due to demand, location, requirements of events, policies of housing facilities, and the preferences of attendees, different methods should be allowed to guarantee housing reservations in a room block.

    b. It is important to communicate all options and policies with all parties (for example, event organizer, housing bureau, attendee, hotel) involved in the housing process.

    c. Policies regarding deposits and guarantees should be stipulated and mutually agreed upon within room block agreements or contracts and a process to communicate any changes to these policies should be in place.

    d. Systems and processes in exchanging commerce between all parties must be secure and comply with the latest standards of personal data encryption (for example, Visa CISP Program http://usa.visa.com/business/accepting_visa/ops_risk_management/cisp.html).

    e. In the event that a rooming list is processed with credit card data, there must be a secure and encrypted method of transferring valid data between parties. Note: Please refer to your Housing Bureau or an Information Technology professional to ensure you are adhering to the latest data encryption standards.

    f. The following are accepted methods by which a reservation for a group block can be properly guaranteed:

        (1) Credit Card – This is the most common form of guaranteeing a reservation and is widely accepted by housing facilities. It is an accepted practice to utilize the latest technology to authenticate credit cards (for example, Verisign) prior to securely communicating this data from one party to another. (For example, make sure credit cards are not expired.)

        (2) Deposits – Based upon what is mutually arranged between all parties, there may be multiple and varying deposit requirements for an ECB and its sub-blocks. Common deposit scenarios are:

- First Night's Room & Tax – This process collects the individual's first night's room rate and tax at the time of reservation. Based upon the established policy this deposit can be collected via a credit card, check, wire transfer, or direct billing. See also "Direct Billing," Part II, Section B-1-3.
- First & Last Nights' Room & Tax – This process collects the individual's first and last nights' room rate and tax at the time of reservation. Based upon the established policy this deposit can be collected via a credit card, check, wire transfer, or direct billing. See also "Direct Billing," Part II, Section B-1-3. This type of deposit is often effective for events where individuals (or sub-blocks) tend to check out early. Note that housing facilities have their own early departure fee policies and it is important to review those policies during the agreement process.
- Full Deposit – This process calculates and processes payment on the room rate and tax for the entire reservation of an attendee. Though not widely used, this is the most aggressive type of guarantee.

(3) Direct Billing – In the event that the credit of an individual, an organization, or a sub-block is pre-approved, an event organizer can guarantee a reservation and invoice for payment at a later date. Direct billing approval policies must be communicated and mutually agreed upon by all parties involved in the housing process (for example, event organizer, housing bureau, attendee, hotel).

2. Reservations Process

a. Prior to an ECB opening for reservations, the event organizer and the housing facility should review and agree upon all aspects of the housing process, including, but not limited to:
   - the housing reservations method;
   - reservation form and/or rooming list format;
   - flow pattern;
   - room types held;
   - additional fees such as energy surcharges and resort fees;
   - rooms audit process and any related costs; and,
   - deposit, confirmation, cancellation, and early departure policies.

   Although some of these items may be addressed in the contract, corporate and organizational policies change and therefore warrant an additional review.

b. All policy changes should be reconfirmed in writing.

c. Each housing facility involved in an event should review all communications (for example, housing forms, on-line information) that mention the housing facility to ensure accuracy prior to the event organizer promoting the event. *See also Security, Part II, Section B-6.*

3. Communications

a. If the event organizer or a designated housing bureau controls the housing process, the organizer or housing bureau should share preliminary pick-up information with the contracted housing facility(s). This information should be shared as reservations begin to materialize. For example, room pick-up should be shared at designated "benchmark" dates of 120 days, 90 days, 60 days and 45 days from the start of the event.

b. Registration numbers, not names (due to privacy concerns), should be shared by the event organizer, if requested by a contracted housing facility.

c. If the event organizer and/or housing bureau has the technological capability, real-time housing and registration data should be made available on-line to contracted housing facilities on a "view only" "," password-protected basis.

d. If the housing facility controls the housing process, the event organizer should have access to real time reservations and room pick-up data, including names and confirmation numbers on a "view only," password-protected basis.

4. Rooms Audit

a. The housing facility should credit all qualified reservations to the appropriate ECB regardless of the rate, package, or method booked. Recoding of such reservations is not essential; however, credit for these rooms to the ECB is necessary, particularly if attrition penalties will be assessed.

b. A rooms audit may be conducted post- and/or pre-event by the housing facility and/or the event organizer, determined by prior agreement in the contract (including process and costs), to the satisfaction of the event organizer while preserving the privacy and confidentiality of each housing facility guest. Post-event audits are the most accurate; however, a pre-event audit can be helpful in room block management.

5. Post-Event Reports (PERs)

APEX accepted practices regarding post-event reports are final. Those guidelines should be referenced for complete details and are available at www.conventionindustry.org. Key points include:

    a. A report of the details and activities of an event is called a "Post-Event Report" or PER.

    b. A face-to-face post-event meeting should be scheduled between the primary event organizer and each venue and facility involved in an event. That meeting should occur immediately following the end of the event and should focus on an evaluation of the success of the event as well as the completion of the Post-Event Report.

    c. The primary event organizer for an event, in partnership with the event's suppliers, should complete all applicable sections of the report within 60 days of the end of that event. Once complete, the primary event organizer should file a copy of the report with each entity, venue or facility that was used for the event (for example, Convention & Visitors Bureau, Hotel, Conference Center, etc.). The event organizer should also file the report internally for future reference.

6. Security

The Secure Sockets Layer (SSL) protocol is a set of rules governing server authentication, client authentication, and encrypted communication between servers and clients. SSL is widely used on the Internet, especially for interactions that involve exchanging confidential information such as credit card numbers.

All e-commerce transactions should utilize an encrypted SSL connection. An SSL connection requires all information sent between a client (for example, event organizer and/or attendee) and a server (for example, housing system) to be encrypted by the sending software and decrypted by the receiving software, thus providing a high degree of confidentiality.

Confidentiality is important for both parties to any private transaction. In addition, all data sent over an encrypted SSL connection is protected with a mechanism for detecting tampering – that is, for automatically determining whether the data has been altered in transit.

III

ACCEPTED

PRACTICES

EXCHANGE

The APEX Post-Event Report Template

Approved by the Convention Industry Council on October 30, 2003
Updated August 10, 2005

Report Section Contents

Instructions for Use
Event Information
Contact Information
Hotel Room Information
Room Block Information
Food & Beverage Information
Function Space Information
Exhibit Space Information
Future Event Dates Information
Report Distribution Tracking
Post-Event Report FAQ

INSTRUCTIONS FOR USE

1. A report of the details and activities of an event is called a "Post-Event Report" or PER. A collection of PERs over time will provide the complete history for an event.

2. A face-to-face post-event meeting should be scheduled between the primary event organizer (the main planning contact person) and each venue and facility involved in an event. That meeting should occur immediately following the end of the event and should focus on an evaluation of the success of the event as well as the completion of the Post-Event Report.

3. The report shall be completed by the primary event organizer of an event and filed with each venue and facility that was used for the event. Detailed recommendations for this process are included in the "Suggested Uses" section of the APEX Post-Event Report template.

4. The most recent PER for an event should accompany any request for proposals (RFP) sent to solicit proposals for future occurrences of that event.

5. In regard to the actual APEX Post-Event Report:
   a. Some information in the APEX PER is required. Information must be included in these sections for the report to be considered complete. These items are designated within the template. While all items are not required, the more that are completed, the more valuable this report will be to the event organizer in the future.
   b. All sections and items will not apply to every event. If a section or item does not apply, it should be left blank.
   c. The APEX PER should be completed for events of all sizes, especially for those of 25 rooms on peak night and larger.
   d. It is recommended that the primary event organizer for an event, in partnership with the event's suppliers, complete all applicable sections of the report within 60 days of the end of that event.
   e. Once complete, the primary event organizer should file a copy of the report with each entity, venue or facility that was used for the event (i.e., Convention & Visitors Bureau, Hotel, Conference Center, etc.). The event organizer should also file the report internally for future reference.
   f. The "Comments" field in each section should be used for any information from the organizer, venue, facility, etc. that does not fit into one of the pre-established fields, but that provides insight or valuable information regarding the event.

6. There will be various stages in the evolution of the industry's Post-Event Report and the processes used to complete it. The Convention Industry Council will remain actively involved in this evolution and will provide resources as needed:

   a. Stage I – The form will be available as a word processing file that will be completed manually and will be filed by planners and suppliers in electronic and/or hard copy form.
   b. Stage II – As industry-related software is updated and new software is developed, programmers will ensure that the APEX data map is referenced so that all data fields are defined correctly and are able to efficiently capture, store, and share historical information. This will allow for more automated completion of the report.
   c. Stage III – When the industry determines that a central event history database is to be developed, this report and the resulting data map, will be the basis for the information collected by and stored in this database. At that time, the Convention Industry Council (CIC) will convene a special APEX panel to address the best practices and processes for the use of such a database.

7. The Convention Industry Council will hold the copyright to the APEX Post-Event Report template. However, members of the meetings, conventions and exhibitions industry are permitted to copy and/or reproduce the template, as permitted by applicable copyright law, provided such use of the APEX Post-Event Report template is for member services and educational purposes and not for commercial advantage or financial gain of any sort. All copies and/or reproductions of the APEX Post-Event Report template must include the following:

   a. the copyright notice of "Copyright © 2003 by Convention Industry Council"
   b. the date the information was copied or reproduced, and

    c.   a reference line that reads: "Refer to the on-line version of this report, located at www.conventionindustry.org for the most up-to-date content."

Any other reproduction, duplication, copying, sale, resale or exploitation of the APEX Post-Event Report template, or any portion thereof, for any other purpose, without the express written consent of the Convention Industry Council, is expressly prohibited.

8.   The Convention Industry Council will annually convene a special committee of professionals from across the meetings, conventions, and exhibitions industry to review all recommendations to the contents of the APEX Post-Event Report that have been be received in the preceding year. This special committee will consult and confirm that changes to the report are required. It will then make a formal recommendation to the Convention Industry Council for action.

9.   The APEX Technology Advisory Council (TAC) will complete its work of defining the data specifications that correspond to the fields of data that the APEX Post-Event Report intends to capture and share. Those data specifications will be included in the APEX Data Map and will be released for industry use by December 31, 2003.

SECTION I: EVENT INFORMATION

*Event Name: _____

*Event Organizer/Host: _____

*Event Location City: _____ *Event Location State/Province: _____

*Event Location Country: _____

*Published Event Start Date: _____   *Published Event End Date: _____

Event Organizer/Host Overview (mission, philosophy, etc.): _____

Event Objectives: _____

Event Web Address: _____

Event Type:	Drop Down Options:
	❑ Board Meeting
	❑ City-Wide Convention
	❑ Committee Meeting
	❑ Customer Event
	❑ Educational Meeting
	❑ General Business Meeting
	❑ Incentive Travel
	❑ Local Employee Gathering
	❑ Product Launch
	❑ Public Show
	❑ Sales Meeting
	❑ Shareholders Meeting
	❑ Special Event
	❑ Team-Building Event
	❑ Trade Show
	❑ Training Meeting
	❑ Video Conference
	❑ Other: _____

Event Frequency:	Drop Down Options:
	❑ One Time Only
	❑ Bi-Annual
	❑ Annual
	❑ Semi-Annual
	❑ Quarterly
	❑ Monthly
	❑ Other: _____

*Primary Event Facility Name (the facility where most of the functions for the event were held): _____

*Primary Event Facility Type:	Drop Down Options:
	❑ Convention Center
	❑ Hotel
	❑ Conference Center
	❑ Other Venue

Was an off-site venue(s) used? Yes/No

Original Expected Attendance: _____

Total Pre-Registered Attendance: _____   Total On-Site Registrations: _____

No-Shows: _____

Number of Exhibitors Attending: _____

*Actual Attendance *(including exhibitors)*: _____

Number of Domestic Attendees *(Domestic Attendees live in the same country where the event is held)*: _____

Percentage of Domestic Attendees *(AUTO CALC: "Number of Domestic Attendees" DIVIDED BY "Actual Attendance" MULTIPLIED BY 100 = _____%)*: _____

Number of International Attendees: _____

Percentage of International Attendees *(AUTO CALC: "Number of International Attendees" DIVIDED BY "Actual Attendance" MULTIPLIED BY 100 = _____%)*: _____

Was shuttle service provided for attendees? Yes/No

Did the event make use of a Destination Management Company (DMC) or Professional Congress Organizer (PCO)? Yes/No

Did the event offer guest tours/guest programs? Yes/No

If a recurring event, complete the following for the last time the event occurred:
    Last Start Date: _____
    Last End Date: _____
    Last Primary Event Facility Name: _____
    Last Event Location City: _____
    Last Event Location State/Province: _____
    Last Event Location Country: _____

Event Information Comments *(Use this space to note important information not captured by the report such as unusual circumstances that positively or negatively affected attendance)*: _____

SECTION II: CONTACT INFORMATION

*Event Contact Type:	Drop Down Options: ❑ Employee of Event Organizer/Host ❑ Employee of Event Management Company ❑ Employee of Association Management Company ❑ Exhibit Manager ❑ Independent/Third Party ❑ Other: _____
*Event Contact Role *(check all that apply)*:	Drop Down Options: ❑ Volunteer ❑ Staff ❑ Event Organizer (Planner) ❑ Informational Contact ❑ Other: _____

Contact Person:

Prefix *(e.g., Mr., Dr.)*: _____   * Given Name: _____   *Middle Name: _____

*Surname Prefix *(e.g., Mac, Vander)*: _____   *Surname: _____

Suffix *(e.g., Jr., Sr.)*: _____   NameTitle *(e.g., CPA, Ph.D.)*: _____

*Preferred Name: _____

*Job Title: _____   *Employer: _____

*Mailing Address Line 1: _____   Mailing Address Line 2: _____

*City: _____   *State/Province: _____

*Postal/Zip Code: _____   *Country: _____

*Phone: _____   Mobile Phone: _____

Fax: _____   Email: _____   Web Address: _____

Repeat for additional contacts as necessary

SECTION III: HOTEL ROOM INFORMATION

*Did the event utilize sleeping rooms? Yes/No

      If No, go to Section V. If Yes, complete the following:

ʸNumber of Hotels Used: _____

ʸTotal Number of Rooms Used on Peak Night: _____

ʸBy whom were housing services performed?	Drop Down Options:
	❑　Event Organizer/Host
	❑　Management Firm – Management Firm's Name: _____
	❑　Housing Bureau – Housing Bureau's Name: _____
	❑　Convention & Visitors Bureau
	❑　Attendees Direct to Hotels
	❑　Other: _____

Hotel Room Comments: _____

ʸ *Denotes Required Information If Hotel Rooms Were Used*

SECTION IV: ROOM BLOCK INFORMATION

This information should be completed for each hotel used. List headquarters hotel first, then others alphabetically.

ˇHotel Name: _____

ˇHeadquarters Hotel? Yes/No

Hotel Type:

Drop Down Options:
- ☐ Airport
- ☐ Downtown
- ☐ Resort
- ☐ Suburban
- ☐ Other

No. of Single Occupied Rooms Used: _____

1 bed/1 person

No. of Double Occupied Rooms Used: _____

1 bed/
2 people

OR

2 beds/
2 people

No. of Suites Used: _____
No. of Complimentary Rooms Used: _____
No. of Staff Rooms Used: _____
No. of Sub-Blocks: _____

Room Block Contracted Date: _____
Final Room Block Date: _____
ˇCut-off Date: _____
ˇWas the Cut-off Date Exercised? Yes/No
What was pick-up at the cut-off date? _____

	Day 1	Day 2	Day 3	Day 4	Day 5	Day 6	Day 7	Day 8	Day 9	Day 10	Day 11	Day 12	Day 13	Day 14	Additional days as necessary
ˇDay & Date (i.e. Monday, March 1, 2003) *Must Be Manually Entered*															
Room Block when contracted															
Final RoomBlock															
90 day pick-up															
60 day pick-up															
30 day pick-up															
21 day pick-up															
14 day pick-up															
7 day pick-up															
ˇActual pick-up															
Requested Oversell Percentage	From event contract														
Actual Oversell Percentage	Manual Calculation: [("Maximum Pick-up" MINUS "Actual Pick-up") DIVIDED BY "Maximum Pick-up"] MULTIPLIED BY 100 = ____%														
Slippage from 21 day pick-up	Auto calc: "21 day pick-up" MINUS "Actual pick-up" = ____%														
% Sold (of contracted block)	Auto calc: "Actual pick-up" DIVIDED BY "Room Block when contracted" MULTIPLIED BY 100 = ____%														
% Sold (of final block)	Auto calc: "Actual pick-up" DIVIDED BY "Final Block" MULTIPLIED BY 100 = ____%														
ˇ% to peak	Auto calc: "Actual pick-up" DIVIDED BY the peak night pick-up MULTIPLIED BY 100 = ____%"														

Room Block Comments: _____

Repeat for additional hotels as necessary

SECTION V: FOOD & BEVERAGE INFORMATION

*Were food & beverage (F&B) functions included in the event? Yes/No   If No, go to Section VI.   If Yes, complete the following:

Attendance at Largest F&B Function: _____

What type of F&B function was the largest in attendance?	Drop Down Options:
	☐ Break/Continental
	☐ Breakfast
	☐ Lunch
	☐ Reception
	☐ Dinner
	☐ Other: _____

What type of F&B function was the largest revenue producer?	Drop Down Options:
	☐ Break/Continental
	☐ Breakfast
	☐ Lunch
	☐ Reception
	☐ Dinner
	☐ Other: _____

F&B Function Schedule (#guar=Total Covers Guaranteed; # fed=Actual Covers Per Function Period):

	Day 1	Day 2	Day 3	Day 4	Day 5	Day 6	Day 7	Day 8	Day 9	Day 10	Day 11	Day 12	Day 13	Day 14	Additional days as necessary
Break(s)/ Continental(s)	Date	Date	Date	Date	Date	Date	Date	Date	Date	Date	Date	Date	Date	Date	
	# held	# held	# held	# held	# held	# held	# held	# held	# held	# held	# held	# held	# held	# held	
	# guar	# guar	# guar	# guar	# guar	# guar	# guar	# guar	# guar	# guar	# guar	# guar	# guar	# guar	
	# fed	# fed	# fed	# fed	# fed	# fed	# fed	# fed	# fed	# fed	# fed	# fed	# fed	# fed	
Breakfast(s)	# held	# held	# held	# held	# held	# held	# held	# held	# held	# held	# held	# held	# held	# held	
	# guar	# guar	# guar	# guar	# guar	# guar	# guar	# guar	# guar	# guar	# guar	# guar	# guar	# guar	
	# fed	# fed	# fed	# fed	# fed	# fed	# fed	# fed	# fed	# fed	# fed	# fed	# fed	# fed	
Lunch(es)	# held	# held	# held	# held	# held	# held	# held	# held	# held	# held	# held	# held	# held	# held	
	# guar	# guar	# guar	# guar	# guar	# guar	# guar	# guar	# guar	# guar	# guar	# guar	# guar	# guar	
	# fed	# fed	# fed	# fed	# fed	# fed	# fed	# fed	# fed	# fed	# fed	# fed	# fed	# fed	
Reception(s)	# held	# held	# held	# held	# held	# held	# held	# held	# held	# held	# held	# held	# held	# held	
	# guar	# guar	# guar	# guar	# guar	# guar	# guar	# guar	# guar	# guar	# guar	# guar	# guar	# guar	
	# fed	# fed	# fed	# fed	# fed	# fed	# fed	# fed	# fed	# fed	# fed	# fed	# fed	# fed	
Dinner(s)	# held	# held	# held	# held	# held	# held	# held	# held	# held	# held	# held	# held	# held	# held	
	# guar	# guar	# guar	# guar	# guar	# guar	# guar	# guar	# guar	# guar	# guar	# guar	# guar	# guar	
	# fed	# fed	# fed	# fed	# fed	# fed	# fed	# fed	# fed	# fed	# fed	# fed	# fed	# fed	

Did the event have any in conjunction with (ICW) F&B functions? Yes/No   If No, go to Section VI.   If Yes, complete the following:

ICW F&B Function Schedule (#guar=Total Covers Guaranteed; # fed=Actual Covers Per Function Period):

	Day 1	Day 2	Day 3	Day 4	Day 5	Day 6	Day 7	Day 8	Day 9	Day 10	Day 11	Day 12	Day 13	Day 14	Additional days as necessary
ICW Breakfast(s)	Date	Date	Date	Date	Date	Date	Date	Date	Date	Date	Date	Date	Date	Date	
	# held	# held	# held	# held	# held	# held	# held	# held	# held	# held	# held	# held	# held	# held	
	# guar	# guar	# guar	# guar	# guar	# guar	# guar	# guar	# guar	# guar	# guar	# guar	# guar	# guar	
	# fed	# fed	# fed	# fed	# fed	# fed	# fed	# fed	# fed	# fed	# fed	# fed	# fed	# fed	
ICW Lunch(es)	# held	# held	# held	# held	# held	# held	# held	# held	# held	# held	# held	# held	# held	# held	
	# guar	# guar	# guar	# guar	# guar	# guar	# guar	# guar	# guar	# guar	# guar	# guar	# guar	# guar	
	# fed	# fed	# fed	# fed	# fed	# fed	# fed	# fed	# fed	# fed	# fed	# fed	# fed	# fed	
ICW Reception(s)	# held	# held	# held	# held	# held	# held	# held	# held	# held	# held	# held	# held	# held	# held	
	# guar	# guar	# guar	# guar	# guar	# guar	# guar	# guar	# guar	# guar	# guar	# guar	# guar	# guar	
	# fed	# fed	# fed	# fed	# fed	# fed	# fed	# fed	# fed	# fed	# fed	# fed	# fed	# fed	
ICW Dinner(s)	# held	# held	# held	# held	# held	# held	# held	# held	# held	# held	# held	# held	# held	# held	
	# guar	# guar	# guar	# guar	# guar	# guar	# guar	# guar	# guar	# guar	# guar	# guar	# guar	# guar	
	# fed	# fed	# fed	# fed	# fed	# fed	# fed	# fed	# fed	# fed	# fed	# fed	# fed	# fed	

Food & Beverage Comments (Use this space to note important information not captured by the report such as green meetings provisions, food bank donations, etc.): _____

SECTION VI: FUNCTION SPACE INFORMATION

*Did the event require function space? Yes/No

> If No, go to Section VII. If Yes, complete the following:

†Attendance at Largest Function: _____

Was the space for the largest function on a 24-hour hold? Yes/No

†Room Setup for the Largest Function:	Drop Down Options: ❏ Theatre ❏ Conference Style Set-up ❏ U-Shaped Set-up ❏ Classroom Set-up ❏ Hollow Square/Rectangle ❏ Rounds for 8 ❏ Rounds for 10 ❏ Other _____
AV Setup for the Largest Function:	Drop Down Options: ❏ Front projection ❏ Rear projection ❏ None ❏ Other: _____
†Facility Type(s) Used for Functions *(check all that apply)*:	Options: ❏ Hotel ❏ Convention Center ❏ Conference Center ❏ Other: _____

Were there extensive AV or technology requirements for one or more functions? Yes/No

> If Yes, Number of Rooms with Extensive AV or Technology Requirements: _____

Total Number of Concurrent Breakout Sessions: _____

†Largest Daily Total of Concurrent Breakout Sessions: _____

Number of Seats Concurrent Breakout Sessions Typically Set For: _____

Typical Room Setup for Concurrent Breakout Sessions:	Drop Down Options: ❏ Theatre ❏ Conference Style Setup ❏ U-Shaped Setup ❏ Classroom Setup ❏ Hollow Square/Rectangle ❏ Rounds for 8 ❏ Rounds for 10 ❏ Other _____

Was pre-function space required? Yes/No

Was a registration area(s) required? Yes/No   # of Registration Areas: _____

Was a lounge(s) area required? Yes/No   # of Lounges: _____

Was office space required? Yes/No   # of Offices: _____

Was table top exhibit space required? Yes/No   # of Table Top Exhibits: _____

Function Space Utilities Required:	Check from the following list:
	❑ Electricity
	❑ Water
	❑ Compressed Air
	❑ Natural Gas
	❑ Analog Phone Lines
	❑ ISDN Lines
	❑ Single Line Phone Set
	❑ Ethernet Internet Service
	❑ T-1 Lines
	❑ Other: _____

Was move-in and/or move-out time required? Yes/No

      If Yes, Number of Move-In Days Required: _____
      If Yes, Number of Move-Out Days Required: _____

Was tear-down time required? Yes/No

      If Yes, Number of Tear-Down Days Required: _____

Function Space Comments: _____

[+] *Denotes Required Information If Function Space Was Used*

SECTION VII: EXHIBIT SPACE INFORMATION

*Did the event require exhibit space? Yes/No

If No, go to Section VIII. If Yes, complete the following:

^Facility Type Used for Exhibits *(check all that apply)*:	Drop Down Options: ❏ Convention Center ❏ Hotel ❏ Conference Center ❏ Other Venue

Number of Exhibits: _____   Number of Exhibiting Companies: _____

^Type of Exhibits *(check all that apply)*:	Drop Down Options: ❏ 8'x10' ❏ 10'x10' ❏ Table Tops ❏ Other: _____

^Gross Square Feet Used: _____   ^Gross Square Meters Used: _____

^Net Square Feet Used: _____   ^Net Square Meters Used: _____

^Number of Move-in Days: _____   ^Number of Move-out Days: _____

^Number of Show Days: _____   ^Show Days (i.e. M–W): _____

Show Hours: _____

Exhibit Utilities Required:	Check from the following list: ❏ Electricity ❏ Water ❏ Compressed Air ❏ Natural Gas ❏ Analog Phone Lines ❏ ISDN Lines ❏ Single Line Phone Set ❏ Ethernet Internet Service ❏ T-1 Lines ❏ Other: _____

Were there extensive AV or technology requirements for one or more exhibitors? Yes/No

If Yes, Number of Exhibitors with Extensive AV or Technology Requirements: _____

Was a general service contractor (GSC) used? Yes/No

If Yes, Number of Move-In Days Required for the GSC: _____

Was food & beverage required for any exhibitors (excluding concessions)? Yes/No

If Yes, Number of Exhibitors that Required Food & Beverage: _____

Exhibit Space Comments: _____

^ *Denotes Required Information If Exhibit Space Was Used*

SECTION VIII: FUTURE EVENT DATES INFORMATION

*Have future dates been confirmed for this event? Yes/No

What is the next open date for this event? _____

Next Published Start Date: _____   Next Published End Date: _____

Next City: _____   Next State/Province: _____   Next Country: _____

Next Facility: _____

Future Dates Comments: _____

Additional future dates as necessary

SECTION IX: REPORT DISTRIBUTION TRACKING

*This report was completed on (DATE) _____ by (FULL NAME) ____, (TITLE) _____, (EMPLOYER) _____. It was delivered via (Checkbox: Postal Mail, Email, Fax, OTHER:_____) on (DATE) _____ to:
- (FULL NAME) ____, (TITLE) _____, (EMPLOYER) _____
- (FULL NAME) ____, (TITLE) _____, (EMPLOYER) _____
- (FULL NAME) ____, (TITLE) _____, (EMPLOYER) _____
- (FULL NAME) ____, (TITLE) _____, (EMPLOYER) _____
- *Additional lines as necessary*

This report was revised on (DATE) _____ by (FULL NAME) ____, (TITLE) _____, (EMPLOYER) _____. A revised copy was delivered via (Checkbox: Postal Mail, Email, Fax, OTHER:_____) on (DATE) _____ to:
- (FULL NAME) ____, (TITLE) _____, (EMPLOYER) _____
- (FULL NAME) ____, (TITLE) _____, (EMPLOYER) _____
- (FULL NAME) ____, (TITLE) _____, (EMPLOYER) _____
- (FULL NAME) ____, (TITLE) _____, (EMPLOYER) _____
- *Additional lines as necessary*

Additional revision notations as necessary

Post-Event Report (PER) FAQ

Information provided courtesy of Holly Hospel & AhhHah! Discovery Tools

What is a Post-Event Report?

A Post-Event Report (PER) is a report of the details and activities of an event. A collection of PERs over time will provide the complete history of a recurring event. A PER is completed by the primary event organizer of an event, in conjunction with the suppliers for that event, and filed with each venue and facility that was utilized.

Why should I complete a report on an event that has already happened?

Once complete, the information a Post-Event Report (PER) contains can do many valuable things – all of which can benefit the event organizer and host.

- **Convey the "Bottom Line":** The APEX PER can be used as a starting point to translate numbers to dollars and cents, which is the universal language of business. What decision makers (whether it is a boss or a supplier) really want to know is "How much did it cost? And how much was our net profit?"

- **Leverage Your Business:** Use it to analyze the numbers and conduct research. Numbers can act as a crystal ball while lending credibility and leverage. Numbers help an event organizer in two critical areas:
  1. Anticipation – Tracking numbers will reveal patterns that will help prepare for and predict the future of an event.
  2. Negotiation – Accurately demonstrating an event's value gives an event organizer the credibility and confidence needed to negotiate effectively. For example, good historical data on room pick-up is vital when leveraging business with a hotel. Without it an event organizer is losing amenities, losing complimentary rooms, and losing discounted exhibit space.

- **Decision Making Tool**: A PER can help answer questions like "How many registration counters and registration personnel will be enough?" or "What food and beverage guarantee should be made?" It can give you insight into the unique characteristics of an event's attendees. A PER can show if attendees bring their children to the event, if they make a vacation out of it, whether they drive or fly in, and whether they care about Saturday night airfare discounts. With this knowledge, an event organizer can make better decisions such as knowing that it is more important to negotiate for free parking instead of free health club passes.

- **Leverage Your Career:** Use it to demonstrate your professionalism and performance as a successful event organizer. If you have been tracking your numbers you can use this information during your annual performance review to demonstrate just how much you have contributed to the organization's bottom line. The value of your professionalism and skill will become indisputable.

Glossary

Information on CD Rom

Accepted Practices Exchange (APEX©)	an initiative of the Convention Industry Council. The mission of APEX© is "To spearhead an industry-wide initiative that brings together all stakeholders in the development and implementation of industry-wide accepted practices which create and enhance efficiencies throughout the meetings, conventions and exhibitions industry."
accessibility	availability or approachability for all persons, regardless of a person's physical or mental limitations
accommodation	guest bedrooms occupied by meeting attendees
accompanying person	any individual who comes with a participant, not necessarily involved with the meeting sessions; guest or spouse of an attendee
accrual accounting	income is entered when it is earned and expenses are entered when they are incurred, not necessarily when they are paid
acetate	transparent material on which information for an overhead projector is written; available in sheets or rolls
advance registration incentives	complimentary or discounted goods, services, or fees that encourage attendees to register for an event before it actually takes place, done through mail, phone, internet, or fax
agenda	program of things to be done; specifically, a list of things to be dealt with at a meeting
ambient lighting	level of illumination from natural lighting sources already existing in an environment
amenities	complimentary items; often in the guest's bedroom
amplifier (amp)	device enabling sound to be intensified

ancillary	those events that are in conjunction with the conference/event, such as guest programs
annual general meeting (AGM)	the yearly General Meeting of an association, corporation
attendee	individual registered for a conference; people who actually come are verified attendees
attendee profile	a description of the typical delegate which includes such details as age, sex, point of origin, companions (demographics)
attendee trend	a following of attendee profiles from conference to conference; to determine general tendencies over a period of time
attrition clause	a specific provision in a contract that has been agreed upon in writing by the hotel and the meeting sponsor; provides for payment of damages by the sponsor to the hotel when the sponsor fails to fulfill its specified percentage of contracted room nights or its specified percentage of food and beverage or both
audio visual aids (AV)	audio and visual support for meetings, usually taking the form of film, slides, overhead projection, flip charts, sound and video equipment
banquet event order (BEO)	detailed instructions for a particular event prepared by the facility; also known as a résumé sheet or function sheet; includes detailed instructions related to room setups, food and beverage
barrier free	absence of obstacles preventing persons with special needs from moving freely to all public areas within a building
blue lines	a copy of filmed camera ready copy, one of the last stages before printing
boom	adjustable support for positioning microphones or lighting fixtures.
booth	one or more standard units of exhibit space. In the US, a standard unit is generally known to be a 10' x 10' space (equaling 100 net square feet).

booth area	amount of floor space occupied by exhibitor. Also known as booth space, exhibition area, or stand area.
brainstorming	group sessions in which all participants contribute creative ideas which are not initially judged for merit
breakeven point	the point at which revenues match expenditures (e.g., no financial loss is incurred)
breakout session	small group sessions, panels, workshops or presentations, offered concurrently within the meeting, formed to focus on specific subjects; the meeting is apart from the general session, but within the meeting format, formed to focus on specific subjects; these sessions can be arranged by basic, intermediate or advanced; or divided by interest areas or industry segment
bulk mailings	large quantity of mail sent at one time at a special rate
budgetary philosophy	financial expectation of the meeting; generate a profit, break-even, or run at a deficit
budget reconciliation	a comparison of the budgeted figures for the meeting vs the actual figures achieved
CD ROM	a compact disk that can hold up to 650 megabytes of data; the data can be read only from the disk, not erased or recorded over
call for abstracts	prospectus sent to potential sources of meeting presenter, exhibitors, speakers or panellist
call for papers	an invitation to submit topic ideas for the conference program; document containing detailed instructions for submission of papers for assessment and selection by a review committee; often referred to as "abstract forms"
cancellation clause	1) provision in a contract which outlines penalties for both parties if cancellation occurs for failure to comply with terms of the agreement; 2) (entertainment) provision with artist's contract that allows artist to cancel

	within a specified period of time prior to artist's play date
carousel tray	circular holder used for projecting 35mm slides; same as round slide tray
cash accounting	a system in which revenue and expenses are counted as they are actually received
cash bar	private room bar set up where guests pay for drinks individually
cash flow	the transfer of monies into and out of an enterprise
Certificate in Meeting Management	Certification program offered by Meeting Professionals International. Global certification in meeting management that focuses on strategic thinking and actions for senior-level meeting professionals.
Certified Meeting Professional (CMP)	accredited designation offered by the Convention Industry Council; this designation certifies competency in 27 areas of meeting management through application and examination
chart of accounts	detailed list of the individual line items that make up the revenue and expense categories in a budget; a numbering system used to identify every line item in a budget, so income and expenses are posted to the correct accounts
client	a customer; may refer to the person/organization hiring the meeting professional
clinic	workshop-type educational experience where attendees learn by doing
communications centre	an area in the meeting venue for telephone, fax, Internet, or teleconferencing facilities
complimentary (comp)	service, space or item given at no charge
complete meeting package (CMP)	an all-inclusive plan offered by conference centres; includes lodging, all meals and support services
concurrent session	multiple sessions scheduled at the same time; programs on different themes or subjects

	offered simultaneously
conference	1) participatory meeting designed for discussion, fact-finding, problem solving and consultation; 2) an event used by any organization to meet and exchange views, convey a message, open a debate or give publicity to some area of opinion on a specific issue; no tradition, continuity or periodicity is required to convene a conference; although not generally limited in time, conferences are usually of short duration with specific objectives; conferences are generally on a smaller scale than congresses
conference résumé	a detailed summary of overall meeting requirements prepared by the organizers for the facilities and/or suppliers. Also called event résumé, manual of operations
confrontation	efforts of a dissident group to obstruct the conduct of an event
congress	1) the regular coming together of large groups of individuals, generally to discuss a particular subject; a congress will often last several days and have several simultaneous sessions; the length of time between congresses is usually established in advance of the implementation stage, and can be either pluri-annual or annual; most international or world congresses are of the former type while national congresses are more frequently held annually; 2) meeting of an association of delegates or representatives from constituent organizations; 3) European term for convention
contingency plan	an alternative plan that may replace the original plan when circumstances change
continuing education units (CEUs)	requirement of many professional groups by which members must certify participation in formal educational programs designed to maintain their level of ability beyond their original certification date

contractor	An individual or organization providing services to a trade show and/or its exhibitors. May be a general service contractor, exclusive contractor of the facility, official contractor appointed by show management or exhibitor-appointed contractor.
contribution margin	amount of the registration fee that is left over once the individual's variable costs have been covered (e.g. how much each delegate contributes towards the fixed costs of the meeting)
convention	lAn event where the primary activity of the attendees is to attend educational sessions, participate in meetings/discussions, socialize, or attend other organized events. There is a secondary exhibit component.
convention and visitors bureau (CVB)	not-for-profit destination marketing organization that represents and promotes a city or geographic area in the solicitation and servicing of all types of travellers to that city or area, whether they visit for business, pleasure or both; CVBs provide destination promotion and sometimes offers personnel, housing control, and other services for meetings and conventions.
corner booth	An exhibit space with exposure on at least two aisles. Some organizations charge premiums for corner booths/stands.
cover	the number of people served at a food and beverage event, the table setting for one person, or in reference to the number of waiters per cover or person
crescent-round setup	uses 60-, 66- or 72-inch (152-, 168- and 183-centimetre) diameter rounds with seating on two thirds to three quarters of the table and no seating with its back to the speaker; used for banquet-to-meeting or meeting-to-banquet quick set; also called buzz style setup or half-moon seating
crisis management	immediate action to control or direct any

	situations which become problematic and which would have a major impact on the meeting
critical path	a listing of significant milestones and achievements, by date, necessary to complete a defined plan
crowd control	direction provided to attendees to ensure smooth traffic flow
culture	the sum total of the attainments and learned behaviour patterns of any specific period, race, or people
currency exchange	exchange of money from country to country
customs broker	person or company which provides customs clearing services to shippers of goods to and from another country
cut-off date	designated date when the facility will release a block of sleeping rooms to the general public; the date is typically three to four weeks before the convention; also called the reservation review date
data projector	the projection of a computer signal from a personal computer, laptop or other computer device onto a screen from an LCD or equivalent projector for viewing by audience
delegate	1) registered meeting participant; 2) voting representative at a meeting
delegate profile	a description of the typical delegate which includes such details as age, sex, hometown, companions
demographics	characteristics that help create a profile of exhibitors and attendees; may include company location, job function, purchase budget, purchase intentions.
demonstration	1) the act of showing how to do something; 2) a group of individuals organized to picket or protest against a group using placards, literature, songs, shouts and, sometimes, marches or sit-ins
destination	a city, area or country which can be marketed

	to groups or individuals as a place to visit or hold a meeting
destination management company (DMC)	company or professional individual engaged in organizing tours, meetings of all types and their related activities; same as professional congress organizer (PCO).
dismantle	1) Take-down and removal of exhibits. 2) To take apart.
dissolve unit	devise that activates fade-out and fade-in of slides from one projector to another by regulating voltage sent to projector lamps
distortion	unclear audio signal that results from giving too much power to a speaker or amplifier
drayage	Delivery of exhibit materials from the dock to an assigned exhibit space, removing empty crates, returning crates at the end of the event for recrating, and delivering materials back to dock for carrier loading. Also known as material handling.
drayage charge	The cost of moving exhibit materials within the confines of the exhibit hall, based on weight. This charge is calculated in 100-pound units, or hundredweight (CWT).
DVD-ROM	this much like a CD-ROM except it can store up to 12 times the amount of data
educational credit	acknowledgement of participation in continuing education as recognized by an accredited authority (CEU)
emergency action plan	procedures for response to any number of emergency situations, such as medical emergencies, fire and bomb threats
end cap	A style of booth space exposed to aisles on three sides and composed of two side by side linear booth spaces
entertainment	activity performed for the amusement and enjoyment of others
entry requirements	specific government requirements people and/or materials must have before entering a country other then one's own (e.g. passport, visa)

ethics	the science of morals; moral principles or practices of a person, company, or association
environmental audit	an inspection completed to assess practices which impact on the environment
evaluation	1) critiquing and rating the overall success of a meeting; 2) developing a meeting profile from accurate meeting statistics.
event	(a) portion(s) of a meeting (e.g., food function, festival)
event resevent resuméumé	a collection of all details relative to a meeting's needs; this document is circulated to all key personnel in the facility and organization
exclusive contractor	A contractor appointed by event or building management as the sole agent to provide specific services or products
exhibit	Individual display area constructed to showcase products, services or convey a message
exhibition	1) An event at which products and services are displayed. The primary activity of attendees is visiting exhibits on the show floor. These events focus primarily on business-to-business (B2B) relationships. 2) Display of products or promotional material for the purposes of public relations, sales and/or marketing
exhibitor	1) Person or firm that displays its products or services at an event. 2) Event attendee whose primary purpose for attending the event is to staff a booth/stand
exhibitor manual	Manual or kit, usually developed by the service contractor with the input of show management, for an event, containing general event information, labor/service order forms, rules and regulations and other information pertinent to an exhibitor's participation in an exhibition.
exhibitor prospectus	Direct mail promotional materials sent to current and prospective exhibitors to encourage participation and promote the benefits of exhibiting in a specific show. Contains

	information about technical points, attendee profile, cost of exhibition space, floor plan of the exhibition and application for participation
exposition	a display of products and/or services; same as exhibition
facility	a structure that is built, installed or established to serve a particular purpose
familiarization tour(FAM Trip)	offered to potential buyers of a meeting site, a program designed to acquaint participants with specific destinations or services and to stimulate the booking of a meeting; often offered in groups, but sometimes on an individual basis
feedback	1) regeneration of sound from audio speakers back through a microphone causing a squealing sound; 2) response about an activity, policy, or idea.
financial procedures	a guide containing accounting and banking techniques
fire marshal	In the United States, Fire Marshals' responsibilities vary from state to state, but they tend to be responsible for fire safety code adoption and enforcement, fire and arson investigation, fire incident data reporting and analysis, public education and advising Governors and State Legislatures on fire protection.
fixed cost	the day-to-day cost of doing business that is pre-committed, such as salaries, insurance, lease expenses, utilities, etc.
fixed expense	expense incurred regardless of the number of meeting attendees
flip chart	large pad of paper placed on an easel and used by a speaker for illustrative purposes
floor plan	a schematic reproduction of the layout for a specific room including placement of every item (e.g., placement of chairs, tables, furniture, plants, entrance doorways, AV, etc.)

focal length	1) distance from the centre of the lens to the film plane; 2) size of lens required to obtain a specific size picture.
follow-up	activities and communications which take place after a meeting; to be distinguished from "evaluation," which is a measurement of the achievement of defined objectives
follow spotlight	manually movable spotlight (a brilliant light projected onto a particular area)
force majeure	contract clause which limits liability should the event or performance be prevented due to Acts of God, Acts of War, civil disturbances, labour strikes or other disruptive circumstances beyond an artist's or a facility's control; (Usually inclement weather does not apply.)
forum	1) open discussion with audience, panel, and moderator; 2) a meeting or part of a meeting set aside for an open discussion by recognized participants on subjects of public interest; also for legal purposes, as part of the proceedings of a tribunal, court or similar body
front screen projection	projection of an image onto the front surface of a light reflecting screen from a projector placed within or behind the audience
function sheet	detailed instructions relevant to a particular event; also known as banquet event order (a BEO) or resumé sheet
function space	space in facility where private functions or events can be held
general session	a meeting open to all those in attendance at a convention; also called a plenary session
general service contractor (GSC)	An organization that provides event management and exhibitors with a wide range of services, sometimes including, but not limited to, installation & dismantle, creating and hanging signage and banners, laying carpet, material handling, and providing booth/stand furniture

goal	a long-term target that may be projected years into the future
gooseneck	flexible support attached to a podium or lectern to support a microphone that can be raised/lowered to suitable height for speaker
graphics	Communicative elements such as color, copy, art, photographs, translites, etc. used to illustrate an exhibit's theme or enhance décor
gratuity	mandatory charge added to food and beverage prices; usually ranging from 15 to 22 percent of food and beverage prices; ostensibly to go to service personnel, some properties take a percentage for administrative costs, confusing it with a service charge
green meeting	a meeting in which methods are used to create an environmentally-sensitive meeting (e.g., use of Internet instead of paper, use of china instead of paper plates, donation of surplus food to a food bank, use of recycling, etc.)
guarantee	the minimum number of servings to be paid for by the client, whether not consumed they are actually consumed; usually required at least forty-eight hours in advance
guest	individual invited to attend or participate in a meeting at no charge; may also refer to an accompanying person who may pay a fee
guest room pick up	actual number of guest bedrooms used
guest/youth program	a program for persons who accompany a meeting attendee and who do not necessarily take an active part in the meeting
herringbone setup	rows of chairs or tables slanted in a V-shape facing a head table, stage or speaker; sometimes referred to as chevron; same as V-shape setup
hidden costs	unexpected charges that need to be anticipated (e.g., gratuities)
hold-harmless clause	part of a contract declaring that neither party will hold the other responsible for any

	damages or theft to materials or equipment owned or rented by either party; clause declaring that one party will take responsibility for damages assessed as the result of another party's inaction
hollow square setup	tables set in a square (or rectangle) with chairs placed around the outside of the table; centre (inside) tables are hollow
honorarium	voluntary payment made for services where no fee is legally required
honored guest	a VIP who is present during a meeting, but is not a participant
horizontal show	An exhibition at which the products or services being displayed represent all segments of an industry or profession.
host organization	an association, corporate body, town, country or other such party that invites an event to take place within or under its jurisdiction or its financial responsibility.
host bar	guests do not pay for drinks, often sponsored; also called an open bar or sponsored bar
housing	controlling a number of guest rooms with room blocks actually occupied during a particular night
housing plan	various types of accommodation facilities that meet the needs of the meeting
housing bureau	reservation office, often within a convention bureau, which coordinates housing for groups
human resources (HR)	paid and volunteer staff; union, and non-union
I & D	Installation & Dismantle. 1) The set-up and teardown of exhibits. 2) Firm that does I & D work
indirect cost	also called overhead or administrative costs, these are expenses not directly related to the meeting; they can include salaries, rent, and building and equipment maintenance
incentive	reward offered to stimulate greater effort

indemnification	a clause appearing in most contracts stating that one party agrees to hold the other harmless (not liable) in spite of what happens and whose fault it is; provides basis for compensation for incurred hurt, loss or damage
in-kind	contributions of goods and services without monetary exchange
installation	A style of booth space comprised of four or more 10' x 10' booth spaces with aisles on all four sides
international delegate	a registered participant who resides outside the host nation
international meeting	1) international/intercontinental: a meeting of an organization with multi-national membership that is available to meet on more than one continent; 2) international/continental: a meeting of an organization with multi-national membership that is available to meet on only one continent; 3) international/regional: a meeting of an organization with multi-national membership that is available to meet in only a given region of one continent
interpretation	oral translation from one language to another
island booth	style of exhibit space that includes four or more booth spaces with aisles on all four sides
itinerary	detailed schedule of a visit or tour
keynote speaker	speaker whose presentation establishes the theme or tone of the meeting
keystoning	distortion of a projected image on a screen, where the image is wider on top and narrower on bottom; (shaped like a keystone in the centre of an arch); the image distorts from a rectangle into a trapezoid because the projector is above or below the centre point of the screen; either the top or the bottom become wider because it is further away from the lens; to adjust for keystoning the top of the screen

can be tilted a little, either forward or back; many of the new data projectors allow you to tilt the lens to solve the problem

lanyard — a cord or string worn around the neck, and attached to a badge

lavalier microphone — portable microphone that hooks around neck or is clipped to clothing; also known as a necklace, lapel, or pendant microphone

lecture — discourse given before an audience, especially for instructional purposes

level of authority — the establishment and description of the level of responsibility and accountability of each person within a specific group

letter of agreement — document outlining proposed services, space, or products which becomes binding upon written approval by both parties; lists services, foods, beverages, and so forth

liability — legal responsibility for damage or injuries to make good a loss or claim

linear booth — Linear booth spaces are generally 10' wide and 8' to 10' deep. They can be combined to create an exhibit of almost any length. Also known as an in-line booth.

liquidated damages — part of a contract dealing with procedures, penalties, and rights of the party causing damages; settling of the damages dispute

logistics — tasks undertaken to ensure the efficient and effective management of materials, information and people for the implementation of the meeting

marketing mix — the combination of the four "p's" of marketing (product, price, place, and promotion) that is used to achieve marketing objectives for a target market

marketing plan — a written guide detailing sales advertising and promotion programs used to attract business

marshalling yard — A holding area where trucks check in and wait for instructions before delivering or picking up freight to an exhibit hall

masking drapes — drapes used to cover storage and other unsightly areas.

master account — all items that are charged to a group; may include room, tax, incidentals, food and beverage, audio visual equipment, décor, etc.; same as master bill

measurable — the standard by which it will be known if an objective has been reached

media strategy — a plan for managing media formats

meeting — a gathering for business, educational, or social purposes; associations often use the term to refer to a combination of educational sessions and exhibits. Includes seminars, forums, symposiums, conferences, workshops, clinics, etc.

meeting agenda — a list, outline, or plan of items to be done or considered at a meeting or during a specific time block

meeting history — record of an organization's previous meetings; usually includes information pertaining to original room block, actual room pickup, meeting space required, and food and beverage revenues generated

meeting specifications — information about a meeting (e.g., hotel occupancy patterns, function space, food and beverage requirements) that is sent directly to a venue or circulated by the convention and visitors bureau

meeting theme — the central motif around which the meeting and elements of the meeting are designed

message centre — the location where participants can pick up messages

mixer — audio unit by which sound signals from all sources feed into one system; allows for dissimilar inputs (microphone and line) to be combined and controlled into one output

move-in — 1) Dates set for installation of an exhibition.

	2) The process of setting up an exhibition including inbound freight movement.
move-in	1) Dates set for dismantling an exhibition. 2) The process of dismantling an exhibition and removing freight.
multimedia	equipment, materials and teaching aides used in sound and visual presentations; includes what is referred to as audio visual (AV)
objective	formalized statements of outcomes to be anticipated as a result of a meeting
official language	initial language in which a document is drafted or a speech is delivered
onsite	at the site of the meeting/program component
onsite registration	process of signing up for an event on the day of, or at the site of, the event
onsite office	a working office located at the site of the meeting
operations manual	the step-by-step procedures developed for the use of staff to conduct the meeting; also known as conference manual, procedural guide, meeting resource guide book, conference résumé
operations sheet	detailed instructions for a particular event prepared by the facility; also known as a banquet order, event order, resumé sheet or function sheet
organization	the corporation/association/client defining the objective(s) of the meeting
overhead projector	equipment which projects an image on a screen by passing light through a transparent slide or other transparency
overset	number of covers set over the guarantee; paid for by the client only if actually consumed
paperless conference	providing all documentation in other media besides print (including marketing, registration, speaker materials); can be on a website, Internet, disk or in CD ROM format
participant	a person attending a meeting; may include speakers (see also attendees, delegates)

participant expectation	specific information regarding what attendees will pay for elements of the meeting, and what they expect to get from the meeting
participant profile	data concerning attendees, including their average age, spending habits, etc.
peninsula booth	A style of exhibit space that consists of a minimum of four 10' x 10' booth spaces with aisles on three sides, and are attached to other exhibit space at one end. Also known as a split island booth
perimeter booth	A perimeter booth is a linear booth that backs to an outside wall of the exhibit facility rather than to another exhibit.
personal digital assistant (PDA)	a pocket-sized personal computer. PDAs usually can store phone numbers, appointments, and to-do lists
physical requirements	the architectural design, furnishings, temperature, and other such factors that are necessary to meet the needs of a meeting
plasma screen	flat screen that has a clear image even in ambient lighting
plenary session	general assembly for all persons actively involved in a meeting
post conference meeting(s)	a meeting between a meeting manager and facility staff to discuss and evaluate an event as soon as it is over; may involve a final review of the master account
post conference report	a report provided by the meeting facility to the meeting professional accounting for the meeting's actual sleeping room pick-up, food and beverage functions, function-room breakdown, exhibit information (if appropriate) and activities; a meeting's history can be compiled from this documentposter session 1) display of reports and papers, usually scientific, accompanied by authors or researchers; 2) a session dedicated to the discussion of the posters shown inside the meeting area; when this discussion is not held

	in a special session, it can take place directly between the person presenting the poster and interested delegate(s)
power drop	describes the location where power is required for any equipment that is necessary during the course of an events; commonly used for lighting rigs, audio rigs and audio visual equipment
pre conference meeting(s)	briefing(s) with meeting professional, facility and/or suppliers to review the purpose and details of the meeting
pre and post program(s)	organized outings taking place before (pre) or after (post) the working conference for both delegates and accompanying persons.
preprocess proof	a copy of filmed camera-ready copy that allows final proofing before printing
pre registration	the process of registering prior to the event; to be distinguished from "onsite" registration which takes place at the site of the event
presenter	person explaining a given topic in an informational session
print broker	a person in charge of managing print arrangements
printing and electronic distribution	two methods of distributing information to stakeholders (via traditional hard copy or electronically)
proceedings	published volume transcribing the conference sessions in full; may or may not include details of discussions
program	schedule of events giving details of times, places and speakers
promotion	the aspect of marketing that deals with generating program awareness amongst the target audience
promotional mix	combination of various strategies to general program awareness
property	establishment such as a hotel, motel, inn, resort, conference centre, or meeting facility

prospectus	information package; prospectus is written for a specific audience (e.g., exhibitor or sponsor) to encourage participation, promoting chief features and benefits
protection clauses	also known as performance clauses; attrition clauses that are the protective contractual device suppliers may use regarding accountability of both parties related to room nights, space needs and food and beverage needs
protocol	customs and regulations dealing with diplomatic formality, precedence, and etiquette
publicity	a media campaign, normally consisting of a series of public notices and advertising activities, aimed at ensuring maximum attendance by focusing attention on an event
rate of exchange	value attached to currency when exchanging from one country to another
reader	one who reads printed material out loud to visually impaired attendees
reader board	board or electronic screen listing the day's events at a venue or facility
ready room	area set aside for speakers to meet, relax, test AV, or prepare prior to or between speeches
rear screen projection	image projected on the back surface of a screen which is placed between the viewer and the projector
receiver	consumer-type television set that has a tuner and accepts regular broadcast signals
registration	1) process by which an individual indicates his intent to attend a conference or stay at a property; 2) method of booking and payment; 3) process of recording data about an attendee (or exhibitor), sending a confirmation and creating a badge used onsite
registration packet (kit) (materials)	packet of meeting materials such as program book, tickets, maps, etc. handed out at the registration desk

registration policy	written rule that outlines how certain situations will be handled during event registration
registration procedure	definition of the method used to carry out the policies so registration can proceed
request for proposal (RFP)	a document that stipulates what services the organization wants from an outside contractor and requests a bid to perform such services
résumé	a collection of all details for a single meeting needs; will include sleeping room information, billing arrangements and meeting requirements including food, beverage and audio visual; distributed to all hotel departments and usually shared with the meeting organizer
return on investment (ROI)	1) net profit divided by net worth; a financial ratio indicating the degree of profitability; 2) determination if objectives met (e.g., did sales increase by 10%? Did attendance increase by 15%?)
rider	expenses and requirements related to entertainment or entertainers over and above their contract fee; includes travel, food and beverage, staging requirements, etc.
rigging	1) The process of attaching the cable on a crane to a piece of machinery or equipment. 2) The process for hanging materials or signs. 3) The assembly or uncrating/recrating of machinery, steel construction and heavy materials
risk management	recognizing the possibility of injury, damage or loss, and having a means to prevent it or provide insurance
riser	platforms of various heights (30.5-45.5 cm [12-18"], 45.5-61 cm [18-24"] or 61-91.5 cm [24-36"]) used to elevate the speaker or headtable so they can be seen throughout the room
room block	the number of guest bedrooms reserved for a specified length of time for those who will be

	attending an event
rooming list	roster of individuals requiring guest bedroom accommodations, including type of accommodation and arrival and departure dates and payment methods
room monitor	the person who ensures that the meeting is proceeding according to plan
room rate	fee charged for guest bedrooms
rounds	banquet table, usually 60 inches (152 centimetres) in diameter; also available in 66- and 72-inch (168- and 183 centimetres) diameters, that seat 8 to 10 people
seminar	1) lecture and dialogue allowing participants to share experiences in a particular field under the guidance of an expert discussion leader. 2) meeting or series of meetings of from 10 to 50 specialists who have different specific skills but have a specific common interest and come together for training or learning purposes; the work schedule of a seminar has the specific object of enriching the skills of the participants
service levels	ratio of servers to banquet guests (e.g. 1:20 or 1:24)
show producer	Company or individual who is responsible for all aspects of planning, promoting and producing an event, including site selection and rental and soliciting exhibitors. Also known as the exhibition manager, show manager or show organizer.
show services	Services provided on show site by various contractors (e.g. material handling, pipe and drape, electrical, communications)
signage	a visual means of communicating either direction, information or instruction
signing authority	person who has authority to sign documents, thereby authorizing charges, guaranteed payment, contracting space, services, and supplies
simultaneous translation	interpretation of the speaker's words into

	another language while the speech is in progress
site	1) area, location, property or specific facility to be used for meeting; 2) a particular platform or location for loading or unloading at a place; see Venue
site inspection	personal, careful investigation of a property, facility, or area
site selection	the process of choosing a location for a meeting
skewing	zigzag pattern on a TV screen due to improper head alignment
slippage	the percentage of guest bedrooms that do not materialize from the negotiated room nights
SMARTboard©	allows notes generated during a meeting to be viewed on a computer screen, where they can be stored, e-mailed to others, or printed
speaker	1) types: keynote; general session and seminar leader who are topic specialists; trainers and workshop leaders who mix presentation with group participation and interaction; and "change of pace" speakers such as humorists and entertainers; 2) device for sound output
speakers bureau	an organization that locates, promotes and books speakers
speaker release form	written permission to record (and sell) audio and visual reproductions of the presentation
special needs	those persons whose needs require special attention
sponsor	1) limited sponsor, one who assumes a specified financial responsibility; 2) meeting sponsor, person(s) or organization assuming full responsibility for all costs and phases of producing a meeting
sponsorship	donated financial or material support, usually in exchange for recognition; paid opportunity for an exhibitor to increase its visibility at the show.
sponsorship agreement	a complete written version of the terms and

	conditions of sponsorship and recognition
sponsorship benefits package	a clear summary of the event, including specific recognition the sponsor will receive in exchange for money, goods, and/or services
sponsorship committee	a group of both meeting staff members and host organization members that focus on gathering sponsorships for an event
staff	paid and volunteer personnel
staging	1) design and placement of all elements being used for a meeting or event; 2) the implementation of a meeting or event
staging guide	compilation of all function sheets, scripts, instructions, room setup diagrams, directory of key personnel, forms, and other material relating to the event
stakeholder	All individuals who are invested in a project or event such as the sponsors, attendees, vendors, media and others
subcontractor	An individual or business, which contracts to perform part or all of the obligations of another's contract. Company retained by a contractor to provide services to exhibitors or event management; outsourcing. Also known as a specialty subcontractor
subsidy	money obtained from bodies or authorities to underwrite an expenditure
supplier	a person, company, facility, agency or other entity who sells space, goods or services for meetings
symposium	meeting of a number of experts in a particular field at which papers are presented by specialists on particular subjects and discussed with a view to making recommendations concerning the problems under discussion
T-shape setup	series of tables set up in the shape of the block T with chairs set all around except at head table.
teleconference	type of meeting which brings together people

	in two or more locations through telecommunications; may involve audio with or without graphics, or full motion video
TelePrompTer®	electronic device which allows display of script for speaker to read during presentation
theme event	an event designed so that food, decorations and entertainment all relate to one central motif
total meeting value	the sum of all revenue that the meeting will bring to the facility; also known as total business value
traffic flow	the movement of persons and vehicles inside and outside a meeting; planning takes into account volume and direction
translation	the changing of written material from one language into another
translator	one who converts a written document in one language to a written document in another language
transportation coordinator	a person in charge of planning and managing transportation arrangements for participants
turnover	1) breaking down and resetting a room with a different setup; 2) a pastry that usually has a fruit filling
valance	an overhead, decorative border normally used as a light baffle
value added tax (VAT)	1) a tax that is added to a product at each step of the manufacturing and marketing process reflecting value which has been added to the product by processing; 2) an additional tax payable in many countries that can be reimbursed partially or in total by completing specific forms and meeting specific criteria
variable cost	an expense item that changes according to the number of attendees present at a meeting
venue	1) site or destination of meeting, event or show; 2) location of performance such as hall, ballroom, auditorium, etc.

vertical show	An exhibition at which the products or services being displayed represent one element of an industry or profession.
very important person (VIP)	those designated for special treatment; may include speakers, visiting dignitaries, officials, sponsors
VIP host	meeting professional, host organization member, or local CVB member assigned to greet VIP participants and/or their staff on arrival, and act as liaison
video cassette recorder (VCR)	playback and recording
video conferencing	a meeting between two or more people or groups across a distance, including video, audio, and potentially other data, utilizing telecommunications or communications satellites for transmission of the signal
virtual conference	any meeting where people at two or more distant locations are linked using video, audio and data for two-way communication via satellite communications or the Internet; each party sees and hears the other through TV screen or computer monitor and audio speakers
virtual trade show	Exhibit of products or services that can be viewed over the Internet, either in conjunction with or in lieu of a physical trade show
volunteer	a person who provides time and/or expertise to a meeting, event or conference with no expectation of compensation
walk policy	guest holding confirmed sleeping room reservation sent to another hotel because of overbooking.
web-based registration	a method of registration using the client's web page or e-mail rather than paper
webcasting	an event that broadcasts the audio and/or video portion of a keynote presentation or other educational sessions over the Web in real-time or on-demand.

white board	used like a chalkboard but utilizes dry erase markers instead of chalk
wings	1) drape that extends from floor to ceiling on either side of the screen; 2) off-stage area out of audience sight lines.
wireless audience response system	hand held infrared or radio signal devices that record polling simultaneously and confidentially
workshop	1) meeting of several persons for intensive discussion; the workshop concept has been developed to compensate for diverging views in a particular discipline or on a particular subject; 2) informal and public session of free discussion organized to take place between formal plenary sessions or commissions of a congress or of a conference, either on a subject chosen by the participants themselves or else on a special problem suggested by the organizers; 3) training session in which participants, often through exercises, develop skills and knowledge in a given field

SOURCES:

Meeting Industry Terminology
International Association of Professional Congress Organizers
(IAPCO), 1992
ISBN 92-826-4036-1

International Meetings Industry Glossary
The Convention Liaison Council and Joint Industry Council, 1993

The Convention Industry Council Manual
7th Edition, December 2000

Convention Industry Council APEX(Accepted Practices) Terminology Panel
©December 2001

Appendix A

CHAPTER 1

1. False
2. True
3. True
4. True
5. False
6. True
7. (c)
8. (d)
9. (c)
10. (e)
11. (c)
13. Determine meeting stakeholders
    Specify thee meeting objectives
    Determine tools to measure the level of success in meeting these objectives
    Develop measurable content that meets the objectives
    Demonstrate results

CHAPTER 2

1. False
2. True
3. False
4. False
5. True
6. (a)
7. (e)
8. (c)
9. (e)

CHAPTER 3

1. True
2. True
3. True
4. True
5. (c)
6. (d)
7. (b)
8. (d)
11. 30 minutes

CHAPTER 4

1. True
2. False
3. False
4. True
5. False
6. True
7. (c)
8. (c)

CHAPTER 5

1. True
2. False
3. (d)
4. (a)
5. (d)
6. (c)

CHAPTER 6

1. False
2. False
3. True
4. (b)

5. (e)
6. (c)
7. (e)

CHAPTER 7

1. False
2. False
3. False
4. False
5. False
6. (c)
7. (b)

CHAPTER 8

1. False
2. False
3. False
4. True
5. True
6. True
7. (c)
8. (d)
9. 1-C, 2-D, 3-A, 4-B
10. Product, place, promotion, price
12. • top of the page should include the date of the release plus the phrase "For Immediate Release".
    • contact name and phone number "for more information"
    • a compelling but short headline or title at the top of the page is needed to help catch the media's attention
    • The format should be a single page, double-spaced letter sized page, double spaced with the event or conference date, time, site or venue, any other event specific information underlined.
    • The announcement should not be any longer than three paragraphs in length. The lead paragraph should tell the main part of the story and then the remaining paragraphs give additional information. Here is the opportunity to provide more information about a special keynote speaker or a VIP to be in attendance

- At the bottom of the page, include the word "more" if you are continuing to another page.
- At the conclusion of the release, use the word "end" or "30".

CHAPTER 9

1. True
2. False
3. False
4. True
5. (b)
6. (d)
7. (b)
8. A temporary marketplace where vendors present products and services, and build relationships with existing and prospective buyers.
9. Linear Booth and Corner Booth
   Perimeter Booth
   End-Cap Booth
   Peninsula Booth
   Split-Island Booth
   Island Booth
   Extended Header Booth

CHAPTER 10

1. True
2. True
3. False
4. True
5. (d)
6 (e)

CHAPTER 11

1. True
2. False
3. False
4. False
5. (e)
6. (a)
7. (a)
8. (e)
9. (d)

CHAPTER 12

1. True
2. False
3. False
4. True
5. (b)
6. (c)
7. (c)

CHAPTER 13

1. False
2. True
3. False
4. True
5. False
6. (e)
7. (f)

CHAPTER 14

1. False
2. False
3. (e)
4. (c)
5. (c)

CHAPTER 15

1. False
2. True
3. False
4. True
5. (e)
6. (d)
7. (d)

CHAPTER 16

1. False
2. False
3. False
4. False
5. (b)
6. (a)
7. (d)

CHAPTER 17

1. False
2. False
3. False
4. False
5. (g)
6. (d)
7. (d)

NOTES

NOTES

NOTES

Meetings and Conventions: A Planning Guide:
With 2006 Updated Forms
A Resource From
Meeting Professionals International (MPI)

CD-ROM USER GUIDE

Welcome to the CD-ROM resource of *Meetings and Conventions: A Planning Guide*. We recommend you take a moment to read this document in order to familiarize yourself with all the tools this CD-ROM offers. (When you load and open the disc you will also see important information under "**Licensing Agreement**". Please be sure to read and understand the contents in that agreement.)

This disc contains 33 online MPI templates that are shown in the book. This means that you can download them into your computer and complete them online, including adding your own logo, etc. and forwarding them to your clients or vendors.

The CD also includes 3 sets of information and templates that are part of an industry-wide project to standardize the forms used in planning meetings, exhibitions, and tradeshows. The project is called APEX (Accepted Practices Exchange) and is being completed by the Convention Industry Council (CIC). The documents from this project are also shown in this book under "APEX". You can also change the logo on the three APEX templates on this CD and then download them as *WORD* documents and write or type on them. If you prefer online templates, you can purchase a software CD with the online APEX versions directly from MPI or the CIC. (www.mpiweb.org and click on Bookstore. Or visit the CIC website at http://www.conventionindustry.org/apex/apex.htm.)

Finally, the disc includes a Glossary of terms from MPI which is also on in the book – but updatable if you use the disc version.

The following is important information to help you use the CD to its fullest advantage.

System Requirements

Minimum

- Windows 98 / ME / 2000 / XP
- 32 MB RAM
- 2 MB free hard disc space
- Internet Explorer Version 4 or above

Recommended

- Word processing program (e.g. Microsoft Word © or Corel WordPerfect ©).
- Spreadsheet Program (Microsoft Excel ©)

Installation

Place the CD-ROM in your drive; the installation process should start automatically. If the installation does not begin after a few moments:

1. Click on Start, and then Run.
2. Type "D:\Setup.exe" (where "D" is the CD-ROM drive) and click on OK. If your CD-ROM drive has a different drive letter, simply type in that letter instead of "D" (for example, "E:\Setup.exe").

Follow the on-screen instructions to complete the installation.

Un-install

To uninstall Meetings and Conventions: A Planning Guide, go to Start > Control Panel > Add/Remove Programs, and choose "MPI CD".

Program Features

❶Menu

You can access all features of the CD from the menu:

- File: Open, save, adjust page setup, preview and print your documents.
- Search: find a keyword in a currently displayed Checklist or Form.
- Settings: Change the logo display in your documents.
- Checklists: Access all checklists.
- Forms: Access all forms.
- Weblinks: Links to online MPI resources.
- Help: a guide to getting the most out of this program.
- For quick access to document templates, use the Create New Checklist and Create New Form drop-down menus. Find the document you wish to view, and click "Go!"

❷ Document Viewer

View and edit documents through the Document Viewer. You can edit certain text information in the documents, including check-boxes, dates, dollar amounts, etc. and logos.

You can also change the document logo. The MPI Foundation logo is the default logo for all Checklists and Forms, with the exception of the <u>APEX © Meeting and Exhibition Specification Guide</u>, <u>APEX © Post Conference Report</u>, and <u>APEX © Housing Form.</u>

You can change the default display logo through the Settings Menu (see below for details).

❸ Open / Save / Save As

- Open: Open a previously saved document.
- Save: save your documents to a hard drive or removable media (floppy disks or CDs).
- Save As: change name or location of previously saved document.

❹Document Assistant

The Document Assistant will help you to make the most use of your Checklists and Forms. Check this area after you open any document for information and tools geared specifically to the document you have open.

Glossary

A lexicon of terms found in the book and CD versions of <u>Meetings and Conventions: A Planning Guide.</u>

To search for a particular word, you can use Internet Explorer's built-in search tool. Click on Edit > Find (on this page), and follow the on-screen instructions.

Click on a letter located at the top and bottom of the document to view words starting wit the letter you clicked.

6 Help

Instructions on the installation and use of this program.

7 Order Book

Order <u>Meetings and Conventions: A Planning Guide</u> online.

Customizing Your Documents

You can customize most Forms and Checklists through the Document Viewer; this allows you to tailor a document for a specific meeting or event.

Before opening and customizing a document, check your page setup by clicking on File > Page Setup. The recommended settings for Checklists and Forms are:

- Paper Size: Letter
- Orientation: Portrait
- Headers and Footers: leave blank
- Margins: 0.5" Top/Bottom and Left/Right

Important! Resetting your page setup options applies to all documents you print through Internet Explorer.

Customizing Text

In most cases, you can:

- modify dates
- edit check boxes (click once to check; click again to uncheck)
- toggle radio buttons (click once to toggle; click again to untoggle)
- edit certain blue-colored text (in the example below, you could change the names of the food and beverage events next to the check boxes)*
- manipulate quantity and dollar amounts where appropriate
- fill in lines (for example, "Instructor" has been added to the "Title:" line)**

* Some blue-colored text is editable directly by the user; other blue-colored text is editable, but automated. For example, a dollar amount total may be calculated automatically from previous budget item entries.

**There are some lines that are considered part of the template and therefore you will not be able to add information to them through the Document Viewer. In the SAMPLE SPEAKER REQUIREMENT FORM below, you cannot add information to "FOR OFFICE USE ONLY".

Remember to Save any changes that you made.

◉ MPI
FOUNDATION

SAMPLE SPEAKER REQUIREMENT FORM

FOR OFFICE USE ONLY

Session: _____
Day: _____ Time: _____
Room: _____

Section 1: General information
Please return by: October 13, [year] ◄—Dates—►
Name: G. Getty   _____
Title: Instructor ◄—Lines—► _____
Company: _____
Address: _____
City: _____ Prov/State: _____ Postal/Zip Code: _____
Bus. Phone: _____ Fax: _____ E-mail: _____
Emergency Name: _____ Tel: _____

Special Needs
Please indicate any special needs: Vegetarian meals _____
_____

For our planning purposes, please check the food and beverage events that you will be attending:
☑ Thursday reception   **Check**   ☑ Friday luncheon
☑ Friday reception   ◄ **boxes** ► ☐ Saturday reception
☐ Monday reception   ☐ Tuesday reception
☐ Wednesday reception   ☐ None of the above

Badge information
Name: _____
Title: _____
                                        Radio
Organization/office: _____   **buttons**

Do you want your business address and phone number listed in the program?
                              ⦿ Yes   ○ No

Customizing Logos

To replace the MPI Foundation logo with a logo of your choosing:

1. Click Settings > Change Logo.

2. Use "Browse" to find a logo.

   NB: the image must be a GIF graphics file. The display is 114 pixels wide x 63 pixels high. Regardless of the size of your image, it will be scaled to fit this dimension.

3. Click "Use Current" button to use the image you are currently previewing.

4. Click "Apply Changes" to complete the operation. This image will now appear in all your template documents.

5. Click "Use Default" to revert to the default MPI Foundation logo.

6. If you do not wish to display any logo, click "Use Blank".

Customizing Logos in APEX © Housing Form

Unlike most documents that contain one default MPI Foundation logo, the APEX © Housing Form has two APEX© logos, one on the top left and one on the top right. This allows you to place both the Event logo and the Event Organizer logo on the customized document you create.

To replace the APEX© logos,

1. Click the Change Logo(s) button in the Document Assistant.

Document Assistant

You can place two logos in the Housing Form: the Event Logo and the Event Organizer Logo.

To replace the APEX® Foundation logos with logos of your choosing:

1. Click the Change Logo(s) button below.
2. Use "Browse" to find a logo.

NB: the image must be a GIF graphics file. The display is 114 pixels wide x 63 pixels high. Regardless of the size of your image, it will be scaled to fit this dimension.
3. Click "Use Current" button to use the image you are currently previewing.
4. Click "Apply Changes" to complete the operation. This image will now appear in this and all future APEX® Housing

Change Logo(s)

Change Logo(s)

Change TOP LEFT Logo

You can change the logo that appears on the top left of this form.

The image specified must be a GIF graphic file.

Logo:

Browse...

Use Blank | Use Default | Use Current

Change TOP RIGHT Logo

You can change the logo that appears on the top right of this form.

The image specified must be a GIF graphic file.

Logo:

Browse...

Use Blank | Use Default | Use Current

Apply Changes | Cancel

2. Use "Browse" to find a logo.

NB: the image must be a GIF graphics file. The display is 114 pixels wide x 63 pixels high. Regardless of the size of your image, it will be scaled to fit this dimension.

3. Click "Use Current" button to use the image you are currently previewing.
4. Click "Apply Changes" to complete the operation. This image will now appear in all your template documents.
5. Click "Use Default" to revert to the default MPI Foundation logo.
6. If you do not wish to display any logo, click "Use Blank".

TECHNICAL HELP
TROUBLESHOOTING

First! Please check with your IT department before contacting MPI to see if you are authorized to install this type of software. (Some organizations do not allow this.)

And Then! If you have technical problems that your IT department determines are not user related, contact MPI's Member Services at 972-702-3093 for referral to the CD ROM company.